"The Pentagon has a secret stash—they call it the black budget—that costs us $100 million a day. This money is still being spent on weapons to fight the cold war, and the Third World War, and World War IV.

"This money is erased from the public ledger.

"In the past three years, $100 billion has disappeared into the Pentagon's classified cache."
—**from** *Blank Check*

PRAISE FOR
TIM WEINER
AND
BLANK
CHECK

✪ ✪ ✪

"The Pentagon's $36 billion black budget is a license to steal. Tim Weiner tells the entire shocking story."
—**U.S. Rep. Patricia Schroeder (D., Colo.),**
member, House Armed Services Committee

✪ ✪ ✪

More . . .

"A carefully detailed unveiling . . . every careful reader is likely to get mad as hell."
        —Grand Rapids Press

✪ ✪ ✪

"Highly recommended. . . . The thesis of this book—that secrecy in government military programs is antithetical to democracy—is hugely important."
        —Library Journal

✪ ✪ ✪

"[Weiner] provides enough well-documented examples . . . to arouse concern even among those who do not share his views."
        —Sea Power

✪ ✪ ✪

"Weiner does a wonderful job exposing this massive absurdity."
        —San Jose Mercury News

✪ ✪ ✪

"Tim Weiner shines his searchlight on dark corners that the Pentagon would like to keep hidden from the American public."
        —David Wise
        author of The Invisible Government

✪ ✪ ✪

BLANK CHECK

CHECK

The Pentagon's Black Budget

By

Tim Weiner

WARNER BOOKS

A Time Warner Company

Warner Books, Inc., 666 Fifth Avenue, New York, NY 10103

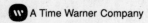 A Time Warner Company

Printed in the United States of Amenca
First trade printing: July 1991
10 9 8 7 6 5 4 3 2 1

Library of Congress Cataloging-in-Publication Data

Weiner, Tim.
    Blank check: the Pentagon's black budget / Tim Weiner
        p.   cm.
    Includes bibliographical references and index.
    ISBN O 446-39275-8
        1. United States—Armed Forces—Appropriations and expenditures. 2. United
States—Armed Forces—Accounting. 3. United States. Dept. of Defense—
Appropriations and expenditures. 4. United States. Dept. of Defense—Accounting.
5. Official secrets—United States. 6. Defense information, Classified—United
States. 7. United States—Military policy. 8. United States—Foreign relations—
1981-1989. 1. Title.
UA25.5.W45 1990   90-50291
355.6'22'0973—dc20   CIP

Book design: H. Roberts
Cover design: Mike Stromberg
Cover illustration: Steve Macanga

To Herbert and Dora, with love

The guarding of military and diplomatic secrets
at the expense of informed representative government
provides no real security for our Republic.

—*United States Supreme Court Justice Hugo L. Black*

Every thing secret degenerates. . . .
Nothing is safe that does not show how it can bear
discussion and publicity.

—*John Emerich Edward Dalberg, Lord Acton*

CONTENTS

Introduction The Panorama Box   1

PART ONE

SECRET WEAPONS

Chapter 1 The Black Budget   5
Chapter 2 Overkill   19
Chapter 3 Toward a Better Armageddon   46
Chapter 4 A Wing and a Prayer   73

PART TWO

SECRET WARS

Chapter 5 Keeping Secrets   111
Chapter 6 A Holy War   143
Chapter 7 From Lebanon to Leavenworth   172
Chapter 8 Laws and Lies   199
Chapter 9 An Open Book   214
Afterword   233
Acknowledgments   236
Notes   237
Selected Bibliography   261
Index   265

BLANK CHECK

INTRODUCTION

The Panorama Box

I BEGAN a journey that took me down the endless pastel corridors of the Pentagon and through the elegant marble entrance to the Central Intelligence Agency by walking down the dark, scarred halls of the county courthouse in Camden, New Jersey, one of America's poorest and most corrupted cities. Down in the basement of the courthouse were thousands of property records. They told the story of a crime.

They were raw evidence that a HUD housing program was being run by thieves. The program was robbing the poor and enriching the greedy. After looking through the records, I knew I was on to something—but I wasn't sure what it was, or how deep it went. So I went searching for an honest man in the lower ranks of the government.

I found him sitting in a dusty room where the county stored copies of old deeds. The keeper of the paper was an old-timer named DeMedio. He kept a kind of archive in his head, an unwritten history of the deals that greased the local political machine.

His jaws worked a skinny cigar as I told him what I'd found and asked him what it meant. He leaned back in his wooden chair. The iron springs creaked. He took the cigar out of his mouth. He looked at it, and then at me, with mild distaste.

"Listen, sweetheart," he said. "You are opening up a real Panorama box here."

You take your revelations where you find them. DeMedio's malaprop sparked an idea. I saw a world of secrets sealed beneath a steely cover. I wanted to pry the lid off the box, find a way inside and see the panorama sprawling within.

I re-read the records, knocked on some doors, and found a cabal of con men manipulating the federal housing agency. All wound up in prison. I came away from Camden with an understanding. The best way to find out what the government is up to is to read the documents that show money flowing. By tracing the movements of money, you can come to understand the workings of power. The people you interview may lie, equivocate or shade their speech to suit their needs. But the document, as the lawyers say, speaks for itself.

Two years later, in April 1986, my newspaper sent me to Washington to try to unlock another box, one that was far larger, far more complex. Something was going haywire in Washington that spring. An uneasiness was in the air, a sense that things were getting out of hand. I listened to Air Force generals refuse to answer congressmen's questions about the Pentagon's most expensive weapons. I read that the CIA director was telephoning reporters threatening to have them indicted for publishing stories that displeased him. I heard the President's men telling transparent lies about what the White House was doing in Central America. Though no one knew it at the time, a manic Marine at the National Security Council was running a lucrative weapons dealership with branches in Tegucigalpa, Tel Aviv and Teheran.

All these secrets and deceptions and arrogations of power sprang from inside the biggest Panorama box of all: the Pentagon's black budget.

PART ONE

SECRET
WEAPONS

1

The Black Budget

THE black budget is the President's secret treasury. It funds every program the President, the Secretary of Defense and the Director of Central Intelligence want to keep hidden from public view. It pays for the weapons for fighting the Cold War, and the Third World War—and World War IV. This money is kept off the books, erased from the public ledger. The secret weapons, secret wars and secret policies it pays for are shielded from public debate.

The black budget began with the Manhattan Project, the crash program to build the atomic bomb during World War II. It became a permanent part of the government with the creation of the Central Intelligence Agency. Most of the money to run the CIA always has been hidden in the Pentagon's ledgers. So is the money for two far bigger intelligence organizations: the National Security Agency, which taps the world's telecommunications, and the National Reconnaissance Office, which operates spy satellites and is so secret that its name cannot be mentioned on the floor of the Congress or in any unclassified government document.

Something new transformed the black budget as the 1980's began. A government obsessed with secrecy began to conceal the costs of many of its most expensive weapons. It enshrouded them in the deep cover once reserved for espionage missions. Under that cover, the black budget exploded. By 1989, at the end of the Reagan administration, it had grown to $36 billion a year. It was bigger than the federal budget for transportation or agriculture, twice the cost of the Education Department, eight times more expensive than the Environmental Protection Agency. It was bigger than the military budget of any nation in the world, except the Soviet Union's.

This cache is kept sealed in covert compartments of the Pentagon's ledgers. The walls around it are designed to be impenetrable. The Pentagon holds the key to the black budget and makes few copies. The classified accounts are called "special access programs," meaning you have to possess a secret code-word security clearance to know about one of them. They are known more familiarly as black programs. "Black" is a word from within the world of spies. It means clandestine, unseen, hidden from the light. Black operations. A black-bag job. When I arrived in Washington in 1986, my assignment was to follow the money disappearing into the black budget, to figure out how much was flowing into it, and to find out what the money was buying. There was only one place to begin: by reading the Pentagon's budget line by line.

Every January, the Pentagon cobbles together a set of computer printouts, binds them in stiff paper, stamps them with the seal of the Department of Defense, a spread-winged eagle clutching three arrows, and ships the books to Congress. This is the version of the military budget made available for public consumption. It is a striking set of documents, if only for the size of its bottom line. In the years of Ronald Reagan's presidency it doubled to roughly $300 billion, or a billion dollars a day, save Sundays and holidays.*

Every spring, a ritual dance takes place around this enormous pile of money, the largest pool of public capital in the world. Generals and admirals emerge from the Pentagon, cross the Potomac and troop up Capitol Hill. They testify to Congress that the latest nuclear missile, bomber, submarine or space satellite is vital to the defense of the United States. The congressmen know well that some two million jobs come from this wellspring of money. Their own jobs depend in part on their ability to direct the flow to their home districts. So while some stand before the cameras and rail at the Pentagon's profligacy, most return to the floor and approve another billion dollars for the military contractors back home. The ranking contractors produce the weapons, display them in patriotic newspaper advertisements, publish impressive profit statements, and provide good jobs for Pentagon officials grown tired of testifying to Congress. This roundelay is the public face of Pentagon spending.

---

* It takes some perspective to think in billions. When you see the word "billion" in this book, keep the following in mind: One thousand seconds is about seventeen minutes. One million seconds is about eleven and a half days. One billion seconds is about thirty-two years.

I learned that this face is a mask. The budget the Pentagon submits to Congress is a cover story.

I began by collecting the Pentagon's budgets for each year of the 1980's, along with copies of briefing books submitted to Congress to justify the spending, and the printed testimony of generals and admirals addressing the armed services committees. The stacks of public documents that grew around my desk were a testament to the openness of American government. But the Pentagon's budget is not an open book. When I looked inside it, I found hundreds of programs camouflaged under code names, their costs deleted, their goals disguised. Code words and blank spaces stood where facts and figures should have been.

I tried to pick the budget apart, to analyze what could be decoded, and to add it all up. That was a way into the black world, the realm of nukes and spooks.

Some of the programs funded by the black budget would make sense if the government explained them. Others would not. People might wonder at a $20 billion military satellite system designed to coordinate a six-month nuclear war. Some might fail to see the logic of spending $60 billion or more on a new nuclear bomber that will gather dust in its hangar until World War III begins. I first became intrigued by these nuclear war technologies, the satellite system called MILSTAR and the Stealth bomber, the latest weapons in the search for nuclear superiority.

Then I looked into three black operations: the CIA's weapons pipeline to Afghanistan, the Army's creation of a new paramilitary force, and the National Security Council's gunrunning schemes—missions that began with high-minded certitude and came apart in moral confusion, financial corruption and political chaos. Again, there was cause to question the common sense of shipping half a billion dollars' worth of weapons halfway around the world to a murderous commando who revered the late Ayatollah Khomeini. There was reason to take offense at American military officers secretly spending hundreds of millions of dollars in disregard for the Constitution they are sworn to defend. As I found myself learning about a system by which public money is spent in secret, I began questioning the system itself, and the secrecy that sustains it.

Ever since the end of World War II, the United States has projected its power around the world by constructing nuclear weaponry and conducting covert actions. Anyone who read the newspapers knew such things existed. But their costs and their component parts were by and large concealed within the black budget.

The secret weapons interested me the most. I didn't see how the Pentagon could stamp "Top Secret" on the price tag of a bomber, a missile or a space satellite. I could understand classifying the details of

fancy technologies or state-of-the-art designs—but not the costs of weaponry. I thought spending money for military hardware in secret went
against the grain of American democracy.

In the Pentagon's 1991 budget, submitted to Congress in January
1990, are three pages listing Air Force programs for strategic weapons
research. "Strategic" is a military euphemism. It means nuclear war
against the Soviet Union. Within those three pages are eleven black
programs long censored by military secrecy, their costs erased by the
Wite-Out of the black budget. But by adding up the costs of the unclassified programs in this sector of the budget, which come to $1.41 billion,
and subtracting that number from the strategic weapons' bottom line of
$4.26 billion, a third-grade student can see that those eleven research
projects cost a total of $2.85 billion. For purposes of comparison, that
is roughly what it costs to run the entire State Department.[1]

What were these projects? Then and now, eight of these nuclear-
war programs are completely hidden under the veil. I do not know for
certain what they are, and if I did, I could be charged with a felony for
telling you. Four have code names: OLYMPIC, BELL WEATHER, ME-
RIDIAN and BERNIE. Four have innocuous, meaningless titles—Special
Analysis Activities, Special Applications Program, Special Evaluation
Program, and Advanced Strategic Programs—which sound more like
graduate courses in accounting. All are unaccounted-for, unaccountable
programs for World War III.

I can tell you much more about the remaining three programs: the
Stealth bomber, MILSTAR and the Advanced Cruise Missile. By order
of the Congress, a few financial facts about them were published for the
first time in the Pentagon's 1991 budget. Their true costs had been a state
secret for ten years.

The Stealth bomber is the perfect symbol for the black budget—an
extraordinarily costly and supposedly invisible weapon. The Air Force
says the bomber's radar-absorbing skin and its sleek boomerang shape
will make it nearly undetectable to an enemy. Its mission is unique: to
dodge Soviet air defenses, drop nuclear bombs on the Soviets' mobile
missile systems, and destroy the Soviet leadership in their bunkers.

The Stealth is the most expensive airplane ever built, the most
expensive secret weapon since the first atomic bomb. The best guess
nowadays is that each one will cost no less than $820 million. That is
only slightly less than if the seventy-ton plane had been built of solid
gold. As of May 1990, the Pentagon wants to build seventy-five of the
bombers, at a cost of $61.5 billion. That is about the size of the annual
budget of the state of California; it is greater than the annual sales of
IBM or General Electric. The Stealth bomber is so expensive that it

almost certainly will never be used in combat unless a full-tilt nuclear war erupts.

If and when that war comes, the Military Strategic, Tactical and Relay system—MILSTAR—will help run it. MILSTAR will cost roughly $20 billion, making it the most expensive space-satellite program in history. It is supposed to be the central nervous system for nuclear war, a space-based brain that can control the immense brawn of nuclear weapons. The system is supposed to be smart enough and strong enough to broadcast the launch orders and coordinate the battle plan through a nuclear war of six months or more—and then stand ready to fight World War IV.

The Stealth bomber and MILSTAR have a common purpose: winning that long nuclear war. I knew that many of the Pentagon's leading strategists had talked a great deal about the United States needing the nuclear firepower necessary for victory in World War III. I had always thought that was saber-rattling designed to cow the Soviets. But I came to understand that plans in the black budget envision this victory. They call for winning a nuclear war that continues long after the nation's major cities and military command posts are destroyed. In these plans, computers run a war no human mind could control. Robot soldiers stalk radioactive battlegrounds. Generals speed down interstates in lead-lined trucks ordering warheads fired from faraway silos. And the MILSTAR satellites act as a computerized concertmaster, conducting the global symphony of destruction. The Pentagon's war-winning rhetoric has been translated into billions of black dollars spent secretly on bombers, missiles, satellites, exotic composite carbons, silicon chips, microcircuitry and computer codes—all immensely costly, technologically exquisite and utterly useless until the air-raid sirens start howling. These plans are known to the Soviet military, which has somewhat similar, though less sophisticated, stratagems. Few Americans know their own government has such plans, or that they are paying for them.

The third of the strategic weapons in the Air Force budget is the Advanced Cruise Missile, or ACM, a slender, twenty-foot-long nuclear-tipped bullet enhanced by stealth technology. It is a rare bird: the first black weapon ever partially declassified and subjected to scrutiny by the General Accounting Office, the government agency that conducts independent audits for Congress. The auditors concluded that the Advanced Cruise Missile was a $7 billion debacle in the making.

The sum and substance of what has been made public on the subject of the ACM is all in the *Congressional Record*. It is as open as any discussion of secret weapons can be on the floor of the Congress. In 1988, Les Aspin, the chairman of the House Armed Services Committee, attempted to put together public reports on the major programs in the Reagan administration's quarter-trillion-dollar nuclear-weapons buildup. Aspin told his colleagues what little he could:

> Most of the committee reports have been publicly released. The report on the ACM is an exception. A report has been done, but because of the high classification, the report remains locked in the committee safe.
>
> The ACM is not a classically black program. I am not barred from acknowledging its existence. I may speak its name. But it is protected in nearly all interesting details by high classification. There is one interesting and important thing I can tell you. It is a procurement disaster. The ACM is the worst of the programs the committee has looked at . . .
>
> Why? Because of classification the reasons will have to remain sketchy, almost nonexistent.[2]

The fact of the matter is that the Advanced Cruise Missile doesn't work. It may not come as a complete shock that the Pentagon produces billion-dollar weapons that prove worthless. But the problem is that the disasters in the black budget usually take place in secret. The likelihood of black-budget boondoggles like the ACM coming to light is slim.

I had a long talk about this with Frank Conahan of the General Accounting Office. Conahan is an affable, white-haired Irishman who runs the GAO's national-security division, which conducts the few outside audits into black programs that the Pentagon permits. He is one of the handful of civilians with the power to look inside black programs.

From 1981 to 1985, while the Pentagon's budget doubled—and the secret spending for black weapons increased eightfold—there was no outside scrutiny of the secret spending, not by the GAO, and not by the Pentagon's own auditors. "Until 1985 we had essentially no coverage of what you call your black programs," Conahan said. It took four more years, until the end of the Reagan administration, for the GAO to begin to get a handle on the black world. Today, for the first time, two dozen auditors are assigned to investigate black programs. What they have found so far is unsettling.

No one in the Pentagon knows how many black programs exist. No one in the Office of the Secretary of Defense keeps track of black programs. The Air Force and the Navy, which have the lion's share of black money, have refused to tell their civilian overseers about new black programs they have created. The most the GAO can say is that there are several thousand special-access compartments, that the military created hundreds of unauthorized black programs in the 1980's, and that civilian control of the black budget has eroded to the point of meaninglessness.[3]

"And," Conahan noted, "in the absence of oversight by anyone, people are likely to do anything."

The Pentagon argues that black programs are better managed, more efficient and less susceptible to fraud than unclassified programs. Conahan said this is nonsense. "I don't see that they're any better managed," he said. "We find the same problems in the black world as exist in the other programs. The only difference between the two is the degree to which things are kept from public debate."

If the black and white worlds of military contracting are run at similar levels of honesty and integrity, then cost overruns and corporate crimes are occurring in secret. We are being asked to take it on faith that defense contractors working under the black budget's cover would never abuse that protection. Given the biggest black contractors' colorful legal and financial histories, this may be a bit much to ask.

Consider their records: Rockwell International, a repeat offender, was fined $5.5 million in March 1989 for criminal fraud against the Air Force on a satellite contract. Lockheed has a criminal history that includes paying millions of dollars in bribes. General Dynamics bilked the Pentagon for $244 million in expenses. General Electric stands twice convicted of defrauding the Department of Defense on an Army computer contract and an Air Force nuclear-weapons contract. Boeing, the biggest subcontractor on the Stealth bomber, has pleaded guilty to paying millions of dollars of bribes to obtain top-secret Pentagon planning papers.

In early 1990, Northrop, the builder of the Stealth bomber, pleaded guilty to thirty-four felonies and paid a $17 million fine for lying to the government about test results on nuclear cruise missiles and fighter jets. And the big three of the black budget—Northrop, General Dynamics and TRW—all were under criminal investigation on charges of paying bribes to obtain secret Pentagon financial plans. The Pentagon's own investigators called that corporate behavior "insidious," "systemic" and "company-approved." But such cases have proved hard to prosecute in court, given the secrecy of the black documents.[4]

Today more than 100 multimillion- and multibillion-dollar weapons systems are being built in secrecy. They include such items as the Navy's A-12 attack plane and an Army ground-to-air missile code-named Grass Blade.

The stealthy A-12 is scheduled to fly for the first time in late 1990. The Navy wants to build 620 of them—at a cost of $75 billion. That fact was a secret until January 1990, when an accidental breach of Pentagon security led to publication of the A-12's cost in a congressional

document. Almost no one in Congress knew that the A-12 will cost about
$120 million a copy—six times the cost of the plane it is designed to
replace. Discovering this by accident was like leafing through your credit-
card receipts and finding out your spouse had swapped your old Chevy
for a Jaguar without talking to you about it.[5]

No one wants to talk about a program like Grass Blade. This missile
is designed to hunt and kill enemy aircraft and missiles with radar and
infrared homing devices. But it has never worked. In early 1990, after
twelve years of tests and nearly $150 million down the drain, the secret
project was a continuing fiasco. Not a single working Grass Blade missile
was in the American arsenal. Yet it remained in the Pentagon's 1991
budget, its funding and its failures still classified.[6]

The Pentagon's secret weapons take shape in windowless buildings
surrounded by fences topped with razor wire, behind locked doors guarded
by armed sentries. The covert procurement of weapons requires the construction of ornate buildings sheathed to shield the weaponry from
eavesdroppers—the *hangars* for the Stealth bombers are going to cost
upwards of $1.6 billion alone. Several hundred thousand civilians seeking
work on black programs must first pass lengthy Pentagon security checks.
The average wait for the security clearance is eight months. Applicants
are paid in full while they wait, producing nothing. The lost time runs
into hundreds of millions of dollars a year. All this and more is charged
to taxpayers in secret as a cost of doing business in the black world.

Toting up the costs of this clandestine system made me wonder:
what right or reason did the Pentagon have for spending the public's
money secretly? I once had the chance to ask Caspar Weinberger, the
corporate lawyer who presided over the black budget's explosion as the
Reagan administration's Secretary of Defense. He had called a press
conference to announce the 1988 and 1989 Pentagon budgets. A press
conference at the Pentagon may not be the best place to go seeking truth.
Still, it was an opportunity to question the man in charge. Why was the
black budget growing so fast? I asked. What were his reasons for keeping
the costs of so much weaponry classified?

Weinberger glanced over his podium with narrowed eyes. He spoke
with an exasperated tone: "This is funding which we believe it is better
for us not to publicize on the very sound premise that we don't see the
purpose of giving additional information to the enemy." Fair enough,
save for one fact: the enemy, under Weinberger's analysis, comes to
include the Congress and the public. The Pentagon's argument for secret
spending is this: disclosing the costs of these programs would be an
exceptionally grave risk to national security. If we reveal the *costs* of
these weapons, the Soviets can figure out our *capabilities*, our *plans*, our
intentions. This rationale strikes me as imperfect. If you tell me what

you paid for a plane ticket, can I tell you where you're headed, or if you'll arrive on time?

I heard another answer to my questions my first week reporting in Washington, my first week combing through the budget, when I was introduced to Tom Amlie at the Pentagon. Of all the people I ever questioned inside and outside of the Pentagon, no one put things in a nutshell quite like Amlie, a grizzled financial analyst for the Air Force. Amlie was also a talented weapons engineer who'd helped develop the Sidewinder, a lethally effective air-to-air missile. He has spent thirty-eight years thinking about weapons, enough time inside the Pentagon to know a few things about the black world, and enough time outside to have some perspective.

Visiting Amlie was my first trip beyond the outermost halls of the Pentagon. My image of the Pentagon had been formed by its architecture: five five-sided concentric rings, each inner ring containing higher levels of power, a concrete fortress of rigorously ordered design. Inside it was an impossibly complicated maze of Lysol-scented corridors, office doors with coded locks, armed guards watching over restricted passageways, signs with incomprehensible acronyms. Amlie helped me decode a bit of the puzzle. We sat down over lunch at a crowded Pentagon cafeteria. I asked him how the Pentagon justified having a secret budget. Amlie picked at his Salisbury steak and explained that there were three basic reasons for having black weapons programs.

"One," he said, "you're doing something that should genuinely be secret. There's only a couple of those, and Stealth ain't one of them.

"Two, you're doing something so damn stupid you don't want anybody to know about it.

"And three, you want to rip the money bag open and get out a shovel, because there is no accountability whatsoever."

There can be no accounting for a black budget. A deeper look into the Pentagon's 1991 request shows how billions of dollars are shielded by secrecy and protected from public debate.

Thirty percent of the Navy's $6.1 billion research budget for tactical warfare—that is, weaponry for something short of Armageddon—is black. Forty percent of the Army's $3 billion budget for tactical weapons research is black. And ninety-five percent of the Air Force's budget for intelligence and communications research is black. Here are $2.26 billion of public funds—and $2.16 billion goes to secret programs. This is the blackest sector of the Pentagon's black budget.

The bulk of this cache goes to an endeavor described only as "Program Element Number 0304111F—Special Activities." That program element number, once deciphered, reveals that the black money for "Special Activities" finances research by the National Reconnaissance Office.

The NRO does not exist, officially speaking. Its letterhead is classified. It operates under the cover of the Air Force Office of Space Systems, behind a double-locked door in Room 4C1052 of the Pentagon. It builds and operates spy satellites that provide instantaneous photographic coverage of the globe, particularly nations the Pentagon has defined as "denied territory," such as the Soviet Union. The urgency of this aspect of the NRO's mission is becoming somewhat murky, now that the Soviets are opening their nuclear-weapons factories and military outposts to everyone from American scientists to members of the Joint Chiefs of Staff.

The satellites also provide crucial links in the nuclear war-fighting network. They help nuclear war planners refine and revise the target list that now contains more than 15,000 dots on the Soviet map. If war comes, the satellites are to transmit photographic data through MILSTAR to Stealth bomber pilots, to help the pilots locate and destroy Soviet mobile missiles stealing through the tundra on camouflaged trucks and trains. The Soviet Union is a big country, 8.65 million square miles, with many roads and railways, and targeting mobile missiles is a task beyond any known powers of man or machine. But the Pentagon is working on it.

The National Reconnaissance Office builds some remarkable satellites, and they are remarkably expensive, up to a billion black dollars apiece. The factories that build the satellites are in the high-tech mill towns of California's Silicon Valley, sprawling suburbs where thousands of people subsist on secret procurement projects. I went out there to interview some of the workers who produce the intelligence satellites. Among them was a systems engineer named Marty Overbeck-Bloem, who worked on satellite intelligence programs at the Space Systems division of Lockheed Missile and Space Company in Sunnyvale. Working on Lockheed's black satellites made Marty a skeptic on the subject of efficiency.

"In a black project, people don't worry about money," Marty said. "If you need money, you got it. If you screw up and you need more, you got it. You're just pouring money into the thing until you get it right. The incentive isn't there to do it right the first time. Who's going to question it?"[7]

It is difficult to question something you cannot see. As I traced the course of Pentagon research and development programs over the 1980's, I saw increasingly huge sums disappearing, in the way stars and constellations are pulled into black holes in space. Between 1986 and 1989, more than $5 billion in previously public Pentagon programs faded into the ether of the black budget. Most of that money was for newer and better nuclear weapons systems and nuclear war technologies. In the same way that astronomers learn about black holes by calculating their gravitational pull, I was learning about the black budget by watching money vanish.

I saw no part of the black budget growing faster than the Pentagon's secret research and development. It multiplied sixteenfold in the 1980's. In fiscal 1981, it stood at $626 million. In fiscal 1990, it reached $10.27 billion. Today, in the 1991 budget, almost twenty-five cents of every dollar for Pentagon research is black.

This foreshadows huge increases in secret weapons spending for the 1990's, as weapons such as the Stealth bomber and the A-12 attack plane progress from the drawing board to the assembly line. Research and development is the acorn from which the defense oak grows. A general rule of Pentagon accounting is that every dollar spent researching and developing a weapon represents at least ten dollars that must be spent building and operating it. And black weapons programs have proved far more expensive than their unclassified counterparts, owing to the technological complexity of their missions and the lack of accountability for money spent in secret. Unless a sweeping set of orders to open the books transforms the Pentagon, the $10 billion black research budget of today augurs that more than ten times that sum will be spent on secretly developed weapons in the next few years.[8]

The costs of secret Pentagon spending are most apparent in the procurement budget—the money for buying weapons. It lists each entry under a column marked MILLIONS OF DOLLARS. Within the ledger for 1991 are line items such as:

Selected Activities:	5354.1
Special Programs:	3101.8
Other Production Charges:	491.5

That is all the public and the Congress as a whole are allowed to know about these three black programs and the nearly $9 billion they consume.

Some of the weaponry this black money buys is used to fight an invisible war, for here is where more of the funds for the empire of intelligence are hidden. At the center of this realm lies the Central Intelligence Agency, which keeps some of its money stowed in that "Special Programs" compartment. The CIA was where the scheme of secret spending started forty years ago. Always resistant to oversight and outside control, the CIA has taught some of its fiscal sleight-of-hand to the financiers in the Pentagon's budget offices.

Together the procurement and the research and development budgets represent only about forty percent of the Pentagon's spending. The blank spaces and the code-word compartments within them contain at least $26 billion in black programs. Within the other sectors of Pentagon spending—operations and maintenance, personnel and construction—lies about $8 billion in secret funding, as near as I can trace it.

After almost four years of taking apart Pentagon budgets, and talking to present and former military officers, members of Congress, congressional staffers, Pentagon consultants and defense-plant workers—all of whom had some knowledge of black programs and a desire to discuss them in some detail—I have found it impossible to nail down the size of the black budget any closer than the nearest billion. There is a level of financial detail that no outsider can hope to know about the black budget. Seemingly unclassified Pentagon programs conceal black programs within them, like a Chinese box holding boxes within boxes. For example, one Pentagon project called the Airborne Reconnaissance Support Program in reality contains twenty-five classified programs whose costs cannot be traced.[9]

But I can say with assurance that the black budget peaked at about $36 billion a year in 1988 and 1989. This year, in the fiscal 1991 Pentagon request, the declassification of the costs of the Stealth bomber and MILSTAR brought the black budget back down toward $34 billion.

In sum, over the past three years, close to $100 million a day has been pumped out of the Treasury into underground pipelines, channeled covertly into nuclear missiles and bombers and spy satellites and hundreds of other secret programs. The black budget constitutes an annual tax of about $150 on every man, woman and child in the United States, though the Pentagon grants no citizen the right to know how that money is spent. You have to account to the government for every dollar on your taxes. The government won't account to you for a dime of the black budget.

The system I have learned about bears little relation to what I was taught in school about how laws are made and funds appropriated. I'd read the Constitution in grade school. I read it again after first poring over the black budget. The Constitution says the government must publish an accurate account of how it spends our money. Its language is plain: "a regular Statement and Account of the Receipts and Expenditures of all public Money shall be published from time to time." Published means printed and made public. From time to time means regularly, every year. The Pentagon's black budget simply doesn't meet that standard. Nowhere is the account demanded by the Constitution published.

Where was the Congress as the black budget grew? Asleep at the switch. Most members of the Congress have no idea of the black budget's size and scope. I have met freshman members of the House Armed Services Committee who have never heard of the black budget. Only a few senior members know much about the Pentagon's secret spending. The first coherent congressional comment on the growth of black weaponry had come out in April 1986, the month I started my reporting in Washington. Les Aspin, the House Armed Services Committee chairman, put out a terse statement saying the black weapons budget had gone up 800 percent since 1981.

"This is grossly excessive," he said. "There is no excuse for having so much of the defense budget hidden from public view." The issue wasn't protecting military technology, Aspin argued. It was the government hiding basic information about how it spends the public's money, information that ought to be available in a democracy.

This issue wasn't being debated openly. Discussing the workings of the black world on the floor of the Congress may be deemed tantamount to an act of treason, and a member who does so runs the risk of being censured or expelled. The same set of national-security laws that allowed the black budget's existence silenced public debate on specific weapons or specific dollars or specific snafus in the black budget. The Reagan administration wanted the laws toughened so that a reporter or a public official who obtained information about a black program and published it could be convicted of high treason. Upon conviction, such a traitor could be shot to death by a firing squad.[10]

Surely there are genuine secrets within the government, things no government would disclose, the kind of secrets a man like Richard Garwin was entrusted to keep. Garwin helped develop the hydrogen bomb in the early 1950's, and he has been a presidential adviser and a highly respected defense consultant over the course of four decades. I wanted to talk to men like him to help me keep my bearings in the black world. I called him to ask what he thought about the growth of the black budget. He said he knew many of the black programs the Pentagon was working on. More than a few were well-intended. But the secrecy had skyrocketed; the Pentagon was keeping far too many secrets from the public for secrecy's sake alone.

"The proliferation of these programs is very bad. It is primarily to avert criticism and evaluation," Garwin said. "And that is profoundly antidemocratic."

Profoundly antidemocratic. That phrase cropped up from time to time as I went about my work.

I walked through the halls of Congress cadging interviews and looking for insight. In principle it was not too different from rummaging around in the Camden County courthouse. Money was vanishing, crimes of a kind were being committed, and not everyone wanted to discuss it.

Some did. I talked to a member of Congress named Denny Smith, an Oregon Republican and a veteran fighter pilot. He knew the military well and styled himself a "cheap hawk," a cost-conscious conservative on defense issues. He talked about the Pentagon having a secrecy program, as if secrecy were a new weapon the Pentagon was deploying. "They control what the Congress gets and sees," Smith said. "As a congressman, I can't get information. . . . They don't want to have us mucking around in their budget."

He paused, and chose his words carefully. "There's a real question here," he said. "Will the military accept civilian leadership when it comes to choosing weapons?"

This was not mere talk. This was a Republican member of Congress asking whether the military was willing to bow to civilian control. It seemed an odd question to be raising about the government of the United States.

The more I learned about the black budget, the less odd the question seemed. As I kept looking into the stark line items and blank spaces containing billions of invisible dollars, I began to see the bones and veins of the black budget, as if it were an X ray developing before my eyes. And deeper still: in time the genetic code that underlay the secrecy became clear. Secret weapons and secret wars were the double helix that gave life to the black budget. To crack the code was to begin to understand the costs of the Cold War.

The black budget began with the decision to build the atomic bomb. The bomb was born classified, and from its seed grew a secret world. In that world, military secrecy reigned supreme. From Hiroshima onward, the military made secret decisions about the bomb that shaped the black budget of today.

2

Overkill

THE secret treasury began growing on October 9, 1941, two months before Pearl Harbor, when President Franklin D. Roosevelt realized it was possible to make an atomic bomb.

Roosevelt sat in the Oval Office as Vannevar Bush, the dean of engineering at the Massachusetts Institute of Technology, explained the force that fission could unleash. A twenty-five-pound atomic bomb could explode with the power of 3.6 million pounds of dynamite. The bomb could be the winning weapon in the world war. The nation that built it first would control the postwar world.

Roosevelt told Bush that the nation should proceed at once on the research to make the bomb. He wanted it done with the utmost speed and secrecy. The President said he could draw upon a hidden reservoir of funds, "a special source available for such an unusual purpose."[1]

The best guess at the time was that the effort might cost $100 million. Over the next four years, $2.19 billion flowed in secret from the Treasury to the Manhattan Engineer District, the code name chosen for the project to build the bomb. Spending so much money in secret required some "rather unorthodox" methods, some "unusual procedures," in the words of General Leslie R. Groves, the gruff and burly commander of the Manhattan Project. Those methods still serve as a blueprint for the black budget.[2]

Most of the funds for the Manhattan Project were disguised under

two line items in the military budget: "Engineer Service: Army" and
"Expediting Production." The balance was buried in other war appropriations. General Groves said "the overriding need for secrecy" required
"a determined effort to withhold all information on the atomic bomb
project from everyone"—especially the Congress, which remained
"completely in the dark about our work" until February 1944.

That month, Senator Harry Truman started raising hell. Truman led
a Senate committee investigating war profiteering. He became intrigued
and then enraged over hundreds of millions of dollars disappearing into
mysterious military plants about which he knew nothing. He dispatched
his investigators to trace the money. They ran into an impenetrable maze
of military secrecy. The Manhattan Project had become an unseen state
within the United States. It had its own laws and language. The thoughts
and words of its citizens were classified. Its factories churned out secrets.

Unable to find a way through the labyrinth no matter what he and
his investigators tried, Truman angrily confronted the Secretary of War,
Henry Stimson. The senator wanted information. The Secretary of War
refused. Stimson said the President had ordered him to keep this matter
"most top secret." On no account would he share it with the senator.
Truman backed down and called off his watchdogs.[3]

General Groves now realized that the complete secrecy could not
go on forever. The Manhattan Project was spending $2 million a day;
"our expenditures were too vast and the project was too big to remain
concealed." Stimson and Groves agreed that a few senior members of
Congress should be told something about the bomb, if only to keep the
secret funds secure. On February 18, 1944, Stimson, Bush and Army
Chief of Staff General George C. Marshall came to the private office of
the Speaker of the House of Representatives. Their briefing dazzled
Speaker Sam Rayburn, House Majority Leader John McCormack and
Minority Leader Joseph Martin Jr. The six men reached a private understanding. The congressmen agreed to keep the money for the bomb
buried in the Army's budget. Only Rayburn would know the precise way
in which the funds were hidden. McCormack and Martin would keep
their colleagues from asking questions.

By late 1944, the United States knew with certainty that the Nazis
could not build a bomb. The secret of the weapon was safe from the
enemy. The original reason for keeping the secret—beating Hitler to the
punch—was gone. The secrecy persisted. It had become as crucial a
component of the bomb as uranium 235.

The secrecy began to take on a life of its own. It became so powerful
that sixteen years passed before a President saw the military's plan for
using the bomb. By then nuclear weaponry had grown into a machine so
powerful that it controlled its creators.[4]

As the monumental effort moved forward in the secret laboratories of the Manhattan Project, no one stopped to ask exactly how or when or whether to use the bomb. Roosevelt and Winston Churchill agreed privately in September 1944 that the bomb "might, perhaps, after mature consideration, be used against the Japanese." The President shared that cautious judgment with no one in the American government. He took it to his grave on April 12, 1945.[5]

Now the secret was to fall into Harry Truman's hands. The onetime Kansas City ward heeler had become Vice President the previous summer through a Byzantine series of backroom deals cut by big-city political bosses. Suddenly he was the President. Truman felt dazed, overwhelmed by the immensity of his power, as he was sworn into office. The Cabinet met briefly at the White House that evening. As the members filed out silently, Stimson lingered. The time had come to tell Truman about the bomb.

The Secretary of War told the new President that the nation had "an immense project" to build "a new explosive of almost unbelievable power"—and said no more. "That was all he felt free to say at the time," Truman remembered. "His statement left me puzzled."[6]

Twelve days later, Truman opened a note from Stimson:

Dear Mr. President,
 I think it is very important that I should have a talk with you on a highly secret matter.
 I mentioned it to you shortly after you took office, but have not urged it since on account of the pressure you have been under. . . . I think you ought to know about it without much further delay.

Stimson and General Groves came to the Oval Office on April 25 carrying a twenty-four-page report on the bomb. Truman flipped through it impatiently. "Mr. Truman did not like to read long reports," Groves recalled. "This report was not long, considering the size of the project. . . . He would constantly interrupt his reading to say, 'Why, I don't like to read papers.' "

The report raised grave political, military and moral issues. As Stimson confided to his diary that night: "The world in its present state of moral achievement . . . would eventually be at the mercy of such a weapon. In other words, modern civilization might be completely destroyed." But Truman never came to grips with these questions. For the next four months, as General Groves put it, "He was like a little boy on a toboggan," propelled down the slope of history by the gravity of the bomb.[7]

The billions had been spent. The bomb was ready to be tested. If it worked, there was no question that it would be used. The question answered itself.

On July 16, a few minutes after midnight, as thunder rolled over the New Mexico desert and lightning flashed in a starless sky, the physicists of Los Alamos began gathering on a barren hill for the first test of the atomic bomb. Robert Oppenheimer, the project's chief scientist, codenamed the test Trinity, after a John Donne sonnet of death and resurrection which begins: "Batter my heart, three-personed God . . ." Oppenheimer had a mind that could connect poetry and physics, the power of the atom and the metaphors of mythology. When, at 5:30 A.M., the unbearably bright light of the Trinity test exploded, it set off a chain of thoughts within him. Oppenheimer remembered an old myth of secrecy and evil: the story of Prometheus stealing the secret of fire from Zeus, and the vengeful Zeus sending Pandora to Earth with countless plagues concealed in an urn. Here was the fire and the concomitant curse.

As dawn came up on the Pacific Coast that morning, the cruiser *Indianapolis* slipped out of San Francisco Bay, carrying the components of the bomb code-named Little Boy. The ship headed west across the Pacific for the Mariana Islands and a rendezvous with the crew of a B-29 bomber. Little Boy was bound for Hiroshima.

As the ship prepared to lift anchor, Truman toured the rubble of Berlin, awaiting Stalin's arrival at the Potsdam conference of the Allied leaders. In the ruined streets, survivors wandered aimlessly, their eyes blank, and starving children tore at dead horses for their meat.[8]

That evening in Berlin, Stimson received a coded cable reporting Trinity's success. With him was an aide, Harvey Bundy, whose sons McGeorge and William were to achieve power in the postwar world. The Secretary of War turned to the elder Bundy and sighed in relief. "Well," he said, "I have been responsible for spending two billions of dollars on this atomic venture. Now that it is successful I shall not be sent to prison in Fort Leavenworth."[9]

Later that night, Stimson shared the secret with the Supreme Allied Commander, General Dwight D. Eisenhower. The revelation saddened Eisenhower: "He told me they were going to drop it on the Japanese. Well, I listened, and I didn't volunteer anything because, after all, my war was over in Europe and it wasn't up to me. But I was getting more and more depressed just thinking about it. . . . I was against it on two counts. First, the Japanese were ready to surrender and it wasn't necessary to hit them with that awful thing. Second, I hated to see our country be the first to use such a weapon." Of the few men in on the secret, nearly no one shared Eisenhower's doubts. Stimson exploded in anger at the general. "The old gentleman got furious," Ike recalled. "And I can see how he would. After all, it had been his responsibility to push for all the huge expenditure to develop the bomb, which of course he had a right to do, and *was* right to do. Still, it was an awful problem.''[10]

The solution was to drop the bomb. It was the President's responsibility but the military's decision. Truman let the military make it. Truman agreed that the bomb should be used, but he never signed an order to drop it or gave his explicit verbal approval. General Groves put it best: the President's role ''was one of noninterference—basically, a decision not to upset the existing plans'' the military had made. ''I didn't have to have the President push the button on this affair,'' he said long after the war was over. The bomb had its own momentum. It pushed its own button.[11]

The momentum was not merely military. Powerful economic and political forces drove the secret weapon. ''As we poured more and more money into the project, the government became increasingly committed to the ultimate use of the bomb,'' General Groves said. The nation could not spend a fortune on the bomb and then put it on the shelf. There had to be a bang for the buck.[12]

''We had spent $2 billion on developing the bomb. And Congress would want to know what we had got for the money spent,'' said Jimmy Byrnes, a savvy political operator whom Truman had just appointed as Secretary of State. ''How would you get Congress to appropriate money for atomic [weapons] research if you do not show results for the money?''[13]

The commanders in the Pacific wanted the bomb dropped without warning. The secret had to be kept until the moment it exploded. It was revealed to the Japanese at Hiroshima on August 6. The results were immediate. Seventy-one thousand people died instantly; many thousands more met death slowly.

''We have discovered the most terrible bomb in the history of the world, the most terrible thing ever discovered,'' the President had written three weeks earlier in his Berlin diary. Now, as he sailed home from Europe aboard the heavy cruiser *Augusta*, Truman was handed a flash message: HIROSHIMA BOMBED. ''This is the greatest thing in history,'' Truman proclaimed. He ran about the ship, spreading the news. ''Mindlessly,'' wrote Truman's most knowledgeable biographer, ''he said he had never been happier about any announcement he had ever made.''[14] He was caught between terror and glee—between his mortal fear of the terrible bomb and his exultation at its great power. He was, at that instant, the most powerful man in the world. He possessed Promethean fire. He never thought of extinguishing it.

The second bomb, Fat Man, fell on Nagasaki August 9. More than 130,000 people died from the blast, the fire and the radiation. The military selected the target, chose the time and gave the final orders. Truman had told Stimson at Potsdam that he hoped only one bomb would be necessary. But once again he did not make a choice or set a policy. The President did not think through the decision to destroy Nagasaki. "Having found the bomb," Truman told a nationwide radio audience that day, "we used it."[15]

The war was over, but it never really ended. As soon as victory came, the military began planning for the war to come. Truman recorded in his memoirs that the Joint Chiefs of Staff insisted, nine days after Hiroshima, that "it was now more than ever necessary to guard and maintain the secrecy of the bomb." They were dead-set on keeping the secret, building as many bombs as possible and making them as powerful as the laws of physics allowed. From the first week of the new age, the military was shaping the nuclear future.[16]

The Joint Chiefs set forth the nation's first secret plans for atomic warfare four weeks after Hiroshima. The plans called for the U.S. to be ready "to strike the first blow if necessary . . . when it becomes evident that the forces of aggression are being arrayed against us." Although many Americans don't realize it, that secret first-strike policy remains in place. There is no other way to win a nuclear war.

The United States made its new war plans without knowing its new enemy. Washington was ignorant of what went on in Moscow. Everyone knew Stalin was a murderous tyrant. No one questioned the danger he presented to America's allies in Europe. But the nature of the threat he posed to the United States was an enigma. The Soviet Union was a sealed fortress led by a paranoid dictator. Its military intentions were a mystery to American intelligence.

Soviet secrecy fed American fears. Lacking facts, the United States assumed the worst. The nation's leaders thought we were weaker than the Soviets when we were far stronger. The newborn Central Intelligence Agency overestimated Soviet troop strengths by the millions. The Soviets had lost twenty million lives in the war, seven and a half million soldiers. Their economy was devastated: 31,000 factories, forty million head of livestock, one-fourth of the nation's possessions destroyed by the Nazis. They had no modern navy, no long-range air force, and as of yet no bomb. Nor would they test a bomb until late in the summer of 1949.

The United States was by contrast a colossus. We had lost fewer than 300,000 soldiers. We controlled two-thirds of the world's capital. We had a near monopoly on technology, science and industry in a devastated and exhausted world. We had the bomb. Still we were afraid.[17]

Fear begat funds. In early 1948, the Pentagon was seeking ways to boost its budget for the coming year. Army intelligence chiefs asked General Lucius Clay, the American military governor of Germany, if he could help prod Congress into appropriating more money for armaments.

On March 5, Clay sent a cable to Washington, disregarding the normal secure communications channels. Clay's communique, based on little of substance, warned that the Soviets were preparing for battle with the United States. The cable said the Third World War "may come with dramatic suddenness." The warning terrified Truman. "Will Russia move first?" he asked. "Who pulls the trigger? Then where do we go?" The Pentagon leaked the cable throughout Washington. The armed forces went on alert. Congress forked over the money the Army sought, and more.

That summer, the Soviets blockaded Berlin by land and water and the Americans broke the blockade by air. Both sides struggled for political control of Europe. The tension deepened. "I have a terrible feeling," Truman wrote in his diary on September 13, "that we are very close to war."[18]

Three days later the newly created National Security Council—the President, Vice-President, Secretary of Defense, Secretary of State, and a White House staff—secretly adopted its first edict on atomic warfare. The highly classified order was numbered NSC-30. It said the military "must be ready to utilize promptly and effectively all appropriate means available, including atomic weapons, in the interest of national security and must plan accordingly." But NSC-30 gave the military no guidance on what kind of plans to make, or how to make them conform to national policy—or what exactly that policy was.

The President's men could not make coherent policy because they knew very little about the bomb. The subject was so secret that the NSC's members could not discuss it in a meaningful way. It was so secret that the President knew almost nothing about it. Truman had no idea how many warheads the nation had, how many it might need, where the cutting edge of weapons technology lay, what war plans the military was preparing. The lawful helmsman of the atomic force was flying blind.[19]

"Secrecy—and also awe—constrained even those with an obvious need to know" about the bomb, said McGeorge Bundy, who served as national security adviser to Presidents Kennedy and Johnson and later spent ten years studying Presidents' decisions about the bomb. "The subject, for everyone, was surrounded by taboos. The result was enormous ignorance, even at the top."[20]

Secrecy, ignorance and fear fed each other in a chain reaction. The secrecy shrouding the bomb led to ignorance, which fueled the deep fear that gripped the men who led the nation. The fear scarred their minds and skewed their thinking. They saw the enemy as if in a funhouse mirror, a distorted image of their own deep terror. The enemy looked at us and saw the same. Both sides began building up their forces for the next war.

The task of creating a strategy for World War III fell to Lieutenant

General Curtis E. LeMay. In October 1948 LeMay became the first chief of the new Strategic Air Command (SAC), the elite Air Force group geared for global warfare. If anyone had the will to create a plan for doomsday, it was he.

LeMay has been caricatured over the years as a cartoon monster, a cigar-chomping warmonger. The image is unjust. He did chew cigars, and he suffered from a facial palsy that twisted his features into a permanent snarl. Behind the grimace lay a superior military mind. LeMay was a patriot given great power. He used that power to the hilt.

As the head of the 20th Bomber Command in 1944 and 1945, LeMay was ordered to build a war machine from a jumble of men, planes and spare parts, and to use that machine to destroy Japan. He was not assigned to assess the consequences. "To worry about the *morality* of what we were doing—Nuts. A soldier has to fight. We fought," LeMay said. "If we accomplished the job in any given battle without exterminating too many of our own folks, we considered that we'd had a pretty good day." His firebombing of Toyko destroyed a third of the city and killed at least 84,000 people in a single night. "We knew we were going to kill a lot of women and kids. Had to be done." LeMay saw his job as saving the lives of his men, American lives. His relentless attacks on Japan's cities accomplished that mission. LeMay saw air war as total war: "There are no innocent civilians. It is their government and you are fighting a people, you are not trying to fight an armed force anymore." His vision of war was shaped by the bombing campaigns.[21]

By the time LeMay took command of SAC in 1948, a series of weapons tests code-named SANDSTONE had confirmed that new kinds of atomic warheads could be built—much smaller, much lighter, much more powerful than before. The fact that they could be built assured that they would be. Within a year the atomic stockpile doubled, and doubled again, approaching 200 warheads by late 1949. But LeMay thought in orders of magnitude: he wanted ten times more, a hundred times more.[22]

LeMay knew he could transform SAC into the air force of the apocalypse. He would destroy not mere cities, but whole nations, on the opening day of the next war. He aimed to make SAC a "cocked weapon." He would divine the enemy's war plans and, "believing I could foresee an attack . . . beat him to the draw." He would strike first, dropping thousands of warheads on the Soviets "in one fell swoop telescoping mass and time." The communist world would collapse instantly beneath the onslaught.[23]

LeMay's vision of an atomic blitz began emerging in 1949. It sparked a flare of dissent from the leading officers of the Navy. This was less an interservice rivalry than a revulsion against plans for mass murder. The argument was based, as Admiral Daniel Gallery put it, on the conflict between SAC's plan and the policy of "a 'civilized nation' like the United States."

"Leveling large cities has a tendency to alienate the affections of the inhabitants and does not create an atmosphere of international good will after the war," Gallery wrote in a private letter to the Deputy Chief of Naval Operations. He condemned SAC's war plan as "an unworthy one for a country of our strength."

Rear Admiral Ralph A. Ofstie argued that "since war was an instrument of national policy, the method of waging it should be adjusted to policy objectives." LeMay's plan "was not related to policy." It called for "the wholesale extermination of civilians." It was "ruthless and barbaric." It was "contrary to fundamental American ideals and would therefore be opposed by the American people on moral grounds."[24]

The revolt was joined by Admiral Louis Denfield, the Chief of Naval Operations and a member of the Joint Chiefs of Staff. He said the war plans were unworkable and unspeakable. When Denfield tried to take his dissent to Congress, he committed an act of professional suicide. On October 27, 1949, Truman fired him.

October 1949 was no time for dissenters. One month earlier, an Air Force intelligence plane patrolling off the coast of Alaska had discovered tiny traces of radioactivity in the air. It had come from an atomic bomb. And it wasn't ours. It was evidence that the Soviets had tested their first atomic weapon.

The political shock waves from that blast reverberated throughout Washington. The United States knew Stalin would have the bomb one day. The secret was in the nature of the atom, not locked in a safe inside the Pentagon. But few in Washington thought the day would come so soon. Now the idea of hitting the Soviets with an atomic barrage became far more ominous. The first strike would have to be a killing blow, or retaliation was certain.

The military decided that it was time to tell the President about the hydrogen bomb, the weapon with the power of a thousand atom bombs. It was time to tell him that the new weapon was within our grasp, to tell him that the nation needed thousands, tens of thousands. The President had never heard of the hydrogen bomb; he had no idea that such a weapon was on the horizon. By that time the possibility had existed for four years. No one ever told him.[25]

Truman asked few questions and learned few facts about the bomb. He never fully understood what it was or how it could be used. "I regarded the bomb as a military weapon," Truman wrote in his public memoirs. "You have got to understand that this *isn't* a military weapon," the

President privately insisted to Air Force officials in a 1949 meeting. "It is used to wipe out women and children and unarmed people, and not for military uses." He could not govern a force he could not understand.[26]

The military controlled the facts presented to the President, and so controlled the choices he made. LeMay and his many like-minded allies in the Pentagon didn't see the bomb as a symbol or a bargaining chip. They saw it as the greatest weapon mankind ever created, and they thought they were going to have to drop it on the Soviets sooner or later. They decided how many warheads the nation needed and how they would be used. The President rubber-stamped their decisions. Only days after discovering that the Soviets had tested their first bomb, Truman approved a tremendous expansion of atomic warhead production, without any debate or discussion among his highest civilian advisers. In January 1950 the President gave the go-ahead to what he called "the so-called hydrogen or Super-bomb." This moment marked a point of no return. The race was on.

A panic swept Washington that winter. Generals and politicians began calling for a war against the Soviet Union. In their minds the war already was under way. This sense that we were at war was no metaphor. "We are in a war worse than we have ever experienced," Robert Lovett, a future Secretary of Defense, told the National Security Council staff in March 1950. "It is not a cold war. It is a hot war." The United States had to "start acting exactly as though we were under fire from an invading army," Lovett said. "In the war in which we are presently engaged, we should fight with no holds barred."[27]

The Secretary of Defense, Louis Johnson, was arguing that the United States should attack the Soviet Union immediately. Johnson had replaced James Forrestal, who'd gone mad in 1949, imagining a menagerie of communist conspirators surrounding him, subverting his thoughts, poisoning his mind. Now Johnson, too, was showing signs of instability, careening around Washington like a man possessed. The Secretary of State, Dean Acheson, believed Johnson's conduct was "too outrageous to be explained by mere cussedness"; he thought the Secretary of Defense was "brain-damaged" or "mentally ill."[28]

Johnson's call for war was one voice in a chorus. The Secretary of the Navy, Francis Matthews, argued for a strike against the Soviets that would "cast us in a character new to a true democracy—an initiator of a war of aggression . . . the first aggressors for peace." The Secretary of the Air Force, Thomas Finletter, spoke of "policing the world with H-bombs" and privately pleaded for authority to launch LeMay's squadrons toward Moscow. General Orville Anderson, the commanding officer of the Air War College, openly advocated "preventive war as a means to keep the U.S.S.R. from becoming a nuclear power." General Anderson wanted Washington to deliver an ultimatum to the Kremlin: Retreat to your borders or we will destroy you. "Give me the order to do it and I can break up Russia's five A-bomb nests in a week," General Anderson proclaimed in a widely reported public speech. "And when I went up to Christ—I think I could explain to Him that I had saved civilization."[29]

The fervors of 1950 found their purest and most controlled expression in another top-secret National Security Council directive: NSC-68, a 25,000-word treatise completed in April 1950, approved as national policy by Truman that September, and kept classified until 1975. The impassioned language of NSC-68 shaped American strategic thinking for nearly forty years.

NSC-68 had two lasting legacies. It defined America's future primarily in terms of a massive and imminent Soviet military threat. And it provided the intellectual basis for a permanent war economy in this country. It remains the central document of the Cold War.[30]

The principal author of NSC-68 was Paul Nitze, a pivotal figure in American nuclear strategy. A brilliant, sometimes arrogant man who possessed great wealth and steely ideas, Nitze had just been named to lead the State Department's policy planning staff, succeeding the leading Cold War theorist of the day, George Kennan. Kennan was a diplomat who saw the world in shades of gray, in nuances and ambiguities. Nitze was a technocrat; he saw a black-and-white world of numbers and absolutes. His mind calculated national policy as if it were an elaborate mathematical equation. Nitze had experienced a revelation at Hiroshima. He had walked through the ruins of the city, taking detailed notes on the destruction. He wanted to "measure precisely the physical effects" of the bomb, he said, "to put calipers on it, instead of describing it in emotive terms. I was trying to put quantitative terms on something that was considered immeasurable." Ever since, he had believed that nuclear war could be translated into a matrix of numbers. The numbers had political value. American policy had to be based on nuclear dominance, on having more nuclear weapons at the beginning and at the end of the next war than the enemy—in short, to have the power to win a nuclear war. The calculus of nuclear superiority would decide the political fate of the world.[31]

Nitze added up the balance of power between the United States and the Soviet Union in the winter of 1950 and arrived at a terrifying conclusion. In four years, the United States would be looking down the barrel of an awesome weapon, a gigantic Soviet military machine. The nation was in mortal danger. Americans had to realize that Moscow aimed to destroy them.

NSC-68 was an air-raid siren echoing down the corridors of power. It depicted the world as a battlefield where the armies of good and evil were fighting to the death. It said the Soviets, "animated by a new fanatic faith," sought to conquer the world. The United States was "the principal enemy whose integrity and vitality must be subverted or destroyed . . . if the Kremlin is to achieve its fundamental design." America was "mortally challenged" by "the conspicuous might of the Soviet military machine." If the Soviets amassed as many nuclear weapons as the United States possessed, "the Kremlin might be tempted to strike swiftly and with stealth." That awful moment was fast approaching. Time was running out.

The United States could shut its eyes and cross its fingers—or choose among three courses NSC-68 offered. One: "capitulate." Surrender, let the Red Army hoist the hammer and sickle over America. Inconceivable.

Two: "precipitate a global war." A possibility. "Some Americans favor a deliberate decision to go to war with the Soviet Union in the near future." But "surprise attack upon the Soviet Union . . . would be repugnant to many Americans. Although the American people would probably rally in support of the war effort, the shock of responsibility for a surprise attack would be morally corrosive."

Three: "a rapid and concerted build-up" of weaponry. Imperative, the only path to peace. "It is clear that our military strength is becoming dangerously inadequate" for "the total struggle in which we are engaged," NSC-68 proclaimed. The buildup had to be immense and sustained. "Budgetary considerations will need to be subordinated to the stark fact that our very independence as a nation may be at stake." The nation had "no alternative" to building thousands of thermonuclear weapons and spending money as if war were at hand.

The secret policy turned the national budget upside down. Truman's defense spending already surpassed any peacetime President's. Still, the military spent only what was left after domestic programs and peaceful foreign-policy initiatives were set. Now every other national concern would be secondary to the military. Nitze privately calculated the policy's price tag at between $40 billion and $50 billion a year—more than the entire federal budget in 1950. The cost-conscious Truman never learned of this calculation. "This was not an oversight," Acheson noted. He told Nitze to keep any mention of money out of the report. To debate the cost of NSC-68's goals would make implementing them impossible. Rather, Acheson said, the task was "to bludgeon the mass mind of 'top government' " with language that was "clearer than truth."[32]

NSC-68 did transcend truth. It gave the clear, but false, impression that the Soviet Union, which only eight months earlier had tested its first crude atomic bomb, presented a monumental and immediate military threat to the United States. It said the Soviets would soon match the United States in nuclear firepower; nuclear parity was in fact some thirty years away. It spoke of 175 Soviet divisions primed for war. The 175 combat-ready divisions were a mirage, Nitze later conceded. The man who would measure the immeasurable destruction of nuclear bombs had tripled the true number of Soviet troops.

The blunt instrument Acheson had described made its impact. U.S. military spending quadrupled from $13.7 billion in 1950 to $52.8 billion in 1953. The Korean War, which began in June 1950, ate up less than one-tenth of this increase. The bulk went to new military bases ringing the Soviet Union and China and to a huge surge of weapons production. NSC-68 had assailed "the war economy of the Soviet world" for spending 13.8 percent of the Soviet gross national product on the military. By 1953, the United States was spending 14.4 percent of its gross national product on the military. Of that, only about one percent financed the Korean War.[33]

That war was a sideshow to Washington. The real enemy was not the Chinese or the North Koreans. It was their masters in Moscow. Acheson put it frankly: the "great trouble" with the Korean War was "that we are fighting the wrong enemy. We are fighting the second team, whereas the real enemy is the Soviet Union."[34]

In November 1950, as Chinese and American troops killed one another in the frozen mud of Korea, Truman fielded a question at a Washington press conference: Would he unleash the bomb on the communists? "It's a matter that the military people will have to decide," the President said. "I'm not a military authority that passes on those things. . . . The military commander in the field will have charge of the use of the weapons, as he always has." As always, Truman was giving the military control of political decisions about the bomb. He already had given commanders overseas direct access to atomic warheads. Now he appeared to place their fingers on the trigger. "It looks like World War III is here," he wrote in his diary that November. "I hope not—but we must meet whatever comes—and we will." Shortly thereafter he declared a national emergency. The military began mobilizing for the next world war.[35]

We would not be prepared to fight that war until we had amassed nuclear forces far in excess of what we imagined the Soviet Union might have someday. With an explosion of Pentagon spending and the rapid development of the new hydrogen bomb under way, the nation's warhead factories began running full-bore. The buildup transformed the Strategic Air Command. LeMay had only thirty or so atomic bombers when he took control of SAC. By 1953 he had more than one thousand. He had at his fingertips an explosive force far greater than all the bombs used in World War II. He had the power to kill a nation.[36]

In 1953 the American people brought to power a retired general promising them peace. General Eisenhower came to the presidency committed to ending the war in Korea. He knew better than any politician the horror of war. And he had a strategy to control the huge military budgets brought on by the war scares of the early 1950's. The new President thought building more nuclear weapons was a less expensive, more effective counter to the Soviet threat than maintaining an immense standing army. The bomb was a bargain. It offered immeasurably more bang for the buck. Eisenhower's thinking mirrored the assurances of the electric industry in the 1950's: nuclear power was going to be clean, efficient and too cheap to meter. In both cases, as the clear light of hindsight shows, the costs and consequences proved greater than imagined.

The policy of building more nuclear weapons was Eisenhower's. But as the plans for nuclear war became more and more complex, with thousands of warheads aimed at thousands of targets, the President lost control of nuclear strategy. He never knew more than the broadest outlines of the developing nuclear battle plans. When he realized that they were growing beyond all reason, it was too late. He tried to limit them, but could not. For six years the President kept his fears to himself. He looked away as General LeMay made bigger and bigger plans to destroy every dot on the Soviet map. He watched silently as the nation's nuclear weaponry became a self-propelled juggernaut.

Eisenhower's public pronouncements sometimes gave the impression that he saw the piling of warhead upon warhead as pure futility. In April 1953, less than three months after his inauguration, at the Statler Hotel in Washington, he gave one of the finest speeches of his presidency, warning of the cost of the arms race. "The worst to be feared and the best to be expected can be simply stated," he said. "The worst is atomic war. The best would be this: a life of perpetual fear and tension; a burden of arms draining the wealth and the labor of all peoples . . .

"Every warship launched, every rocket fired signifies, in the final sense, a theft from those who hunger and are not fed, those who are cold and are not clothed," Eisenhower said. "The cost of one modern heavy bomber"—one among LeMay's one thousand—" is this: a modern brick school in more than thirty cities. It is two electric power plants, each serving a city of sixty thousand population. It is two fine, fully equipped hospitals. . . ." Bathed in a cold sweat, trembling from an intestinal infection, Eisenhower raced to his summation: "This is not a way of life at all, in any true sense. Under the cloud of threatening war, it is humanity hanging from a cross of iron."[37]

Eisenhower was no pacifist. His fears of the costs of the arms race led him to think hard about destroying the Soviet Union. The logical way to end the Cold War might be to wipe out the competition. He discussed this idea several times with his fiercely anticommunist Secretary of State, John Foster Dulles, whose brother Allen ran the CIA. The subject arose the week after the Soviet Union exploded its first hydrogen bomb in August 1953. John Foster Dulles argued that the moment was upon us: "Sooner or later," he told the President, "we must manage to remove the taboo from the use of these weapons." The United States had an overwhelming advantage in nuclear firepower. We might soon lose it. If we were going to hit the Russians, the time was ripe. In early September, Eisenhower wrote to Foster Dulles that the "vastly increased expenditures" of an endless arms race might prove insufferable for the United States. "The cost would either drive us to war—or into some form of dictatorial government," the President said. "In such circumstances, we would be forced to consider whether or not our duty to future generations did not require us to *initiate* war at the most propitious moment."[38]

Eisenhower turned the idea over and over in his head, and rejected it. "I want you to carry this question home with you: Gain such a victory, and what do you do with it?" he asked the Joint Chiefs in June 1954. "Here would be a great area from the Elbe to Vladivostok"—all of the Soviet Union and Eastern Europe—"torn up and destroyed, without its communications, just an area of starvation and disaster. I ask you what would the civilized world do about it? I repeat there is no victory except through our imaginations."[39]

The imaginations of the military ran differently from Eisenhower's. They envisioned victory. "There is no question that a nuclear war can be 'won,' as wars of the past have been won—by the side which is best prepared to fight it," said General Nathan F. Twining, the Air Force Chief of Staff and chairman of the Joint Chiefs of Staff under Eisenhower. That vision—not Eisenhower's—shaped the nation's nuclear forces.[40]

The military's vision was flawed. By 1955, the nuclear arsenal was too powerful to be used. A Pentagon war game conducted that year revealed this dilemma. The war game was code-named CARTE BLANCHE.

CARTE BLANCHE was conceived as an exercise in moderation. The American players allotted themselves only 335 small nuclear warheads, about one-tenth of the available firepower. They planned a conservative attack against a Soviet invasion of Western Europe. In the first two days of the game, 270 of the American warheads exploded upon Germany. Immediate civilian casualties were estimated at 1.7 million dead and 3.5 million wounded. CARTE BLANCHE showed that a nuclear attack against a Soviet invasion would destroy Europe in order to save it. The conundrum went unsolved.[41]

LeMay wanted a nuclear force that could defeat any enemy, and made his plans accordingly. But the enemy he planned to defeat was far less powerful than he feared. For SAC's war plans were based on imaginary projections of a huge Soviet bomber force. The fears of a bomber gap began building in 1955. U.S. Air Force intelligence estimated that the Soviets would have between 500 and 800 intercontinental Bear and Bison bombers in five years. In reality, the Soviets never built more than 200 Bears and Bisons. The intellectual machinery that churned out these Air Force estimates was more like alchemy than analysis. Air Force intelligence took leaden fragments of data—twelve Soviet bombers spotted at a Moscow air show, guesses about assembly line efficiency, old Nazi reconnaissance photos of Russian industrial plants. Then it mixed the data into Air Force studies showing that Soviets would need at least 500 long-range bombers to attack the United States. Suddenly the data were gold. They proved the Soviets were building at least 500 bombers, and if the Soviets were building that many bombers it could only be for an all-out attack.

In time, this way of thinking earned a name: threat inflation. It continually corrupted American estimates of Soviet strength. The nuclear commanders built a force. Then they feared the Soviets had an equal force. So they built a greater force, and a defense against that force, and another force to counter that defense. They never realized that their spyglass on the Soviets was a mirror.

They were like medieval mapmakers trying to chart an unknown world. Out on the edge of the map, out where knowledge dissolved into dreadful conjecture, they drew dragons and inscribed the warning: Here Lie Monsters.

"The U.S. . . . was fighting a bogeyman," said Jerome Wiesner, scientific adviser to Presidents Eisenhower, Kennedy and Johnson, and president emeritus of the Massachusetts Institute of Technology. In retrospect, "we were running against our own intelligence, which wasn't very good. In fact, our assessments of the Soviet capabilities tended to be a mirror image of what we were doing. That is really very dangerous." The bomber gap was not the first such nuclear hallucination masquerading as hardheaded realism, and far from the last.[42]

The hardest questions the weapons posed were left for the weapons' greatest proponents to answer. How do you fight a nuclear war? How much firepower is enough? Can the war be controlled once it starts? The answers rested in the mind of the man who ran the Strategic Air Command. LeMay believed that he alone had the nerve and foresight to win a nuclear war. For four years running he simply refused to submit his annually revised war plan to the Joint Chiefs. It was his secret. He alone would determine the exact manner in which SAC would fight the war.

Finally, on June 9, 1955, General Twining sent LeMay a letter that said, in effect, please tell us what your war plan is. Four months later,

LeMay provided a short briefing to the Joint Chiefs. The plan called for the instantaneous destruction of 645 military targets, 118 cities and sixty million people in the Soviet Union. It stunned the few officers from outside SAC headquarters who were briefed on its dimensions. One naval officer left a SAC briefing with the vivid impression that "virtually all of Russia would be nothing but a smoking, radiating ruin at the end of two hours."[43]

By now the United States had two policies for the bomb. National policy—the openly declared policy of the United States—was one thing. SAC's was quite another. The public policy announced for political effect was restraint, control, Atoms for Peace. If war came, the enemy faced massive retaliation, but nuclear weapons would not be used for a first strike.

The real policy was Curtis LeMay's. He was convinced a first strike was absolutely essential for victory. If he perceived the Soviets were readying their bombers for war, he said, "I'm going to knock the shit out of them before they get off the ground." And he planned to launch that strike without the President's go-ahead if he had to.[44]

Presidents have told the people time and again that only the Commander in Chief has the authority to push the nuclear button. That is not so. Since at least 1957, the SAC commander has had that power.[45]

General Thomas Power became the SAC commander after nine years as LeMay's deputy, when LeMay was promoted to Vice Chief of Staff, second in command of the Air Force, in October 1957. Officers and civilians from outside SAC's closed world found General Power genuinely frightening. He was bombastic, a shouter, a table-pounder. He believed deeply in the wisdom of the secret first-strike policy.

On November 22, 1957, General Power received a memorandum from the Air Force Chief of Staff, General Thomas White. The memo gave Power the authority to launch his nuclear weapons in an emergency "if time or circumstances would not permit a decision by the President."[46] General LeMay may not have had the written authority to launch a nuclear war in a crisis. But General Power certainly did. And General Power had an arsenal the likes of which the world had never seen.[47]

By 1958 nuclear weaponry was an infinitely expanding dynamo. SAC's target list had grown to some 20,000 dots on the communist map, with the help of photographs from the CIA's new U-2 spy plane, a winged eye in the sky that was mapping the Soviet Union. The target list included every city in Russia, Eastern Europe and China; railroad switching yards, airfields, dams, power stations, oil rigs, bridges, fertilizer plants, machine-tool factories, anything that conceivably could be identified as a military or economic target. Every target needed to be destroyed by at least one warhead. So SAC needed more warheads, many more. Soon there were enough warheads to assign two or three to each target. More warheads required more missiles to carry them, more bombers, more computers for SAC to sort out all the missions, more computer-generated plans requiring more warheads, and so on in an endlessly rising spiral.

In 1945, the Little Boy bomb had destroyed Hiroshima with an explosive force of about 12.5 thousand tons of TNT. In 1952, the arsenal held 128 million tons of radioactive firepower. In 1959, it peaked at nineteen billion tons. If that arsenal were a freight train with 100-foot-long boxcars, and each of its boxcars carried one Hiroshima, the train would reach around the world. It carried the death and destruction of more than 1.5 million Hiroshimas.[48]

SAC's strategists did not have 1.5 million targets to hit. They had far more firepower than places to fire. So they figured on hitting a Soviet city the size of Hiroshima with nuclear bombs 600 times more powerful than the Little Boy.[49]

As SAC worked on the war plan, Eisenhower gradually grew more and more aware of the power of the secret arsenal. The more he learned, the more he worried. In 1958, the military sought and received more classified funds to build more nuclear reactors, to make more plutonium, to triple the number of warheads within a year. Why did they need so many? Eisenhower asked John McCone, the Atomic Energy Commission's chairman and a future CIA director. Where was the logic? What was the point? "They are trying to get themselves in an incredible position—of having enough to destroy every conceivable target in the world, plus a threefold reserve," he told McCone in January 1959.

Eisenhower was not talking about banning the bomb. But he was becoming afraid that if SAC unleashed even a fraction of its weapons, the radioactive fallout would drift back to destroy life in the United States, all of Europe, half the planet. "There just might be nothing left of the Northern Hemisphere," he told Gordon Gray, his national security assistant, in February 1959.[50]

The weaponry had grown too powerful. So had the complex of forces that produced the weapons. "How are we ever going to scale our programs down?" Eisenhower asked his dying Secretary of State, John Foster Dulles, in April 1960. If we did not, "in the long run, there is nothing but war—if we give up all hope of a peaceful solution."[51]

For years the President had told the Joint Chiefs of Staff to impose some control over the plans for nuclear war. They left the job to SAC. And SAC kept its plans secret from the President. It was not until August 1960 that the President told the nuclear commanders to show him their order of battle. Three months after Eisenhower's order, General Power produced a unified program with an unwieldy name: the Single Integrated

Operational Plan—SIOP. Finally, in late November 1960, the President took his first full look at the military's plan for nuclear war.

What Eisenhower saw shocked and disgusted him. He understood war. He had seen cities in ruin, he knew death and destruction. The President thought the plan was a monstrosity. He thought it was pure overkill.[52]

The plan began World War III with a devastating first strike. Three thousand two hundred and sixty-seven nuclear warheads annihilated the Soviet Union, China and Eastern Europe in a single blinding blow. And the first strike was just that: the beginning. SAC planned to follow this apocalyptic spasm with thousands and thousands more bombs, everything we had on hand. Ten nations would be obliterated. Five hundred million people would die.

The plan accurately reflected General Power's thinking. "The whole idea is to *kill* the bastards!" Power said in December 1960. "At the end of the war, if there are two Americans and one Russian, we win!"[53]

The plan did not reflect the thinking of the President. There had to be some limit, Eisenhower told his naval aide, Captain Pete Aurand: "We've got to get this thing right down to the deterrence"—to cut the arsenal down to the minimum necessary to deter the Soviets from going to war. He never did.

No President has. The military then had roughly 23,000 nuclear warheads in the arsenal, almost exactly the same number as today. More than 90 percent were in their possession and ready to be fired at any time. The President did not know—because he was not told—that the military planned an automatic and total escalation to nuclear war anytime that U.S. and Soviet soldiers clashed. Once that tripwire was triggered, once the war began, there was no way to control it. Presidential control of nuclear weapons had become a convenient fiction.[54]

Eisenhower realized he had lost command over the power of the nuclear arsenal. He did not share this knowledge with the nation. He did not say what he knew. The subject was too secret. But he felt compelled to deliver as clear a warning as he could. Two months after his first look at the SIOP, on January 17, 1961, Eisenhower took to the airwaves to deliver his farewell address to the nation. What he said was startling. People remember the gist of it to this day:

> Our military organization today bears little relation to that known by any of my predecessors in peacetime, or indeed by the fighting men of World War II or Korea. Until the latest of our world conflicts, the United States had no armaments industry. American makers of plowshares could, with time and as required, make swords as well.

But now . . . we have been compelled to create a permanent armaments industry of vast proportions. Added to this, three and a half million men and women are directly engaged in the defense establishment. We annually spend on military security more than the net income of all United States corporations.

This conjunction of an immense military establishment and a large arms industry is new in the American experience. The total influence—economic, political, even spiritual—is felt in every city, every statehouse, every office of the federal government . . .

In the councils of government, we must guard against the acquisition of unwarranted influence, whether sought or unsought, by the military-industrial complex. The potential for the disastrous rise of misplaced power exists and will persist.

We must never let the weight of this combination endanger our liberties or democratic processes. We should take nothing for granted.

The President, a five-star general, was calling the Pentagon's power a threat to the nation. He was describing the growth of the national arsenal grinding against the law of the land, corroding the Constitution.

Yet what the Pentagon feared most about American nuclear forces in these years was their inadequacy. No sooner had it moved to close the bomber gap than it discovered a missile gap. The Air Force thought the Soviets soon would have as many as 3,000 intercontinental ballistic missiles, the new and terrible ICBMs, missiles that could fly from the U.S.S.R to the U.S.A. in half an hour—3,000 of them, far more than American forces possessed.

The augury again was a delusion. General Power was looking at reconnaissance pictures of Russian territory and pointing out ICBM sites that were in reality war memorials, cathedrals, grain silos, haystacks and fallow fields. Intelligence estimates of the number of missiles the Soviets *might* have in the future were cited as evidence of how many they *did* have.[55]

Secrecy prevented the fraud from being exposed. The knowledge that the missile gap was heavily in America's favor was held by only a few. The knowledge had been gleaned by the U-2, and confirmed by the new intelligence satellite, *Discoverer*—but Eisenhower thought the existence of the spy planes and satellites was too secret to be shared. Four civilians in the American government knew about the espionage flights. Yet the Russians had known about the U-2 ever since its first violation of Soviet airspace in 1956. So did the governments of at least six nations which provided air bases for the spy plane. The Congress and the American people did not.

To shield that secret, the falsehood of the missile gap went unchallenged for four years. The missile gap was revealed as a mirage once the secret was out—long after the Soviets shot down a U-2 on May Day 1960 and the Eisenhower administration had been caught lying to the public about the spy plane.

"The 'bomber gap' of several years ago was always a fiction, and the 'missile gap' shows every sign of being the same," Eisenhower finally told the public in his last State of the Union Address, in January 1961. The first American intelligence satellites were making an amazing discovery. The Soviet Union did not have 3,000 ICBMs loaded with multimegaton warheads and aimed at America's head and heart, as Air Force intelligence feared. They did not have 1,000 ICBMs, as SAC insisted. They did not have 200, as the CIA cautiously estimated. They had four. All sat above ground at a single launch site. One well-placed warhead could wipe them out. The nation's war plans and policies had been created in secret with the Russia of imagination in mind, an enemy conceived in ignorance and fear of the unknown.

John Kennedy had made the spectre of Soviet missiles a central issue in his presidential campaign. He had assumed that the United States faced a heavily armed nuclear enemy and yet had no plan to strike first. But he learned soon after his swearing-in that we had far more missiles than the Soviets, we were indeed planning to strike first if war threatened, and if that time came we were planning to shoot off everything at once.[56]

Kennedy was as unnerved as Eisenhower by the brute force and inflexibility of the Single Integrated Operational Plan. He received his first briefing on the SIOP from the Joint Chiefs on September 13, 1961. He was told he had little choice but to fire the entire arsenal if war came—the plan was "designed for execution as a whole." A limited attack had "little practical meaning as a humanitarian gesture." It would still kill "many millions" of civilians. The weapons were so powerful that "there is considerable question that the Soviets would be able to distinguish between a total attack and an attack on military targets." After absorbing the war plan Kennedy walked out of the Oval Office, turned to his Secretary of State, Dean Rusk, and muttered, "and we call ourselves the human race."[57]

The arsenal kept growing under Kennedy, its momentum too strong to stop. A bitter struggle over the nuclear-war machine now began between the military and the civilians. The new defense secretary, Robert McNamara, began to ask heretical questions. How much was enough? How many missiles, how many bombers, how many warheads? The brightest minds of the Rand Corporation, the Air Force's civilian think tank, were recruited by McNamara to seek the answers.

The Air Force was demanding 10,000 ICBMs as the minimum force needed to ensure national security. But the civilian analysts calculated that roughly 400 one-megaton nuclear missiles striking Soviet territory would destroy the nation. Anything beyond 400 only made the rubble bounce. Anything beyond 400 was overkill.

Had the fears behind the missile gap prevailed, 10,000 ICBMs might have been built. Once facts replaced fear and ignorance, 400 looked like plenty. A political compromise was forged. One thousand ICBMs was the minimum force deemed necessary to deter an attack on the White House—not by the Russians, but by the American military and Congressional conservatives. One thousand was enough, more than enough. Today, thirty years later, in the aftermath of the Soviets' building up their nuclear forces to equal ours, 1,000 is still more than enough.

By the early 1960's America's nuclear forces began to look much as they do today: the triad of land-based ICBMs, sea-going submarine missiles and airborne bombers. The central problem that confronted the nuclear strategists of the day still remains the same: how to fight the war and win.

The first SIOP called for the United States to unleash all its weapons if the Soviets invaded Europe. If the Soviets did not believe we would destroy Europe in order to save Europe, then the strategy was worthless. The war planners of the Kennedy administration—a group ranging from General Power to Paul Nitze to Daniel Ellsberg—were ordered to come up with something more sophisticated, more flexible than blowing up whole nations.

They began searching for ways to fight a limited nuclear war. They wanted the ability to choose clearly defined levels of nuclear violence, a ladder of escalation with many rungs ranging from peace to total war. A new order was needed to control the levels of escalation and thus the flow of battle. The struggle to impose reason on the SIOP proceeded from this point.

The Rand analysts already had thought long and hard about rationalizing nuclear war, imposing limits on the number of weapons fired and the nature of targets to be destroyed. In the summer of 1961, the SIOP grew to include five escalating options. First, Soviet missiles, bomber bases and submarine docks would be destroyed. Air defenses along U.S. bomber flight paths would go next; then air defenses near cities. Then Soviet command centers and major military bases would be bombed. Finally came the full-blown SIOP, an all-out war.

The whole strategy rested on the controlled use of nuclear weapons. When the United States government discovered to its horror on October 16, 1962, that the Soviets had smuggled nuclear missiles into Cuba, it also discovered that its nuclear arsenal was fundamentally useless as a military weapon. For now the bomb worked both ways, and once one was fired, once the taboo was broken, the war could not be controlled.

The worst nuclear crisis the world has known came at a moment of complete American nuclear superiority. The United States possessed more than 25,000 nuclear warheads, and could have launched at least 2,000 strategic missiles at the Soviets on a few minutes' notice. The Soviets had about 340 warheads capable of striking the United States, including the forty believed emplaced in Cuba. Yet all the men gathered in the White House as the crisis unfolded knew that one of those Soviet warheads could have killed five million Americans.

Late on the first day of the confrontation, President Kennedy tried to weigh in his mind what forty more missiles aimed at the United States meant in the strategic balance. "I would think that our risks increase," he said. He mulled that over and then said: "What difference does it make? They've got enough to blow us up now anyway."

Three hundred enemy missiles were enough to explode all thoughts of nuclear victory. From that moment on no one spoke of using nuclear weapons in the Cuban missile crisis. Nuclear superiority meant little or nothing when men thought of the disaster a single Soviet warhead would create.[58]

The men in the crisis missed the meaning of the moment. The stockpile kept increasing, the missiles became more accurate, the warheads simultaneously smaller and more powerful. Computer technologies created the MIRV, the Multiple Independently Targeted Reentry Vehicle, which allowed up to fourteen warheads to dance on the head of a single missile, take separate trajectories in midflight and hit fourteen different targets. Still the quest for ways to fight and win through superior nuclear strength remained a search in a trackless desert. The fine-tuned SIOP of 1961 went essentially unrevised for the next thirteen years, as the Soviets slowly built their nuclear forces up to the level of the United States. The attention of those still focused on perfecting the art of nuclear war turned to the arcana of basing modes and missile accuracy and silo vulnerability and MIRV technology—and to the idea of arms-control negotiations. But by the mid-1960's the theoretical war began to wane in intensity. A real war was on the rise.

America spent more than a decade lost in Vietnam looking for technological solutions to the struggle. Nothing worked—no electronic fences, no smart bombs, no computerized bombing patterns, no statistics or analyses or charts—nothing. The limited war carried out in Vietnam and the limited war conceived by nuclear strategists had their similarities. Each turned on the quantification of death—the body count, the burning city, the precise allocation of pure force. Each attempted to translate violence into language the enemy could understand. Each assumed that bombing cities would transmit a message, that the explosions would be a clear signal, easily translated into peace with honor.[59]

Vietnam made some nuclear strategists realize, with a start, that their well-laid plans might have no meaning in a real war. Some began to look upon the pursuit of rational nuclear warfare with disgust, and they turned away from studying war. For they had found no answer to the mournful questions posed in July 1974 by Secretary of State Henry Kissinger: "What in the name of God is strategic superiority? What is the significance of it politically, militarily, operationally at these levels of numbers? What do you do with it?"[60]

By the time Saigon fell in April 1975, a schism was emerging in the nuclear church. In one faction were the faithful. They still believed in limiting and fine-tuning war plans, while working to limit and fine-tune the superpowers' arsenals through the SALT negotiations, the Strategic Arms Limitations Talks. In the other camp stood rebels. They believed that the United States again faced great danger from Soviet nuclear forces, just as they had believed in the 1950's. Nuclear superiority mattered to these apostates. It mattered a great deal. If the United States were superior, then the world would be a safer place. But if the Soviets were, the world was in danger. Arms-control negotiations were pointless unless the United States mustered the will to completely rebuild its nuclear forces against the coming threat of Soviet nuclear aggression.

Early in 1976, the new Director of Central Intelligence, George Bush, began hearing rumblings from the schismatics. They maintained that the CIA was understating the Soviet threat in its annual estimate of Soviet strengths and weaknesses. They saw a subtle treason in the Soviet estimate. What Bush did in response to those complaints had never happened before and has not happened since at the CIA. He joined and supported an ideological coup. Bush chose a team of generals and neoconservatives and invited them to come over to CIA headquarters and rewrite the Soviet estimate. Ray Cline, a former CIA deputy director of intelligence whose anticommunist credentials were paid up in full, said Bush's move subverted the intellectual honesty of the CIA's analyses. He called the squad Bush picked "a kangaroo court."[61]

The outsiders were known as Team B, and the team's star player was Paul Nitze. Nitze had resigned from the SALT delegation and condemned the arms-control talks as a fool's errand. His rebellion was the beginning of a crusade that soon gained a powerful following.

As Team B completed its work in 1976, the CIA suddenly doubled its estimate of Soviet military spending. The discovery of a spending gap created a far grimmer picture of Soviet intentions and capabilities than had been perceived since 1950. In retrospect, the CIA now appears to have made a serious miscalculation, overstating by many billions the amount of money the Soviets were devoting to military hardware. But its fearful guesswork was taken as gospel. The immense Soviet military machine was looming again.[62]

Nitze once more foresaw a nuclear Pearl Harbor drawing near. The Soviets were pursuing a "war-winning capability." The United States was lagging behind in its power to wage nuclear war. Nitze had charts and graphs and numbers to prove it. They showed that the Soviets' missiles were now so accurate that they could launch some of their ICBMs, destroy all our missiles, and then threaten to fire off the rest of their arsenal. And it was "highly plausible" that the Soviets would be tempted to strike first in a crisis and destroy the United States with a bolt from the blue. Every surviving American would be a nuclear hostage. The United States would be forced to surrender. The nation faced a nuclear war-fighting gap. The fateful hour was near.[63]

In his search for the road to wisdom in the nuclear wilderness, Nitze always sought truth in numbers. Ever since his tour of the atomic ruins of Hiroshima, he had tried to find equations and mathematical models that would prove a grand thesis—that strategic superiority meant something: diplomatic victory in peacetime, military victory in war.

Nitze nailed his thesis to the White House wall. He started by creating a coalition of born-again cold warriors in March 1976. The Committee on the Present Danger was a National Security Council in exile. The committee's members believed that the Soviet Union was hell-bent on world domination and a war-winning nuclear strategy. They declared that "a window of vulnerability" had opened wide, and the evil wind of Soviet power was blowing through it. The United States was approaching a state of nuclear defenselessness.[64]

"Providing for the common defense now requires the same kind of priority that it had in 1950," Nitze wrote in a 1976 manifesto. Few who knew their history could misapprehend his meaning. The wailing sirens of NSC-68 were returning with a vengeance.

America had to rearm for the coming war, and rearm mightily so we could win it. "The United States may have no practical alternative to waging a nuclear war," wrote Colin Gray, an influential member of the committee. And if only the nation found the will to fight, "Victory is Possible," Gray proclaimed in a seminal 1980 essay of that title. Gray said "the United States should plan to defeat the Soviet Union and to do so at a cost that would not prohibit U.S. recovery." That cost, Gray said, was twenty million American dead.[65]

In January 1981, as Ronald Reagan was sworn into office, the board of directors of the Committee on the Present Danger took over the foreign policy machinery of the United States. Fifty-one of the committee's members found work in the Reagan administration. The most prominent was Reagan himself. William Casey took the CIA. George Shultz became Secretary of State; Richard Allen, National Security Adviser. Paul Nitze became a chief arms-control negotiator. John Lehman became Secretary of the Navy, and promptly announced that we "have to have a war-winning capability." Fred Ikle, an architect of the new nuclear war–fighting doctrine, took under secretary of defense for policy. Richard Pipes, who saw no likely alternative to war with the Russians, became the leading Soviet analyst on the National Security Council. Colin Gray, the nuclear war–fighting advocate, became a leading adviser on nuclear arms control.

Men obsessed with victory and secrecy took control of nuclear policy. "The crazier analysts have risen to higher positions than is normally the case," said Dr. Herbert York, a preeminent nuclear-weapons scientist who once ran the Pentagon's research and engineering programs. "They are able to carry their ideas further and higher because the people at the top are simply less well-informed than is normally the case."[66]

The analysts bent over their computers, transfixed by scenarios of a seemingly endless war: eighty million dead on either side, a government gradually crawling from the wreckage, a new series of nuclear salvos and counterstrikes. "The war never really stops," said a State Department official briefed on the scenarios. "One side gradually builds back its communications and its bomber runways. The other side destroys them again. . . ."[67]

Spurgeon Keeny, a nuclear-weapons adviser to three Presidents and the former civilian head of the Air Force's nuclear-weapons directorate, looked over the new leadership at the Pentagon and said: "A lot of them think that nuclear war–fighting is not only possible, but very probable. . . . There is a big difference between just declaring this policy and actually believing it."[68]

The beliefs were stark: The United States was in a national emergency. The survival of the nation was at stake, and the expense be damned. Dr. James P. Wade Jr., the principal deputy under secretary of defense for research and engineering, put it straight to the Senate subcommittee on nuclear forces: "There can be no price tag on national survival."[69]

The cost of national survival, Reagan announced to the nation on October 3, 1981, was $180 billion. That was the price of rebuilding the nation's nuclear forces. That number was roughly $100 billion shy of the truth. For the costliest technology for fighting the long nuclear war was to be funded by the black budget.

The Stealth bomber, the stealthy nuclear-tipped cruise missiles, the satellites and computer programs and command posts for the envisioned nuclear war of the future began taking shape under cover. The extraordinary secrecy of the Manhattan Project became an everyday practice inside the Pentagon. Now it was not only nuclear strategy that would be conducted in secret. The weapons themselves would be secret.

The nuclear strategists had looked long and hard into their mirror and had seen the Soviets gearing up for victory. So we would do the same. Now billions of black dollars began flowing to build the strangest secret weapon of all, the space-based brain to control a nuclear war that would go on for weeks, months, maybe years, the war that would not end until the nation emerged triumphant.

3

Toward a
Better Armageddon

Sometime in 1992, a Titan 4 rocket is scheduled to blast off from Cape Canaveral. The precise launch date is classified. The cargo is secret. The Pentagon will describe it only as a "communications satellite," which has the soothing sound of a telephone company commercial reminding us to keep in touch with our loved ones.

When the rocket takes off, the press may identify the satellite as the first in the Military Strategic, Tactical and Relay system, MILSTAR for short. But the nature of this satellite, and the message it is supposed to communicate, will most likely go unmentioned. The public may see a ten-second clip of the lift-off on the evening news, enjoy the glowing image, and let the memory of the rocket's glare fade away.

No one will explain this mission the way Air Force Major General Gerald Hendricks did at a closed-door conference in 1982. "MILSTAR is designed to be a war-fighting system," General Hendricks said. "The first of its kind."[1]

MILSTAR is built to be the military's global switchboard for World War III and World War IV. It is at the core of the Pentagon's plans for a nuclear war that will last for months and end in victory. MILSTAR is supposed to endure that long war, to stand ready, after the war is over, long after the White House and Pentagon are reduced to rubble, to help fight World War IV. Strange as that may sound, it is the nation's battle plan: to fight and win a six-month nuclear war, and to be ready to strike and win again when the next war erupts.

MILSTAR is to be the central nervous system for nuclear war. Its satellites will be a constellation in space, its interwoven signals an electronic brain to coordinate the brawn of the nation's nuclear forces. If Washington is destroyed, if the chain of command is shattered, if no one human voice can direct the war plan, the Pentagon wants MILSTAR to help run the war, to weave together our fragmented forces and orchestrate the flight of nuclear weapons over the world's battlefields.

MILSTAR will be the Pentagon's worldwide nuclear-war communications network, broadcasting in uncrackable codes on its own exotic frequency. Imagine it as a military radio and television station whose satellites, broadcast towers, antennas, receivers and state-of-the-art control rooms are placed strategically in space, around the earth and under the seas. It is a good deal more elaborate than the systems that brought us live broadcasts from the Olympics and the moon. This network is built to bring us a far bigger spectacle.

Throughout the 1990's, up to nine MILSTAR satellites will rise one by one from launching pads, on the new Titan 4 boosters dedicated to secret military missions. Once in orbit, 22,300 miles from earth, the satellites will link up electronically with one another, with intelligence satellites and sensors, and with computer terminals on earth. The Pentagon is building between 3,000 and 4,000 of these MILSTAR terminals. Each one costs at least $1 million. President Bush's new black limousine will have one. His doomsday plane, the flying Oval Office that can carry him away from Washington in a crisis, will have one. The auxiliary Pentagon, carved deep in a mountainside north of Camp David, will have many. Everyone with nuclear weapons at his disposal may have access to one, from special operations commandos to Stealth bomber pilots.

MILSTAR is supposed to connect the President and the generals commanding U.S. forces around the world to the soldiers with their fingers on the nuclear trigger. The nuclear-war commanders and officers will be huddled in underground bunkers, hidden underwater in nuclear submarines, hurled aloft in airborne command posts and hurtling down interstate highways in lead-lined tractor-trailer trucks and panel vans. All will be trying to get a connection to MILSTAR, in their roles as human adjuncts to the computer software of the global war-fighting system. As the war explodes, the MILSTAR satellites are supposed to help the software coordinate the hardware of the nuclear triad, the bombers aloft, the submarines at sea and the missiles on land.

Through it all, as the warheads take out great modern cities and isolated military outposts, MILSTAR is to keep the channels of nuclear command and control flowing. Its satellites are to elude Soviet attack by maneuvering in space, outwitting efforts to jam its signals, and piercing the ferocious electronic static of nuclear war. Should political control of the war collapse while the war continues, with surviving soldiers in submarines and missile silos fighting to their last warhead, MILSTAR is supposed to carry on regardless. It is designed to stay in its orbit, to keep transmitting and relaying, without a human mind to direct it, for months on end, until the final missile screams across the sky.[2]

Before President Reagan came to office, the whole idea behind MILSTAR was considered impossibly expensive. But when the President announced his program to rebuild the nation's nuclear forces in 1981, the Pentagon dusted off its plans for the nuclear-war network and put them back onto the drawing board. It began pouring billions of dollars into Lockheed Missile and Space Co., the company given the primary MILSTAR contract. And it waited to take the results out onto the launching pad.

Now the first lift-off is drawing near. By 1990, roughly $5 billion was spent on secret research and development of the MILSTAR system. The project was two years behind schedule and far over budget. The cost of each satellite had doubled to nearly $900 million. Combined with the cost of the rocket to launch it, each new satellite carries a price tag of at least $1 billion. And if the dream MILSTAR embodies is realized, if the system is completed, that realization will come at a total cost of roughly $20 billion, making it by far the most expensive satellite communications program in history.

Though much about MILSTAR remains secret, one hard fact about it has become clear. It represents only a small down payment on a working wartime communications network, a system that actually can endure a long nuclear war. The truth is that no one knows if MILSTAR will work, and no one will until a nuclear war erupts. No one wants to fight that war. No one knows how to fight it, with or without MILSTAR. No one knows how to control a nuclear war once it starts. And no one has any idea how to end one.

Ever since armies have clashed, commanders have dreamed of ways to pierce the smoke and fog of war, to control the flow of conflict, to communicate orders that will be carried out instantly, to act on intelligence fresh from the front. To command. As General Thomas Power of the Strategic Air Command once put it: "Without communications, all I command is my desk." To *command* his forces in a nuclear war, the general has to know his officers will receive his orders. To *control* the forces, he has to hear back from them; this requires two-way *communications* that will work amid nuclear detonations. He needs electronic *intelligence* networks to receive warnings of attack and to know how the war is going. And, ideally, the President of the United States should command and control the generals.

The Pentagon's shorthand for a command, control, communications and intelligence network is C^3I, pronounced see-cubed-eye. The ideal working state of a C^3I system is "connectivity," the state of being connected. MILSTAR is intended to be the highest technological expression of this ideal, the solution to the C^3I equation. It is designed to provide answers to these critical questions: If a nuclear war begins, will the President's commands be carried out? Can the generals control the nation's nuclear forces? Or will chaos prevail?

The command and control of nuclear war rests on the communications links between those who hold legitimate political power and those who hold the lethal weapons. No communications means no control. No control means chaos. And chaos in a nuclear crisis means a planet pointlessly destroyed.

For the past ten years, the Pentagon and the President of the United States have demanded the ability to fuse all the elements of nuclear warfighting—command decisions, control of the weapons, wartime communications and battlefield intelligence—into a perfect web that will withstand an attack by thousands of nuclear warheads. MILSTAR is supposed to be that seamless system.

It is not. That system has not been built and never will be, even though the MILSTAR satellites' first launch date is drawing near. The reason that system was not built has little to do with a lack of funds, or a lack of will to build it. The money is being spent, the war plans are set. The system has not been built because no one has the slightest notion of how to do it. The challenge has confounded the leading military minds of two generations.

The power of nuclear weapons grew far faster than the ability of the human mind to control the weapons in battle. Today the nation's nuclear weapons contain the equivalent of seven thousand billion pounds of TNT, ten pounds of radioactive explosive for every pound of human flesh on earth. For all the years the Pentagon strengthened and rebuilt the nuclear arsenal, expanded and refined its war plans, all the money and all the minds in America never created a system that could command and control nuclear weapons in a real war. What the Pentagon created instead is a mammoth creature with a primitive brain—"an enormously complex but stupid organism," as Paul Bracken, a leading C^3I analyst, describes it —a rough beast whose awesome power far outstrips the ability of men to command it.[3]

The intellects of hundreds of thousands of people and secretly appropriated funds totaling tens of billions of dollars have been fused into immensely powerful weapons and immensely complicated systems for fighting a nuclear war. The warning radars and sensors and satellites, the underground centers for assessing an attack and coordinating a response, the launch-control centers and computerized guidance systems, the safety catch and the trigger and the explosive power of nuclear weaponry, taken together, comprise the most elaborate technological system in human history. But it is still incapable of orchestrating a nuclear war.

As the arsenal grew bigger and better, and the technology more ornate, the war plan grew more and more complicated. Curtis LeMay's "one fell swoop telescoping mass and time," his single blinding blow, became obsolete. Defense secretaries, members of the Joint Chiefs, SAC commanders and civilian technocrats kept fine-tuning the brutal, all-or-nothing war plan that the Eisenhower administration left behind. Applying the methods of economists and mathematicians and systems analysts, the war planners kept refining the attack into ever subtler sets of "limited nuclear options" and "flexible responses."

The Single Integrated Operational Plan grew to encompass scores of different computer-driven scenarios for fighting a war that would not be over in an hour or a day, but would go on and on, with pauses, sorties, parries and thrusts and counterstrikes, all the grand tactics of a chess match played with cities and nations. Today's plan, SIOP 6-F contains some 15,000 Soviet targets. If the war comes, the President—armed with intelligence from four new secret satellites, code-named IKON, LACROSSE, MENTOR and MAGNUM, launched at a cost of five billion black dollars—must choose among the SIOP's options. A restrained attack? Here's a small target set— the Soviets' biggest cement plant. A stronger message? Here's a target set of major munitions plants. Have the Soviets destroyed Detroit? Here are three Soviet cities of equal size and strategic importance. Does the President want to exterminate the Soviet leadership? War planners postulate these exchanges of millions of tons of nuclear firepower as if they were a coherent conversation being conducted by rational men.[4]

But without a working command-and-control system, programming nuances and subtleties into the SIOP is like trying to teach ballet to a brontosaurus. The nation's nuclear strategy is senseless if the government's commands cannot be followed. There is no point in developing more and more complex war-fighting strategies if the wiring of the war machine will short out under attack, if an attack on the command-and-control system causes the war plan to go haywire.

In a limited nuclear conflict, in anything short of total war, the nation's leaders are supposed to attune war-fighting with diplomacy, so that the war can be ended before it escalates out of control and consumes the planet. There is no room for error. The President—or whoever survives the first minutes of a nuclear attack to assume the President's role in the nuclear chain of command—has to perform a juggling act under unimaginable pressure. He has to fight by commanding his forces to attack the enemy, and simultaneously negotiate with the enemy, and control his forces to limit the war.

If in the first few minutes of a war, Washington is attacked, and commands from the capital dissolve into electronic static, how will the war be fought? This problem of nuclear strategy has a suitably unpleasant name: decapitation. The head of the government is lopped off by an attack on Washington. Communications links between the national leadership in Washington and the nuclear commanders are destroyed. Without communications links to commanders, the control of a nuclear war falls away rapidly from the political leadership. It cascades down the chain of command into the hands of young officers with their fingers on the nuclear triggers, isolated soldiers in Nebraska and Alaska and a hundred other sites, terrified beyond comprehension, with no way of knowing if Washington is still standing. Disconnected from political control, expecting to die at any minute, the officers make themselves heard in a language the enemy will understand: by launching every weapon they can. The enemy responds in kind. The nuclear war escalates beyond control.[5]

Anyone who has seen the film *Dr. Strangelove* can understand this dilemma. An insane SAC commander has launched nuclear-armed B-52s at the Soviet Union. The President has ordered the bombers recalled. All but one receive the order. The single bomber that keeps heading for its target has had its communications gear destroyed in a dogfight. The pilot cannot receive the President's command; the President cannot control the bomber. At the moment it unleashes its payload, political control of nuclear weapons has failed. As a consequence, the world explodes.

The problems presented by command-and-control vulnerability have haunted the Pentagon ever since the days of the "missile gap." In those days, the problem was not seen as the threat of uncontrolled escalation. What frightened the Pentagon the most was the possibility that a bolt-from-the-blue attack on the White House, the Pentagon and a few other targets could paralyze the United States' power to strike back. The decapitated state would collapse and die. Our own nuclear strategy has long been based on the theory that it would be wisest to decapitate the Soviet leadership in the first hours of World War III.

The Pentagon recognized the problem of protecting itself, the President and their power in a nuclear war in the late 1950's and early 1960's. It addressed the problem energetically. In the 1950's, the nation built underground command centers in which Presidents and generals could survive a nuclear barrage and keep on fighting. In the 1960's, we erected a worldwide network of radar and satellites and early-warning systems to sound the alarm if the Soviets attacked. The Soviets began closing the missile gap that had stood in America's favor, and by the mid-1960's had the power to launch their nuclear forces in sufficient numbers to destroy the United States. In the 1970's, we built better weapons, put multiple warheads on the missiles, pinpointed their accuracy, fortified their silos. When all this proved inadequate to calm our fears, we began to completely rebuild our nuclear forces in the 1980's.

To prevent the decapitation of our nuclear forces, and to ensure massive retaliation should the Soviets strike first, the authority to launch a nuclear weapon was delegated to generals no later than 1957, when SAC's General Power received the go-ahead. Today a multitude of American generals and admirals around the world have that predelegated authority. This system has nothing to do with the lawful line of succession to the presidency laid down by the Constitution. That line runs from the Vice President to the Speaker of the House of Representatives, to the president pro tempore of the Senate, and on down through the cabinet secretaries in order of the year their departments were created. But the Pentagon did not want to take orders from the Secretary of Agriculture in the midst of a nuclear firestorm. In the missile age, the constitutional chain of command could not suffice. The authority to push the button could not rest with the President alone, not if he would be among the first to go when the war began. So in 1958 the Pentagon invented a new system outside the constitutional line. It is called the National Command Authority. The Pentagon defines this entity as "the President and the Secretary of Defense *or their duly authorized alternates and successors.*"[6] The nuclear chain of command runs from the President to the Secretary of Defense to the Joint Chiefs of Staff to the unified and specified commanders—such as the chief of SAC—and on down to generals in the battlefield.

How far down the chain of command does the ability to give the launch order go? All the way down to a set of Minuteman missiles sitting in their silos in Missouri. The missiles have a tape recorder instead of a warhead in their nose cones. The tape carries a preprogrammed Emergency Action Message—the launch order for nuclear weapons. The nuclear commanders can order the Emergency Rocket Communications System, as it is known, to take to the air and broadcast the go-codes to SAC's bomber pilots in the sky and missilemen in the silos. The system is in effect a robot built to order the troops to carry out the war plan.

The programs for running the nation in a nuclear crisis and a nuclear war—the plans for "continuity of government"—are as highly classified as any item in the black budget. What is known is this: in order for the government to continue, the government as we know it will cease to exist. It will dissolve into several alternate governments huddled in vast underground headquarters.

The Pentagon began burrowing into the earth in the late 1950's to build two nuclear-war command centers. The subterranean shelters are the wartime capital of a military government. The twin seats of this provisional government are at the Alternate National Military Command Center, buried inside Raven Rock Mountain in the Alleghenies northwest of Camp David, Maryland, and at Mount Weather, Virginia, the alternate national capital under the Blue Ridge mountains an hour west of Washington. These two enormous strongholds, each staffed by hundreds of full-time employees, are subterranean cities with streets traversed by electric cars, reasonably comfortable offices and residences, copious fresh-water reservoirs and tons of freeze-dried food.

The alert system that sends the civilian and military bureaucracies fleeing for the bunkers has five levels of vigilance. The levels are called DEFCONs, short for Defense Conditions. At each escalating level, the political control of nuclear weapons travels further down the chain of command. The safety on the nuclear trigger gradually comes off.

In peace, we stand at DEFCON 5, save for SAC's bomber crews. Ever ready for battle, they always maintain DEFCON 4. Continuously, since 1961, one of several airborne command posts carrying a SAC general and battle staff has been in flight over the Midwest, ready to take charge if SAC headquarters is destroyed. The planes have a code name that sounds lovely, if fragile: LOOKING GLASS. In December 1989 the Air Force proposed cutting back on the Looking Glass flights to save some $20 million a year. The Bush administration rejected the idea, and Looking Glass continued unbroken.

At DEFCON 3 the nuclear-war system's nerves and muscles begin to tense and twitch like a cat waiting to pounce on its prey. The Minuteman crews finger their keys and codebooks for launching their missiles. A team dispatched by the Joint Chiefs of Staff heads for Raven Rock Mountain, and civilian leaders telephone one another with orders to evacuate their offices and homes for Mount Weather. Trucks and vans loaded with communications gear for relaying the launch orders are tuned up and tested. The President's four "doomsday planes" rev their engines. The planes are part of the Pentagon's fleet of airborne command posts. The President's planes are formally known as the National Emergency Airborne Command Post (NEACP), and informally called Kneecap. The Pentagon has built President Bush a new model, a military version of the 747 converted to withstand nuclear war, at a cost of $300 million each. Three of these planes are based on SAC's command at Offutt Air Force Base in Nebraska, the fourth at Grissom Air Force Base in Indiana.

The last time we were at DEFCON 3 was in the closing hours of the 1973 Arab-Israeli conflict, the Yom Kippur War. The Soviet Union wanted the United Nations to call for a joint dispatch of U.S. and Soviet troops to the battlefront to enforce a cease-fire. The U.S. balked. Soviet leaders threatened to move their troops unilaterally. On October 24, 1973, at 10:40 P.M., the Secretary of State, Henry Kissinger, convened an urgent meeting in the White House basement. The Secretary of Defense, the director of Central Intelligence and the chairman of the Joint Chiefs were there. The President was not. Richard Nixon was incapacitated with drink and anger following the Saturday Night Massacre, his firing of the Watergate special prosecutor and Justice Department officials. The White House chief of staff, Alexander Haig, told Kissinger that the President was "too distraught" to function. There was no Vice President: Spiro Agnew had resigned facing criminal indictment. No one disturbed the President. Just before midnight, the men in the White House basement took the United States to DEFCON 3. Within twenty-four hours Kissinger decided the Soviet threat was a "big bluff," and the alerted forces stood down.[7]

At DEFCON 2 the nation is on the verge of war. The provisional governments shape up underground. The Vice President helicopters to a rendezvous with one of the four doomsday planes. A second of the planes flies to Andrews Air Force Base near Washington to prepare to meet the President. SAC's bombers go on a continuous airborne alert, to avert being caught on the ground by a Soviet missile. Roughly 300 bombers take off, armed with more than 3,000 nuclear bombs and missiles. The Navy's submarines fan out through the seas, carrying more than 5,000 warheads. Convoys of lead-lined tractor-trailor trucks head down the interstate highways to secret destinations. Each convoy will be headed by a one-star general with the predelegated authority to give the go-codes to missile and bomber crews. In an all-out nuclear war, Pentagon planners realize, few major command posts would avoid direct nuclear hits. The Soviet Union knows where to find crucial nerve centers such as the Pentagon and the SAC. Figuring that a moving target is harder to hit, the Pentagon has a $3 billion investment in black programs to create mobile command posts. The idea is to have a large number of command-and-control centers that the Soviets cannot target.

Inside the ordinary-looking tractor-trailers, the road warriors can operate computerized command centers. Each will have a million-dollar MILSTAR transmitter, receiver and antenna, all contained in a satellite dish the size of a trash-can lid. Other details of the trucks' mission—for example, where they might refuel or change a flat tire in the midst of a nuclear war—remain unknown. But the convoys' communications links through MILSTAR to bombers and missilemen would make the trucks into tiny Pentagons coordinating the nation's nuclear forces.

Once the trucks start rolling, DEFCON 1 is near. The declaration of DEFCON 1 completely transforms the political structure of the United

States. We are under martial law. Warning of a possible attack has come. Nuclear war is imminent.[8]

The nation has a multibillion-dollar warning system that encircles the world. But it still is capable only of telling the President that he has ten minutes to choose a strategy for World War III. Today warning of a nuclear attack can come from a dizzying array of systems: the National Reconnaissance Office's black satellites, with their powerful photographic and infrared imaging; ground-based radars in the United States, Canada, Greenland and England; the Navy's Sound Surveillance System, secret underwater microphones that track Soviet submarines and warships; more than thirty highly classified National Security Agency and Air Force electronic eavesdropping posts ringing the Soviet Union; a variety of aircraft and space-based sensors; and many, many other sources.

The data from all the military and intelligence agencies are supposed to be analyzed by watch officers and fed to the Pentagon, the NSA, the CIA, the State Department, the White House Situation Room and the National Security Council's new Crisis Coordination Center in the Executive Office Building across from the White House. The people manning these operations centers are supposed to assess the data, confer on the NSA's voice-scrambling National Operations and Intelligence Watch Officers network, and tell the nuclear commander in chief whether war is imminent.

No President is likely to be aware of the military's contingency plans for a nuclear alert at this level. No President has ever been fully briefed on them. Only two civilians in the Pentagon, the Secretary of Defense and his chief deputy, are allowed to look at the plans. No civilian and no President has ever reviewed them in the depth of detail needed to grasp their complexity. The Joint Chiefs refused to allow anyone out of uniform to inspect these alert plans. They said that would be "civilian intrusion into strictly military matters."[9]

One inescapable fact will be clear to the President. If the missiles start flying, he has next to no time to decide what to do. The flight time of a land-based Soviet ICBM aimed at American soil is a half hour at most. It takes at least ten minutes to detect the attack, make sure that it is truly an attack and not some malfunctioning computer chip in the warning system, identify the trajectory of the missiles and the target of the attack, and notify the Pentagon and the White House. Once the President is alerted, it takes at least ten minutes to convey an order from the President to the nation's nuclear forces, confirm its authenticity and launch American ICBMs before the Soviet missiles detonate. That leaves ten minutes at the outside for the President and his military advisers to grasp the situation and make a decision. An attack by Soviet submarines would cut the time down to less than five minutes. Tens of billions of black dollars poured into satellites and sensors only provide the President with a cascade of warnings that he has minutes to go.

As time ticks away, the President must confer electronically with the ranking nuclear commanders and arrive at a decision. Assuming the President is in control, still in command of the nuclear forces and sitting in the White House, he will look across the wide conference table in the Situation Room and demand the authorization codes for unleashing the war plan.

The SIOP and the go-codes are locked inside a briefcase handcuffed to an unobtrusive officer who follows the President at every moment. The briefcase is known as the Football. The President is likely to be unfamiliar with what is inside it. Bill Gulley, director of the White House Military Office under Presidents Johnson, Nixon, Ford and Carter, has noted that none of them ever had more than one short briefing on the contents of the Football. None ever had an update, though its details change constantly. "Not one President could open the Football—only the warrant officers, the military aides and the Director of the Military Office have the combination. If the guy with the Football had a heart attack or got shot on the way to the President, they'd have to blow the goddamn thing open."[10]

Once the Football is opened, the President has a long, long list of choices for destroying thousands of targets grouped in four major categories: the Soviet Union's political leadership, its nuclear forces, its conventional military forces and its major industries. He can order attacks with strategic long-range bombers and intercontinental ballistic missiles and submarines. He can blow a quarter of the planet off the map or fire a single warning shot. Only first he must connect. The links in the C^3I system must interlock for the war plan to work.

But the Pentagon has known for years that its communications network does not work—not in peacetime, not in crisis. This did not enhance its confidence that the system would work in war. The President facing a nuclear crisis could find himself in an awkward position. He would be like a general in battle who turns to his second-in-command and orders him to inform the troops that the communications are out.

A series of communications failures caught the Pentagon's attention in the late 1960's. Most concerned the Worldwide Military Command and Control System (WWMCCS, pronounced Wimmix), the rudimentary network which was—and still is—the primary crisis communications system for the Joint Chiefs of Staff and the President of the United States. Throughout the 1960's and 1970's, the Wimmix failed to connect. It is the kind of military system described by the famous acronyms of World

War II—SNAFU and FUBAR, politely rendered as "situation normal: all fouled up" and "fouled up beyond all recognition."

There are dozens of horror stories about the Wimmix. The most famous one concerns the USS *Liberty*. In June 1967, the *Liberty*, an intelligence-gathering ship bristling with National Security Agency gear for intercepting electronic communications, was headed for the coast of the Sinai Peninsula to monitor the 1967 Arab-Israeli war. The Joint Chiefs tried to send it a top-secret message to steer clear of the coast, for fear the ship might come under attack. The urgent communique went out on the Wimmix, stamped "immediate." It was addressed to the commander in chief of U.S. forces in Europe, the Chief of Naval Operations, every commander with authority over the Sixth Fleet and to the *Liberty* itself.

The *Liberty* never got the message. Nor did it receive a copy of the orders from any of the commanders. Nor did it receive several other urgent messages over the following twenty-four hours. The Wimmix sent the *Liberty*'s copy of the message to the Naval Communications Center in the Philippines; the men at Subic Bay sent it back to the Pentagon, advising the Pentagon that it should route the message through a relay station in Morocco; the Pentagon then sent the message to NSA headquarters at Fort Meade, Maryland, where it was filed and forgotten. A second copy of the message ricocheted around the Mediterranean all the next morning, bouncing from station to station in search of a secure channel cleared for top-secret messages. That afternoon, Israeli jets and torpedo boats attacked the *Liberty*, destroying the ship with bombs and napalm and heavy artillery, shooting up the life rafts, killing thirty-four men and wounding more than 100.

It was "one of the most incredible failures of communications in the history of the Department of Defense," in the words of a congressional investigating committee. For this reason, and to preserve the sanctity of the NSA's secrecy as well as U.S.-Israeli relations, the U.S. government stamped nearly every aspect of the tragedy secret, and attempted to stop public investigation. Nearly five years passed before the barest details of the snafu became known.[11]

And nearly ten years passed before the Pentagon came to grips with the fact that the Wimmix did not work, that it might be an inadequate system for executing the nuclear-war plan. Running the broadcast network for nuclear war is more complicated than sending a teletype to a ship in peacetime. A special channel of the Wimmix, the Minimum Essential Emergency Communications Network, might have been able to communicate one short, unmistakable message to all U.S. nuclear forces, a flash signal ordering execution of one of the many options in the SIOP before any Soviet missiles arrived. But the system would collapse under attack.

Albert Babbitt, a prominent systems engineer given the unenviable task of trying to debug the Wimmix in the late 1970's, reported that its capabilities were "not sufficient to support and sustain nuclear operations." It could not even support a war game, and crashed for twelve hours during a worldwide military exercise called Proud Spirit in November 1980. The General Accounting Office reported that the Wimmix malfunctioned in every military crisis from the fall of Saigon in 1975 to the failed Iran hostage-rescue mission of 1980. After the Pentagon had spent $600 million tinkering with the computers and rewriting almost all the software, the Wimmix was 300 percent over budget—and obsolete.

The Pentagon and the GAO conducted study after study of the failures of the global communications network. Secretaries and Deputy Secretaries of Defense testified to Congress again and again that the United States needed a system that would work in a crisis. The Pentagon and the Congress turned the problem over and over, each report confirming the previous one, each new task force reaching the same basic conclusion: "The nation is failing to deploy command and control systems commensurate with the nature of likely future warfare [and] modern weapons systems," as the Defense Science Board reported in 1978.[12]

The implications for the war plan were enormous. A few nuclear weapons could cripple the command-and-control system. That meant that the elaborate "limited options" of the war plan could not be carried out under an attack. The fragility of the network made our nuclear weapons useless—except if they were used at first warning, when a buzzer or a blinking light signaled an attack on any radar, any early-warning post, any link at all in the communications chain. The only way to carry out the war plan would be to fire off as many weapons as we could, as quickly as possible, before the command-and-control network collapsed. If attacked, the United States could still execute the SIOP—but not the carefully tailored set of plans we had created. The SIOP we were capable of executing was General Curtis LeMay's blitzkrieg—the one that so terrified President Eisenhower thirty years ago.

This harsh fact meant, among other things, that the conventional wisdom of nuclear strategy was dead wrong. We assumed that it truly mattered how many warheads we possessed, how many hardened silos, how many missiles. But it did not matter—not if the vulnerabilities of the command-and-control system put the United States back to the days of all-or-nothing, of use-it-or-lose-it.

This is where MILSTAR comes in. It took me the better part of a year to grasp the meaning of MILSTAR after I first saw the word, a single acronym in a Pentagon printout with no other word in any official text to explain it. No one in the Pentagon or on Capitol Hill would discuss it. Air Force officers shied away when I spoke the word. Only a half dozen obscure technical papers and war-college doctoral theses mentioned it. Only a handful of academics, most of whom had spent long years inside the Pentagon, had both the knowledge and the courage to talk about it in depth.

MILSTAR is a technological fix for three decades of frustration among nuclear-war strategists. It is a $20 billion answer to an impossible conundrum: how do you win a nuclear war? George Bush succinctly stated the solution to that question ten years ago, when he first ran for President: "You have a survivability of command and control . . . and you have a capability that inflicts more damage on the opposition than it can inflict on you. That's the way you can have a winner." The survivability of command, control, communications and intelligence in a nuclear war, and thus the path to victory, lies with MILSTAR.[13]

The infuriating inability to build a command-and-control network that would survive a nuclear war was first recognized as a serious national-security problem in the late 1970's. The problem finally percolated up to the President of the United States. Jimmy Carter had been a nuclear abolitionist. He vowed in his inaugural address to work for the elimination of all nuclear weapons from the face of the earth. The week before he made that pledge, at his first briefing by the Joint Chiefs of Staff, he asked them if it were possible to cut the nuclear arsenal by roughly 90 percent—down to 200 submarine-launched missiles, a force more than powerful enough to destroy every major Soviet city. Carter's question, echoing Eisenhower's wistful plea to cut the arsenal "down to the deterrent," appalled the Joint Chiefs. General George Brown, their chairman, was reported to have stared at Carter in utter disbelief. The President was suggesting that the Chiefs put on sackcloth and take a vow of poverty.

Carter's view of nuclear weapons evolved fairly quickly from fastidious abhorrence to a form of grim fascination. At first attracted and finally addicted to the complexity of nuclear strategy, and under immense political pressure to prove himself capable of endorsing new weapons systems, he agreed in short order to build the biggest, most accurate new missile he could under existing arms treaties. In the fall of 1977 American intelligence monitored Soviet missile tests that suggested their new missiles might be as accurate as our old missiles. In response, Carter gave the go-ahead to the MX missile, a ten-warhead weapon. The accuracy of the new MX warheads would supposedly be measured in yards. That meant more options for war planners; they could pinpoint whole new sets and subsets of Soviet targets. There was nothing vague or subtle about the MX. Its power and precision made it a potentially devastating first-strike weapon.

The weaponry was way out ahead of a strategy to use it. Technology was driving policy; a new Soviet weapon demanded a better American weapon, and a new war-fighting strategy to go with it. The improving accuracy of both sides' weapons meant that nuclear battle plans could be further refined. It meant that a nuclear war might not be over in a day, or a few days, or a week. The war plans needed more elaboration to embrace that understanding. A more sophisticated war plan demanded a working command-and-control system.

Over the next two years, Carter and his top aides devoted much time and energy to devising new nuclear stratagems. A great deal of the burden fell on General William Odom, the National Security Council's top military assistant. A former military attaché at the U.S. embassy in Moscow, Odom knew a great deal about the Soviet Union and its nuclear-war doctrine. Largely through Odom's efforts, Carter became the first President to immerse himself in the details of nuclear war-fighting scenarios. The President "really got into the procedures, ran through numerous scenarios, and became very comfortable with it," Odom told a Harvard seminar in 1980. "He wanted to be awakened at three o'clock in the morning and not be confused, and understand what he was going to have to see, or what he was about to hear, what the voice would sound like on the other end of the line." What Carter was hearing from Odom became clear in a series of top-secret presidential directives. Odom was an intellectual architect and author of the orders. Taken together, they called for a command-and-control system that could survive a nuclear war.[14]

Presidential Directive 53, signed on November 15, 1979, said it was "essential to the security of the U.S." to have C^3I connectivity between surviving leaders and the nation's nuclear weaponry—a connection that would "support flexible execution of retaliatory strikes during and after an enemy nuclear attack." Presidential Directive 58, signed June 30, 1980, called for improvements in the systems for "continuity of government" during and after a nuclear war: better evacuation plans, new emergency shelters for leaders, better emergency computer and communications systems for the war bunkers. "For the first time," wrote Carter's national security adviser, Zbigniew Brzezinski, "the United States deliberately sought for itself the capability to manage a protracted nuclear conflict."[15] And Presidential Directive 59, signed July 25, 1980, required the U.S. to develop the capability to fight and win a nuclear war that would last for months, not an hour or a day.

The Carter administration, badly outflanked to its right in the campaign against Ronald Reagan in the summer of 1980, leaked the substance of PD-59's goals to the press. An understanding emerged of how long the envisioned war would last. The war-fighting theorist Colin Gray wrote: "PD-59 said that [World War III] could be protracted, with six months as the consensus guess for the duration of a protracted nuclear war."

This capability could only be achieved by a revolution in the technology for command and control.[16]

The President who vowed to try to rid the world of warheads wound up signing the first truly significant war-fighting plan since the heyday of Curtis LeMay. But PD-59 was a paper tiger. In practice, the directive never had time to take effect. Carter was out of office before the order filtered down to the nuclear commanders.[17] Still, he had tilled the ground for MILSTAR. The next President planted the seed and provided billions of black dollars for fertilizer. The Reagan administration came to power proposing an altogether new nuclear reality. And it was willing to match nuclear war-fighting rhetoric with nearly a quarter of a trillion real dollars. By the fall of 1980, Ronald Reagan, George Bush and some of the Pentagon's leading strategists were talking openly about winning a nuclear war.

The band of believers in nuclear victory that came to power in January 1981 soon drew up a secret decree for the President to sign. In October, Reagan put his signature on National Security Decision Directive 13. This still-secret directive called for the creation of a new command-and-control system that could do what the new war-fighting rhetoric demanded. It said that the United States must have the power to fight a six-month nuclear war and force the Soviets to surrender. And it said the nation must then control a reserve of nuclear forces large enough to be ready to fight again. It said flatly that "the United States must prevail" in a nuclear war against the Soviets. A great deal of discussion ensued as to what "prevail" meant. Prevail meant to win. To win a nuclear war.[18]

To achieve that goal, the Pentagon needed MILSTAR. The Pentagon did not care to fix its broken command-and-control system. It wanted an entirely new system with war-fighting capabilities. "The people on the right wanted a win-the-war policy . . . and so money was siphoned off from ten good, solid, less-ambitious programs to pay for MILSTAR," said Bruce Blair, a former Minuteman launch-control officer who conducted an unprecedented study of the nuclear command-and-control network at the Pentagon. "The people on the right made a case for spending the money. In the Office of the Secretary of Defense, Weinberger would say that his job was to get the money." The Secretary of Defense got the money. The Pentagon promoted MILSTAR in Congress as an essential upgrade to the C^3I network. More truthfully, it was the tool to carry out the goals of the new nuclear strategy.

The Pentagon happened to have a dusty blueprint for a war-fighting satellite network in its files. The system was called the Strategic Satellite System—STRATSAT, for short. The Air Force was deeply enthusiastic about the idea, and endorsed it as a "survivable" system, meaning one that could live through the first days of a nuclear war. STRATSAT would have put four satellites in space at a projected cost of at least $3 billion. The satellites were to orbit at 110,000 miles from earth, nearly halfway to the moon, making them impervious to Soviet attack. They would be linked by radio transmissions of extremely high frequency (EHF), wavelengths up to fifty-five billion cycles a second, a bandwidth at the edge of known physics. EHF theoretically allows more data to be transmitted more quickly, and makes it harder for the enemy to jam transmissions. The Carter administration's Air Force Secretary, Hans Mark, told Congress in 1980 that STRATSAT "surely would survive a nuclear exchange."

STRATSAT could not survive informed scrutiny. Congress could not stomach the idea of spending $3 or $4 billion on such a system. The Navy's strategists bad-mouthed STRATSAT in private conversations with Armed Services Committee staffers, pointing out that the system could not communicate with its submarines at all, much less sustain communications with them in wartime. Congress rejected STRATSAT three years running.

But now the Reagan revolution had come, and everything was different. Defense Secretary Weinberger told Congress in 1982 that a new C^3I network was "perhaps the most urgently needed element" in the administration's buildup of nuclear war-fighting forces. Without it, the Pentagon could not achieve the goals it laid out in a secret policy statement, a strategic five-year plan which it leaked to the press in 1982. The plan said the nation's nuclear forces must "maintain, throughout a protracted conflict period and afterward, the capacity to inflict very high levels of damage against the industrial/economic base of the Soviet Union." And it said the United States needed command-and-control networks capable of "supporting controlled nuclear counterattacks over a protracted period while maintaining a reserve of nuclear forces sufficient for trans- and post-attack protection and coercion." In plain English, this meant fighting a long nuclear war and emerging victorious, our strength undiminished, with enough nuclear firepower left over to wipe out any Soviet forces still standing. The policy made a "survivable" C^3I system an outmoded goal. The goal now was an "enduring" system, one that could fight and win and fight again.

The task was enormous. As MILSTAR took shape over the 1980's, the Pentagon had to create new computer programs to run a nuclear war, to write tens of millions of lines of debugged and error-free computer code, at a cost of at least one hundred dollars a line. It had to weave the data into the computer banks of newly created links in the nuclear-war network—the space satellites, the ground terminals, the convoys of trailer trucks, a MILSTAR mission control center in Colorado Springs—so that the orders for launching nuclear weapons could continue after Washington was destroyed. It had to develop transmitters and receivers that would operate at the esoteric electronic frequency, EHF. It had to build a maneuvering capability into the satellites so they could detect and evade attacks in space. It had to shield the satellites and terminals and trucks against the devastating effects of nuclear explosions.

The goal was a system that could endure an all-out nuclear war, coordinating the detonation of five or ten or fifteen thousand nuclear warheads, choreographing the ballistic ballet down to the millisecond. The Pentagon tried to transform the dinosaur into an electronic Hydra, a creature that would continue to fight intelligently even as it was being decapitated. It tried to perform a feat of nuclear brain surgery, to implant an indestructible nervous system in the great brawny beast.

The assignment drove legions of computer programmers and nuclear strategists beyond their limits. The Pentagon "consistently sent the signal: They want an enduring system. They've told the weapons and systems designers to do it. And they've driven the designers crazy," says John Steinbruner, the director of foreign-policy studies at the Brookings Institution and an expert on nuclear-war strategies. "The designers don't know how to do it, even spending tens or hundreds of billions of dollars. We do not know how to build a system that could endure a large-scale attack. But the money's being spent, no question about it."

The money for MILSTAR's satellites, earth-bound control centers, ground terminals and hookups for most of the war planes in the Air Force started flowing in 1982. The cost of the system will exceed $1 billion a year in 1991, before the first scheduled satellite launch. Lockheed Missile and Space is the prime contractor. Its MILSTAR contract is a cost-plus arrangement; the taxpayer picks up 70 percent of Lockheed's cost overruns, which may be considerable in years to come. The Pentagon's initial guess was that MILSTAR might be bought for a total of $10 billion. Analysts I have interviewed inside and outside the Air Force think that once you add up the overruns, the two years of delays beyond the projected schedule, the costs of launching the satellites and the costs of keeping them in space, $20 billion is a more accurate price tag.

From MILSTAR's first days, skeptics inside and outside the military have thought no amount of money could buy the war-fighting network the Pentagon envisioned. They warned Congress and the Pentagon repeatedly that the vision of a working nuclear-war machine was precisely that—a phantasm, a dream, a mirage. General David Jones, upon his retirement as the chairman of the Joint Chiefs of Staff in 1982, told Congress that the military was throwing money into "a bottomless pit" by planning for a long nuclear war. "I don't see much chance of nuclear war being limited or protracted," he said.

The Pentagon's response to the strategic critique was to take MIL-STAR to a higher level of secrecy, wrapping its components in ever-more-classified compartments. The debate was silenced. And so the questions remain unanswered: Can MILSTAR survive a long nuclear war? Can it fulfill the Pentagon's vision of winning a nuclear war of three or four or six months' duration?

"The idea of having it run safely at 120 days strikes me as insane," says Paul Bracken, a Yale professor who has studied command-and-control issues since the early 1970's and wrote the most widely acclaimed unclassified study of the problem. After fifteen years of researching C^3I, he says flatly: "It is a waste of money to spend money on protracted nuclear war."

Ashton Carter was a ranking civilian in the Pentagon's systems analysis branch. As a professor of public policy at Harvard's Kennedy School of Government, he has published pioneering studies of C^3I. He says MILSTAR is "a very complicated system that's prone to failure. No command-and-control system can be expected to do the job it's supposed to do. It's in the nature of the beast—fighting a war we've never waged, in circumstances we can't foresee, on a time line dictated by technology and weapons, not human decisions."

"At what price have we bought survivability?" he asks. And, he continues, how long can any command-and-control system be expected to survive a nuclear war? "The question is whether the system can survive for a day, not six months."

The war machine MILSTAR must coordinate has many moving parts. One hundred and twenty thousand people on some fifty American bases and 160 foreign posts have direct responsibility for carrying out the nuclear-war plan. Thousands of them must receive commands and acknowledge them through MILSTAR. The mind of the President or the surviving nuclear commander in chief must be married to the military's missiles at ICBM silos, aboard the submarines plying clandestine routes through the seas, upon bombers thousands of miles from home. Enormous amounts of intelligence data must flow through MILSTAR's channels. Will MILSTAR handle the onslaught of data and messages in a nuclear crisis? Can it receive and transmit messages to all the forces in time for a coherent war plan to be carried out? It seems unlikely. Each MILSTAR satellite can handle no more than fifteen communications at a time. The sixteenth caller is going to get a busy signal. That was the price the Pentagon had to pay for protecting MILSTAR's transmissions from being jammed or intercepted.

An enemy jams a signal by broadcasting in the same wavelength, creating static and garbling messages. MILSTAR's satellites will use a trick called frequency hopping. Its messages jump from frequency to frequency, creating a moving target to foil the enemy's jammers. The effect on an enemy would be like turning on a television with sixty cable channels, finding the MILSTAR show on channel 2, only to see the program disappear, then searching with the remote control to find MIL-STAR again on channel 49, seeing it for a second and then watching it vanish again. MILSTAR also will encrypt its voice and data transmissions, scrambling the signals just like a pay-TV station on cable blocks you from seeing movies for free.

But as with all technologies, there is a cost. All the effort spent on deceiving the foe takes away from MILSTAR's ability to connect with its friends. Encoding and decoding signals takes time. Frequency hopping takes energy. So MILSTAR will be hard to jam, but it can receive and transmit data only at a very slow rate for such a state-of-the-art system.

Even if MILSTAR works perfectly in the midst of an exploding war, no more than 135 users at a time can communicate through its nine satellites. If the Pentagon prudently decides that two of the nine satellites should be kept earthbound as spares, the system could handle barely more than 100 urgent calls at a time.[19]

A far longer line of soldiers will be queuing up for a connection. Part of MILSTAR's great cost lies in its attempt to satisfy three very different, very large, military communities. The tactical forces, the soldiers manning ground terminals and battle stations and mobile command posts, need only to receive and transmit quick messages. They also need small terminals to fit in their truck and vans. The strategic users, the Stealth bomber pilots and SAC launch-control officers and submarine commanders, need relatively small amounts of message traffic, too. But they must have instant MILSTAR communications to survive an attack, receive their go-codes, find their targets, fire their weapons and report back to command posts. The nuclear commanders in chief, the intelligence community and the watch officers manning command centers all need extremely high rates of message traffic, given the enormous amount of information they must absorb and the number of commands they must issue.

MILSTAR satellites must also handle huge amounts of data from other military hardware. They must receive and transmit photoreconnaissance data from spy satellites, providing eyes in the sky to survey the progress of the battle; from NAVSTAR satellites, a system built to guide our missiles to within fifty feet of their targets; and from space-based sensors that will pinpoint nuclear explosions, assess the damage done and report the results back to commanders in their airborne posts and underground bunkers.

MILSTAR is supposed to receive digitized photo images of the nuclear battlefield from the multibillion-dollar network of intelligence satellites, and relay the images via ground stations to Stealth bomber pilots, who would then survey the Soviet battlefield to stalk and kill Soviet mobile missiles. This would be an impressive feat. In fact, hardly anybody in the Air Force thinks it can be done.

If war comes, all of America's nuclear forces around the world will need immediate access to MILSTAR. Every minute counts in nuclear war. Ashton Carter places himself in the position of a nuclear commander in chief: "I've built my plans around making all my decisions within a few hours of an attack. I may have resolved to launch my ICBMs under attack, in which case I've said: 'Look, guys, we're going to make all the crucial decisions within half an hour.' " But the forces whose mobility best enables them to evade Soviet nuclear attack—the covert ground units, the airborne forces and naval battle groups at sea—can expect to wait up to half an hour to receive and transmit messages through MIL-STAR.

The MILSTAR satellites have a set of antennas to communicate with mobile forces. But the antennas can cover only a small broadcast area. They must reposition themselves to track MILSTAR's communicants as they move through the air, land and sea. "As task forces or mobile platforms traverse the oceans and skyways, [MILSTAR's] satellite coverage beams will have to reconfigure to maintain their coverage of these platforms. This can incur extremely long processing delays," according to a 1987 study by Navy Lieutenant Richard Landolt, who had the security clearances necessary to learn about some of the system's weaknesses. Landolt concluded that the transmission delays would last up to thirty minutes.[20] Thirty minutes is a long time in a nuclear war. It is enough time for life-and-death decisions to be made, as Ashton Carter points out. It is also the flight time of a missile from Omaha to Moscow. If enough time ticks by, a cease-fire message sent through MILSTAR might not reach a nuclear triggerman in time for him to cease firing.

The MILSTAR network is also going to have to cope with a much-debated, little-understood phenomenon called the electromagnetic pulse. A nuclear blast high in the atmosphere creates an enormous electromagnetic charge. A Soviet warhead exploding 300 miles above Omaha would instantly zap the United States from coast to coast with a tidal wave of charged electrons. Every electronic system, every radio transmission, every computer bank in the country would experience something like a lightning strike magnified a millionfold. An intense surge of up to 50,000 volts per meter would flow through the circuitry that wires the entire nation. This phenomenon was discovered in 1962, when the U.S. exploded three nuclear weapons high over the Pacific. Although the test took place 800 miles from Hawaii, street lights went off across Oahu and burglar alarms went haywire in Honolulu. The tests showed that airbursts of nuclear weapons created a temporary but terrifying effect, previously unimagined over seventeen years of nuclear tests. Today, more than seventeen years later, the effects of the electromagnetic pulse remain what engineers call a "known unknown"—a problem that is known to exist but has no known solution.

The entire structure of the nuclear-war network rests on computer systems. If the computers cannot function, almost nothing will. Nuclear experts disagree emphatically on the possibility of defending against the electromagnetic pulse. Those who consider it a grave threat say it could disrupt every computer chip in the system, overloading low-voltage circuits with a tremendous high-voltage surge. In theory, the whole electronic architecture of command and control could be undone by a single nuclear bomb. The Pentagon is seeking ways to prevent the network from being disconnected. The cables that connect Minuteman missile silos to their launch centers are encased in six inches of lead. At Kirtland Air Force Base in New Mexico, Pentagon scientists shoot ten million volts of electricity through aircraft and electronic equipment, testing ways to protect them. The President's "doomsday plane" has $100 million worth of armor against the electromagnetic pulse. For the same cost, every MILSTAR satellite will have some similar form of shielding.

Yet there is a link in the MILSTAR network that cannot be shielded at any cost. It is the most important one: the human mind. And MILSTAR would weaken the role of the only truly reliable safety catch on the hair trigger of nuclear weaponry.

The Pentagon's early-warning systems have gone berserk repeatedly. When a defective forty-six cent computer chip caused SAC computer data displays to report an attack by thousands of Soviet missiles in 1980, when faulty radars interpreted the rising moon and a gaggle of geese as warheads heading for Washington, when a technician ran a test tape through the warning system and set off a full-scale alert, a special safety device stopped the false alarm from spreading: the human mind. It rejected the computer messages signaling the beginning of World War III. The mind reasoned, saw discrepancies in patterns, sought independent confirmation of an isolated event. The mind has a uniquely human characteristic called common sense, a capability still beyond computers.

The new command-and-control technologies incorporated into MILSTAR increasingly take human reason out of the loop. A former director of the Pentagon's Defense Advanced Research Projects Agency (DARPA), George Heilmeier, has testified that "human limitations in formulating and communicating demands [are] a central difficulty in increasingly complex command, control and communications systems."[21] Jacob Gilstein, the Pentagon's former director of ballistic missile defense, goes further: "No human being can enter the real-time decision-making loop and control the system. It has to be preprogrammed with logic so the computer can make the decision and run the game."[22]

The solution, DARPA reported in an obscure budget document in 1987, lies in thinking that machines can supplant foot soldiers and generals alike in wartime. The agency said it was developing computer programs for artificial intelligence to "assist, advise and/or relieve military personnel in complex decision-making tasks [which are] dangerous or rapidly changing." DARPA is working on a variety of robots—"hexapods" that move with a tank's agility and speed, "quadrupeds" that gallop and trot, "walking vehicles," and robot hands and fingers. It is developing robot intelligence, focusing on "flexible software systems that show unique promise for solving complex military problems." Commanders will communicate with robots through "a state-of-the-art man-machine interface called IRUS." DARPA envisions a robot soldier of the future that takes orders "but does not generate discourse"—no back talk or balking. The robot soldiers will give commanders the ability to have their commands carried out in "an enhanced nuclear environment," the Pentagon's language for a lethally radioactive battlefield.[23]

The Pentagon clearly thinks that the barrage of computerized data that will flood the command-and-control system in a nuclear crisis is going to overwhelm the human mind. Its solution is to let the computer run the show. This may be an unavoidable consequence of the technology of nuclear war. No electromagnetic pulse shielding, no extremely high-frequency antenna and no computer software will change the fact that many of the people assigned to interpret the sounds and signals of the battle would die in the first minutes and hours of a nuclear war. Without them, the safety mechanism on the nuclear-war machine will be damaged. Decisions of life and death will take on the rigidity of a preprogrammed drill determined by a computerized script. You cannot replace the intelligence community with a covert MILSTAR receiver in a truck. And you cannot replace human reason with a satellite relay.

But you can place a command-and-control network dedicated to nuclear war in space. MILSTAR is the first truly space-based war-fighting system. It will take the arms race into space in new, destabilizing and potentially dangerous ways. It will be an obvious target. Everyone in the Pentagon who has studied the problems of command and control realizes that the way you win a nuclear war is by paralyzing the enemy's ability to strike back—by knocking out his brain, his C^3I network. More boxing matches are won with shots to the head than with body blows. Obviously, war planners in the Kremlin understand this concept.

Unless the U.S. and the U.S.S.R. sign a treaty banning antisatellite wars in space—a treaty the United States has resisted vigorously—MILSTAR may become the first step in a race for antisatellite weapons and anti-antisatellite weapons. Existing international treaties ban the use of space for military purposes, but the Pentagon takes issue with the treaties. The Pentagon has told Congress, in a policy statement on antisatellite warfare, that the United States interprets "the right to use space for peaceful purposes to include military uses of space to promote peace in the world."

Finally, things go wrong with complex systems. The more complex they are, the more can go wrong. If there is any lesson to be learned from the *Challenger* and Chernobyl, it is that. The nuclear command-and-control network under MILSTAR's aegis will be the most complicated system the human mind ever has created. But despite its complexity, a computer crash in a crisis could be interpreted by another computer as an attack on the C^3I system. This alone could trigger a massive response.

If a nuclear war actually begins, the man in the loop must understand the pattern of the attack. This understanding must be reached at the very moment the C^3I network comes under fire. An attack by only a few weapons on the C^3I system would be interpreted *by the system* as an attack designed to decapitate the dinosaur, to destroy its brain. Enormous pressure would build on the nuclear commanders to fire off every weapon they can before their command-and-control system collapses. At best, MILSTAR will endure a nuclear attack long enough to glue together some of the fragmented and frightened forces still surviving. The best they can do is to strike back at the easiest targets to hit. Those targets are not Soviet missiles, nor Soviet military forces. Those targets are cities, and a second-strike attack on cities serves little purpose save blind revenge.

Ultimately, an attack by a few weapons on any part of the command-and-control system could trigger a response that would compress the death and destruction of World War II into a few hours. "Ten weapons aimed at key political and command nodes could be interpreted as a blinding decapitation strike," Paul Bracken has written. All preconceived plans for limited and controlled warfare would then collapse. "A decapitation attack aimed at a command system is likely to produce a nuclear war that is difficult to end without firing hundreds or even thousands of nuclear weapons. Wars of this magnitude could easily produce tens of millions of fatalities."[24]

The nation's nuclear strategy in the 1990's rests on a system built to realize a vision of victory in a long nuclear war. That is the aim that led the Pentagon to create MILSTAR. What MILSTAR leads us toward is the promise of a better Armageddon, a more efficient, more sophisticated nuclear war.

This vision of victory is a dangerous illusion. We pursue it at great cost even as the rationale for nuclear warfare disappears. The United

States does not want to destroy the Soviet Union. Yet we still are building this secret system in search of a way, as President Bush himself has said, to win a nuclear war.

The idea behind MILSTAR strikes some people well versed in nuclear-war plans as insane, the cost unsupportable, the secrecy undemocratic. But our elected representatives cannot debate the idea openly. It remains part of a closed world.

Bruce Blair, the former nuclear triggerman, studies the problems of command and control at the Brookings Institution, one of Washington's foremost public-policy centers. Blair has an ashen complexion and haunted eyes. Now forty-three years old, he served as a missile launch-control officer—the man in the bunker with his finger on the button—in the early 1970's. He went on to join Strategic Air Command and served as a soldier aboard the Looking Glass plane, the airborne command post that becomes a nuclear-war nerve center if SAC's headquarters is obliterated. The experience started him thinking about nuclear war. He thought long and hard, and he has reached some clear conclusions. He has spent a decade engrossed by the nation's war plans and, increasingly, by the secrecy that sustains them.

When he left the Air Force, he went to Yale University to mull over issues of command and control. He earned a graduate degree and was hired by an arm of Congress, the Office of Technology Assessment. In 1982, Congress commissioned Blair to study the Pentagon's nuclear-war plans and the network designed to execute them. Blair became one of the few outsiders ever to see the entire Single Integrated Operational Plan, the blueprint for nuclear war. He saw the SIOP and its many annexes, the command-and-control procedures, the muscles, bones, tendons and nerve endings of the nation's strategy for nuclear war laid bare. He read almost everything every Pentagon agency had written on the subject, interviewed generals and admirals, and wrote a pioneering study over the course of two years. Very few people in the Pentagon ever see more than a part of the SIOP. No civilian ever had this kind of access before. No one inside or outside the Pentagon had ever pulled the facts together coherently.

Blair concluded that the vulnerabilities of the command system may make nuclear war impossible to control—and may actually increase the risk of a conventional crisis escalating into nuclear holocaust. One implication of his study was that no technological solution to the problem of fighting a nuclear war has been invented, and none may exist.

Congress commissioned this study. Blair wrote it. But the Pentagon seized it, stamped it with the highest security classification in the government and destroyed all but a few of the existing copies. The clearance to read Blair's report—now classified "Single Integrated Operational Plan/Extremely Sensitive Information"—was restricted to four people: the President, the Secretary and the Deputy Secretary of Defense and the chairman of the Joint Chiefs of Staff.

Congress cannot see Blair's study. *Blair* cannot see Blair's study. And only three people at the Pentagon are authorized to see Blair's study. This was a case of classification gone wild. It forestalled informed discussion of a central issue—perhaps *the* central issue—of modern military strategy: the control of nuclear weaponry in crisis and in war. George Orwell wrote in *1984* that freedom is the ability to say that two plus two makes four. Blair put two and two together. The Pentagon forbade him to say four.

Blair is prohibited from discussing details of his work. He can discuss the political climate in which his study was suppressed. "Part of the story of black programs is this loss of faith in the democratic system, the adversarial system, to produce consensus on weapons programs," Blair said as we sat in his tiny, cluttered office at Brookings. "Taking things black relieves the pressure of give-and-take, of the adversarial process. You don't have this messy business of democratic debate. . . .

"The black programs are a travesty of our political system," he said. "What it means is that nuclear-weapons decisions, decisions that have always eluded democratic controls, are now being delegated to a small inside group. And we can't delegate decisions on national goals and objectives to a few insiders. It's an illicit evasion of the adversarial process, and it leads to tremendous distortion in the public debate and, potentially, a grave misallocation of resources."

Bruce Blair also has reached some conclusions about MILSTAR. "If MILSTAR is dedicated to protracted nuclear war-fighting, then all democratic debate on the traditional objectives of defense has been muted. And that's wrong," he said. "By hiding the specific means to goals like MILSTAR, you're hiding the goals themselves. That's sabotaging our form of government.

"Look," Blair said, "I've read the SIOP. I've looked through our plans for postattack operations. They don't amount to a hill of beans. All this baloney about multiple exchanges is a lot of loose rhetoric. It can't be done, no matter how much money you spend. I still believe in the Big Bang theory. The war starts. SAC lays down its best hand. The end."

In the end, if MILSTAR will not work, we are spending $20 billion chasing a chimera. And if it will work, the survivors of its success will be too busy hunting for food, searching for shelter and coping with a mortally wounded planet to care.

Late in his life, Albert Einstein was asked what weapon would be used to fight the Third World War. Einstein replied that he really didn't know, but he had an idea what weapons would be used in World War IV.

"Sticks and stones," Einstein said.

4

A Wing and
a Prayer

ON November 22, 1988, at a top-secret Air Force post in the Mojave Desert, the Pentagon unveiled its biggest secret weapon since the first atomic bomb.

A military band played "Those Magnificent Men in Their Flying Machines" and a specially composed air, "Stealth Fanfare." Security guards with police dogs stood watch. Cameras clicked as a hangar door rattled open and a tractor pulled a winged war machine into the morning light.

The mechanical creature loomed over the tarmac, conjuring all sorts of lethal images in people's minds: some saw a stingray, some saw a hellish bat, some saw a pterodactyl from a Japanese science-fiction movie; *Time*'s man on the scene saw "a death machine out of Darth Vader's workshop."

The machine had an evil beauty. Its skin was the color of shadows, a leaden shade, gray fading to black. Its body was a needle-nosed bullet, its single wing a sharp machete, its tail a set of shark's teeth. In its belly hid a cylinder like a revolver's, its chambers fitted for nuclear bombs.

Here at last was the Stealth bomber, the B-2, the wonder weapon for World War III. The audience on the airstrip went wild. Air Force brass, employees of the Northrop Corporation, which built the bomber, and congressmen applauded, whistled and cheered. The Secretary of the Air Force, Edward C. Aldridge Jr., took the microphone. "Let us all remember America's enduring hope and prayer—that the B-2 will strengthen the cause of peace—and that this magnificent aircraft will never fly in anger."

The Air Force was hoping and praying that the plane would fly at all. For nearly ten years, the Air Force promoted the bomber with song-and-dance briefings to select congressmen. It was a tremendous technological breakthrough. Its sleek flying-wing design and its radar-absorbing skin made it nearly invisible to Soviet early-warning sensors. It rendered obsolete hundreds of millions of dollars of Soviet air defenses. It would revolutionize nuclear warfare. It was the greatest bomber ever built.[1]

But what would it cost? The Stealth went through its research and development in complete secrecy. It existed: that was all most anyone knew. It was so highly classified that Congress couldn't debate it. It was invulnerable to informed criticism. There was no informed criticism because there was no public information. But by the time the Air Force rolled the bomber out before the cameras, its staggering cost could be classified no longer. Trying to hide the Stealth bomber in the black budget was like trying to hide an elephant with a handkerchief.

It slowly became clear that the program was running a bit ahead of its original cost projections. Back in 1981, the Air Force thought it could complete 132 of the planes for as little as $22 billion. Eight years later, it had already spent that sum, and it had but a single plane to show for it.[2]

The cost had grown in secret as Northrop struggled to build the black bomber. The Stealth was ferociously complicated, and a committee of computers was designing it. Now, in the days before the rollout, the Air Force was conceding that their estimates had been a bit off—$44 billion would cover the program. That figure had an asterisk on it, though. Those were 1981 dollars the Air Force was counting. Those dollars now were worth less than seventy cents. Adjusted for inflation, the Air Force's revised figure was a tad under $68 billion—more than half a billion dollars per plane. That was an understatement. I talked to three civilian Air Force analysts the week the Stealth debuted. They all said there was no way the Air Force could bring the bomber in at less than $80 billion for the fleet. That was only if Congress pumped enough money into the plane to meet a heavy production schedule in the early 1990's; the longer production was stretched out, the more the plane would cost. Members of the House Armed Services Committee were saying the cost could reach $1 billion a plane. And at that price, the Stealth would never fly.

Back out on the tarmac that November morning, the Air Force Chief of Staff, Larry D. Welch, was waxing proud. "The B-2 is a superb example of the inherent technological advantage of a free society," he said. "This aircraft combines all the best attributes of the penetrating bomber—long range, efficient cruise, heavy payload, accurate delivery, reliability and maintainability."

Welch's rave review rested on a wing and a prayer. That bomber standing behind him was a flightless bird. The Stealth on the tarmac could not have flown that day. The date for its first flight test had been pushed back for four years. The Air Force had built a revolutionary craft without building a test prototype. So had the makers of the *Titanic*. If the Stealth bomber ever went end over end when pushed to its limits on one of its test flights, there were going to be some serious questions asked. But the questions had already started, now that the Stealth had emerged from blackness. The questions proved more dangerous to the bomber than any anti-aircraft weapon could be. From the moment the Stealth began to be stripped of its secrecy, once its invisibility began slipping away, it was revealed as an act of folly: a plane so expensive the nation couldn't afford to build it. That was the Stealth's blackest secret.

The first open congressional hearings on the plane began in the spring of 1989. That April, in his first public testimony on the bomber, Defense Secretary Dick Cheney stated the obvious: the Stealth was "enormously complex" and "enormously expensive" and "there are a lot of unre-solved questions there about how ultimately we are going to finance it and what it ultimately will cost." At the time, Cheney said he couldn't find anybody in the Air Force willing or able to tell him what the plane's true price tag would be. "I would be less than forthright with you today if I didn't highlight for you the fact that we've got problems with the B-2," Cheney testified. That was the most forthright anyone in the Pentagon ever had been about the Stealth. Cheney's refreshing flirtation with reality on the subject of the Stealth proved an intoxicating experience. People's tongues were loosened; hard figures and harder truths began flowing.

A few days after Cheney's testimony, Robert B. Costello resigned as Under Secretary of Defense for Acquisition, the "procurement czar" of the Pentagon. I called him up a few weeks later at the Hudson Foundation, a think tank in Indianapolis. Costello said the Stealth should be written off as an impossibly expensive mistake.

"I don't think we can afford any at the price we have to pay for it," Costello said. "Whether the price is more than $500 million, as the Air Force says, or more than $700 million, like Les Aspin says, whatever it turns out to be, at that price the target subset you can use it against becomes smaller and smaller."[4]

Costello was talking about targets in the nuclear-war plan. Clearly no one would send the Stealth to blow up a cement factory or a railroad yard. The targets the Air Force has chosen for the Stealth are far more valuable: the Soviet leadership and their mobile missiles, the SS-24 and SS-25, which roam the tundra on trucks and trains. But the Air Force has a problem with targeting mobile missiles, Costello said. No one knows how to hit a small moving target hidden somewhere in the vastness of the Soviet Union. And the trouble with targeting the Soviet leadership is that there are far less costly and risky ways to do it than flying black bombers over Red Square. Costello said he hated to use the term, but the Stealth's "cost-per-kill" ratio was unconscionable: "If I want to hit the men's room in the Kremlin, I've got a lot of cheaper ways of doing it."

He said that in the six months between the Stealth's rollout and his resignation in May 1989, he had argued that the plane should be killed. "I recommended that we cancel it," he said. "I got a good deal of covert support for that argument around the Pentagon, but not much overt support." The lack of open enthusiasm was unsurprising. They don't hand out stars and medals at the Pentagon for killing momentous weapons projects.

Costello said the Stealth still had value as a test program. "I mean, test it, sure, take it up and test the avionics, test the design," he said. "But cut your losses. It's like going to Las Vegas. You quit while you're ahead, quit while your losses can be minimized." The man who'd been in charge of buying weapons at the Pentagon was likening the building of the Stealth bomber to a crap shoot in a casino.

As the 1990's begin, the Pentagon has spent roughly $30 billion building one working Stealth bomber. The cost per plane has risen to $820 million, and it keeps rising. And "the overriding purpose of this new bomber," as Air Force chief Larry Welch said that November morning, "is to ensure that we never need to employ it."

If deterring nuclear war is a matter of displaying symbols of strength, then the Stealth bomber is a ruinously expensive icon. It serves the nation primarily as a monument to the costs of secrecy.

The manned bomber has a special place in modern warfare. It has ever since late 1944, when the B-29s of Curtis LeMay's 20th Bomber Command began laying waste to Japan, and newsreels lit American movie theaters with the reflected light of the firebombings. The destruction of Tokyo and a thousand other towns and cities in Europe and Asia was the triumph of a new and merciless war technology. The manned bomber changed the face of war. It was the first machine that could level great cities at will.[5]

From the beginning of World War II, the Allies dreamed of a bomber that could fly from the safety of American airfields, soar across the Atlantic and strike Nazi strongholds in Europe. Jack Northrop thought he could build that bomber. Northrop began designing planes for Douglas Aircraft in Santa Monica, California, in the early 1920's. Ever since, he'd been thinking about streamlining aircraft so they could soar greater distances at faster speeds, thinking about how to slim down the body of a plane until it became one with the wing.

In 1939, Northrop started his own aviation company. He was one of the handful of daring, innovative men capable of building war planes with little more than their rich imaginations (and a generous application of government funds). Before the war ended, Northrop developed a unique design for an intercontinental bomber, a propeller-driven plane in the shape of a flying wing. The experimental bomber was dubbed the XB-35. After the war was over, Northrop worked closely with the new armed service formed in 1947, the Air Force. The search for the long-range bomber continued as the Cold War took hold. Northrop kept the basic design of the XB-35, applied the lessons he'd learned from the flight tests and the new science of jet propulsion, and created the YB-49.

Northrop's new bomber looked like a jet-propelled boomerang. He'd buried the fuselage and engines within the flying wing. The plane had a sleekness to it that cut wind resistance and increased fuel efficiency. And the Air Force couldn't help but notice how the YB-49's slender profile reduced the radar cross-section of the plane. There is nothing mystical about this quality. Radar is simply radio waves that bounce off an object in space, revealing the object's location. The radar cross-section of an object is a measure of how much radar the object reflects. A B-52 bomber has a big radar cross-section, because it looks like a steroid-swigging football linebacker carrying his bench on his shoulders. Its bulky body has fat wings, pendulous engines and a jutting tail. Not for nothing was the B-52 nicknamed the Stratofortress. It reflects a lot of radar, about 100 square meters' worth.

Jack Northrop's bomber was supple and aquiline. Its wings blended into its body, forming a softly curving surface. Its radar cross-section was more like ten square meters. If the United States went to war against the Soviets in the 1950's, the YB-49 would be an elusive target for a Russian radarman.

The flying wing was an inherently stealthy design. It was also inherently unstable. The YB-49 gave test pilots fits. One of the best, Glen Edwards, took it up again and again, trying to master the new machine. "Flew the YB-49 again today," Edwards recorded in his flight notes. "Too rough to get any data. Darndest airplane I've ever tried to do anything with. Quite uncontrollable at times."[6]

Edwards took the plane up for the last time on June 5, 1948. Along with four crew members, he was killed when the YB-49 tumbled out of control and crashed in the California desert. Not far from where he died stands Edwards Air Force Base, named in his memory.

The Air Force, discouraged by the flying wing's shaky performance, killed the YB-49 in 1951. Embittered, Northrop quit the company he'd founded. The dream of a stealthy bomber survived. The Air Force showed no great interest in building such a craft for the better part of three decades, but the enticing technological challenge persisted. Throughout the 1950's, 1960's and 1970's, a doctrine of stealth technology slowly grew.

Stealth technology is nothing more than a high-tech version of an old trick: camouflage. The uniforms of European armies used to be gaily colored; in the 1770's, the British army learned the hard way that a bright red coat made for poor cover when fighting a revolutionary army in green fields. Now every infantryman's uniform in every army in the world is a dull khaki or mottled green. Fighter pilots knew enough to camouflage their craft with paint in the days when the naked eye was the only way to detect a war plane.

Radar and infrared sensors have supplanted the naked eye. Stealth technology is the search for different ways to camouflage a plane against these detectors. "Stealth," writes Bill Sweetman, one of a handful of civilian experts in the field, "is a philosophy, not just a single technology."[7] None of these technologies is a secret, any more than Einstein's equation of $E=MC^2$. A high-school physics student understands the equation, but still can't build a bomb. It's the combination of many technologies that makes a plane stealthy, and it's the search for the right combination that has proved so difficult. Every choice of a design, a material or a system has drawbacks, trade-offs and shortcomings. Stealth technologies have limits: no plane can become invisible.

Changing the design of a plane is the simplest camouflage. A B-52 carries its engines outside its body. A stealthy plane hides its engines within. An infrared detector finds a plane by tracking the heat of its engines. A stealthy plane insulates its engines and mixes their exhaust with cool air. Metal is an excellent reflector of radar, so a stealthy plane can't be a big metallic box. The Stealth bomber's skin is made up of materials transparent to radar. These include heat-resistant thermoplastics, and composites like carbon/carbon, made of reinforced graphite fibers bound together by plastic epoxy, and Kevlar, the synthetic used in bulletproof vests. But the slightest scratch will damage the skin's stealthiness; the bomber must be handled with care.

A transparent skin is useless if the underlying muscles and bones show up on radar. Between one-third and one-half of the Stealth bomber's 140,000 pounds are structural components made of materials that absorb, deflect, diffract and dissipate radar waves. These materials work on the same basic principle as your microwave oven. The reason your microwave doesn't hurt you when you turn it on is that its fixtures absorb the radiating waves that cook your roast. A variety of materials, some dating back to the 1940's, have this radar-absorbing quality. Ferrite materials, which are tiny bits of rusty iron suspended in layers of plastic, work well in breaking up incoming radar. Another trick is to shape sheets of radar-absorbing materials in triangular wedges, like the bottom of an egg carton. The wedges trap and muffle incoming radar like the baffled walls of a soundproof room soak up sound waves.[8]

Again, these methods have shortfalls. Radar comes in a variety of wavelengths. To create enough layers of radar-absorbing materials to capture all the different wavelengths would require making a plane's walls at least eight feet thick. Such a plane would be very stealthy, but it probably could not fly. The combined weight of the Stealth's radar shielding is one reason the plane is relatively sluggish, with a top speed of less than 600 miles an hour, less than three-fourths the speed of sound. If detected, it cannot outrun a supersonic MiG jet fighter. In fact, it can't outrun the red-eye from L.A. The Stealth bomber is unarmed, except for its warheads. Once spotted it is a sitting duck.

The Stealth's designers built it with modern radars in mind. But the Soviets rarely throw anything away, and about a quarter of their air defense is based on old-fashioned long-wave radars. Such radars work on roughly the same frequency as television, very high frequency or VHF, with wavelengths of between one and ten meters. The Stealth bomber's body, wheels up, is a little more than five meters high. When the wavelength of a radar is similar to the dimensions of the body being illuminated, the radar wave resonates as it flows around the body. Radar-absorbing materials cannot stop this resonance. In short, long-wave radars, a shopworn technology of the 1950's, can detect the Stealth, the dazzling high-tech weapon of the 1990's.

The time-honored way to defeat radar is to jam it, by sending out signals at the same frequency as the radar. A bomber pilot also traditionally uses radar to find his targets, and to guide him through rough terrain on a low-altitude night flight. Unfortunately, both techniques defeat the whole idea of stealthiness.

The Air Force's Tom Amlie, who was the technical director of the China Lake Weapons Center, a secret missile-testing post in the California desert, knows a thing or two about weaponry. For a variety of reasons —mainly the unbending laws of physics—he says there is no way to reduce the radar cross-section of a bomber the size of the Stealth beyond the point where radar can detect it. Amlie's old boss, Edward Aldridge, the former Air Force Secretary, has conceded that the Stealth "will be detectable to enemy radar [but] only when it is close." How close? Amlie says the air traffic control radar at an average commercial airport could pick up the Stealth at a distance of no less than thirty-five miles, or about four minutes' flying time at top speed. The Soviets' air defenses are more sophisticated than the control tower at O'Hare. And four minutes is a long time when the nuclear stakes are high.[9]

To escape being detected, the Stealth bomber pilot has to fly at low altitudes, hugging the ground. To do that, he must use terrain-following radar. And if he uses his radar, or his jamming devices, he is no longer stealthy. The second he turns them on, he lights up his plane like the White House Christmas tree. He becomes an easy target for an enemy's sensors, and an enemy's weapons. The pilot and his enemy are like a policeman and a criminal in a dark and empty warehouse, each holding a flashlight and a gun. Whoever turns his flashlight on first dies.

Finally, no amount of tinkering can change the fact that two wings are better than one. The flying-wing design is unstable in flight, and always will be. Such a plane stays aloft only if hundreds of on-board computers continuously calculate and correct its aerodynamics. If the computers crash, the plane crashes.

These were some of the fiendishly complex problems confronting tens of thousands of engineers, technicians and scientists assigned to work on stealthy aircraft throughout the 1970's and 1980's.

The origins of the Stealth bomber are obscured in the shadows of military secrecy. The Air Force apparently became interested in building stealthy war planes after the Arab-Israeli war of 1973. The Arab nations' Soviet-made SA-6 anti-aircraft missiles proved highly effective against Israel's American-made aircraft, including F-4 Phantoms, the most advanced fighter-bomber of the day. The Israeli planes were equipped with the best electronic countermeasures, sophisticated jammers, and chaff, bits of metal tossed from a plane to dazzle radars and confuse missile homing devices. They didn't confuse the Soviet-made missiles. The Israelis lost more than seventy aircraft in the first forty-eight hours of the Yom Kippur War.[10]

The after-battle reports evidently started some wheels turning in the Air Force, and sparked some creative thinking about stealth technology. In early 1974, the Defense Advanced Research Projects Agency, which is the Pentagon's own venture-capital firm, began funding a black research and development project code-named HAVE BLUE. HAVE BLUE was a program to develop a prototype of a small stealth aircraft. Three years later, in early 1977, at a test site called Dreamland, in the sprawling desert surrounding Nellis Air Force Base, an experimental stealth fighter took off from the badwater flatlands near Groom Lake, Nevada. Although at least three of the black fighters crashed in test flights over the years, the program proceeded full-bore.[11]

And then, on June 30, 1977, the Air Force suddenly became extremely interested in the idea of a stealthy bomber. That was the day the President of the United States canceled the B-1 bomber, the plane the Air Force wanted to replace the B-52. Jimmy Carter thought the B-1 was an expensive anachronism, a technology left over from the 1960's, an old warhorse loaded down with costly new computer systems; the nation didn't need it. Besides, he'd been briefed on the secret stealth programs, and on the promise they held. Six months after his inauguration, Carter announced "one of the most difficult decisions I've ever had to make." He made it in the face of enormous opposition by everyone from the Joint Chiefs to the union workers who would help build the B-1 for the Rockwell International Corporation. The United States would not buy the new strategic bomber. The B-1 was dead.

The B-1 did not die. The Air Force had been trying to build a new strategic bomber for two decades, and it would not stop trying now. The ranking generals of the Air Force led an underground campaign to save the B-1. They enlisted top Pentagon officials, congressional staffers and Armed Services Committee members with thousands of B-1 production jobs in their districts.

The generals revolted against the President, and Carter detested them for it, raging that they "treat me like an enemy." Among those opposing Carter was the man in charge of Air Force research and development, Lieutenant General Thomas Stafford, a veteran test pilot who'd commanded Apollo 10's circumnavigation of the moon in 1969. The President and the astronaut developed an abiding mutual contempt. The President thought Stafford insubordinate. Stafford referred to the President as "that peanut farmer." Stafford flew figure-eights around the President on the embattled bomber program, helping to transfer at least $450 million from different Pentagon accounts, including stealth research funds, to keep the B-1 alive in 1978. He was second to none in his efforts to build a new bomber—any new bomber.[12]

Late that year, Stafford received a visit at the Pentagon from a dapper salesman drumming up business. His visitor was Thomas V. Jones, the chairman and chief executive officer of the Northrop Corporation. Jones was an aeronautical engineer who'd run Northrop since 1960. The company never had risen to the first rank of defense contractors, and it hadn't built a big airplane since Jack Northrop's flying wing, the YB-49. It flourished mainly as a subcontractor, building radar-jamming gear and missile guidance systems. Jones himself was something of a star in the aerospace industry. Suave and handsome, a trustee of Stanford University and a member of the board of the *Los Angeles Times*, he lived in a sprawling home decorated with Impressionist paintings on the edge of Bel Air, the most elegant neighborhood in Los Angeles, where he threw great barbecues for his wide circle of friends.[13]

Jones and his company were also convicted corporate criminals. In August 1972, Jones had reached into his office desk and handed a package of $75,000 in hundred-dollar bills to a lawyer named Herbert Kalmbach, who happened to be President Nixon's chief campaign fund-raiser. Those bills became hush money. The President's men gave the cash to the CIA-connected burglars who'd been arrested ransacking the Democratic National Committee headquarters at the Watergate hotel and office complex the previous June. Once this payoff was traced back to Northrop, the Watergate special prosecutor had some questions for Jones. He wanted to know why Jones happened to have that kind of cash on hand. He also wanted to know if Jones and Northrop were in the habit of handing out large sums of money to crooked lawyers and power brokers.

They were. Under Jones' direction, Northrop laundered millions of dollars of corporate funds through foreign banks in the 1960's and early 1970's. The company used the money to wine, dine and bribe generals and politicians in the United States and abroad. Jones pleaded guilty to a felony in 1974 for his role in creating the secret Northrop slush fund that channeled a total of $150,000 in cash to Nixon's reelection campaign. The corporation was convicted of the crime as well. And Jones had to step down for a while as chairman in 1975 after the company's own board of directors held him responsible for Northrop's paying hefty bribes to win military contracts overseas.

Jones persevered and regained control of his company. But times were harder now. The war in Vietnam was over. The arms business was slowing down. The weapons market in the oil-rich nations of the Middle East was glutted. The only big deal Jones had landed in recent years was a $2 billion contract to build the computerized brain of the ten-warhead MX, the new land-based missile approved by President Carter in 1978. In order to meet a deadline imposed by Congress, Northrop rapidly expanded its payroll, hiring 2,000 new workers and in the process transforming the character of its workforce from "Swiss watchmakers to a bunch of guys in Grateful Dead T-shirts," as one aerospace industry analyst put it. The MX guidance system was giving the company fits. Serious snafus marred the Deadheads' work. Eventually, the Pentagon sued Northrop for fraud and stopped $130 million in payments for the MX, saying the company faked test results to make a flawed system look good on paper.[14]

Back in 1978, it looked like there might not be a great deal of profit in the MX, and nothing else of promise was coming down the Pentagon's pike for Northrop to build. The company's cash flow was in danger of stagnating. Northrop needed new business. General Stafford was sitting on billions of research dollars. Might he have a job in mind?

Stafford saw a gambit. He would set Northrop to work researching plans for a new penetrating bomber, a bomber that would incorporate the exotic new technology being tested at Dreamland. If the B-1 didn't survive, perhaps an advanced-technology bomber could capture the imagination of the President. Stafford jotted down some ballpark numbers for the plane: the miles it could fly on a tank of fuel, the weight it could carry, the square meters of its radar cross-section. Jones glanced at the specifications, said he'd be in touch, and flew home to headquarters in Los Angeles. Northrop studied the numbers, looked back to the future, and saw its founder's visionary bomber, the YB-49. By the summer of 1979 the company came up with a radical flying-wing design for the Stealth. The secret bomber was born.[15]

Its birth was announced within the year. The President of the United States declassified the secret, and used it as a weapon in a fight for his political life. Jimmy Carter's fortunes began failing badly in 1979. The Shah of Iran fell. The Ayatollah Khomeini rose and unleashed Islamic rage across the world. Fifty-two Americans were seized in Teheran and their plight was televised nightly to the nation. The Russians launched their murderous invasion of Afghanistan. And a seismic rumble was rising in California. Ronald Reagan was gearing up to run for the presidency, battering Carter as hard as he could on his weekly syndicated radio shows and on the campaign trail. The cancellation of the B-1 was a lightning rod for Reagan, and he used the decision to paint Carter as a sell-out, a quisling, the Neville Chamberlain of national defense. On his radio show, Reagan said the B-1's downfall "must have been good news in Moscow. They must be toasting in the Kremlin." When Jimmy Carter vetoed defense programs, Reagan said in 1979, "the Soviets smile happily."[16]

Carter badly needed to broadcast a sign of strength in the presidential election of 1980. Voters were weary of his ineptitude and skeptical of his devotion to defense. Carter's aides leaked news of his decision to build the Stealth in August 1980, trying to wring some political advantage out of the secret weapon. The distinct impression the leak left was that the Pentagon had a fleet of invisible bombers in the works.[17]

The Stealth became a political plane. The Democrats needed a big military program to call their own. They chose the Stealth as their weapon, and stood by it. Republicans had to admit they liked the idea behind the bomber. But few politicians from either party knew anything about the technology—and no one dreamed of its potential cost.

The cost of a new weapon was not a matter of political controversy in 1981. Reagan's election galvanized the Pentagon and its contractors. "Defense," the new President kept saying to his advisers, "is not a budget issue. You spend what you need." Jimmy Carter's parting budget, reflecting his rightward drift, gave the Pentagon $20 billion in new programs for 1981. The new team at the White House added $33 billion to that sum, and promised more, much more, to come: more than $250 billion in new military spending in the next four years. The Congress, for the most part, went along happily. It made few difficult choices among defense programs in Reagan's first term. Almost nothing was forbidden, almost everything permitted. David Stockman, Reagan's first budget director, looked back cynically on the Pentagon's spending spree. "They got a blank check," Stockman said. "But it worked perfectly, because they got so goddamned greedy that they got themselves strung way out there on a limb."[18]

The GAO's Frank Conahan tried to track the floodtide of defense funds during the first Reagan administration. "In those four years, the Pentagon's budget doubled, from $142 billion in 1981 to $282 billion in 1985," he said. "Well, that's a lot of money, and the Pentagon was not prepared to spend it wisely. The whole rewards system in the Pentagon is to get money, to get programs funded. This environment led to some foolish things."[19]

The Reagan administration had to make a difficult choice: build the B-1 or the Stealth? The B-1 was a political weapon too; Reagan had made it a potent campaign issue, an issue not just of defense but of patriotism, and of morality. The Moral Majority was keeping lists of congressional voting records on important issues, and building the B-1 was high on the list. Reagan would be seen as a hypocrite if he shot down the B-1.[20]

And the Stealth—well, no one knew much about the Stealth, but it sounded as if it were too sweet a possibility to pass up. The secret technology was too tantalizing. If the United States truly could build an invisible bomber that could slip past the Soviets' defenses, that bomber was a winning weapon.

Northrop's Tom Jones was pushing for the Stealth as if his company's life depended on it. He buttonholed anyone who might have a say in the Stealth's future, petitioning the Pentagon, working the chambers of Capitol Hill, twisting the arms of Armed Services Committee members and staffers. The contract was going to be the biggest in the history of national defense. It would be a cost-plus contract, of course; a set margin of profit would be guaranteed and cost overruns picked up by the government. The job was potentially worth billions, perhaps a billion dollars' clear profit during research and development, and $2 billion a year in profits at peak production. Landing this bomber could make or break the corporation.[21]

Jones had a unique status among his peers in the aerospace business: he was a pal to the President. He stood in the innermost circle of conservative businessmen who'd been close to Reagan since the actor's stint as General Electric's corporate spokesman in the 1950's. His wife Ruth was a dear friend of Nancy Reagan's from Hollywood days; Ruth's father was Conrad Nagel, a silent-movie actor of some note. During the Reagans' cinematic years, Nagel was president of the Academy of Motion Picture Arts and Sciences, the organization that gives out the Oscars. Every New Year's Eve, the Joneses celebrated with the Reagans at the publishing magnate Walter Annenberg's palatial Palm Springs estate. In February 1981, the Joneses were on the guest list for the President's birthday party at the White House. In May, the Joneses hosted a small formal dinner party for the Reagans at the Georgetown Club, a private establishment in a charming old house in the capital's most fashionable district. Tom Jones pursued his plane on the fastest track in Washington.[22]

Jones made his case for the Stealth. Buz Hello, Rockwell's B-1 manager, made the case for his resurrected plane, now dubbed the B-1B. The President, typically, couldn't choose between the two. Reagan's package of weapons to rebuild the nation's nuclear forces included 132 Stealths and 100 B-1s. The problem for the Defense Secretary, Caspar Weinberger, was finding a rationale for both. It only made sense if there was a bomber gap to be filled. But where was it? Tom Jones was swearing up and down that he could build the fleet of Stealths by late 1987. Rockwell pledged to make a crash effort to complete 100 B-1s by 1985. Weinberger, a lawyer by trade, prepared his case as if going to trial with a difficult client. A two-bomber budget didn't appear to be a decision any advocate could win, even amid the bonanza beginning at the Pentagon. "Weinberger hasn't a prayer in hell of getting the money to build two bombers," declared Senator Barry Goldwater of Arizona, the grand old man of conservative Republicans. "We have too much stuff coming along to pay for that and he knows it."

The Senate Armed Services Committee and its subcommittee on strategic and theater nuclear forces began answering Weinberger's prayer during ten days of hearings in October and November 1981. The hearings were like most others on Capitol Hill, despite the unusual subject matter of a secret plane. The transcripts of the hearings show senators apologizing for wandering in late from debates on shale-oil drilling, television talk-show appearances, lunch with King Hussein of Jordan. Many stayed ten or fifteen minutes, asked a few questions and scurried off to their next appointment. Most had barely enough time and energy to focus on the issue.

Weinberger argued both sides of the case to his restless audience. On November 3, he warned of a coming bomber gap. He said the B-1 must be built immediately to replace the B-52. But by 1988, sending the B-1 against Soviet air defenses would be "suicide." By then the Stealth squadrons would be ready, if work started immediately. So the nation had to build both.

On reflection, this did not sound like a ringing endorsement of the

B-1. So on November 11, in a complete reversal, Weinberger produced a CIA study showing the B-1 *could* penetrate Soviet air defenses well into the 1990's. But the Stealth—at the time known by a generic name, the Advanced Technology Bomber, or ATB—was a far greater aircraft, Weinberger said. It was crucial to national security through the end of the century and beyond. So the nation had to build both.

Air Force Chief of Staff Lew Allen Jr. told the senators that the Air Force had studied the question thoroughly. "The answer was clear and unambiguous. Acquiring the B-1 while continuing to pursue the ATB was the most cost-effective approach." Why the most expensive approach was also the most cost-effective remained unclear.[23]

Pressed by Senator John Warner of Virginia to choose between the two, Allen squirmed. "Sir, I would regret having to make a choice like that. . . . However, I would see no alternative, if I were forced to make that choice, and that is that I should go ahead with the B-1. The ATB alone would be a risky course to follow," since the technology was so new and unproven. The B-1 was practically ready to roll down the production line; the Air Force had been set to build it for years. The Stealth was still a paper airplane.

SAC Commander Bennie Davis agreed with his chief, in a roundabout way. He testified that both planes were necessary, and the Stealth was a better plane on paper, but if forced at gunpoint he'd take a B-1 in the hand over a B-2 in the bush. "If put to the test and this country says we cannot afford two bomber programs at the pace proposed, I must go with the near-term capability, which is the significant capability, and that is the B-1," Davis said. "That does not say that we kill the [Stealth] forever."

General Davis' explanation left the junior senator from Indiana confused:

Senator QUAYLE: If I could take five minutes, I have to go to another meeting. I will limit it to five minutes. Your statement on the B-1 is that it may be thirty years before we build that plane. [The SAC commander had said nothing of the sort.]. . . . But that is not my question. The B-1 was designed to penetrate defenses at high speed and high altitude, is that correct?
General DAVIS: No, Senator, we went to low altitude in the 1950's and early 1960's. . . . We have been at low altitude for years.
Senator QUAYLE: We have gone from high to low altitudes, and we are now at low altitude. . . . Which is better as a penetrator, the Stealth or the B-1? Which would be preferable, if

you could have your choice today, or in 1987? Which would you choose, the B-1 or the Stealth?

General DAVIS: As I said earlier, I chose the B-1. . . .

Senator QUAYLE: Even if you could have Stealth by 1986?

General DAVIS: Well, I don't think that is a good assumption. . . .

Senator QUAYLE: I just want to know which is the better penetrating bomber.

General DAVIS: Of course, the theoretically lower radar cross-section.

Senator QUAYLE: That would be the Stealth?

General DAVIS: Yes.

Senator QUAYLE: So the Stealth would be. If you could get the Stealth earlier on, would you focus on Stealth rather than the B-1?

General DAVIS: I think the question is very hypothetical, Senator.

Senator QUAYLE: Sure it is; a lot of questions are hypothetical, General.

General DAVIS: If we had aircraft that would travel four times the speed of sound, that would be preferable.[24]

Quayle's confusion was forgivable. Which was the better bomber? Few senators could make up their minds. The Stealth was a highly secret, highly theoretical plane in 1981. There was very little hard information, classified or unclassified, for Congress to go by. B-2 or not B-2? CIA studies and SAC studies and Pentagon studies supported every side of the argument. "We have one expert testify and they come in and totally convince us they are correct, and four or five days later we have another expert and they come in and convince us they are correct," sighed Senator Sam Nunn of Georgia. "We never isolate the differences. . . . If we can isolate the differences, we can make some meaningful decisions."[25]

The Congress never did. Military questions, economic questions, technological questions all were overwhelmed by politics. Reagan's 1980 landslide made the Republican bomber, the B-1, a shoo-in. The Democratic bomber, the Stealth, had bipartisan backing; few Republicans rejected the President's weapons proposals. On November 18, the House voted 335–61 to build both bombers. On December 3, the Senate sealed the deal, 66–28.

Tom Jones had played the Congress masterfully. He'd selected the LTV Corporation of Dallas as the major Stealth subcontractor. That did not offend the Republican chairman of the Senate Armed Services Committee, John Tower of Texas. He brought in the Boeing Corporation of Seattle to work on the Stealth's design. That had some influence on the most influential Democrat on Armed Services, Senator Henry "Scoop" Jackson of Washington, an ardent hawk known as "the senator from Boeing."

"Boeing had great experience, LTV had a good reputation, and along with choosing them came this happy happenstance," said Donald Hicks, at the time Northrop's senior vice president for marketing and technology. "That was thinking to the future." Hicks left Northrop in 1985 to become the under secretary of defense for research and engineering, the Pentagon's chief overseer of the Stealth's research and development. He left the Pentagon in 1987 and today is a Northrop consultant.

Hicks thought building both bombers made good sense from a political and economic perspective: "It was a good quick way of pouring money into the community"—the defense community.[26]

The black money for the B-2 started flowing like an oil spill, and it slowly spread through the food chain of the military-industrial complex. A Northrop manager in charge of sharing the wealth had a map of the United States in his office that looked like a flattened porcupine. The map bristled with hundreds of pins. Each pin was stuck in a town with a company that had a Stealth subcontract or sold equipment to subcontractors. Forty-six states containing 383 of the nation's 435 congressional districts were pinned.

Northrop's black money washed back up on Capitol Hill as well. The company's political action committee gave $605,747 to members of Congress' armed services and appropriations committees between 1979 and 1988. On top of that, Northrop gave $62,000 in honoraria in 1988 alone to defense-minded congressmen who gave inspirational speeches at Northrop's Advanced Systems Division, a huge, windowless plant in a smoggy Los Angeles suburb called Pico Rivera.[27]

In early 1982, its cost-plus contract signed and sealed, Northrop began working on the Stealth in earnest. The contract was demanding: the company was supposed to build the fleet from scratch in six years. Northrop rolled up its sleeves, hiring 13,000 workers, creating a 3-D computer graphics network for design and production work, building tons of robotic equipment for its new production line adjacent to the Air Force's secret Plant 42 in Palmdale, a desert town north of Los Angeles. The pressure to produce was intense. Pressed for time, Northrop adopted the techniques of fast-track construction for its bat-winged bomber. In a fast-track building, the stages of construction overlap; you pour the concrete before you complete the blueprint. In Pentagonese, the practice is called "concurrency"; research, engineering, testing and production take place concurrently. The whole idea of concurrency is to save time and money.

Northrop didn't have the time to construct a test model and wring the bugs out of it. It created the Stealth straight from its 3-D data bases. It bought machine tools and constructed assembly lines immediately, well before the data bases were debugged. It started work on the first production model three years before research and development was close to complete. A secret Rand Corporation study conducted for the Pentagon in 1988 warned that the tight schedule had invited serious technical snafus in a system as complex as the Stealth.

Northrop badly underestimated the time it would take to build the bomber. The company calendar on the office wall set a rigorous schedule that the workers on the factory floor couldn't meet. As a consequence the company badly miscalculated the Stealth's cost. The mistake cost taxpayers at least eleven billion black dollars, Frank Conahan's GAO investigators told Congress in a classified 1988 report. But the Air Force said concurrency was more important than cost.[28]

So was the Stealth's war-fighting abilities. In 1983, the Air Force suddenly ordered a major design change in the Stealth. As SAC Commander Davis explained to Senator Quayle, there are high-altitude bombers and low-altitude bombers. The Air Force decided it wanted the Stealth to be both. "The Air Force decided it wanted the B-2 to be more secure in its ability to penetrate," Hicks said. "It wanted to guard against threats nobody could foresee and still can't foresee."

The plane's original mission was to destroy the Soviets from the relative safety of 40,000 feet or more. Now the Air Force ordered Northrop to make the Stealth perform at 400 feet and less. A warplane's aerodynamics and fuel-efficiency are quite different in the thin air eight miles up and the rich atmosphere at sea level. The stresses on its frame are far greater when manuevering at high speed through mountains and over hilltops. To make the Stealth a low-altitude bomber, the plane had to lose some weight and gain some strength. Northrop had to go back to the drawing board.

"You had to go back and start from scratch and reconfigure" the bomber, Hicks said. There would be no fine-tuning the Stealth once the first production model was complete. There could be no flaws in the machine. The computer-driven design meant that the first Stealth built would be the same as the last one off the line.

The design changes alone cost more than $1 billion and set the bomber back a year. The setback cost as much as $1.5 billion in lost productivity and wasted time.

Why was the change made? There is really only one reason for a pilot to fly low: to avoid being detected by radar. If the Stealth were truly stealthy, why would it have to hug the ground? One motive for the redesign was the bomber's new and unprecedented mission: hunting and killing Soviet mobile missiles. The fact that no one knew how to accomplish this mission did not deter the Air Force. The fact that those mobile missiles would most likely have been fired long before the subsonic Stealth found them on the first day of World War III was irrelevant. The fact that the idea could not be debated made it a done deal. The fact that billions had been spent on this afterthought stayed secret for nearly six years.[29]

Another monkey wrench in the machinery was the time it took to investigate the honesty, patriotism and integrity of the thousands of new workers Northrop hired for the Stealth. The Pentagon's Defense Investigative Service was assigned to the task. The DIS was badly overburdened. It had 250 investigators on its staff, and they had other responsibilities—for example, overseeing security in 13,500 buildings at defense plants and private corporations where black weapons projects were under way.[30]

The security program for the Stealth bomber was the biggest and most thorough in the nation. It had a special component called Seven Screens: videotaped lie-detector tests for 2,500 workers a year. The Pentagon investigators couldn't keep up with the backlog. A newly hired worker had to wait an average of six to eight months for the government detectives to interview his neighbors, check his credit ratings, peruse the records of his life. The cost of thousands of workers drawing full salaries and performing no work while waiting for security clearances ran to more than $1 billion a year throughout the defense industry in 1984, the GAO reported. The cost was balanced against the threat of Soviet espionage.

The new hires spent months sitting in waiting rooms at Northrop's Pico Rivera plant drinking coffee, reading magazines and staring into space, like travelers waiting for a long-delayed flight. These holding pens had different names at different companies. At Lockheed Missile and Space in Sunnyvale, California, the detainees called their waiting room the Icebox. At Pico Rivera they called it the Drunk Tank.

Inevitably, a few crooks slipped through the cracks. In March 1984, Northrop hired a man named William Reinke as an engineer for the Stealth project. Reinke noted on his application form that he had a graduate engineering degree and had been working for Rockwell International on a top-secret satellite project. In reality, Rockwell had just fired him for inflating his expense accounts. A few other facts were missing from the form. Reinke said he'd graduated from engineering school. He was actually an alumnus of a Florida chain gang. He'd spent three years at hard labor for stealing cars and passing bad checks. He was a tenth-grade dropout who'd been arrested thirteen times. The Pentagon's elaborate security screening failed to reveal any of these facts to Northrop. At a time when all but four members of Congress were barred from gaining access to the Stealth program, Reinke received his special-access clearance.

Reinke was nothing if not resourceful. He set up his own defense-contracting firm, RF Engineering, and he managed to steer $600,000 in Stealth subcontracts to himself. Even by the generous standards of the defense industry, Reinke's prices were high. RF Engineering sold $20 Radio Shack headphones to Northrop for $90, and marked up ordinary cable costing $1.24 a foot to $4.50. Each markup added a little more to the bomber's price tag. It took Northrop auditors seventeen months to notice that Reinke was buying equipment from himself. They called in the Defense Investigative Service.

"I find it astonishing, almost frightening, that a person of Mr. Reinke's background was able to achieve his position," said the federal judge who sentenced him to five years in prison for fraud. "I don't find Mr. Reinke astonishing. The world is full of Mr. Reinkes. I find Northrop, Rockwell and the government astonishing."[31]

Two weeks after Reinke went on Northrop's payroll, Ronald Brousseau, a Northrop manager in charge of buying parts for the Stealth, sat in his living room chatting with a business acquaintance named Richard Haskell. Haskell was a part-owner of RH Manufacturing, a local machine shop that built some of the Stealth's parts. The two had a relationship that was more than purely professional. Brousseau was a swindler. Haskell was a government informant.

The FBI had paid Haskell a visit earlier that winter as part of an investigation of corruption in the southern California aerospace industry. Haskell told his visitors he had some information that might interest them. RH Manufacturing was paying Brousseau a 5 percent kickback on Stealth subcontracts. The practice was so routine in the industry that it had a nickname: "a nickel job."

The government granted Haskell immunity from prosecution if he'd help snare Brousseau. On March 16, 1984, as the two discussed deals more lucrative than five cents on the dollar, a tiny microphone strapped to Haskell's body captured the conversation:

BROUSSEAU: Let's say you look at a job. . . . Let's say it's worth, let's say a hundred bucks a part. Okay? . . . Now I'm gonna bump it seventy-five dollars [up to $175]. That hundred-dollar price that you originally bid was a good bid. You know? In your eyes. It was a small profit job for you. Okay, I'm gonna bump it seventy-five dollars. . . . What I would like is I would

like twenty-five percent of the seventy-five-dollar bump. You
keep the other seventy-five percent. You know?
HASKELL: Okay.
BROUSSEAU: And that seems like an equitable position.

Brousseau regarded the Stealth bomber as a first-class flight to early
retirement.

BROUSSEAU: We are . . . in the ground floor of this program.
I'm forty-four years old right now. I firmly intend to retire at
fifty-five. And if I just take a little piece here and a little piece
there, put 'em in a shoebox and bury the shoebox, bury 'em in
the backyard. . . .
HASKELL: And don't get greedy.
BROUSSEAU: And don't get greedy, you know, a nickel here
and a nickel there. Everybody's gonna get fat and everybody's
gonna be happy and at fifty-five I'm gonna say goodbye, guys,
I'm gonna buy my little cabin and my fishing boat on a river. . . .
HASKELL: There you go. That's good.
BROUSSEAU: It's the people that get greedy are the people that
get caught.

Brousseau and his favorite Stealth subcontractors stayed fat and
happy by practicing the fine art of courtesy bidding. Courtesy bidding is
an illegal price-fixing scheme. It requires a secret understanding between
buyers and suppliers.
Here's how Brousseau explained it to Haskell. Brousseau meets with
three Stealth subcontractors. They cut a deal. The three agree to take
turns playing low bidder. When Brousseau has a Stealth job to let, he
pencils in a small "c" on the contract, makes three copies and sends
them to his friends. The "c" stands for courtesy. By prearrangement,
two submit impossibly high bids. The third submits a winning "low"
bid. It is almost as high as the high bids, bumped up to cover the cost
of Brousseau's kickback, plus a hefty profit. The illusion of competitive
bidding is created. Brousseau happily awards the classified contract and
lets out another. The price of building the Stealth bomber goes up again,
bloated by the costs of corruption.
Brousseau told Haskell he worked with a circle of like-minded
Stealth buyers and suppliers. And he marveled at how easy it was to steal
money from the Stealth project:

BROUSSEAU: We don't have any heads, we don't have any
supervisory people. . . . I take what I want, and give them what

I want. Or what I want them to have. . . . Nobody questions dollars or anything like that. As long as I can show competition, whether it's true competition or courtesy competition or bullshit competition. . . . Everybody looks good. We make money.[32]

Confronted with this tape, Brousseau pleaded guilty to fraud and spent the next three years in prison. Fred Heather, the federal prosecutor in the case, said Brousseau had used the Stealth's invisibility as a shield: "The shroud of secrecy enabled him to do things he wouldn't ordinarily be able to do." Heather's boss, Robert Bonner, the U.S. Attorney in Los Angeles, told me he thought the Brousseau case was "the tip of the iceberg" of fraud on the Stealth project. But he said the Stealth's secrecy made such cases almost impossible to investigate and prosecute without willing undercover informants. Bonner's office wasn't awash with volunteers.

A transcript of the Brousseau tape, with sections censored by the Department of Defense to protect the Stealth's secrecy, found its way back to Washington. It created a bit of a stir. FBI transcripts of undercover tapes often have a distinctive aroma. This one made congressional investigators' noses twitch.

In January 1986, a powerful congressman read the transcript. The congressman was John D. Dingell, Democrat of Michigan, an oversized, gruff muckraker nicknamed the Truck. Dingell drove a big rig: the Committee on Energy and Commerce, specifically its subcommittee on oversight and investigations. By its name alone, Dingell's committee would not appear to have jurisdiction over the Pentagon. But the way Dingell saw it, "commerce" meant anything involving business. And the Pentagon's contracts constituted the biggest business in town.

Dingell delighted in roasting generals and defense-industry executives called before him to explain the mysteries of the Pentagon's finances. His finest moment, he thought, was grilling a General Dynamics executive, Dr. A.M. Lovelace, who'd charged his personal expenses to corporate overhead accounts. Taxpayers picked up 94 percent of the defense giant's overhead tab. Dingell thumbed through the expense records as the cameras rolled. "Fursten," he read aloud, "boarding at Silver Maple Farm, $87.25." Dingell peered over his thick glasses and fixed Dr. Lovelace with a withering glare. "Who," he said, "is *Fursten*?" Fursten was Dr. Lovelace's dog. All told, General Dynamics had charged the Pentagon more than $244 million in improper expenses, and poor Fursten became a symbol for defense companies chowing down at the public trough.

In 1985, congressional investigations introduced Americans to the $9,606 Allen wrench and other wonders of Pentagon procurement. A good Allen wrench costs less than a dollar at your local hardware store. The outrageous prices the Pentagon paid for ordinary tools and spare parts were a tiny part of a very big picture, but they were a clear image, easy for people to understand. Dingell's committee sought to broadcast such images. One that stuck in the mind was the brainchild of the committee's part-time consultant, Ernie Fitzgerald, a civilian Air Force analyst and the Pentagon's most famous in-house critic. Fitzgerald testified that, in order to understand the cost of a military aircraft, one should see it as "a collection of vastly overpriced spare parts flying in close formation."[33]

A rare consensus was emerging in Congress in 1985: the defense budget was out of control. Spurred by the hearings, a congressional Military Reform Caucus, whose members ranged from ardent doves to cheap hawks, was slamming the Pentagon with the procurement horror stories. In the House, where all spending bills originate, Les Aspin, an economist by profession, had taken over the chair of the Armed Services Committee, the primary source of the defense dollar. For four decades the committee had been controlled by chairmen who'd formed protective relationships with the Pentagon, men like Carl Vinson of Georgia and Mendel Rivers of South Carolina, leaders who gave the generals and admirals everything they wanted and more. Aspin was different. He and most of his colleagues decided that $300 billion a year was enough. The Pentagon's budget stopped growing.

Pentagon insiders were well aware that the black budget was still growing. It had grown far faster, with far less oversight, than the total Pentagon budget. A September 1985 editorial in *Defense News*, a widely read trade journal, warned of a coming crisis: "The public furor over spare parts pricing will pale by comparison with the public backlash against defense spending that is likely to come. In the coming months, the taxpayers gradually will realize that too many weapons projects and too many billions of dollars are hidden from public view in the rats' maze of highly classified 'black' programs. . . . It is only a matter of time before the public gets a peek inside the rats' maze and is repelled by what is there. A huge systems failure? Another crash of a black plane? A billion dollars squandered? Where is the $650 hammer of the black system? It is there. And it will be put to the same purpose as was the scandal over spare parts pricing: to damage public faith in the Pentagon and in the defense industry."[34]

Dingell, whose faith in the Pentagon had faded, wanted a peek inside the black budget. He wanted a grip on that black hammer. The Stealth bomber, the biggest weapons program in the Pentagon, had been too secret for too long. The congressman wanted to make an issue out of it. "The Pentagon keeps these programs of almost unbelievable size secret from Congress, from the General Accounting Office, from its own auditing agencies,'' he told me. ''And every time they have kept secrets from us, the facts, when they come out, have been surrounded by a bodyguard of lies.''[35]

On January 16, 1986, Dingell wrote an angry letter, stapled it to a copy of the Brousseau transcript and mailed it to the Secretary of Defense. Dingell's letter to Caspar Weinberger was one of the first audible shots fired in Congress' battle with the Pentagon over the black budget.

''The Subcommittee is concerned about the rapidly increasing size of the Air Force's so-called 'black' programs and . . . is aware of an increasing number of abuses involved in these 'black' programs,'' Dingell wrote. ''Secrecy is being used by the contractors as a device to cloak mischarging, overcharging and, in some cases, outright illegal activities. . . . It appears the Air Force has given the contracting community a blank check. . . .

''Compounding this problem,'' Dingell continued, ''the Air Force has been hiding virtually all relevant data on 'black' programs from the Congress.'' Dingell wanted information from the Secretary: a list of all Air Force black programs over $10 million. The cost of each program. The names of black programs being investigated for fraud by the Air Force. And he wanted it all in ten days.[36]

He got nothing. Weinberger would never respond to such a request. He did not answer the letter for three months, and when he did, it was to assure the congressman that nothing was amiss in the black world. Yet not all was well. On April 9, 1986, Weinberger received another letter from Capitol Hill, and this one couldn't be ignored. It came from Les Aspin and the ranking Republican on the House Armed Services Committee, Bill Dickinson of Alabama. Aspin and Dickinson spoke for all forty-seven members of the committee.[37]

''Dear Cap,'' the letter began:

We are concerned over the growing volume of defense programs that now fall under the . . . ''black'' umbrella. Of course, there is a need for special access programs; regrettably, not everything can be done in public. However, it is essential that the maximum portion of our defense effort be conducted in the open. The need to mobilize support for our defense programs alone demands that. But equally important, it is simply bad public policy to hide increasing amounts of government spending.

A major portion of the special access funding now goes toward the [Stealth] Bomber and the Advanced Cruise Missile. We are not convinced that there is a legitimate requirement to keep the wraps any longer on the most basic numbers involved in these programs—the funding requests for the current fiscal year, and the estimated program costs. In fact, it appears to us that about 70 percent of the funds contained in [the black budget] could be declassified. . . .

The calm language of the letter masked a serious challenge. The congressmen were telling the Secretary of Defense that he was hiding the costs of the Stealth bomber—and 70 percent of the military's black budget—for illegitimate reasons.

The Pentagon's own regulations define what can properly be classified as Top Secret: information whose release could cause "grave damage to national security." Aspin and Dickinson were saying that declassifying the costs of most secret weapons could not damage national security in the slightest. They were saying that keeping the cost of the Stealth secret was damaging other ideals: openness, accountability, public debate, rational decision-making. They wanted the price tag revealed. Now.

Weinberger refused to declassify "the most basic numbers": the bomber's annual budget, and an up-to-date figure for the whole fleet. But he realized that the cost of the Stealth would have to be revealed someday. His realization led to the publication of some remarkable figures.

On June 3, 1986, Weinberger issued a "fact sheet" on the Stealth bomber. It gave a "cost estimate" of $277 million for each plane, or $36.6 billion for the entire project—in 1981 dollars. "The program is on schedule," Weinberger said. "The technology is well understood and working." None of this proved to be true. The cost estimate, even when adjusted for inflation, was more than $11 billion shy of reality. The cost was growing by the day. Northrop was having trouble on the production line. The technology was untested. The "fact sheet" was dead wrong.[38]

These misleading facts and figures may have been honest errors. They did not contribute to an informed debate. In the fall of 1986, the Pentagon began issuing security clearances to select congressmen who wanted factual briefings. But what they got was "a song and dance," said one conservative Republican, Congressman John Kasich of Ohio. The briefings, conducted jointly by the Air Force and Northrop, amounted to a public-relations spiel. "They were not straightforward. They were not candid," said Congressman Mike Synar, an Oklahoma Democrat. Synar told me after his briefing that he'd been deceived by the Department of Defense: "It's obvious that DOD will not be truthful with Congress and the American public when they think it's in their interest." A House Armed Services committee staffer I interviewed in 1988 said the briefings were "a sales pitch, a total hose job. It was like somebody telling you about the neat parts of *Top Gun*."[39]

By late 1986, the B-1B, the penetrating bomber the Air Force had been trying to build for a generation, was ready at last. Like the Stealth, it had been built under the principles of concurrency. Perhaps the experience could provide some useful lessons. So, too, might the hands-off approach the Congress took. The Pentagon had insisted that the Congress not "micromanage" the B-1B; the Congress had agreed in exchange for putting a cap on the plane's budget.

On January 16, 1987, Air Force Chief of Staff Larry Welch called the B-1B "the most advanced bomber in the world." So it may have been—on paper. But it couldn't fly very well. It simply didn't perform. Its flight controls didn't work. It was often too unstable to be refueled by a tanker in midair. Its terrain-following radar didn't work. It couldn't evade enemy defenses by flying close to the ground. And the core of its computerized nervous system, its electronic countermeasures for evading enemy radars, was brain-damaged.

Nearly three years later, in late 1989, the electronic countermeasures still didn't work, and the Air Force was begging Congress for $1.9 billion to fix them. Three of the 100 bombers had crashed in training missions. On September 27, 1987, three B-1B crewmen were killed when their plane hit a pelican. The bird pierced the bomber's skin, damaged its electronic controls and brought it down. On November 6, 1988, a second B-1B burst into flames in midair and crashed; fortunately, all four crew members ejected safely. Eleven days later, a third crashed and burned; the crew survived.

There were lessons to be learned from the B-1B, but they were bitter ones. Its creators—the Air Force, Rockwell and the Congress—demanded concurrency. They paid for it with a faulty plane. This pointed to potential problems with the far more complex Stealth, for concurrency drove every aspect of the secret bomber's construction. The B-1B was largely an unclassified program. Yet it, too, was marked by secrecy and deception. The Air Force hid known defects in the plane to protect the program. The Pentagon said the B-1B was going to be a great plane if Congress only kept its fingers off and left the Air Force alone. The Congress took it on faith. "What the Congress did was to accept exactly what the Pentagon wanted . . . and the Air Force screwed up and . . . did not tell anyone about it," Aspin said after the B-1B was unveiled. He later told his colleagues in Congress: "When problems mounted, the impulse of the Air Force Systems Command, the organization in charge of the B-1B [and the Stealth], was to cover up. It wasn't only Congress and the public who were kept in the dark. It was also Defense Department civilian leaders and even Air Force higher-ups."[40]

On May Day 1987, Larry Welch confessed to a degree of uncertainty about the Stealth. "I am not going to say that we understand all of the costs and risks," the Air Force chief said at a breakfast with Pentagon reporters. "Because clearly, that's a naive thing to say at this point." The due date of the Stealth's first test flight was drawing near. The date already had been pushed back two years by the design change and other delays. Now word went out that opening day was postponed indefinitely. Something was amiss at Pico Rivera and Palmdale.

One clear sign of trouble was financial. Northrop's accountants wrote off $214 million against profits for reasons they did not explain in 1986 and 1987. Aerospace analysts said the reason had to be the Stealth; they'd pored over Northrop's financial records and the source of the write-offs was a very big black program.

Another cause for concern was the purchasing division at Northrop, which bought the myriad parts of the bomber from subcontractors. The purchasing division flunked a review by the Air Force in the fall of 1987. As a result, the Pentagon suspended some payments to Northrop, accounting for part of the 1987 write-off. The amount the Air Force withheld was, of course, classified.

A third, clearly related problem was a nuts-and-bolts issue. When I talked to Robert Costello, the former Air Force under secretary in charge of buying weapons, he'd said that the quality control on the Stealth was "terrible." Costello has some experience with quality control in manufacturing; he used to be a top executive at General Motors. Costello said there had been big problems with the Stealth's fasteners, the nuts and bolts and flanges that hold the different parts of the bomber together.

"You got a fancy machine here that they started to assemble . . . with fasteners from suppliers that were defective," he said. "Fasteners are always a bitch. You've got to test them all, or demand that your suppliers have statistically verified quality control. They hadn't gotten that far yet with the B-2" in 1988, even though the first six planes were rolling down the production line in Palmdale.

Many of the titanium fasteners in the Stealth bomber came from a company called Voi-Shan in Chatsworth, California. In 1988 Voi-Shan attracted the interest of a federal task force investigating fraud in the aerospace industry. The fraud squad suspected Voi-Shan was supplying defective fasteners stamped as approved by a fictitious "Inspector 11." Voi-Shan sold its nuts and bolts to Boeing Advanced Systems in Seattle. The Boeing subsidiary used them in the Stealth's wings and many other of the bomber's components. It sold the finished parts to Northrop's purchasing division, the division that couldn't pass Air Force inspection in late 1987.

In February 1988, the same month that the federal task force began its work, a quality-control manager at Boeing Advanced Systems ordered the routine testing of Voi-Shan's fasteners stopped. A *Seattle Times* reporter dug up a memo from the manager. It said: "Effective immediately, routine receiving inspection of fasteners will be stopped." Why? The manager said Boeing could save nearly $9,000 a month by testing only "suspect" fasteners.[41] To save time and money, Boeing Advanced Systems cut its inspections of the fasteners. But in the eyes of the federal investigators, *all* of Voi-Shan's fasteners were suspect. And as Costello says, when it comes to fasteners, "you've got to test them all." Northrop, Boeing and Voi-Shan didn't.

The winter of 1988 was turning out to be a bleak one for Northrop and its secret plane. At the end of January, the Air Force secretly postponed the first test flight of the Stealth again, this time until August. The meter kept running: every month of delay cost taxpayers at least $100 million. Then, on February 25, four Northrop employees filed a lawsuit against the company. The employees' lawyer called a press conference and, sounding outraged, charged that Northrop was billing the government for the time of hundreds of employees who "sit around all day reading newspapers and drinking coffee." This was neither illegal nor surprising. It was normal. Life in the Drunk Tank at Pico Rivera was part of the cost of doing business in the black world. Northrop was no worse an offender in this instance than any other defense contractor with large classified contracts.

But the lawsuit went beyond the Drunk Tank and into Northrop's corporate offices. It also alleged that Northrop auditors had prepared a draft study showing that there had been $400 million in overcharges on the Stealth bomber—and that Northrop managers shredded and burned the audit. The suit itself quickly became caught in a procedural snarl complicated by the Stealth's secrecy. It went nowhere for a year and a half. But the charges it contained set off a chain reaction.

The suit was filed under a nineteenth-century law, the False Claims Act, that obliged the Justice Department to open a civil investigation into the employees' charges. Federal investigators in Los Angeles heaved a sigh and went to work. Eight months later, they wrote to their Justice Department superiors in Washington, saying they couldn't make a dollars-and-cents case against Northrop for overcharging the government—because the Air Force had approved all of Northrop's overcharges.[42]

The law works in mysterious ways. The raw data of the civil investigation became fresh meat for a criminal investigation. If the Air Force approved the overcharges, or overlooked them, or simply ignored them, then in all fairness the federal government couldn't sue Northrop and demand its money back. But if those same Pentagon employees had cut a secret deal with Northrop managers to conceal overcharges—that was conspiracy. That was fraud. The Justice Department's criminal division took over the investigation in late October 1988, barely three weeks before the Air Force band struck up the "Stealth Fanfare" and the Air Force put the bomber on display.

The year of the Stealth's premiere should have been pure bliss for Northrop, the highlight of Tom Jones' three decades at the corporation. Instead it was an unending gantlet of financial, political and legal misery. Northrop's stock took a nosedive. The Stealth was mocked in editorial cartoons, a sure sign of political trouble. And all year long, it looked like Northrop was a candidate for a corporate Ten Most Wanted list. The Occupational Safety and Health Administration began looking into why people on the Palmdale production line were falling deathly ill. Workers blamed the exotic compounds in the Stealth's skin. The Justice Department became interested in Northrop's paying $7.75 million to South Korean businessmen while the company was trying to sell its least successful product, the F-20 Tigershark fighter jet, to the South Korean government. The Defense Investigative Service said Northrop was suspected of dealing in a black market for black documents—bribing government officials and defense consultants in exchange for copies of secret Pentagon papers reflecting long-term weapons-buying plans.

On April 11, 1989, the Northrop Corporation was indicted for conspiracy and fraud. A federal grand jury charged the company and five top managers with deliberating falsifying tests on components for nuclear cruise missiles and fighter jets.* Two weeks later, Thomas Jones announced he was stepping down as Northrop's chief executive officer by the end of the year. He was sixty-eight and he said he had no intention of running the company at seventy. He looked back over his long career, and said he was proudest of "that chain of events" that led to Northrop's landing the B-2 contract.[43]

The long wait for the Stealth's first test flight continued in May and June. The defense budget was being debated in Congress and the Air Force still had not released any hard numbers on the cost of the Stealth. Finally, on June 23, 1989, after ten years of secret research and development, one and a half years after the Congress had passed a law demanding that the cost be revealed, seven months after the Stealth went on display, the Air Force released the budget of the Stealth bomber.

It was a shock. First off, if all the planes were funded immediately, if all went perfectly in testing, if there were no more glitches or delays —all of which would be fairly miraculous—the price tag for 132 planes came to $70.2 billion.

It was hard to get one's mind around that number. Seventy billion dollars was more than the Defense Department wanted for the entire Star

---

*The company pleaded guilty and paid a $17 million fine in a secret agreement with the Justice Department in February 1990.

Wars program through the end of the century. It was more than the cost of purchasing every other weapon in the Pentagon's 1990 budget. It was more than the deposits on hand in any bank in the country but one. It was more than the annual sales of any American corporation save two.[44]

The Pentagon wanted $40 billion of that sum up front to build forty-four bombers before research and development was completed in 1993. That was the cost of concurrency. The $40 billion would be spent before the plane was fully tested, and at the time the plane never even had taxied under its own power. Forty billion dollars was more than twice the cost of all federal programs to feed the hungry.[45]

Finally, the Pentagon wanted $4.7 billion for the Stealth in 1990. That was more than three times what the government was spending to fight AIDS. The Pentagon wanted $5.3 billion in 1991. That was more than the budget of the Environmental Protection Agency. And the Pentagon wanted at least $8 billion a year after that. "It's an impossible proposition," Aspin said. "They must be smoking something over there if anybody thinks that we're going to spend $8 billion in one year on a single weapons system."

"Now," said Senator John Glenn, Democrat of Ohio, "for the first time, the American public can see how expensive this program is."[46]

Aspin and Glenn, two very senior members of the armed services committees, had known roughly what the bomber might cost for at least two years beforehand. But they couldn't talk about it. They couldn't debate it openly. They couldn't argue against it. And the public couldn't be told.

At dawn on July 17, the Stealth bomber made its maiden flight on live television. It revved its engines in neutral, sending up great clouds of gray smoke. It pirouetted onto the runway at Palmdale. It chugged down the runway at 200 miles an hour. And it lifted off in a gorgeous arc towards the desert sun. An Air Force captain unfurled an American flag as a woman watching from the roadside sang "The Star-Spangled Banner." The bomber made a few leisurely circles at 10,000 feet over the desert and, less than two hours later, touched down thirty miles away at Edwards Air Force Base.

The air show got mixed reviews. There were stunning pictures, but the pictures had stories along with them. And the stories told of a secret bomber with an unclear mission, an uncertain future and an unbelievable price tag. Now the veil was lifted, and the debate began. The debate was most intense.

"Today's flight is a giant leap for Northrop and one small step for the B-2 program," Aspin said. "The Stealth program today proved that it flies. . . . But yet to be determined is whether it flies with the American people and with Congress." Patricia Schroeder of Colorado, a liberal

Democrat on the House Armed Services Committee, was more blunt: "One test flight does not a blank check get."[47]

The Stealth could not be sold simply as a beautiful nuclear bomber—not when every poll of American voters showed that they liked the idea of the Cold War ending and wanted the defense budget cut. The Stealth needed a rationale that had nothing to do with nuclear war.[48]

President George Bush mentioned one: "competitive strategies." Put simply, the B-2 would force the Soviets to spend a fortune to defend themselves from the threat the bomber posed. The concept made the Stealth a weapon of economic warfare.

Under Secretary of Defense Donald Hicks wrote shortly before leaving the Pentagon in 1986 that the Stealth "will render Soviet air defenses—defenses in which they have already invested rubles to the tune of more than $100 billion—obsolete." To defeat the Stealth, "the Soviets will need to spend hundreds of billions more." Hicks' estimate of the Soviet investment in air defenses came from Air Force intelligence. It matched the CIA's; the Agency's analysts figured that Moscow had spent roughly $6 billion a year on air defenses over the past fifteen or sixteen years.[49]

Yet in early 1989 Air Force Chief of Staff Larry Welch told Congress that the Soviets already had invested *$350 billion* in air defenses. Suddenly the Air Force had discovered a quarter of a trillion dollars' more value in the Stealth. But neither the CIA nor the Pentagon had any evidence that the Soviets had a crash air-defense program under way. In the year after the Stealth made its bow, U.S. spy satellites revealed no new big Soviet radars or other early-warning sensors to detect the Stealth in the works. The Soviets had known about the Stealth ever since President Carter's aides announced its existence in 1980. They did not appear overly concerned. Perhaps the Russians also subscribed to Bruce Blair's big bang theory: that a nuclear war would be fought with intercontinental ballistic missiles, that SAC and the Soviets would lay down their best hand first, and that war planes following the first strikes would only smash the rubble into dust.

If the Stealth was built to bankrupt the Red Army, then nuclear strategy was not the intricate chess game strategists supposed it to be. It was a late-night game of seven-card stud. The United States was ready to throw $80 billion in the pot to bluff the Soviets into raising the bet.

"Competitive strategies" wasn't winning the Stealth new support in Congress. No matter how the Air Force played it, the argument was a losing hand.

The Air Force then tried to argue that the Stealth could be used in tactical combat—against Libya's Muammar Qaddafi, for example. The cheap hawks in Congress found the idea ludicrous—send a $600 million bomber to blow up a $6 million bridge? And risk being shot down by a $60,000 anti-aircraft missile? The cost-per-kill ratio was off the chart. "It's the equivalent of saying we're going to send a Rolls-Royce down into a combat zone to pick up groceries," said Senator William Cohen, Republican of Maine.

On July 21, 1989, the Air Force upped the ante. Welch told the Senate Armed Services Committee that if the Congress didn't buy all 132 bombers, he would walk away from the Strategic Arms Reduction Talks, the arms-control negotiations between the U.S. and the U.S.S.R. And Welch said he'd take the rest of the Joint Chiefs of Staff with him. The SAC commander, John T. Chain, made the same threat. Chain had argued that the Air Force would "need a hell of a lot more than 132 B-2s" if the START talks succeeded in cutting back SAC's missile forces. And if the Air Force got fewer than 132 Stealths, General Chain told the senators, "I can tell you right here, up front, that I could not support a START agreement." The most powerful generals in the Air Force were saying they'd sacrifice arms control on the altar of the Stealth bomber. This sounded a little extreme. Senator Timothy Wirth, Democrat of Colorado, wasn't buying in. "That's a very high-stakes poker game for the Air Force to be playing," he told the generals.[50]

Northrop did its part to win the pot. In mid-July, the company spent more than $100,000 blitzing Washington with television commercials and newspaper advertisements hawking the Stealth. Northrop's advertising was funded by tax dollars provided by the Congress. Since few Americans had the money or desire to buy one of the bombers, there was little question about the target of the advertising. It was Congress. Northrop's ads had a ludicrous aspect. Until a few months earlier, it was a crime to discuss the bomber in public. Now here was this prime-time publicity campaign for the secret weapon.

Northrop and the Pentagon also put out a list of 156 major Stealth subcontractors in forty-six states, members of "The B-2 Nationwide Industrial Team . . . supported by tens of thousands of men and women." The roster was an unsubtle reminder of the jobs each member of Congress created by paying for the bomber. Congressman David Skaggs, a Colorado Democrat, thought it was a tasteless appeal. "The Air Force," he said on the floor of the House, waving the list in his hand, "is now working with the Northrop Corporation to sell the B-2 as a jobs program." The list was "a clear attempt to persuade legislators to vote for the project based on home-state interests. There can be no other reason for it. That's offensive," Skaggs said. "Our debate should be about the national defense, not local jobs." The hard sell was backfiring.[51]

Then, bad news broke on July 25, the worst possible day, the day the House of Representatives first took up the B-2's budget in public.

The Pentagon announced that it had joined the Justice Department in the criminal investigation of Northrop for cooking its books and overcharging the government on the Stealth. By this point, Northrop was under one federal felony indictment and six separate criminal investigations.

The day marked a terrible violation of the Stealth's secrecy. The Stealth's books would be open now, revealed to the prying eyes of FBI agents, IRS criminal investigators, Pentagon auditors, every manner of nitpicking accountant, all poring over the classified ledgers. And in Washington, everyone in Congress was arguing over the secret bomber, praising it, criticizing it, talking about cutting its budget.

The full debate on the floor of the House the next day lasted more than three hours. It was the first time ever that a black weapons system was debated openly in Congress. The floor debate on the Stealth was rancorous, rhetorically excessive, often illogical and ultimately inconclusive. It was also democracy in action.[52]

Nearly $23 billion already was down the tubes on the Stealth's production line. Perhaps $50 billion more—and probably much more than that—would be needed to complete the fleet. If fewer than 132 bombers were built, the cost of each plane would rise as high as a billion dollars, or beyond. Did the nation need this war machine? Was it worth it? These were questions that secrecy had stifled for ten years.

An avid supporter of the bomber, Congressman Ike Skelton, a Missouri Democrat, called the decision on the Stealth "the most important national security vote that will be cast in this chamber this year or possibly in this decade." On this day the House would vote for one of three Stealth programs: to proceed full speed ahead, to apply the brakes gently, or to stop. Skelton characterized these choices as "The Good, the Bad and the Ugly."

Skelton's bill gave Stealth the green light. It provided for $3.9 billion, $800 million less than the Pentagon wanted for fiscal 1991, but with no strings attached.

Les Aspin and his Armed Services Committee colleague Mike Synar provided nearly as much—$3.76 billion. But their bill required the Stealth to pass many performance tests before it got another nickel. This was the yellow light. It slowed the program down enough for Congress to take a deep breath, study the facts and make an informed decision. The problem was that every year of delay now cost the public between $2 and $3 billion.

The red-light bill came from the deeply conservative John Kasich of Ohio and the deeply liberal Ron Dellums of California. It mothballed the program, at a savings of $40 billion or so. The nation would then have thirteen Stealths, each costing close to $2 billion apiece.

Kasich, a fresh-faced young Republican, called himself "a strong advocate of defense spending.'' He'd voted for 99 percent of the weaponry Reagan and Bush proposed in the 1980's. But he said secrecy had destroyed the Congress' ability to make a rational decision about the Stealth. "In a secret world, we did not have an appropriate forum to actually raise the kinds of questions that needed to be raised," he said. "We now find ourselves $23 billion down the road with the military, arguing that we are being held hostage." Kasich made the cheap hawk's argument: paying for the bomber would force the Pentagon "to cut back on training and spare parts, the building blocks of the military establishment."

John Edward Porter, an Illinois Republican, took up Kasich's point. "This is a program that would rob dollars from more important weapons systems," he said. "It is an unbelieveably expensive, poorly conceived weapon."

Dellums, a graying dove from Berkeley, attacked the Stealth from the left: it would rob dollars from people, not weapons. "We ought to deal with the problems of poverty, hunger, disease, inadequate education," Dellums said. "The national security ought to mean a healthy economy, healthy children with a bright future. This bomber would not give them that."

The rare coalition of the right and the left could not hold the center. The death-to-the-Stealth bill was defeated, 279 to 144. Then the bomber's strongest supporters took the floor. Skelton led the way. "All future warplanes will be made of Stealth technology," he said. "Is it not important for the future generations of our country to be secure behind this technology and behind the great American know-how that has given us the Stealth B-2 bomber?"

Some of the Stealth's advocates spoke as if the world were at the brink of war. "Our job here today is to best decide how we can defend this country, not to take steps to unilaterally disarm this country," said Floyd Spence, a Republican of South Carolina. "It seems that every time we come up with a good, effective weapons system, we hear the cry that it is provocative, it is destabilizing, it has a war-fighting capability. My God, I hope it does. We spend billions to insure it does. We have to have effective weapons of war to deter war." This was the traditional logic of deterrence, fervently expressed.

"If the B-2 bomber can help keep us free, then it is one of the most cost-effective programs we have," Spence said. "Cost?" he shouted. "What price tag do you put on freedom?"

The build-the-Stealth-now bill failed the test, 247 to 173. It was clear now who held the cards. Aspin and Synar had a lock. They used most of their time on the floor trying to educate their colleagues. Aspin was pithy. "If we go ahead with the program, and it is only $70 billion, it would be a miracle," he said. At some point the Congress was going to have to decide what to do with the Stealth. But not now. "We ought to at some time make a go/no-go decision on the B-2," Aspin said. "I feel uncomfortable making that decision today." Aspin didn't want to give the Stealth the green light or the guillotine.

What was needed, Synar said, was "a massive restructuring" of the Stealth program. "We will require testing before we buy the plane. We will strengthen the program's oversight. And finally, and probably most important to this debate, we will break the back of excessive secrecy, which has existed for too long in this program and too many weapons systems." Synar had argued this point for years to no avail.

"Maybe we have learned a lesson," he said. "That lesson is that special access programs may be the worst thing we can do, not only in behalf of the taxpayer, but in behalf of our national security."

The Congress failed to grasp that lesson. The House finally voted 257 to 160 to give the Air Force $3.76 billion for 1991, to subject the Stealth to the same kind of tests that any new weapon would have to pass, and to build as many as the nation could afford. The next day, the Senate passed a bill to give the Air Force $4.3 billion for the Stealth. And in the end, the Senate's bill was approved by both houses in an exhausted and confused Sunday session on November 19. The $4.3 billion would pay for two Stealths, along with some spare parts and some production costs for the next five bombers.

On that very day, Defense Secretary Cheney said the production of the bomber might have to be reconsidered, given two inescapable facts: the United States was going broke and "the likelihood of all-out conflict between the U.S. and the Soviet Union . . . is probably lower now than it's been at just about any time since the end of World War Two."[53]

Six months passed before Cheney and the Congress sat down together again to discuss the Stealth in April 1990. The Berlin Wall had fallen, the Warsaw Pact had vanished, and the military threat the Soviets posed to America appeared less immediate than the economic threat of the Stealth. Cheney announced that the Pentagon now sought only 75 Stealth bombers—and the projected cost of each one immediately and inevitably jumped to at least $820 million. The Congress professed shock at the cost. And yet the Stealths moved on down the production line. Christened in secret in the name of national security, the Stealth bomber had become a gigantic ship churning full speed ahead under classified orders toward a dangerous destination. Its course could not be easily reversed. Even if an order came down from the bridge to change direction, the ship's momentum would carry it forward on its original heading for years.

The debate over the Stealth's mission, over why it was needed, over what it might cost, had come far too late. The silencing of that debate for a decade meant that the technology had no policy to justify its existence. As the plane made its debut, a realization was dawning on its creators: the enemy, and the threat it represented, was beginning to disappear. The rationale that brought the Stealth into being was vanishing; the thinking that had shaped it was outmoded. The bomber faced a future in which it might soon be an irrelevant relic, doomed to gather dust in a top-secret hangar. The Stealth, for all its twenty-first-century technology, was an anachronism. This most modern weapon belonged to the past.

The Stealth lived on because it had stayed secret. The Pentagon was now so pregnant with the bomber that it could not be aborted. The money already spent could not be written off. Congress had given $23 billion to the Pentagon, and to a company with a record of misfeasance and corruption, in exchange for a single warplane, without a dollar being subjected to the give-and-take of public debate. Behind closed doors, the Congress had agreed to keep the Stealth's costs hidden for ten years running, and now its howls of outrage rang hollow.

"The fault lies with the Congress," Congresswoman Pat Schroeder told me. "If we forced the release of this information, there would be no issue. As long as the Congress goes along with the Pentagon's secrecy program, we have no complaint."[54]

The Stealth bomber stayed too secret too long because Congress consented to it. The black budget itself exists because Congress agreed to let it grow. The Central Intelligence Agency talked Congress into creating the secret treasury a long time ago.

PART TWO

SECRET
WARS

5

Keeping Secrets

THE black budget is a creature of the Cold War. The policy of secret spending began as an emergency measure at the dawn of the postwar world. It was conceived as a shield to conceal the secret wars of the Central Intelligence Agency.

In short order the shield of secret appropriations became a sword. As America began trying to reform foreign governments by acts of sabotage, economic warfare and subversion, the nation's statecraft was conducted increasingly in secret, at night, under cover. Secret spending, though it had no constitutional sanction, was essential to the war against the Soviets, their satellite states, their surrogates and all of America's real and imagined enemies abroad and at home.

The obsession with secret operations spread throughout the great machinery of the American presidency. Soon the CIA and its sister agencies were reading Americans' mail, poring over their telegrams and tax returns, tapping their telephones, infiltrating church groups and college organizations, penetrating the press and manipulating the news. The Agency tried to fix elections in democratic nations overseas, and when that failed, to overthrow fairly elected governments by force. Its access to unlimited, unaudited, unaccountable secret funds buried in the Pentagon's budget made the CIA immune from outside control. The secret forces created to fight communism abroad evolved into a power that threatened constitutional government at home.

The CIA's glory days are over now. No longer is it free to roam the world, hiring assassins, running guns and toppling foreign leaders without accounting to anyone for its actions. The CIA of old proved incompatible with American democracy. But in its heyday the Agency existed as a government unto itself. From humble beginnings in ramshackle offices scattered throughout Washington, it quickly grew to become the President's secret army.

The United States had won two world wars without setting up a permanent clandestine branch of the government. Americans shied away from secret agencies by instinct. "Everybody knows that corruption thrives in secret places, and avoids public places, and we believe it is a fair presumption that secrecy means impropriety," Woodrow Wilson told voters on the campaign trail in 1912. "Government ought to be all outside and no inside." What Wilson said was a fair summary of 150 years of American political tradition. The American way was to shun secret government.

The Cold War created "a new culture" in this country, said the late Senator Mike Gravel of Alaska, "a national security culture, protected from the influences of American life by the shield of secrecy."[1] The war against the Soviets demanded a new order of battle, new weapons wielded by secret agents and funded by secret appropriations. The culture of secrecy came into its own when Congress created the CIA.

Congress gave its blessings to the CIA without knowing exactly what it was doing, without understanding what it was creating. When it established the Agency, Congress gave up its constitutional power of the purse. It gave up its right to know how the President's men were spending the people's money, whether that spending made sense, whether it was legal. It was a quiet but spectacular abdication of power. By the time Congress tried to assert control, the CIA had piled up twenty-five years' worth of skeletons, the detritus of hundreds of secret operations. In the boneyard lay assassination plots and tiny vials of deadly poisons, missions to overthrow scores of foreign governments and files on 300,000 Americans.

After years of struggle, Congress reined in the Agency in the late 1970's, and created oversight committees to make the CIA accountable. But the clandestine service soon slipped its bonds again, trying to recapture the lost magic of its youth. When the Congress stayed the Agency's hand, banning covert actions in Central America, the White House, the CIA and the Pentagon set up their own secret operations off the books. Deception replaced open discourse. The results piled up again: dismal failures, criminal indictments and dead mercenaries in foreign lands. The congressional intelligence committees now feel compelled to keep watch over the CIA much as a parole officer tries to supervise a recidivist second-story man.

Short of dissolving Congress and smashing printing presses, no way existed for conduct that defied the Constitution's checks and balances to be kept secret. Keeping secrets from the people challenged the greatest strengths of the American system. After fifty years, no one has resolved the paradox of running secret operations in an open democracy.

The CIA traces its beginnings to June 18, 1941, the day President Roosevelt invited William J. Donovan into the Oval Office and appointed him the Coordinator of Information: the nation's first spymaster. Donovan was a brilliant New York lawyer who'd fought Pancho Villa with the U.S. Cavalry in Mexico and won the Congressional Medal of Honor in World War I. He drew up plans for a civilian espionage council to direct paramilitary operations in World War II, and his proposals led directly to the creation of the Office of Strategic Services, the OSS, America's first modern intelligence agency. Like the Manhattan Project, the OSS was bankrolled through secret accounts controlled by President Roosevelt.

Donovan chose an unusual insignia for his outfit, a golden spearhead on a field of black. One of the patches is preserved in the CIA's Historical Intelligence Collection. The CIA archivists note that the gold spear symbolizes "opening the way to subduing the enemy's defenses." The black field? "Black is associated with activities which may be performed under cover of darkness."[2]

Just as the firebombing of Japan shaped the soldiers who made nuclear strategy at Strategic Air Command, the black operations of the OSS defined four men who became directors of Central Intelligence: Allen Dulles, Richard Helms, William Colby and William Casey. From the safety of Switzerland, Dulles intercepted Nazi cables and plotted with leaders of resistance movements. Helms organized intelligence networks from Scandinavia and London. Colby parachuted behind enemy lines in France and Norway, scouting German troop movements and blowing up bridges. Casey was chief of the London branch, plotting operations throughout the European theater.

The memoirs of OSS veterans have the lyric quality of an aging man recalling his sporting days. The secret agent at war was an independent operator, a creative artist, a legal criminal. " 'Donovan's private army' was recruited from the highest and lowest strata of society—bankers and tycoons, safecrackers and forgers, printers and playwrights, athletes and circusmen," Casey recalled in an unfinished manuscript. The foreign-policy establishment despised the freewheeling clandestine service: "Donovan created the OSS against the fiercest kind of opposition from everybody—the Army, Navy and State Department, the Joint Chiefs of Staff, regular army brass, the whole Pentagon bureaucracy, and, perhaps most devastatingly, the White House staff."[3]

President Truman was deeply skeptical when Donovan sought to keep his secret service after the war was over. The President knew almost nothing about Donovan's intelligence work, save Washington newspaper columnists' breathless descriptions of OSS members as "dilettante diplomats, Wall Street bankers, amateur detectives," "ex-polo players, millionaires, Russian princes, society gambol boys . . . the blue bloods of democracy." The service chiefs blocked Donovan's ascension. In September 1945, Truman was presented with a military intelligence report accusing the OSS of more than 120 instances of "incompetence, corruption, 'orgies,' nepotism, black-marketing" and other wartime offenses. The report did not increase the President's desire to preserve the office. Truman broke up the OSS six weeks after Hiroshima, and scattered its branches among the Departments of State and War.[4]

Still the idea of a clandestine intelligence service persisted. The United States needed an intelligence agency in the postwar world, an agency to provide warning against another Pearl Harbor, to anticipate political and economic revolutions, to serve as the President's eyes and ears abroad. What the United States got in addition to all this was a secret army capable of subversion, sabotage, insurrection and other acts of war. For under the shield of secret intelligence lay the sword of secret wars. An internal CIA history of Donovan's imprint on the Agency says he saw intelligence analysis as a convenient cover for subversive operations abroad. This subterfuge proved useful down the years.[5]

On January 23, 1946, Truman signed an executive order creating the Central Intelligence Group and swore in Rear Admiral Sidney Souers as the nation's first director of Central Intelligence. The next day, the President held a private little ceremony for Souers in the Oval Office. He called the admiral to his side, presented him with a black cloak and a little wooden dagger, and jokingly knighted him "director of centralized snooping" and "chief of the Gestapo."[6]

The Central Intelligence Group's birth was illegitimate. It had no legal power; the President cannot singlehandedly create a new arm of government with the stroke of his pen. The agency was financed with funds secretly diverted from the armed forces' budgets, not by lawful appropriations. This meant the "CIG was technically illegal," recalled Lawrence Houston, who served as the CIA's general counsel for twenty-six years. "You cannot have an operating agency going on for more than a year without a statutory basis."[7]

Bastard child or not, the CIG was father to the CIA. As it became clear that the United States was about to create a new and permanent secret intelligence agency, many in Congress and the White House expressed fears that it would become a secret police, an American version of the Nazi storm troopers. Truman heard warnings from Secretary of State George C. Marshall, who told the President that "the powers of the proposed agency seem almost unlimited." Marshall felt strongly that covert operations inevitably would be exposed, and that their exposure would disgrace the nation. Dean Acheson, Marshall's successor as Secretary of State, said he had "the gravest forebodings" about the CIA.[8]

These fears were quieted by the CIA's future leaders. They said time and again that this was going to be a civilian agency constituted to collect, analyze and collate information. Nothing more. Allen Dulles, who had run his OSS operations from a 500-year-old house in Berne, Switzerland, now ran a bit of an operation on the houses of Congress. Dulles, who was to serve as CIA director under Eisenhower and Kennedy, submitted secret written testimony on the proposed agency to Congress in April 1947. Dulles described an agency that sounded like a graduate-school colloquium in foreign affairs, an office filled with tweedy men puffing pipes and mulling over the problems of the postwar world. The agency's "prime objectives" would not be "strategic or military, important as these may be," Dulles said. "They are scientific. . . . They are political and social." He also gave his best guess on how many people it would take to run the CIA. "I should think that a couple of dozen people throughout the United States could do it. Abroad you will need a certain number of people, but it ought not to be a great number. It ought to be scores rather than hundreds."[9]

By the time Dulles became director of Central Intelligence, just five years later, the CIA had a covert-action department, politely entitled the Office of Policy Coordination. The OPC had forty-seven foreign stations, a budget of at least $84 million and 5,954 employees. A far cry from Dulles' modest vision.[10]

Those present at the creation of the CIA may genuinely have thought that it would be a small affair. They surely believed, and believed sincerely, that the need for secrecy was as great as it had been in the secret weapons laboratories of Los Alamos. But they began by concealing their actions and intentions from the Congress, and they built their power by secrecy, and their power grew rapidly.

The power formally began when the National Security Act was signed into law on July 26, 1947. The act does not define "national security"; the institutions it created do. The act transformed the Department of War into the Department of Defense, a watershed event in the etymology of political language. It created the National Security Council and the Air Force. It brought the CIA into being, but curiously left the job half finished. The agency now existed, but in name only, without a legal birth certificate from Congress. It would be nearly two years until that task was completed. In the interim, the CIA's money kept flowing from the Pentagon's budget in secret, without any lawful sanction.

What the Congress needed to create a democratically chartered intelligence agency was a clear idea of what the CIA was going to do, based on honest information. The information should have come from Truman; from the new Secretary of Defense, James Forrestal; and from Dulles. What the Congress got instead were half truths and evasions, a wink and a nudge and a warning not to wade into deep waters. Truman, in a letter transmitting the National Security Act to Congress, said nothing about secret operations overseas—nothing at all about an intelligence agency. Dulles said nothing about covert actions. Forrestal testified in no uncertain terms that the CIA never would conduct secret operations. Congress wound up legislating in the dark.[11]

The National Security Act itself said nothing about the CIA's power to conduct espionage or paramilitary actions or secret wars. Nothing in the legislative history shows that Congress intended to give the Agency that power. But a loophole in the law gave the CIA authority to "perform such other functions and duties . . . as the National Security Council may from time to time direct." From that open-ended phrase sprang more than a thousand covert actions over forty years—revolutionary acts that subverted governments, conspiratorial acts that led to assassinations and attempted assassinations, violent acts that over time contributed to the deaths of tens of thousands of people. The men who carried out these acts thought they were part of the costs of containing the Soviets, preserving American power and keeping the Cold War's uneasy peace.

In December 1947, not quite five months after the CIA's creation, the National Security Council met for the first time. The NSC acted as a board of directors exercising the President's foreign-policy powers. At that first meeting, Defense Secretary Forrestal demanded that the CIA begin a secret war against the Soviet Union. Forrestal wanted action on every front; the threat was everywhere. Elections were coming up in Italy, and money and propaganda had to flow to defeat left-wing political parties. All over Europe, American interests in the struggle for postwar power had to be fueled, and pro-American social opinion shaped.

There was an actual Stalin to be fought, a real tyrant to oppose, but Forrestal's demands had a tinge of mania to them. His demands grew along with his madness. In 1948 he began to hallucinate, seeing communists around every corner, sensing invisible microphones planted in his path. He lost his mind, and killed himself in May 1949, in some sense an early victim of the Cold War.

Forrestal's initiative at that first meeting in December 1947 led the NSC to issue a secret order, NSC-4A. It instructed the CIA's new director, Rear Admiral Roscoe Hillenkoetter, to begin psychological warfare operations in Europe. Deeply uneasy, Hillenkoetter consulted Lawrence Houston, the CIA's general counsel: Psy ops in Europe? Was that legal? Did he have the lawful power to carry out this order?

Houston prepared a memorandum saying it wasn't legal and the Agency had no authority to do it. The CIA was an intelligence ministry, not the President's secret strike force. It couldn't set up foreign offices and buy radios and rifles and finance insurrections on its own. Houston wrote that this would be "an unauthorized use of funds made available to the CIA." If the NSC or the President gave proper orders, the CIA would have to go to Congress to ask for the money to carry them out.

The lawyer's reading of the law displeased Forrestal. So Hillenkoetter asked Houston for a second opinion. Houston recalled that he already had told the CIA director the facts: nothing in the law "specifically gave us authority for such activities. Hillenkoetter then asked was there any way, and we wrote another opinion saying that if the President gave us the proper directive and the Congress gave us the money for those purposes, we had the administrative authority to carry them out. So that's how we got into covert operations."[12]

Congress had not given the CIA money for covert operations. But the communist threat abroad took precedence over constitutional questions at home. In this legal netherworld, the CIA plunged forward.

NSC-4A was supplanted within six months by a far more sweeping command. The CIA's powers were recast by a new secret presidential order, entitled NSC-10/2. It established the Agency's covert-action branch, the Office of Policy Coordination, and it became the blueprint for the CIA's work abroad. It authorized the CIA to engage in "economic warfare; preventive direct action [in other words, paramilitary operations], including sabotage, anti-sabotage, demolition, and evacuation measures; subversion against hostile states," anything short of armed combat. These were the marching orders for the secret war.

The President would approve and hold ultimate responsibility for these covert operations. But his hand had to be hidden. NSC-10/2 set forth the notion of plausible deniability: the idea that the CIA's operations should be "so planned and executed that any U.S. Government responsibility for them is not evident . . . and that if uncovered the U.S. Government can plausibly disclaim any responsibility for them."

This was a formal assertion by the President of the government's right to lie. The lie must be convincing and must protect the government. It had to convince the American people as well as the enemy. The fog of the secret war wafted up from the theater of conflict, rode the wind and drifted back home. Lies during wartime predate the crossbow and the catapult; they served as a shield to protect troops in the field. This was something more: a double-edged sword of presidential power.

That rulers lie is hardly news. In *The Republic*, Plato endorsed the "noble lie" as a political fable by which the powerful could convince the poor to accept poverty and injustice as God's will. The Renaissance scholar Erasmus defined these lies as "deceitful fictions for the rabble, so that the people might not set fire to the magistracy," and "falsifications by which the crass multitude is deceived in its own interests." The political tradition justifies lying—but only in the way that parents lie to their children and doctors deceive a dying patient. The lies were noble only if they served as bitter medicine spooned up for the public's own good.[13]

Plausible deniability was something else. It let the President lie to protect his own power.

The doctrine of deception was laid down in May 1948. The year passed, and 1949 was passing, and still the CIA had no formal legal charter, no formal budget, nothing beyond secret executive edicts to legitimate its power. The CIA still subsisted on funds taken surreptitiously from the armed services' appropriations. This had been going on for nearly two years. It was hardly legal. The CIA's Hillenkoetter came to Carl Vinson of Georgia, the Democratic chairman of the House Armed Services Committee, to tell him that the CIA needed a law giving it operating authority passed immediately. It was "a matter of urgency." Frankly, the CIA director said, "we find ourselves in operations up to our necks." The CIA already was beyond the law. It needed the law enlarged.[14]

The Central Intelligence Agency Act of 1949 is the sole legal basis for secret government spending in America. It remains one of the more unusual acts of legislation in the nation's history.

The CIA Act was reviewed behind closed doors by the ranking members of the Armed Services committees of both houses. Vinson summed up the secret sessions by saying: "We will just have to tell the House they will have to accept our judgment and we cannot answer a great many questions that might be asked." The same cloaking of the bill took place in the Senate. The "highly confidential nature" of the bill precluded open debate of its contents.[15]

As a result the Congress had no clear idea of what it was doing. It enacted the law "without knowing what all its provisions meant," said Senator William Langer of North Dakota.[16]

The first black budget received its formal baptism over the course of a half hour or so on the floor of the House of Representatives on March 7, 1949. Vinson introduced the bill and gave a very brief and highly circumspect description of its contents. The language of the bill was not discussed. Vinson said it would not be "wise" to reveal the CIA's budget.

The closest he came to candor was to suggest that Congress had to "legalize" the confidential funding of the CIA.[17]

Debate focused on the secrecy surrounding passage of the bill, not the bill itself. Congressman Emmanuel Celler of New York, who voted for the bill, protested the refusal of the few in the know to share their knowledge: "If the members of the Armed Services Committee can hear the detailed information to support this bill, why cannot the entire membership? Are they the Brahmins and we the untouchables? Secrecy is the answer."[18]

The only member who spoke out against the bill was Congressman Vito Marcantonio of New York, a left-winger. "The Committee informs us through its report that the Members of the House must pass this bill without any explanation of all its provisions," Marcantonio argued. "This makes every single section of the bill suspect." For the congressmen to pass a law kept secret was "to abdicate their functions." The members were "evading their duty to the people." The CIA Act had the force of "suspending all laws with regard to government expenditures."[19]

Dewey Short of Missouri, the ranking Republican on the House Armed Services Committee, expressed the more conventional wisdom: "We are engaged in a highly dangerous business. It is something I naturally abhor but sometimes you are compelled to fight fire with fire. . . . The less we say in public about this bill the better off all of us will be."[20]

So not much else was said. The bill passed without amendment by the convincing margin of 348 to 4.

Even less debate was heard after Armed Services Committee chairman Millard Tydings of Maryland brought the bill before the Senate on May 27, 1949. Tydings warned that discussing the mechanics of the bill would be a grave mistake. He assured his fellow senators that "every possible democratic safeguard" surrounded the new law. In other countries, Tydings said, governments funded their intelligence agencies by fiat; they would "simply appropriate a disguised sum of money, without any authority of law. . . . If the Senate knew the details, it might be willing to do as other countries do, but we do not do business that way."[21]

The Senate, not knowing the details, passed a bill legalizing the appropriation of disguised sums of money. The implications of the bill, the secret funding mechanisms, the lack of any formal oversight all remained obscure. By a voice vote, without a roll call, the Senate enacted a law like no other.

The CIA Act said any arm of the government could transfer money to the CIA "without regard to any provisions of law." That meant a legal appropriation for weapons, public welfare or water-pollution control could be earmarked for the CIA and smuggled into its classified accounts.

The new law said "sums transferred to the Agency . . . may be expended . . . without regard to limitations." That meant the CIA could spend as much money as it wanted on whatever it wanted. And it said the CIA could spend its money "without regard to the provisions of law and regulations relating to the expenditure of Government funds." That meant there was no need for the Agency to account for the money it spent—the word of the director of Central Intelligence was good enough.[22]

Most significantly, the CIA Act kept the Agency's budget secret. That flatly contradicted the Constitution's demand that Congress publish an account of the receipts and expenditures of all public money. By creating a clandestine treasury for the CIA, the Congress reverted to the days of kings who taxed the public and spent their money in secret, never accounting for their actions. The first Americans had fought and won a revolution over this principle.

Like the CIA, the armies of the American revolution faced a distant enemy drunk with power and addicted to secrecy and deception. But this war was different. The rules of engagement were new. The old ideas of openness and accountability had to be suppressed in the service of the secret war. The CIA could not be constrained by the Founding Fathers' distaste for concealment. It was in a knife fight in the back alleys of the world, and no holds could be barred. So a blank space appeared where a constitutional boundary had stood. The budget of the United States became a cover story.

A U.S. intelligence veteran, James McCargar, has explained the concept of cover deftly: "As open warfare depends on weapons, so does the secret war depend on cover. Weapons are not in themselves the purpose of war, but they shield the soldier and enable him to advance to his objective—or they protect his retreat. Cover shields the secret agent from his opposition. . . . The budget of the United States Government is itself a cover." Under that cover, the secret war expanded on all fronts.[23]

The cover grew progressively deeper with each new intelligence agency created by the President, the Pentagon and the CIA. In 1952, Truman signed a still-secret seven-page charter establishing the National Security Agency. The NSA's mission is to intercept electronic communications around the world. No public law defines or limits its powers and responsibilities. The only known mention of the agency in the public laws of the United States is a 1959 statute that states: "Nothing in this act or any other law . . . shall be construed to require the disclosure of the organization or any function of the National Security Agency."[24]

The NSA's listening posts include ground stations around the world and spy satellites orbiting the earth; it sucks up electronic information from telecommunications, microwave transmitters and telemetry, the computer language controlling missiles and satellites. It owns the most powerful array of computers in the world, and has the capability to pick out specific conversations from the babble of international telecommunications traffic. The agency controls the nation's cryptography program, making the codes for U.S. forces and breaking the codes of foreign nations.

The NSA also spent a great deal of time and money spying on American citizens. For twenty-one years after its inception it tracked every telegram and telex in and out of the United States, and monitored the telephone conversations of the politically suspect. The NSA now employs at least 60,000 people and spends about $10 billion a year, all hidden in the Pentagon's black budget.

The National Reconnaissance Office, established in 1960, is still more secret. As we have seen, its spy satellites serve the causes of both peace and war. They are crucial for verifying arms-control treaties. And they provide raw data for nuclear-war planners. No one can openly discuss the NRO in Congress or question its $5 billion annual budget.[25]

The CIA similarly was set apart from scrutiny for a generation. In theory, the CIA Act gave Congress limited powers to control the Agency. In practice, Congress did not assert that power for more than two decades. The freedom from control made the 1950's and the 1960's the CIA's golden age. Tom Braden, chief of the CIA's international organizations division in the 1950's, described the heady atmosphere of the days when the CIA accounted to no one:

> It never had to account for the money it spent, except to the President—if the President wanted to know how much money it was spending. But otherwise the funds were not only unaccountable, they were unvouchered, so there was really no means of checking them—"unvouchered funds" meaning expenditures that don't have to be accounted for. . . .
>
> Since it was unaccountable, it could hire as many people as it wanted. It never had to say to any committee—no committee said to it: "You can only have so many men." It could do exactly as it pleased. It made preparations therefore for any contingency. It could hire armies; it could buy banks. There was simply no limit to the money it could spend and no limit to the people it could hire and no limit to the activities it could decide were necessary to conduct the war—the secret war.[26]

The CIA depended on the Brahmins of the Congress for its freedom from accountability. Power in Congress then lay in the hands of a few stalwart men who, when it came to foreign affairs, trusted in God and Allen Dulles.[27] When budget time rolled around, Dulles met in private with one or two of the deeply conservative Southern congressmen who headed the armed services and appropriations committees. They reached gentlemen's agreements as to how many billions the CIA and the military intelligence agencies might need. Few questions were asked. Senator John Stennis of Mississippi, one of those Southern gentlemen, said it behooved his colleagues "to shut your eyes some and take what is coming" when it came to the CIA's conduct. Senator Allen Ellender of Louisiana, chairman of the rarely convened intelligence subcommittee of the Senate Appropriations Committee, said he simply didn't want to know what the CIA was up to—he was afraid he might blurt out secrets talking in his sleep.

Few protested the practice of secret spending. One who did was Senator Mike Mansfield of Montana, who in 1954 warned his colleagues: "Secrecy now beclouds everything about the CIA—its cost, its efficiency, its successes, and its failures. . . . Once secrecy becomes sacrosanct, it invites abuse." Mansfield's colleagues in the Senate rejected his proposal that a congressional committee should oversee the CIA and "reduce the threat to our democratic processes which this uncontrolled agency by its very nature now possesses." The prevailing mood in Congress was defined in 1955 by Senator Leverett Saltonstall of Massachusetts, long a leading member of the Armed Services Committee: "It is a question of our reluctance, if you will, to seek information and knowledge on subjects which I personally . . . would rather not have."[28]

The congressional review of the black budget was a brief, tightly controlled affair dominated by the committee chairmen. The briefings from the CIA director were a half-hour package tour, a quick cruise through the straits of foreign policy, with glimpses of distant cloud-capped islands where volcanoes rumbled. Members asked few or no questions. All understood that anything sensitive would be handled one-on-one between the CIA director and the chairmen. When the archconservative Richard Russell of Georgia headed the Senate Armed Services Committee in the 1960's, he was the only senator who met regularly with the CIA leadership. Years went by in which the Armed Services subcommittees on intelligence never convened. Some years they met once, for less than two hours. Eventually the House subcommitee was disbanded and the Senate subcommittee simply never met. Congressional control of the CIA faded away.[29]

That gave the CIA unlimited freedom to conduct its secret wars. And as the CIA geared up for battle, a great fear was sweeping the land. The Soviets threatened everyone everywhere, at home and abroad. The tone of the times was the high-pitched radio signal of the emergency broadcast system. The sense of near-panic resonates in the Top Secret report of a 1954 presidential commission calling on the CIA to be:

> [A]n aggressive covert psychological, political, and paramilitary organization more effective, more unique, and, if necessary, more ruthless than that employed by the enemy. No one should be able to stand in the way of prompt, efficient and secure accomplishment of this mission. . . . It is now clear that we are facing an implacable enemy whose avowed objective is world domination by whatever means and at whatever cost. There are no rules in such a game. Hitherto acceptable norms of human conduct do not apply. If the U.S. is to survive, long-standing American concepts of "fair play" must be reconsidered. We must . . . learn to subvert, sabotage, and destroy our enemies by more clever, more sophisticated, and more effective methods than those used against us. It may become necessary that the American people be made acquainted with, understand, and support this fundamentally repugnant philosophy.[30]

Americans remained unacquainted with this philosophy for many years. The philosophy and the policies it supported stayed secret. Nowadays we know that the chronicle of the CIA's subverting, sabotaging and destroying its enemies is an unhappy one. The Agency started out trying to save small, weak European nations from communism, and fared poorly. It found success overthrowing small, weak Third World governments in the name of democracy. Its power expanded to the point where it could advocate murder as a tool of American values.

The CIA tried to export the American revolution to lands threatened by communism. But it began its work in years when the birthrights of the revolution went unfulfilled at home. Segregation was the law. Southern blacks had no right to vote, no rights the law was bound to respect. The government demanded and received loyalty oaths from its workers. Citizens were jailed for unpopular beliefs. Teachers and actors and scientists and longshoremen lost their jobs in the name of national security. The Agency itself defaced its charter by spying on Americans to enforce political orthodoxy.

The revolution did not travel well. The CIA became the bogeyman for every real and imagined sin of American foreign policy, the same spectre abroad that communism was to Americans. Too often the CIA played the role of a Christian missionary who brings true religion to the natives but carries a case of measles along with the gospel. God's kingdom is served, but the innocent die.

The secret agent in a foreign land is the President's invisible emissary. His covert acts are designed to influence and alter political events. The plans he makes and the steps he takes can trigger political furies— a riot, an assassination, a revolution. He can find himself in the position of a pilot who intends to seed the clouds to quench parched crops, and who watches as the rains turn to torrents that touch off a flood. The CIA often set in motion forces it could not control. These forces sometimes proved to be as malevolent as the enemy, or worse.

In Iran, a 1953 covert operation code-named AJAX overthrew Prime Minister Mohammed Mossadegh, *Time* magazine's "Man of the Year" the previous winter. The CIA pegged Mossadegh as a communist dupe because he rejected Anglo-American dominance over Iran's oilfields. In reality, the prime minister was a nationalist who simply despised the British. Operation Ajax reestablished Western control of Iranian oil and put the Shah of Shahs, Reza Pahlavi, on the Peacock Throne, where he reigned for the next twenty-five years. Ajax looked like a great victory at the time. But as the years passed, the Shah's repressive rule and his CIA-trained secret police enraged Iranians. Their rage brought the Shah's downfall, and brought on the regime of the Ayatollah Khomeini, the long tortured decade of hostage-taking, and the rug-merchant diplomacy of the Iran-contra debacle.

In Guatemala, the CIA's 1954 Operation SUCCESS toppled President Jacobo Arbenz Guzmán with a combination of psychological warfare, economic pressure and a cadre of soldiers who received CIA training and weapons. The CIA shipped them airplanes and rifles through a maze of charitable foundations and dummy companies. Arbenz, too, had been fingered by the U.S. as a communist, though he had served loyally as a defense minister, he was elected democratically, and he never appointed a communist to his cabinet nor sought Soviet support. His fatal offense was confiscating some of the vast rural holdings of the United Fruit Company with the idea of transferring the land to peasants. United Fruit got its land back and the U.S. got a more compliant Guatemala. But the overthrow of Arbenz ushered in an era of military rule notable for its brutality, even by the harsh standards of Central America. The era of the death squads has not ended in Guatemala.[31]

A little more than ten years after Congress gave it a hunting license, the CIA became the President's own death squad. Conspiracies to commit murder began blooming like night flowers in the White House. Very few in the CIA opposed the assassination plans for religious, moral or political reasons. The President had the power to give such orders and the CIA was duty-bound to carry them out.

The avuncular Eisenhower approved a political killing in the summer of 1960. The Cold War had come to the Belgian Congo, the huge nation at the heart of Africa. The Belgians granted their colony a measure of independence in June 1960, but kept control of the country's economy and army. The new government's prime minister, Patrice Lumumba, faced Belgian officers and paratroopers leading a secession of the nation's richest province. The struggles led the CIA's station chief in the Congo, Lawrence Devlin, to cable headquarters in June warning that Lumumba was leading "a classic Communist-effort takeover government." Spurred by Devlin's dire reports, Eisenhower authorized the CIA to eliminate Lumumba. In August, Dulles cabled Devlin to say that Lumumba had to go: "His removal must be an urgent and prime objective . . . of our covert action." In September, the CIA's resident expert in poisons, Dr. Sidney Gottlieb, prepared biological toxins for an assassination. The CIA hired and trained two professional killers for the mission to murder Lumumba. They flew to meet Devlin in the Congolese capital, Leopoldville. A kit of Dr. Gottlieb's poisons arrived concealed in a diplomatic pouch.[32]

Devlin cultivated the allegiance of a twenty-nine-year-old army colonel named Joseph Mobutu. The CIA team went after Lumumba, but Mobutu got him first. Mobutu's troops captured the prime minister November 30. He was murdered, probably by Mobutu's soldiers, on January 17, 1961. Mobutu still rules the nation, now known as Zaire. He still works closely with the CIA in Africa. He has used his power to amass a personal fortune estimated by the State Department at roughly $5 billion. His country remains one of Africa's poorest and least fortunate.[33]

Planning for another assassination began in early 1960, after Dulles signed a memorandum advocating that "thorough consideration be given to the elimination of Fidel Castro." By September 1960 the Agency joined forces with Mafia bosses, who had more experience in the killing of rivals. The leaders of Operation Success—among them, E. Howard Hunt, case officer, spy novelist and jack-of-all-trades—regrouped to plan the Bay of Pigs invasion.

The disaster now has the aura of a myth: the Cuban exiles training in Guatemala, their CIA coaches pumping them up with pep talks, President Kennedy and his advisers sitting in the Oval Office at two in the morning reading anguished dispatches from the beachhead, the collapse of the invasion and, finally, what Dulles called the "disposal problem."[34]

The disposal problem was the dilemma of what to do with the thousands of Cubans armed and trained for the invasion. Some went to work on the CIA's continuing attempts to kill Castro. From 1963 to 1966, hundreds were employed by the CIA's Miami station for the futile war against Cuba. When the war wound down, the exiles felt bitterly betrayed. Some formed their own terrorist group, Omega 7, and began assassinating political opponents. Cuban diplomats assigned to the United Nations were their favorite targets. Many Bay of Pigs veterans remained available for odd jobs requiring special skills—the break-in at the Watergate Hotel, the smuggling of weapons to the Nicaraguan contras. They became the lost patrol of the Cold War, their anger simmering like heat waves rising from the land.

What did the CIA's foreign adventures accomplish? What lasting good did covert action achieve? In January 1961, on the eve of the Bay of Pigs, a panel appointed by Eisenhower concluded that covert action was an unworthy tool of presidential power. The President's Board of Consultants on Foreign Intelligence Activities was led by Robert Lovett, the former Secretary of Defense, who a decade earlier defined the Cold War as "a hot war . . . a war worse than we have ever experienced." The group reported that secret operations could not justify their costs and dangers: "We have been unable to conclude that, on balance, all of the covert action programs undertaken by the CIA up to this time have been worth the risk or the great expenditure of manpower, money and other resources." This conclusion was not shared with the Congress or the public.[35]

The Bay of Pigs fiasco was cause for some introspection at the CIA. The Agency's general counsel, Lawrence Houston, noted in a January 1962 memorandum that the raising of secret armies for revolutions and insurrections was not within the CIA's legal power. Just as he had fifteen years earlier, Houston said "there is no statutory authority . . . for the conduct of such activities."

The loophole in the National Security Act giving the CIA the power to carry out "such other duties and functions" as the President and his men commanded covered only *"intelligence* affecting the national security," the CIA's counsel emphasized. "It would be stretching that section too far to include a Guatemala or a Cuba." So when covert action came to acts of war, "the Executive branch under the direction of the President was acting without specific statutory authorization"—acting outside the law. What the CIA had been doing was illegal. Houston was hard-pressed to find a legal basis for covert action where there was no law to support it. "Congress as a whole knows that money is appropriated to CIA and knows that generally a portion of it goes for clandestine activities," he wrote. "To this extent we can say that we have Congressional approval of these activities."[36]

This was absurd: Congress was supposed to have approved specific secret operations it knew nothing about—by approving an omnibus secret budget it knew next to nothing about. This was the CIA's legal rationale for covert action. It led to some grand deceptions. For example, in the late 1960's, Congress appropriated tens of millions of dollars a year for refugee aid in Southeast Asia. The CIA used the money on paramilitary operations in Laos. Was Congress approving money for a secret war by voting to feed and shelter war refugees?

The power to conduct covert operations could remain unchallenged only if the operations stayed concealed from Congress. The CIA's power flowed from the President: it was *his* secret army. Sharing information in this realm was sharing a power presidents were loath to share. So Congress stayed ignorant of the CIA's Cold War activities.

Nor was it alone in its ignorance. Dean Rusk, Secretary of State under Kennedy and Johnson and a statutory member of the National Security Council, said he knew next to nothing of what the CIA was doing abroad in those years. He never even saw a CIA budget. Each and every member of the National Security Council, the body that by law directed and approved covert actions, later swore he knew nothing of the attempts to kill Castro. In fact, under Presidents Kennedy, Johnson and Nixon—three Presidents deeply involved in covert action—the National Security Council formally approved only one of every seven covert operations the CIA undertook. Constitutional control of covert action in the 1960's became as fictitious as presidential control of nuclear policy was in the 1950's.[37]

Secrecy now enveloped the government's most ambitious policies, and the White House had to start lying openly to keep the secrets. When the CIA's U-2 spy plane was shot down over the Soviet Union in 1960, the Eisenhower administration lied about the plane's mission. When newspapers reported that the American-backed invasion of Cuba was imminent in 1961, the Kennedy administration lied about it. The next covert operation to spin out of control was the war in Vietnam. When official lies about the war became an almost daily event, a new phrase came into the American language: the credibility gap. With its echoes of the phony missile gap, the expression implicitly recognized that lies were a weapon the government used against its own people. It slowly dawned on Americans that their government could not be trusted. This realization was one of the reasons that the American political system began breaking down in the 1960's. Millions of people simply stopped voting. They declined to follow leaders who misled them. They withdrew from the system and withheld their consent to be governed.

The mistrust of secret government extended to ex-Presidents. Late in his life, Harry Truman, who had helped create the CIA, coldly denounced it. Truman had used the CIA as enthusiastically as any President, approving eighty-one covert actions abroad. In 1963, ten years out of office, he pronounced the CIA a danger to democracy: "Those fellows in the CIA don't just report on wars and the like, they go out and make up their own, and there's nobody to keep track of what they're up to," Truman said. "They spend billions of dollars stirring up trouble so they'll have something to report on. . . . It's become a government all of its own and all secret. They don't have to account to anybody."[38]

Congress had demanded no accounting. It made no attempt to control the President's secret wars until January 1971. That winter, the press reported that the CIA controlled an army of 36,000 men in Laos. Congress had sanctioned no such army. Five congressional leaders had been told that some sort of Laotian operation existed, but they did not know that the CIA was spending more than $300 million a year trying to build a mercenary army in the jungles of Laos. Senator William Fulbright of Arkansas, chairman of the Foreign Relations Committee, asked Senator Ellender, chairman of the Appropriations Committee's intelligence sub-committee, what he knew about the operation. Their conversation was the first open discussion on the floor of the Senate about the mechanics of financing the CIA:

Mr. FULBRIGHT: It has been stated that the CIA has 36,000 there. It is no secret. Would the Senator say that before the creation of the army in Laos they came before the committee and the committee knew of it and approved it? . . . Did the Senator approve it?
Mr. ELLENDER: It was not—I did not know anything about it. . . . I never asked, to begin with, whether or not there were any funds to carry on the war in this sum the CIA asked for. It never dawned on me to ask about it. . . .
Mr. FULBRIGHT: You do not know, in fact?
Mr. ELLENDER: No.
Mr. FULBRIGHT: As you are one of five men privy to this operation, in fact you are the No. 1 man of the five men who would know, then who would know what happened to this money? The fact is, not even the five men, and you are the chief one of the five men, know the facts in the situation.
Mr. ELLENDER: Probably not.[39]

This rattled Congress. The whole system was built on taking the CIA on faith, and trusting in the wise old men nominally responsible for overseeing the Agency. After twenty-two years, the system was being revealed as a charade.

Director of Central Intelligence Richard Helms was moved to give a rare public speech in April 1971. Addressing the American Society of Newspaper Editors, Helms asserted that the press and the public should "take it on faith that we too are honorable men." His audience applauded warmly and accepted his word. But this speech marked the beginning of a very bad stretch for the CIA, the beginning of the end of that faith.[40]

Now members of Congress were beginning to put questions to the CIA. Few received answers. Ed Koch, the longtime mayor of New York, tells the story of his first visit to the CIA in 1971, when he was a newly elected member of Congress. Koch and seventeen other congressional freshmen were invited out for a chat with Helms. The CIA's headquarters stands in a clearing in the woods of Langley, Virginia. In winter, when the trees are bare, the compound may be glimpsed from the George Washington Parkway along the Potomac. As a whole, the CIA looks like the campus of a Midwestern state college, but the director's office on the seventh floor of the main building is a sumptuous Ivy League affair, complete with an elegant dining room.

The congressmen had breakfast up on the seventh floor, "a great breakfast on gold service," Koch recalled. As the lawmakers polished off their eggs, Helms pushed back his chair and opened the floor. "Gentlemen," he said, "this is probably the only time you will ever have an opportunity to ask any question of the CIA. So ask."

Koch raised his hand and said, "Mr. Helms, I really only have two questions. How many people do you employ and what is the size of your budget?"

Helms recoiled. "There are only two questions I can't answer and those are the two," he said.

"Mr. Helms," Koch said, "are you telling me, a member of Congress, that I can't learn the size of your budget? After all, I vote on that budget. Somehow or other I ought to be able to see it."

"That is exactly what I'm telling you," Helms shot back. "That budget item is buried under some other items and you will not know what it is. . . . You will never know what it is."

"You mean it could be buried under Social Security?" Koch asked.

"We have not used that one yet," Helms said, "but it is not a bad idea."[41]

Savvy members of Congress began to realize that the money for the CIA's secret wars was buried in the Pentagon's inventory of weapons and hardware. But Helms was right: they would never find it. This fact was addressed openly in the Senate for the first time in April 1971. Again, Fulbright opened the door. The liberal Senator Alan Cranston of California and the longtime Armed Services Committee member Stuart Symington of Missouri followed Fulbright inside.

The first public discussion of the black budget in Congress began as Fulbright waved a copy of the Pentagon's budget in the air:

Mr. FULBRIGHT: Billions of dollars of intelligence funds are contained in this appropriation. No one can tell where in this bill those funds are. When they read a line item and find that there is so much for aircraft, or for a carrier, those may or may not be the real amount.

This practice gives rise to questions about every item in the appropriation. . . .

Mr. CRANSTON: Are there references in the appropriations bill to funds for intelligence uses?

Mr. SYMINGTON: No.

Mr. CRANSTON: How are they provided for; by padding other categories?

Mr. SYMINGTON: I am not sure I have enough knowledge to answer. Presumably yes.

Mr. CRANSTON: . . . Is that the way these items are handled, inflated, or bloated, in fact—some of them at least—that will cover up what is in this bill for intelligence?

Mr. ELLENDER: Yes, the Senator is correct—some of it.[42]

By now, senators were up in arms. Symington introduced a measure to cap the intelligence budget at $4 billion a year. Senator George McGovern of South Dakota proposed to the Senate that it simply reveal the black budget. Both ideas were deemed too dangerous to consider. But in December 1971, a bill introduced by Senator Clifford Case of New Jersey won overwhelming support and became law: it cut off funds for the secret war in Laos. For the first time, a CIA paramilitary operation had been exposed and shut down through the democratic process. It was a harbinger.

The old guard did their best to keep the secrets. Senator Stennis tried to deal with the revolt against secret spending by shutting down the Armed Services intelligence subcommittee, holding no meetings at all, to dam the trickle of information. But Senator Ellender began seeing faults in the dam. He surveyed the domain of the black budget in late 1971 and exclaimed: "If you knew how much we spend and how much money we waste in this area, it would knock you off your chair. It's criminal!"[43]

No one knew. Such crimes were not investigated or prosecuted.

The crimes of Watergate almost undid the CIA. When the whole sordid affair was over, and the public realized that their government was run by liars and could not be trusted, Congress began to mount an assault on the fortified walls surrounding the intelligence community.[44]

On June 17, 1972, a team of burglars was arrested inside the Democratic National Committee headquarters at the Watergate Hotel. The team's captain was E. Howard Hunt, veteran of Operation Success, bearer of psychic scars from the Bay of Pigs. The burglars included James McCord, a former chief of security at the CIA; Bernard Barker, Hunt's aide-de-camp during the Bay of Pigs; Eugenio Martinez, a CIA boat captain with 354 missions to Cuba under his belt and still on the Agency's payroll as an informant; and Frank Fiorini, alias Frank Sturgis, a longtime CIA agent inside Cuba. The mercenary Sturgis took his alias from a character in one of Hunt's spy novels, *Bimini Run*.[45]

The team was not working for the CIA. It was working for CREEP, the Committee to Re-Elect the President. Six days later President Nixon captured himself on tape ordering the CIA to block the FBI's investigation of the burglary. This tape proved to be the punch line of a long story. Nixon refused to release the tape to the Watergate Special Prosecutor on the grounds of "national security" and "executive privilege." It took a year of unrelenting political pressure and a unanimous Supreme Court decision before Nixon turned it over. By then, the House had voted articles of impeachment against the President—among them a charge of "endeavoring to misuse the Central Intelligence Agency."

The damage the CIA sustained from the Watergate virus took longer to incubate. The first signs of the sickness appeared after Nixon fired Helms on November 20, 1972, most likely for refusing to cooperate fully in the Watergate cover-up, and appointed him ambassador to Iran. In his stead Nixon chose an arrogant professor named James Schlesinger, who had served Nixon as a budget director and chief of the Atomic Energy Commission. He stayed at the CIA only four months before moving on to become Secretary of Defense. A number of unpleasant surprises confronted Schlesinger in his brief tenure at the CIA. Chief among them was the anger of the federal judge presiding over the trial of Daniel Ellsberg, the former nuclear strategist and present-day peace activist, charged with espionage for distributing the Pentagon Papers, the secret history of the Vietnam War.

On April 27, 1973, the judge read aloud, in open court, a Justice Department memorandum. It said that Howard Hunt, using cover provided by the CIA at the White House's request, had led Barker and Martinez in a burglary of Ellsberg's psychiatrist's office, looking for dirt on the defendant.

Hunt had served the CIA loyally for twenty-three years, rising to chief of covert action in the Domestic Operations Division in the 1960's. That was a problem right there; the CIA was not supposed to have a domestic covert-action chief as such. The CIA's charter barred it from spying on Americans. In his speech to the newspaper editors Helms swore the CIA would never do so. The Domestic Operations Division had done little else. Hunt had officially retired from the CIA in April 1970. He still had his CIA security clearances three months later when he signed up as a $100-a-day consultant to the Nixon White House. In his consultancy, Hunt obtained CIA-issued identification and disguises, notably an ill-fitting red wig. He used CIA tape recorders, CIA microphones and CIA friendships in his dirty work for the White House.

The CIA had developed and copied the photos Hunt took while casing the psychiatrist's office. The Agency also had prepared two psychological profiles of Ellsberg at Hunt's request. In the charged atmosphere of the day, the CIA was seen as part of a conspiracy to destroy Ellsberg and crush political dissent.

Alarm bells started ringing up on the seventh floor at Langley. "This was a shocker," said William Colby, then the CIA's Deputy Director for Operations. He said Schlesinger vowed to "tear the place apart and 'fire everyone if necessary,' but we had to find out if there were questionable or illegal activities hidden in the secret recesses of our clandestine past that we didn't know about and that might explode at any time under our feet." Many such land mines lay beneath the surface.[46]

On May 9, 1973, two days before Schlesinger announced he was leaving Langley for the Pentagon, he issued a directive drafted by Colby. The order shook the CIA to its bones:

I have ordered all senior operating officials of this Agency to report to me immediately on any activities now going on, or that have gone on in the past, which might be construed to be outside the legislative charter of this Agency.

I hereby direct every person presently employed by CIA to report to me on any such activities of which he has knowledge. I invite all ex-employees to do the same. Anyone who has such information should call my secretary (extension 6363). . . .[47]

Colby had to answer the calls. It was a harrowing assignment. Colby had spent most of his adult life fighting secret wars. He'd worked diligently as a CIA clandestine operator from 1950 onward, serving as chief of the Far East Divison from 1962 to 1967 and overseeing the CIA in Vietnam. He took time out only to run the Phoenix program, a civilian-led counterinsurgency operation that had led to the deaths of more than 20,000 Vietnamese.

Colby was a Princeton graduate, Princetonian in demeanor and speech: proper, almost patrician, in bearing; mild-mannered but capable of being cold-blooded. He wore clear-framed glasses that sometimes caught the light in a way that hid his eyes. Colby's family background was military and devoutly Roman Catholic; both facts are clues to his apostasy. He would follow any legitimate order, and he had a sense of guilt and redemption.[48]

He now had a mission that violated every rule of secrecy: to make a list of the secrets. It was an encyclopedia of dirty tricks. The CIA's officers called it the Family Jewels, or the Skeletons. The CIA's files teemed with them. The list eventually grew to 693 single-spaced pages.

There was a long entry under "Activities directed against U.S. citizens." Most were illegal or immoral. The CIA had put thousands of Americans under steady surveillance, tapped their telephones, bugged their bedrooms, scrutinized their tax returns, combed through their office files at night. The CIA had been opening Americans' mail for twenty years; the NSA had been intercepting millions of telegrams and telexes. The unpleasant subject of Dr. Gottlieb's poisons arose. There were the CIA's mind-control experiments with LSD, the drugging of unwitting human guinea pigs. Some had lost their minds; two had died. And then there were the assassination plots. Every President had used the CIA in ways that violated standards of human decency.

None of this was revealed at first. But as Watergate raged on, and as it became clear that Nixon's secrecy and deception would destroy him, Colby developed a conviction that revelation and confession were necessary to save the CIA's soul. Trained as a lawyer as well as a secret warrior, Colby knew some of the CIA's operations violated its charter, the law and the Constitution. He realized, as he told me, that the days of total secrecy at the CIA were over. Plausible deniability wouldn't work anymore: "It went out the window, finished, over. It was a nice theory when the spy business was a tiny little service that sat at the knee of the President. . . . It had become too big for that kind of fiction." The CIA's denials no longer sounded plausible, not when the President himself was being exposed as a liar. It was time to start telling the truth.[49]

At first Colby moved very cautiously, making selective disclosures. In the summer of 1973 he revealed some of the Family Jewels to Senator Symington and Congressman Lucien Nedzi of Michigan, who chaired the Senate and House Armed Services intelligence subcommittees respectively. He kept the secrets from the Nixon White House, sensing that Nixon would spill them to make his own excesses look less grievous by contrast. But the list of secrets kept growing. Extension 6363 kept ringing off the hook.

One of the worst calls was from a mid-level CIA official. He warned that Helms had lied to the Senate Foreign Relations Committee three months earlier, during his confirmation as ambassador to Iran. The subject was the CIA's still-secret subversion of Salvador Allende, the democratically elected president of Chile:

Senator SYMINGTON: Did you try in the Central Intelligence Agency to overthrow the government of Chile?
Mr. HELMS: No, sir.
Senator SYMINGTON: Did you have any money passed to the opponents of Allende?
Mr. HELMS: No, sir.

Senator SYMINGTON: So the stories you were involved in the war were wrong?
Mr. HELMS: Yes, sir.[50]

The CIA was working very hard to overthrow Allende, a socialist who'd won a fair and free election. In 1970, Nixon had ordered Helms to block Allende from taking power by any means necessary. The CIA started out buying votes and painting slogans on walls. It wound up passing automatic weapons to right-wing soldiers who shot and killed the Chilean army chief of staff. The military overthrew Allende in 1973. He died in the coup.

Helms was in an impossible position. He was unable to reconcile the secrecy of his past with the present truth-telling spirit. He was under oath. He was being questioned point-blank about a covert operation. He had been asked to divulge a dangerous secret. He could not speak the truth.

Reluctantly, Colby asked the CIA's Inspector General, William Broe, to look into the matter. Broe knew perfectly well what the CIA had been up to in Chile. He had been chief of clandestine operations in Latin America when the covert action against Allende began. He also knew what Helms had been through, the tension between keeping secrets and telling the truth. Broe had been the first CIA official ever to testify openly before a congressional committee. The subject was Chile.

Broe appointed a team of CIA analysts to report on Helms' testimony. The analysts insisted that Helms had committed perjury. Helms' allies at the Agency regarded the report as pure poison. A long and bitter tug-of-war ended in early December 1974, when the report finally arrived at the Justice Department. The word "perjury" stayed in it.*

The dam broke two weeks later. Seymour Hersh, a reporter for the *New York Times*, came to see Colby on Friday, December 20. Hersh had followed the trickle of secrets from the CIA's reservoir for a solid year. Hersh told Colby he was prepared to break a story about Operation CHAOS, the CIA's program of keeping taps on antiwar activists. Colby admitted to Hersh that "on some few occasions" the CIA had wiretapped, monitored and opened the mail of Americans and "overstepped the boundaries of its charter." The headline two days later across the front page of more than a million copies of the Sunday *Times* read: *Huge CIA Operation Reported in U.S. Against Anti-War Forces, Other Dissidents in Nixon Years*. Harry Truman's amusing little joke with the cloak and the dagger in the Oval Office had turned bitter.[51]

---

*In 1977, Helms pleaded no contest in federal court to a charge of "failing to testify fully" under oath to Congress. The judge gave him a harsh lecture, a suspended sentence and a $2,000 fine.

The golden age was over. The skeletons were beginning to tumble into the open. The Congress had to face the fact that it was ignorant of the CIA. "Fewer than a dozen Members of Congress have any idea how much money the CIA spends a year, and probably none of them has much of an idea what the Agency actually does with that money," said Representative Paul Findley, Republican of Illinois. "We are uninformed," Senator Harold Hughes, an Iowa Democrat, told his colleagues. "We have not even had the capacity or responsibility to know even when we were given information whether it was right or wrong, or what was happening."[52]

Things had to change. Public knowledge and debate were what kept democracy's machine greased and oiled. The machine was groaning and smoking. No one wanted it to fail.

The new President, Gerald Ford, was an unlikely man to preside over an era of reform at the CIA. He had been a leading member of the old guard in Congress. He was one of the sleeping watchdogs on the House Appropriations Committee's intelligence subcommittee from 1957 to 1965. He had served on the Warren Commission investigating President Kennedy's assassination, a group that was hardly a model of investigative zeal, and he had secretly informed the FBI on the commission's progress. Now he was compelled to change his ways, and the CIA's as well.[53]

On December 30, 1974, "plausible deniability" was buried in a simple White House ceremony. Ford signed into law a bill written by Senator Hughes and Congressman Leo Ryan of California. Passed in reaction to the revelation of the CIA's role in Chile, the Hughes-Ryan act barred the CIA from spending money on covert actions abroad "unless and until the President finds that each such operation is important to the national security of the United States and reports, in a timely fashion, a description . . . of such operation to the appropriate committees of Congress." The President now had to sign a piece of paper—a "finding"—to authorize a secret operation. His name and his authority were on the line. His secret service had to go to Capitol Hill to report its covert actions.

The CIA found itself facing the same paradox Richard Helms had confronted: how could it keep secrets if it was forced to be part of an open government? It was confounding, and damned demoralizing. Many of the old pros at the Agency began packing their bags.

The President met with Colby in the Oval Office five days later, on January 3, 1975. Ford decided to appoint a commission to look into the CIA's domestic activities, one that would not run wild and ask too many questions. The blue-ribbon commission—led by Vice President Nelson Rockefeller, and including the former governor of California, Ronald

Reagan—was intended to control the damage being done to the power of secrecy.

Colby told the commissioners truths they did not want to know. Rockefeller drew the CIA director aside at one meeting and said, "in his most charming manner, 'Bill, do you really have to present all this material to us?' I got the message quite unmistakably, and I didn't like it," Colby recounted. Rockefeller was letting Colby know "that he would much prefer me to take the traditional stance of fending off investigation by drawing the cloak of secrecy around the agency in the name of national security." Colby threw off the cloak. He thought he had to "educate the Congress, press and public" in order to save the CIA: "The Agency's survival, I believed, could only come from understanding, not hostility, built on knowledge, not faith." The Agency had breached its trust. The truth had to come out. The CIA could be taken on faith no longer. Understanding and knowledge could only come from facts.[54]

The public education began on January 21, when the Senate voted 82 to 4 to create a select committee to investigate the CIA. Unlike its counterpart in the House, a disastrous outfit that self-destructed in bickering and recrimination, the Senate committee did about as good a job as could be expected. Over the next two years, it produced thorough, balanced reports on the assassination plots, the dirty tricks and domestic spying, on the CIA's role in a democracy. There were some awkward moments. On September 16, in its first public hearing, the committee sandbagged Colby. It compelled him to produce an odd-looking pistol from the CIA's storehouses. Colby memorably described it as "a nondiscernable microbioinoculator." It was a gun that shot poison pellets, tiny darts tipped with a toxin. Pictures of committee chairman Frank Church posing with the gun ran around the world. But the Church Committee generally conducted its work in a sane and coherent way, and Colby's cooperation kept the CIA from being destroyed, disenfranchised or emasculated by congressional outrage.

Colby's cooperation also cost him his job. He had gone over the President's head in presenting his case. He had compelled the disclosure of the assassination plots. He had disclosed the secrets. And he had produced the poison gun. "The administration did not approve of my cooperative approach to the investigations," Colby said. "I had been blamed for not categorically denying Hersh's story at the very beginning; I had been criticized for turning material on Helms over to the Department of Justice; I had been chided for being too forthcoming to the Rockefeller Commission. . . . But the impact of the toxin spectacular, and especially the fact that I had delivered the dart gun when Congress demanded it, blew the roof off." Colby had spoken truth to power. He paid the price. On November 2, 1975, the President fired him.[55]

Election Day was a year away. Ford's accidental presidency was faring poorly. To shore up support from his party's right wing, he needed to put a genuine conservative with solid Republican credentials in charge of the CIA. He chose a colleague from his days in Congress, the man who had run the Republican National Committee during Watergate, the head of the liaison office in the People's Republic of China: a fifty-two-year-old millionaire named George Herbert Walker Bush. Bush served as a caretaker, soothing the CIA's nerves. "He was initially viewed with suspicion as an ambitious politician who might try to use the Agency for partisan purposes," wrote Cord Meyer, a well-traveled senior CIA officer. But Bush "put politics aside" and worked at "restoring the morale of an institution that had been battered enough."[56]

Bush had a few other significant accomplishments in his year at the CIA. For one, he helped stop the final secret from being spilled. He helped stop the Congress from publishing the intelligence community's black budget.

The Rockefeller Commission's newly issued final report on the CIA, most of which was a bland and themeless pudding, contained one riveting recommendation: "Congress should give careful consideration to the question of whether the budget of the CIA should not, at least to some extent, be made public, particularly in view of the provisions of Article I, Section 9, Clause 7 of the Constitution." In a fine-print footnote, the commission printed the crucial clause: "No money shall be drawn from the Treasury, but in Consequence of Appropriations made by Law; and a regular Statement and Account of the Receipts and Expenditures of all public Money shall be published from time to time."[57]

So the Church Committee took up the elemental question: was the black budget constitutional? The committee reached a conclusion in April 1976. The answer was no:

> The budget procedures which presently govern the Central Intelligence Agency and other agencies of the Intelligence Community prevent most members of Congress from knowing how much money is spent by any of these agencies or even how much money is spent on intelligence as a whole. In addition, most members of the public are deceived about the appropriations and expenditures of other government agencies whose budgets are inflated to conceal funds for the intelligence community.
>
> The failure to provide this information to the public and to the Congress prevents either from effectively ordering priorities and violates Article I, Section 9, Clause 7 of the Constitution. . . .
>
> The Committee finds that publication of the aggregate figure

for national intelligence would begin to satisfy the Constitutional
requirement and would not damage the national security.[58]

The committee voted 8 to 3 to disclose that aggregate figure, the
sum total of the national intelligence budget. There were few secret
weapons programs at the time; they were largely a phenomenon of the
1980's. So the disclosure would let the Congress and the public know,
with a fair degree of accuracy, how much money the Pentagon, the CIA
and the White House spent in secret.

All the Congress really knew for certain was that the intelligence
community spent more than it revealed. Members of Congress had tried
to estimate the black budget before. Their reckonings varied wildly.
Senator William Proxmire of Wisconsin read into the *Congressional
Record* rough figures that placed the total intelligence budget at $6.2
billion in 1973. Some of Proxmire's figures appear to have been on the
mark. Others were way off. He pegged the National Security Agency's
budget at a round $1 billion. That was far too low. The House Government
Operations Committee, in an unpublished 1976 report, placed the NSA's
budget at $15 billion. That was far too high.[59]

The black budget actually contained somewhere between $7 billion
and $8 billion in 1976, secret weapons programs accounting for less than
one-tenth that sum. The senators on the Church Committee thought revealing that fact would not shock the sensibilities of the American people
nor harm the nation's security. They were ready to share that secret.[60]

Bush pleaded with them to stop. The CIA director privately argued
to the senators that the revelation would be a disaster, compromising the
CIA beyond repair. Bush's appeals worked. By a single vote, the Church
Committee agreed to hold off. It voted 6 to 5 to refer the issue to the
full Senate. The question never reached the Senate floor.[61]

The Senate leadership handed the controversy to its newly created
Select Committee on Intelligence, a new body formed to oversee the CIA.
The Senate intelligence committee took up the question in April 1977.
It held two days of public hearings and a lengthy closed session. The
senators heard from Colby and Helms, from the new CIA director Stansfield Turner, from former high officials of the CIA and the military
intelligence agencies. They interviewed the President, the Vice President,
the Attorney General of the United States.

No one—not a soul—argued that disclosing the secret number would
endanger national security. Many said it would be in the public interest.
The CIA's Admiral Turner testified that it would "help the public put
into perspective the intelligence activity of their country."[62]

In June 1977 the committee voted 9 to 8 to reveal the secret. The
majority thought releasing a single figure for the 1978 intelligence budget

to the public would be a salutary dose of sunlight for the world of secrets. This moment was the high-water mark in the tide of openness and disclosure. "The public has a right to know as much as possible" about intelligence spending, the majority report said. "Now they know nothing." The decision to unveil the black budget was "a reflection of the qualities that distinguish our democracy from all other nations," the majority said. "Pressure for information is the mark of a healthy democracy."

The idea that secret spending was illicit, and that the black budget should be published, now had been endorsed by a presidential commission, by a Senate investigative committee and by a majority of the Senate intelligence committee. Each recommendation carried with it strong suggestions that the practice was unconstitutional. The idea that publishing the black budget in some form would damage the national security of the United States had been rejected by a former CIA director, by former national security advisers, by a former chairman of the Joint Chiefs of Staff.

And still the power of secrecy prevailed. The minority report of the Senate intelligence committee was scathing: the revelation "would wholly undermine the effectiveness of our entire intelligence apparatus." It "would be a grave mistake." One member of the minority, Senator Malcolm Wallop, a Wyoming Republican, went further: "It is indeed a move of weakness, a betrayal of the trust bestowed upon us. . . . IT WILL NOT STOP HERE. . . . We will needlessly harm the country we seek to protect, all in the name of satisfying the curiosity of the press lords of America." It stopped there. The minority position won out. The measure died, for no one in the majority had the will to press it. The Senate never voted on the question. "The intensity of the issue faded away," said William G. Miller, then the intelligence committee's staff director. "The constitutional question was unresolved."[63]

Constitutional questions were much on William Colby's mind as he sat at home writing his memoirs. Colby concluded that the meaning of the ordeal the CIA had been through was clear. The point of it all had been to resolve "the previously unacknowledged contradiction between the old tradition of intelligence and the Constitution."[64]

The old tradition was best represented by the CIA's James Jesus Angleton, breeder of orchids, weaver of conspiracies and seer of Soviet intentions. Immensely influential inside the Agency, he had been the longtime chief of counterintelligence, the liaison with the FBI, and sole proprietor of the Israeli account. Angleton was called to testify before the Church Committee. He was asked why the CIA had disobeyed a direct order from the White House to destroy the Agency's stockpile of poisons. His interrogators heard twenty-five years of CIA history in his reply. "It is inconceivable," he said, "that a secret arm of the government has to comply with all the overt orders of the government."[65]

This doctrine placed the CIA outside the law. It meant that there was no law the CIA was bound to obey, none save its own secret creed. This was a zealot's code. It was incompatible with the Constitution.

The Constitution stands mute on most of the mechanics of foreign policy. Its silences create what a Supreme Court Justice once called "a zone of twilight" in which the President and the Congress must struggle for power. But what the CIA did was done in darkness. What the CIA did amounted to a secret foreign policy of the United States, and a secret foreign policy was not what the framers of the Constitution had intended.[66]

Where the Constitution speaks clearly, its rules are absolute. The Constitution gives Congress sole power "to raise and support Armies." The CIA had raised and supported secret armies. The Constitution prohibited the President from going to war without Congress' consent. Presidents had used the CIA to mount secret acts of war. And the Constitution says the President and his agents cannot spend a cent without a lawful and public appropriation. The CIA could carry out any order so long as it could get and spend money secretly.

If the conflict between secrecy and democracy could be resolved, it had to be settled in the Constitution's favor. The CIA had to start acting as if it were part of a constitutional government.

By 1980, a cautious consensus on covert action had been forged after a long struggle between Congress and the President. All agreed America needed the CIA to gather and analyze facts, to foresee distant dangers approaching, to understand a fiendishly complicated world—in short, to provide intelligence. And when the CIA set out to win friends and influence enemies, to buy the allegiances of foreign leaders, to ship arms to guerrillas or subvert governments, the intelligence committees now would be consulted—preferably in advance. They had to be told about the flight plans and takeoff procedures of covert actions, not simply called in to comb through the wreckage after a crash.

The intelligence committees in the Senate and the House asserted the right to know when the President authorized a covert action. Consultation and consensus could create a standard for secret operations. If revealed, the schemes would have to make sense to the American people. In unusual circumstances, the CIA could narrow the circle of knowledge to eight men—the chairmen and ranking minority leaders of the intelligence committees and the majority and minority leaders of the House and Senate. In exceptional circumstances, it could tell the intelligence committees "in a timely manner" after the fact. The CIA was the only agency that could conduct covert actions unless the President explicitly ordered otherwise.

The one unsettled issue was the secrecy of the black budget. Though the Constitution's overt order flatly prohibited it, and though two reform-minded Senate committees found the secrecy unconstitutional and undemocratic, the issue remained unresolved. And now the era of reform was passing quickly.

"Reform committees . . . were mornin' glories," a wise and thoroughly corrupt Tammany Hall fixer named George Washington Plunkitt said long ago. "Looked lovely in the mornin' and withered up in a short time, while the regular machines went on flourishin' forever, like fine old oaks." The reformers had their triumphs, but the effort to learn the CIA's secret history had been exhausting. In January 1981, the counter-reformation began.[67]

Ronald Reagan saw the world as the cold warriors of the 1950's did: a world of good and evil. "The Soviets," he said at his first press conference as President, "reserve unto themselves the right to commit any crime, to lie, to cheat." So once again the United States had to subvert, sabotage and destroy the enemy by more clever, more sophisticated and more effective methods.

Reagan's field marshal was CIA director William Casey—"the last great buccaneer from OSS," as the chief of the CIA's clandestine service, Clair George, affectionately memorialized him. Casey came to power with his freebooting days as a secret agent fresh in mind. His leadership brought back to American intelligence some of the sense of limitless possibilities from the era of the OSS. He worked hard to make the CIA the most powerful foreign-policy arm of the United States government once more.

To shield that power, the Congress had to be kept at bay. Casey had genuine contempt for his congressional overseers, and duped them with his mumbling, evasive testimony. "We are like mushrooms," one member of the House intelligence committee, Norman Mineta of California, said in 1983. "They keep us in the dark and feed us a lot of manure."[68]

In one of his few public speeches, Casey defined the war he was waging and the nature of the enemy. "This is not an undeclared war," Casey said. "In 1961, Khrushchev, then leader of the Soviet Union, told us that communism would win—not through nuclear war, which could destroy the world, or conventional war, which could quickly lead to nuclear war, but by wars of national liberation in Africa, Asia and Latin America. We were reluctant to believe him then—just as in the 1930's, we were reluctant to take Hitler seriously." Casey seemed to see subverting the Sandinista government of Nicaragua as the moral equivalent of defeating the Nazis.[69]

Reagan and Casey were living in the past. The rules of the game as they stood when Reagan came to office had been defined clearly after a decade of debate. Reagan and Casey knew the rules, or should have. They broke every one.

They made war in violation of the law and made secret deals with thugs and terrorists. It was hard to explain these actions to a congressional committee, or obtain funds for them. So the Reagan administration kept them secret, and found the money elsewhere, and deceived the Congress. Ultimately, the United States came ''to rely on covert activity as the core of our policy,'' said the President's morose national security adviser, Robert McFarlane.[70]

The administration knew the legal restraints on covert action left only three courses open to a President who wanted his foreign policy carried out in secret. Reagan chose all three.

The President could ignore the law and run covert operations from the White House. Reagan did. His national security advisers were convicted as criminals. His secret policies were exposed as follies and failures.

The President could use the armed forces as a surrogate CIA. Reagan did. His generals created a hard-charging brigade of soldiers turned spies. The secret army accomplished precious little. Its crimes landed some of its leaders in Leavenworth.

Finally, he could follow the law, play by the rules, win Congress' consent for covert actions and use the CIA the way its creators intended, as a tool for containing communism. The Congress, the White House and the CIA all collaborated on the biggest and most ambitious covert operation in decades—an immense arms pipeline to Afghanistan.

The Afghan operation was the CIA's greatest success of the 1980's. But it left a legacy of corruption, betrayal and murder.

6

A Holy War

MAHMOUD Rahman, a white-bearded, hawk-eyed soldier of God, knelt atop a barren mountain. He faced the setting sun, looking out over Afghanistan, west toward Mecca. He chanted in Pushtu, his native tongue, praising Allah and praying for vengeance. Before him lay a Stinger missile launcher, a five-foot talisman labeled: *Confidential— National Security Information—Unauthorized Disclosure Subject to Criminal Sanctions*. The Stinger had come to the mountaintop through a worldwide weapons pipeline run by the Central Intelligence Agency.[1]

At dawn, Rahman had left a refugee camp outside Peshawar, Pakistan. He traveled in a caravan of Japanese jeeps through the stony wilderness where his grandfather and great-grandfather had fought the armies of Great Britain. Along the road to the border where Afghanistan begins, green flags symbolizing martyrdom flew over rough stone graves. He clutched a Chinese-made Kalashnikov rifle. The jeeps and the rifle, too, were bought and paid for by the CIA.

The convoy swerved past two-humped camels loping through a frontier village of tiny huts made of mud and straw and dung. The jeeps climbed a perilously narrow trail and stopped at a mountain pass nearly 9,000 feet high. Rahman and a hundred other men marched over the pass into Afghanistan, into a landscape harsh and beautiful as the mountains of the moon. They had come to fight the *jihad*, the holy war against the infidels of the Soviet army.

The Soviets invaded Afghanistan in December 1979, and made war against the nation for nearly ten years. The invasion was an act of murder on a grand scale. Hundreds of thousands died, perhaps one million or more. No one ever will know the true number. The Soviets destroyed thousands of villages and farms and mosques. Five million Afghans, a third of the nation, fled eastward to Pakistan and west to Iran.[2]

The CIA bought an immense arsenal for the Afghan rebels. The Agency enlisted Chinese generals, Saudi princes, Swiss bankers and Iranian radicals in a global gunrunning network. The weaponry that reached the guerrillas bled the Soviets badly. For the first time in history, American missiles, the Stingers, shot down Soviet pilots. The Afghans' struggle became the CIA's holy war as well.

Over the course of the 1980's, the CIA spent nearly $3 billion smuggling weapons to the *mujaheddin*, the holy warriors of the Afghan resistance. The operation started small: $30 million of weaponry a year in 1980. It grew to $100 million, then $500 million, then $700 million a year. The CIA's arms shipments to Afghanistan became the biggest covert operation in its history, save its wars in Vietnam, Laos and Cambodia twenty years ago.

The arms shipments began as the very model of a moral covert action. Few in Washington imagined that the CIA's clandestine pipeline would be corrupted, its funds would help finance the heroin trade, its Stingers would fall into the hands of Iran, the *jihad* would collapse into a civil war and the CIA's mortars and rifles would one day be killing the people they were meant to save.

The holy war erupted in a year of religious fervor and political revolution throughout the nations of Islam. On January 16, 1979, the Shah of Iran fell. Only nine months earlier, the Shah had told the former CIA director, George Bush, that he feared the Soviets would one day encircle Iran and destroy it in a bid to seize power in the Persian Gulf. On February 11, the Shah's army disintegrated and the Ayatollah Khomeini took power. Three days later, the American ambassador in the Afghan capital of Kabul, Adolph "Spike" Dubs, was killed in a bungled kidnapping. In November, Iranian zealots seized the American embassy in Teheran and held its luckless inhabitants hostage. The flames of fundamentalism swept into Saudi Arabia; armed religious radicals took over Islam's holiest site, the Grand Mosque in Mecca.[3]

The world of Islam was burning with rage, and the wildfire crept all the way up to the Soviet border. The Soviets looked south nervously. Moscow's domain included about forty million Muslims living in the tier of Soviet republics north of Iran and Afghanistan. The Kremlin did not want the fire to spread.

In Kabul, a heavy-handed regime had taken power in an April 1978

was a tough question, morally, to answer. The whole program of feeding freedom fighters is one of feeding people who cannot win militarily.

"But at the time, back in 1979, there was surely a benefit to the United States in this. So I said: 'Okay. I think I can morally accept this.'"[7]

A look at the map showed there was only one way for the CIA's arms shipments to reach the *mujaheddin*. Afghanistan's neighbor to the west and south was Iran, now fallen under Khomeini's spell. To the north lay the Soviets. The pipeline had to run through Pakistan. That posed a particularly thorny problem. Relations between the United States and Pakistan were at an all-time low at the hour of the Soviet invasion.

Pakistan's military ruler, General Mohammad Zia ul-Haq, cheerfully described himself as a dictator. With his deep-set eyes and his handlebar moustache, Zia looked a bit like the villain in a silent movie. He jailed his opponents and banned dissent. In April 1979 he ignored worldwide protests and executed the president he had overthrown, Zulfikar Ali Bhutto. Bhutto was dragged from a prison cell and hanged in the middle of the night. To make matters worse, the CIA learned that Pakistan was using smuggled technology in an attempt to build a nuclear warhead— the first Islamic bomb. Under U.S. laws aimed at stemming the spread of nuclear weapons, Carter cut off all military and economic aid to Pakistan in April 1979. Then, on November 21, the month before the Soviet invasion, Pakistanis caught the pandemic fever of Islamic fury. Anti-American mobs burned and ransacked the U.S. embassy in Islamabad and the American cultural centers in Rawalpindi and Lahore.

The CIA approached its marriage of convenience with Zia in this atmosphere of hatred and mutual mistrust. But now his nation was transformed. Pakistan was no longer a hostile Islamic dictatorship; it was a stalwart ally on the front line of the war against the Soviets. In time, the CIA made stranger alliances in the holy war.

The Agency began shipping armaments into Pakistan in January 1980, two weeks after the Soviet invasion. As the new year began, Turner cabled the CIA station in Cairo, one of the Agency's largest overseas posts. He told the station chief that the President of the United States had a favor to ask of Egypt's President Anwar el-Sadat. The Egyptian leader had something the CIA needed: huge stockpiles of Soviet-model automatic rifles, land mines, grenade launchers, antitank and anti-aircraft missiles. They were left over from the 1960's and early 1970's, when Egypt was on friendly terms with Moscow.

"The first moment that Afghan incident took place," Sadat recalled in a September 1981 interview with NBC News, two weeks before his assassination, "the U.S. contacted me" and "told me, 'Please open your stores for us so that we can give the Afghans the armaments they need to fight,' and I gave the armaments. The transport of armaments to the Afghans started from Cairo on U.S. planes.''

The CIA took Sadat's Soviet weapons—about $15 million worth in 1980—and replenished Egypt's stockpiles with newer American arms. Some of the weapons went to a CIA-controlled factory near Cairo. The factory began stamping out copies of the Soviet weapons, replicating them for the *mujaheddin*. The CIA hired the Hughes Aircraft Company, a frequent CIA contractor, to refurbish Egypt's Soviet SA-7 anti-aircraft missiles.[8]

The weapons began arriving in Pakistan within a month after the Soviet invasion. But the most important link in the arms pipeline still had to be constructed. The CIA could not set up a weapons dealership in some Pakistani garrison and openly dole out guns and ammunition to the Afghan rebels. It needed a front.

Carter's national security adviser, Zbigniew Brzezinski, flew to Islamabad in January. Islamabad is an artificial city constructed to serve as Pakistan's new capital. Its government center looks like a gigantic international airplane terminal, a soulless pile of stressed concrete. Brzezinski came directly from his military jet to meet with the CIA's chief of station, who was working out of temporary quarters after the burning of the American embassy. The two then sat down with Zia's intelligence director, General Aktar Abdul Rehman. The message from the White House was simple. U.S. military and economic aid would be restored to Pakistan if Zia would help ship the CIA's weapons to the Afghan resistance. "When Zia heard that, it was 'all the way with CIA,' " said a Pakistani familiar with the meeting.[9] After some haggling—the dictator pointedly dismissed Carter's initial offer as "peanuts"—the U.S. agreed to give Zia $3.2 billion, half in cash, half in high-tech weapons, over the next six years. The deal transformed Pakistan from an international pariah to the third-largest recipient of American foreign aid, after Israel and Egypt.

Zia agreed to provide the vital connection in the CIA's pipeline. But he imposed a strict condition. He demanded that once the weapons shipments reached Pakistan, they would be under Pakistan's control—specifically, the control of Zia's military intelligence unit, the Inter-Services Intelligence directorate (ISI), a kind of combination CIA, FBI and secret police.

The CIA agreed quickly to Zia's terms. It had no alternative but to consign its arms shipments to Zia's spies. An "absurdly small" number of American intelligence personnel oversaw the weapons deliveries on the most crucial leg of their journey, according to Senator Gordon Hum-

phrey, a New Hampshire Republican who was among the most avid
supporters of the *mujaheddin* in Congress. Over the years, the head of
the ISI—first General Rehman, then General Hamid Gul—met regularly
with the CIA station chief to discuss logistics and tactics. But the ISI
was in control. It distributed the weapons to the political leadership of
the Afghan guerrillas. It decided which factions in the resistance received
which weapons, and in what quantities.

There were seven separate major political parties among the rebels.
Though their American benefactors kept referring to the *mujaheddin* as
The Resistance or The Alliance, as if they were a single fighting force,
the rebels were united only in their hatred of the Soviets. The leaders of
the seven parties depised one another. Their internal politics were a
minefield of religious, political and personal rivalries. Their alliance was
mythical. Syed Ahmed Jhan, a *mujaheddin* field commander, said the
seven headmen had only one thing in common: "They all want to be the
king of Afghanistan."[10]

The Pakistani intelligence chiefs who doled out the CIA's guns and
money favored the four factions they deemed most effective in the battlefield. Those factions also were the most politically extreme, religiously
fundamentalist and anti-Western of the groups, the factions also receiving
support from their Muslim brothers in Iran and Libya. In particular, the
ISI favored the most radical of the *mujaheddin* leaders—a gaunt man
with a foot-long black beard named Gulbuddin Hekmatyar.

Hekmatyar received more than half a billion dollars' worth of the
CIA's weaponry over the years, a heavily disproportionate share, despite
his well-earned reputation as a brutal zealot. A man who stood for almost
everything the West despises became the biggest beneficiary of the CIA's
arms shipments.

The head of the *Hizb-i-Islami*, or Islamic Party, Hekmatyar rose to
power as a student leader in Kabul before the Soviet invasion. He deeply
admired Khomeini and his Islamic revolution in Iran. His followers first
gained attention by throwing acid in the faces of women who refused to
wear the veil. CIA and State Department officials I have spoken with
call him "scary," "vicious," "a fascist," "definite dictatorship material." A democrat he is not. If Hekmatyar becomes the king of Afghanistan, he will ascend upon the bodies of countrymen he has killed with
the CIA's weapons. Hekmatyar's guerrillas kidnapped and assassinated
hundreds of rival rebels over the years. He and his men habitually murdered their prisoners and mutilated the corpses. He hijacked shipments
of weapons destined for battle. He stole truckloads of food and medicine
at gunpoint. He received money and weapons from Libya's Qaddafi. He
hates the United States almost as much as he hates the Soviets. His

followers screamed "Death to America!" along with "Death to the Soviet Union!" at his political rallies in Peshawar, where the rebels maintain their political headquarters in exile.[11]

Peshawar has long been a city of murderous intrigue. I spent much of the fall of 1987 in the venerable frontier town near the foot of the Khyber Pass, preparing to go into Afghanistan with the *mujaheddin*, talking with Afghans, Americans and Pakistanis caught up in the war. Though Peshawar's center was laid out in an orderly grid imposed by the British conquerors of the last century, its streets dissolved into dusty tangles of back alleys where sellers of rubies, radishes, hashish, sheep's heads, spices, stilettoes and pomegranates prospered. Turbaned Afghans daubed with *kohl*, an Asiatic eyeshadow of powdered antimony, walked the rough roads holding hands and carrying Kalashnikovs. Car bombs set by rival rebel factions and Soviet-trained infiltrators blew up with terrible regularity. Intelligence operatives posed as free-lance reporters and freelancers posed as secret agents. Peshawar is the last outpost of law in the land, for from its outskirts west to the Afghan border the power of the state ceases and tribal codes rule where the paved road ends.

It was in Peshawar, a natural haven for spies, smugglers and thieves, that the CIA lost control of the Afghan operation. Nobody from the Agency saw that the arms pipeline had a deep flaw built into it, a flaw with a high cost for the American covert operators and the Afghan foot soldiers.

The CIA's pipeline leaked. It leaked badly. It spilled huge quantities of weapons all over one of the world's most anarchic areas. First the Pakistani armed forces took what they wanted from the weapons shipments. Then corrupt Afghan guerrilla leaders stole and sold hundreds of millions of dollars' worth of anti-aircraft guns, missiles, rocket-propelled grenades, AK-47 automatic rifles, ammunition and mines from the CIA's arsenal. Some of the weapons fell into the hands of criminal gangs, heroin kingpins and the most radical faction of the Iranian military. Others were held out of battle by leaders such as Hekmatyar, stockpiled for the struggle for Afghanistan that would begin the day the Soviets left.

"There are many temptations in Peshawar," said Gulam Ahmed, a rebel commander inside Afghanistan. "There are not too many honest people to do the political jobs honestly. A lot of people are putting a lot of money in their pockets."[12]

The *mujaheddin* leaders sold some of the CIA's weapons in the arms bazaars of Pakistan. The weaponry was sold and resold all over the nation. Criminal syndicates in Pakistan's cities armed themselves with guns once destined for the Afghan battlefield. Life in small villages was punctuated with fire from the CIA's automatic rifles and rocket-propelled grenades. "There's been a tremendous proliferation of weapons all over the coun-

tryside," a State Department official in Peshawar observed. "Every shep-
herd boy guarding his flock has got an AK-47."[13]

At least a dozen of the CIA's deadly Stinger anti-aircraft missiles
wound up in the hands of Iran's Revolutionary Guards. The Iranians
obtained the Stingers from one of the most prominent guerrilla groups,
led by a hard-liner with a hennaed beard named Yunis Khalis. Khalis
maintained that the Iranians stole the Stingers in an ambush near the
Iranian border. Skeptics in the American embassy in Islamabad said
Khalis' men sold them. Whatever the true story, close ties exist between
the fundamentalist factions of the *mujaheddin* and their Islamic brethren
in Iran. Many shared a vision of Khomeini as a hero, not the dangerous
fanatic the West saw him to be. On October 8, 1987, Revolutionary
Guards on an Iranian gunboat fired one of those Stingers at American
helicopters patrolling the Persian Gulf. American weapons, shipped
abroad by the CIA, were aimed back at American soldiers.

"It was assumed that some Stingers might fall into the wrong
hands," the U.S. ambassador in Islamabad, Arnold L. Raphel, told me
the week after the incident. "This was taken into account." The United
States had calculated the danger of shipping the Stingers and then shut
its eyes.

"Sure, there's leakage," the ambassador acknowledged. "If a commander has plenty of weapons, and he needs money—well, he's going
to be pragmatic about it. Not much we can do or say about that."[14]

No Americans died in the Stinger episode in the Gulf. But death
came to America from the holy war. It came in the form of heroin. Guns,
drugs and money are interchangeable commodities for the *mujaheddin*.
The rebels make a great deal of money growing and dealing in opium,
the raw material from which heroin is refined. *Mujaheddin* commanders
inside Afghanistan personally control huge fields of opium poppies, some
stretching for miles across the country's southern plains. According to
State Department officials and U.S. Drug Enforcement Administration
agents in Pakistan, lands controlled by the rebels produce a harvest of
as much as four million pounds of opium a year. Missiles and mortars
that make their way into Afghanistan travel on trucks and mules the CIA
bought for the guerrillas. The trucks and mules often carry opium on the
return trip to Pakistan. There, in laboratories along the border, the opium
is refined into heroin. The heroin flows around the world.

"I don't doubt that the *mujaheddin* carry dope across the border,"
said a State Department official in Islamabad charged with combating the
drug trade. "We talk to the commanders about it. But they say, 'I need
those people—I can't alienate them.' We've been terrified all along of
discovering a really big drug conspiracy among the *mujaheddin*."[15]

American drug-enforcement agents in Pakistan said the *mujaheddin* sold automatic weapons, rocket-propelled grenades and even anti-aircraft guns diverted from the CIA supply line to rebel commanders who grow opium and heroin traffickers who buy the opium. "Every doper down country has got RPGs and AK-47s," a DEA agent in Islamabad said. "I mean, dope peddlers anywhere in the world are going to have guns, but these guys are armed to the teeth. . . . Where do you think those weapons come from? Allah? There's no question that a lot of these guns are coming from our friends."[16]

Very little heroin was refined in Pakistan before the *jihad* began in 1979. By 1989, Afghanistan and Pakistan produced and transshipped as much heroin as the rest of the world combined. Between one-third and one-half of the heroin used annually by American addicts—roughly three tons of the drug, worth billions of dollars—came from opium grown on land in the hands of the *mujaheddin*.[17]

Finally, the Pakistani armed forces under General Zia saw it as their right to take weapons and ammunition from the CIA's shipments. "The Pakistanis were siphoning off a reasonable amount of the aid we sent," said Congressman George E. Brown, Jr., a California Democrat who served on the House intelligence committee from 1985 to 1987. The CIA condoned the thefts as a kind of a commission. "It's a contrived way for us to give more [military] assistance to Pakistan," said Senator Dennis DeConcini, an Arizona Democrat serving on the Senate intelligence committee.[18]

But the corruption of the CIA program was primarily the work of the political leadership of the Afghan resistance. These men are politicians first and foremost, more interested in personal power than in the danger of the battlefield. While their troops eked out hard lives in Afghanistan's mountains and deserts, the guerrillas' political leaders maintained fine villas in Peshawar and fleets of vehicles at their command. The CIA kept silent as the Afghan politicos converted the Agency's weapons into cash.

"In a clandestine operation of this sort, you must be prepared for these kinds of corruptions, diversions and losses," said General Kemal Matinuddin, a retired Pakistani Army general who runs the Institute of Strategic Studies, Pakistan's leading military think tank, a campus carved out of a hillside on the outskirts of Islamabad. "It is unwise for the U.S. to feel that whatever they send is going to be received. There are so many agents in between, so many people who can make money along the line. Between the weapons that have been sold to criminal elements and the weapons being stockpiled for a rainy day, the men who handle these weapons have taken advantage of an opportunity given to them."[19]

Estimates of the thefts and diversions of the CIA's arms shipments, made by intelligence officials and members of Congress receiving intelligence data, range from $600 million worth of weapons to $1 billion or more. The most conservative estimate of the losses came from the CIA. Agency analysts told members of the congressional intelligence committees in 1986 that at least 20 percent of the weapons shipped to the Afghan resistance were siphoned from the pipeline. Another study, conducted by the National Security Agency, estimated that 30 percent of the CIA's weapons were stolen and sold. The NSA's estimate matched the educated guesses of several intelligence professionals. It placed the losses over time at roughly $900 million. State Department officials and members of Congress I interviewed said the losses could be 50 percent or higher. By any measure, the cost of the weapons stolen from the Afghan effort far exceeded the $350 million Congress appropriated for the Nicaraguan contras in the 1980's.[20]

Such losses are normal in a covert operation, or so say men who have spent their lives in the CIA. "You have to be willing to accept that kind of attrition in a covert operation of this nature," said William Colby, the former CIA director, who oversaw the arming of CIA-backed militias in Laos during the Vietnam War. "A 20 percent attrition is not all that bad."[21]

Stansfield Turner, the CIA director who began the Afghan operation, said he'd be amazed if only a quarter or a third of the CIA's weapons failed to reach their destination. "I wouldn't figure it would be a 20- to 30-percent loss," said Turner. "You're not going to get arms through Peshawar without a lot of graft. It is not a clean, neat operation. Weapons are going to fall into the wrong hands. The Pakistanis are going to take something. The various Afghan factions are going to take their share. . . . If we only got 20 percent *through*, I wouldn't be surprised.

"But you've got to keep your eyes open," he said. "You've got to ask yourself if the cost of Stingers going astray, if the cost of what's being stolen, is more than it's worth. You have to ask yourself: 'Am I being taken beyond all reason?' "[22]

American officials in Pakistan knew about the thefts, but could do little to stop them. A State Department official in Islamabad said he was resigned to the losses. "If 50 percent of everything we send gets through, it's a miracle," he said. "But that's life in this part of the world." The members of the congressional intelligence committees accepted the thefts as well. "Can you sign off on those kind of losses?" Senator DeConcini said. "I guess this country has said yes."[23]

The CIA knew the risks of running guns into an ungoverned war zone seething with religious fervor, a land where opium poppies swayed in the breeze and the rule of law was a slender reed. The Agency knew the most powerful of the rebel groups were openly anti-American and sought to impose a rigidly Islamic regime in Afghanistan. The Agency knew the guerrillas were neither parliamentarians nor models of rectitude.

The thievery, the fanaticism, the drug-running—these were costs of doing business in the covert world.

What mattered to the CIA was that the *mujaheddin* were more than willing to fight and die in their war against the Soviets. The Afghans have been fighting such battles for many centuries. Its warlords and tribesmen lived in one of the last untamed lands on earth. They accepted no laws save those of Allah and brute force. Their prowess as warriors was legendary.

In November 1987 I left Peshawar and traveled with a band of *mujaheddin* over the border into Afghanistan. We traversed a mountain ridge high above the Kunar River valley in northeastern Afghanistan and made camp near a ghost town named Narang, one of the untold Afghan villages destroyed in the *jihad*. Artillery screamed across the sky, a constant aimless shelling from enemy positions down in the valley.

For days men from three of the seven guerrilla groups filed down steep trails to the camp, leading caravans of skinny mules hauling missiles and mortars. They stored the weaponry in caves carved into the mountainside. They slept in mud hovels and under the stars. A new phase of the war was beginning, or so the political leaders of the resistance had said in Peshawar. No more would the rebels fight in small hit-and-run operations against the Red Army. They would band together and make war as one. They planned to attack six outposts along the Kunar River, six strongholds of the infidels. The first major Soviet offensive of the war had taken place in this once-fertile valley in February 1980. Many of the *mujaheddin* gathered near Narang once lived along the Kunar, and lost their homes and their families. The aqueducts that sent water flowing to their fields had been destroyed, and the fields lay barren below us. As they prepared for battle, they sipped tea and told stories of those first days of the war.

"The Russians bombed our village and killed our children," said Mahmoud Rahman, who'd been a shopkeeper before the invasion. "I lost my son and my brother. I gathered up the rest of my family and we walked into Pakistan. All the time we were under helicopter attack. . . .

"Always I am thinking about my village and my gardens," he said, gazing into a campfire. "We had land, we had woods, we had good fruit and good water. I grew walnuts, grapes, apples, peaches and tangerines."

Everyone had a litany of loss to recite. "Every Afghan has lost someone in their family—a mother, brother, cousin, father," said a commander named Zamrey, who like many Afghans has only one name. "They killed our children, our women, our old people. They destroyed our villages, our gardens, our mosques."

The talk ceased as the call to prayer rose within the camp and echoed off the mountains. For the fifth time that day, in accordance with the laws of Islam, the men laid down their automatic rifles and their ancient muskets. The holy warriors praised God and prayed for victory.

I had a copy of the Koran with me, and read through it by flashlight that night. The Koran is the word of Allah as heard by the prophet Mohammed. The story of the *mujaheddin* was written there: "How many gardens, how many fountains they left behind them! Cornfields, and noble palaces, and good things in which they took delight. All this they left. . . .

"You shall be called upon to fight a mighty nation," their God told them. "Make war on the leaders of unbelief. . . ."

"They were the first to attack you. Do you fear them? . . ."

"Make war on them. . . . Whether unarmed or well-equipped, march on and fight for the cause of Allah."[24]

Late that night, the guerrillas' disorganized offensive began with mortar and artillery fire. Foot soldiers with automatic rifles waited throughout the next day for their marching orders. No directives came. They slept that night on the hard ground. Their political leaders, who organized this set-piece battle, spent the night in a fort inside Pakistan, sleeping on cushions and gold-embroidered pillows.

The *mujaheddin* waited and complained bitterly about promised arms and ammunition that never arrived. They said the flood of weaponry sent out by the CIA was reduced to a trickle in Afghanistan. "There are never enough weapons," Zamrey said as he cradled his rifle. "We know the United States is helping us, the weapons coming from the American people. But it is not enough." He picked up a handful of stones, symbolizing weapons, to illustrate his point. "This amount should be distributed." He took a few of the stones in his other hand. "This is what we receive. The Pakistanis are stealing the best of them, and keeping some. In Peshawar they are stealing, too."

A hubbub arose from the bombed-out farmhouse that served as a headquarters in the mountain encampment. Three ragged Afghan army soldiers had defected and walked into the *mujaheddin* camp. Tens of thousands of Afghan army soldiers had done the same over the years. All three said they had been press-ganged into service, seized from their fields and villages and taken to battlefronts far from home.

"There are no posts of the government and no Russians in my area. We were free," said one of the defectors, Mahmoud, who came from a remote sector of Helmand province in southern Afghanistan. "Then one day the soldiers come and take us away to here." The Afghan army officers told him that the *mujaheddin* were tools of foreign infidels and that it was his patriotic duty to fight them. "The officers told us you must defend your country. The *mujaheddin* are supported by the Chinese, U.S., European people, they are fighting with foreign money. We don't believe it. If we did we wouldn't surrender to the *mujaheddin*." This was a sore point with the rebels. They did not want their fellow Afghans to see them as instruments of foreign powers. So they maintained the fiction that they received no outside aid.

At sunrise the next day, Asraf Khan crouched on the mountainside cleaning his antique Enfield rifle. He was seventy, or so he thought, his rifle nearly as old, his gray beard a storm cloud gathered around his face. With him were two of his sons, Mohammed Yunis, thirty, and Salahuddin, thirteen, both armed with automatic rifles.

"I want to be killed for Afghanistan," Asraf Khan said. "I want to be martyred. I will fight until the last moment of my life. I have trained my sons to fight until their last moment."

Salahuddin did not remember when the *jihad* started, but he knew why. "The Russians came to finish our religion and finish our people," he said. "They said they came to help the Afghan people, but they came to kill us."

Everywhere in the camp were boys too young to marry but old enough to fight and die. Sharim was eighteen. He had been fighting for six years. He lost his father, his friends and his childhood to the war. "Before my father was martyred, he told me never to surrender," Sharim said. "I will fight until the last of my soul, until my death."

Mohammed Ali was fourteen. He had been fighting since he was twelve. "My father and one of my brothers were martyred down there," he said, gesturing to the Kunar River valley. "I was with my brother when he died. . . . Our home was down there. We had sheep and goats. I took care of them. Now my home is destroyed and the sheep and goats are gone." I asked him what he wanted to do when he grew up. He wondered if he would. "I don't know about my life," he said. "I can't predict it. Maybe I will die and become a martyr. Maybe that is best."

An anti-aircraft gun erupted and Mohammed Ali looked into the blinding sun. The MiGs had come again.

Many Afghans first became acquainted with modern technology when Soviet MiG jet bombers and Hind helicopter gunships came out of the sky trying to kill them. Soviet air power ruled the war for nearly seven years.

Then the Stingers started arriving from the CIA pipeline in late 1986. The Agency hired retired U.S. military men and sent them to the guerrillas' camps in Pakistan to teach the tribesmen how to use the Stinger, which finds its targets with a homing sensor that locks on to the heat of an aircraft's engines. The shoulder-carried missiles were so effective that Soviet helicopters all but stopped flying in daylight, and Soviet bombers flew at higher altitudes, sacrificing accuracy.

But it takes some training to use the Stinger. The man trying to draw a bead on one of four silvery MiGs overhead had none. Wali Khan was

proud that he had been entrusted with the valued weapon. Now he staggered on the mountain ridge, $50,000 worth of firepower bouncing in
his arms. The ground shook as a MiG dropped a 500-pound bomb near
a *mujaheddin* mortar position 200 yards away. This was the fourth MiG
bombing run he'd faced in two days, his fourth clear shot. He fired. The
Stinger soared into the air. It left a long white squiggle in the blue sky
as it disappeared harmlessly.

"We wanted to scare them," he said with false bravado. "They
won't be back."

Three days later, the *mujaheddin* offensive, planned as a crucial two-
week assault, collapsed. It turned out that each of the three groups had
its own battle plan, and none of them worked. The recoilless rifles, the
surface-to-surface missile launchers, the mortars—all hauled here to this
mountainside at great expense and danger—were useless. The *mujaheddin's* political leaders had hoarded their ammunition and held it out of
battle. Rival guerrillas were killing one another that same month in dis-
putes over the precious armaments. While murderous fights broke out
over weapons caches, and warring guerrilla factions attacked one another's strongholds with rocket-propelled grenades, this offensive failed for
want of ammunition. The rebels retreated as the MiGs returned and blasted
their abandoned camp into dust. They had lost nineteen men and gained
no ground.

This was the way of the war. The bravery of the *mujaheddin* in the
face of the Soviet army was undeniable. The morality of their struggle
against the invaders was understood. The political chaos and corruption
of their leadership was a cost the CIA was willing to pay.

Washington was willing to pay almost any price to win the *jihad*.
The Congress in particular came to love the war in Afghanistan. It pumped
more money into the Afghan war than the CIA wanted, or could spend
wisely. For every dollar the CIA requested over the years, the Congress
gave it two. For many conservatives, any war in which American arms
could kill Soviet soldiers was a godsend. For many liberals, the romance
and bravery of the Afghan rebels proved compelling, and their support
for the war provided political protection from charges of insufficient
anticommunism.[25]

The near-unanimous enthusiasm for the war was in marked contrast
to the struggle over the other great anticommunist cause of the Reagan
administration—the Nicaraguan contras. "That was the 'bad war,' " said
a congressman who served on the House intelligence committee, his
fingers drawing quotation marks in the air. "Afghanistan was the 'good
war.' "[26]

"It was a holy war from the first day," said Congressman Charles
Wilson, a Texas Democrat who became the *mujaheddin's* best friend in

Washington. "Oh, you had some liberals who were personally opposed to killing people, including Russians," he said. "But this war—even liberals on the wrong side of the contra issue got behind it."[27]

Charlie Wilson is a long tall Texan with an appetite for Texan pleasures. He kept a collection of souvenirs of the Afghan war in his office on Capitol Hill. A color picture of him riding a white horse with *mujaheddin* equestrians was prominently displayed. A Stinger missile launcher hung over the doorway to his office. A handcarved plaque leaning on his desk read "Be Prepared: THINK WAR." I met Wilson leading a congressional delegation on a tour of Darra, a Pakistani town near the Afghan border where all manner of guns and drugs—most prominently automatic rifles and balls of opium the size of boulders—are sold openly in shops along the town's single street. When I saw the congressman in Darra, he was cradling a mean-looking longarm from one of Darra's many weapons dealers on his shoulder, pointing the muzzle skyward and firing shots into the air.

"It's a total gun culture," he said happily. "It's like Abilene in the 1870's." The cowtown congressman felt right at home on the Afghan frontier.

Wilson campaigned tirelessly for more money and better weapons for the *mujaheddin*. "I viewed this operation as an opportunity to defeat the Soviets in the battlefield," he said when we talked in Washington in 1987. "I looked at it this way," Wilson said. "We lost 58,000 men in Vietnam. The Russians have lost maybe 25,000 in Afghanistan. I figure they owe us 33,000 dead."[28]

He said CIA director William Casey agreed wholeheartedly. "Casey viewed this as a possible profound setback to the Soviets—politically supportable in the U.S., with a minimum of financial commitment and political risk—and as an absolutely morally right thing," Wilson said.

In an unprecedented struggle behind closed doors, Congress kept increasing the CIA's budget requests for the Afghan operation. In late 1983 Wilson led an effort to double the $40 million appropriation for arms to Afghanistan hidden in the Pentagon's black budget—and won. But some dissent over the Afghan operation arose within the CIA early in the Reagan administration. Agency analysts could not ignore the facts that "the pipeline was full, and we had intelligence reports of corruption, of weapons being sold off by the *mujaheddin*," as the congressman on the House intelligence committee told me.

In 1984 and 1985 the internal battle over the Afghan operation grew bitter. One faction within the intelligence committee did not believe that the rebels could win a military victory over the Soviets and favored keeping the annual aid at less than $100 million. This group was led by the CIA's deputy director, John McMahon, a CIA veteran of thirty-two years. McMahon wanted to keep the operation as "deniable" as possible—using only communist-bloc weapons, keeping sophisticated American armaments out of the battle, controlling the size and scope of the arms shipments. McMahon was a pro, and more than anyone else in Casey's CIA, he kept the Agency honest. But his position on the Afghan war destroyed his career.

"He was beaten up pretty badly by an element that was accusing him of being soft on the issue," said Thomas Twetten, now the CIA's associate deputy director for operations. "There was a big letter campaign that had been mounted in 1985 against John McMahon personally that really disturbed him. This was a public campaign, thousands of letters to Congressmen attacking John McMahon for being soft on Communism and not letting the 'muj' push back the Russians. It was nasty stuff." The attacks were the primary reason McMahon left the CIA in March 1986.[29]

The rival faction won battle after battle. The "bleeders," as they came to be known, thought the rebels could defeat the Soviets in the battlefield, if only the United States gave them the weaponry to win. They wanted to make the Soviets pay the highest possible price for their invasion—in blood, in human lives. In 1984, conservatives in the Congress assailed the CIA program as weak and ineffective. "From 1980 to 1984 the CIA was a little gun-shy," Congressman Wilson said. "They had serious reservations. They didn't want to step in another pile of shit. But in '83, '84, we were doubling their requests, insisting that they send anti-aircraft missiles. . . . And we won. McMahon's departure was the key to the victory."

The bleeders achieved their first victory of sorts in October 1984. They pressured the CIA to buy bigger and better weapons for the *mujaheddin* to shoot down Soviet aircraft. The CIA succumbed to the pressure and withdrew $50 million from a Swiss bank account to buy forty Oerlikon anti-aircraft cannons. The bulky Swiss guns were complicated and expensive weapons, not ideal for hauling up a mountainside or lugging through a desert. The Oerlikons never saw much action in Afghanistan. Of the forty the CIA purchased, only eleven made it to the battlefield. Somewhere along the way twenty-nine of them, worth $36.25 million, disappeared.[30]

By 1985, the bleeders were in control of the Afghan operation. Early that year, they tripled the CIA's budget request for the Afghan program to $250 million. The sum represented more than 75 percent of the CIA's spending for all covert operations that year. Then, in April 1985, President Reagan declared himself a bleeder. He signed a secret order, National Security Decision Directive 166, that called for the CIA to drive the Soviets from Afghanistan "by all means available." In October, the

White House reached into a pocket of the black budget, a $2 billion line item in the Air Force budget for "special activities." The secret order reprogrammed $200 million in intelligence funds, channeling the money into the Afghan battle. The CIA now was spending close to half a billion dollars a year on the holy war.

Nearly six years after the Soviet invasion, the United States finally had an official Afghan policy. The bleeders had won. In spirit, and to a large degree in substance, American policy in Afghanistan was Charlie Wilson's policy: revenge for Vietnam.

The *mujaheddin* needed another source of money beyond the black budget of the United States and the oil revenues of the Arab nations. They had to pay exorbitant fees to mule drivers and truckers hauling supplies inside Afghanistan. Bribery also is a regular cost of doing business in Afghan life. Sometimes, the rebels could buy guns and ammunition from corrupt Afghan army troops. What they needed was cash, Afghan currency, and lots of it. So the CIA counterfeited at least $20 million of it. Afghanistan is in a part of the world where paper money almost always is dirty, battered and torn. Yet the rebel commanders I met in Afghanistan all had big wads of Afghan bills, invariably crisp, clean and in mint condition. The counterfeiting program appeared to be highly successful.

Still the CIA's aid was never enough. No matter how much money the Congress and the CIA poured into the war, the vision of a *mujaheddin* military victory proved elusive.

CIA director Casey looked abroad for new sources of covert cash. He had been a stellar fund-raiser for the Republican party in the 1970's. He knew how to twist a donor's arm when he had to. He saw foreign governments as a rich source of funds for CIA operations. He used them to create a secret CIA treasury that could be hidden from Congress. Casey's CIA formed partnerships with China, Saudi Arabia and Iran. Those nations sent more than $750 million in guns, money and material aid into the Afghan arms pipeline. The United States sold them billions of dollars in weapons and gave them tens of millions more to encourage their silent support.

The CIA director turned first to the royal family of Saudi Arabia. During Casey's tenure, the CIA and the Saudis discovered that where their interests coincided, they could work together. "There's no reason not to do that," said Casey's predecessor at the CIA, Stansfield Turner. "It's nice to get some money from a rich uncle. If you have joint interests with another country, you may want to collaborate. Where Casey misled everybody is that he didn't tell Congress what was going on."[31]

The U.S.-Saudi relationship was cemented with American weapons. In October 1981, the United States sold the Saudis five AWACS surveillance planes, a state-of-the-art intelligence-gathering instrument, along with a large package of weaponry. The price was $8.5 billion. The sale was hotly contested in the U.S. Senate, which must approve foreign military sales of that size. Heading up one of the White House teams seeking the Senate's approval was Air Force Major General Richard Secord, then a deputy assistant secretary of defense with years of experience selling American weapons to foreign countries. A Marine major newly appointed to the National Security Council staff, an indefatigable worker named Oliver North, was part of the sales team prodding the senators. Under intense pressure from the White House, the Senate approved the sale, 52 to 48. Saudi Arabia was grateful to the Reagan administration, and Casey capitalized on their gratitude. After the AWACS planes were delivered, Casey began urging Saudi Arabia's royal family to work with the CIA to finance the Afghan resistance. The Saudis, proficient practitioners of checkbook diplomacy, were willing and able.

In November 1981, when Saudi Arabia's King Fahd was still crown prince, he told an American friend, a Palestinian-born businessman named Sam Bamieh, about a tacit understanding in the AWACS sale. Bamieh described the conversation in sworn testimony before a House Foreign Affairs subcommittee in July 1987. In exchange for the AWACS, Bamieh testified, the Saudis committed themselves to contribute money to the CIA's biggest covert actions. In the world of secret diplomacy, this was a quid pro quo between sovereign nations. No one would call it a kickback.

The CIA set up a joint U.S.-Saudi bank account in Switzerland for the benefit of the Afghan resistance. Like a donor to a matching fund in a telethon, Saudi Arabia contributed sums equal to the CIA's annual allotment to the resistance, dollar for dollar. In early 1984, Casey personally persuaded Fahd and his ambassador to the United States, Prince Bandar bin Sultan, to help pay for the Nicaraguan contras' war as well. Once the arrangement for Saudi funding for the contras was set and the joint Swiss bank account for the Afghans opened, President Reagan used special emergency powers to bypass bitter congressional opposition and send 400 Stinger missiles to the Saudis. In 1984 and 1985, the Saudi government funneled more than half a billion dollars to CIA bank accounts in Switzerland and the Cayman Islands. Between $500 million and $525 million was invested in the Afghan resistance. At least $32 million was earmarked for the contras and hidden from Congress. The money for the two causes was commingled in a single CIA account in Switzerland. When the Iran-contra inquiry blew the lid off this secret account, congressional investigators suspected that Casey had taken money appropriated for the Afghans and transferred it to the contras. Their suspicions were never proven or disproven.[32]

Casey also had an unlikely pact with the world's largest communist nation: China. The American intelligence relationship with China dated back to 1971, when Henry Kissinger met in secret with Premier Chou Enlai. The Chinese established formal diplomatic ties with the United States in 1979, and the two nations began sharing secret intelligence about the Soviets. When Khomeini came to power in Iran late that year, the U.S. had to abandon its two sophisticated electronic eavesdropping stations in northern Iran used to spy on the Soviets. The Chinese quickly allowed the U.S. to set up two new listening posts in the isolated towns of Korla and Qitai, some 600 miles from the common border of China, the Soviet Union and Afghanistan.

In May 1980, the Chinese Defense Minister, Geng Biao, visited Washington and agreed to work with the CIA to coordinate shipments of Chinese-made weapons to the Afghans. For two years the CIA paid the Chinese to ship the weapons, mostly automatic rifles, over the Kandahar pass from western China into Pakistan. In January 1983, Casey stepped up the quantity and the firepower of the Chinese arms shipments. The CIA began buying anti-aircraft guns, missiles, bazookas and mortars directly from the Chinese and flying them into Pakistan. The pact with China was unaffected by the fact that the Chinese government sold Iran $1.6 billion worth of jets, tanks, heavy artillery, rocket launchers and surface-to-air missiles in 1985. Nor did the 1989 massacre of hundreds, perhaps thousands, of Chinese dissenters alter the intelligence relationship. "The Chinese have been the one constant factor throughout the Afghan operation," said a State Department official.[33]

The Chinese-made, CIA-supplied weapons were a mainstay of the Afghan rebels' arsenal. I saw many on my trip inside Afghanistan. One was a 1950's-vintage 75-millimeter recoilless rifle. It was unusual in one respect: the Chinese armed forces usually do not adorn their weapons with U.S. government tags, complete with shipping dates and English-language identification. The weapon was as clear a symbol of a secret operation as one is likely to find.

The constitutionally dubious tactic of tapping foreign governments for secret funds gained currency early in Reagan's second term. The search for ways to keep the administration's favorite freedom fighters financed sparked some innovative thinking.

In 1985 Casey received a highly intriguing proposition from GeoMiliTech Consultants Corp., a Washington arms brokerage secretly shipping weapons to the contras. GeoMiliTech was run by Barbara Studley, a former Miami radio talk show host with platinum-blond hair, three-inch fingernails and fervent beliefs. "Barbara . . . believes that she had a commission from God to form this company," said Robert Schweitzer, a retired Army general who had been Oliver North's immediate superior on the National Security Council staff. Schweitzer had been fired from the NSC in 1982 for giving a hellfire-and-brimstone speech in public about an imminent Soviet invasion of Poland and eastern Europe. He later became GeoMiliTech's executive vice president.[34]

GeoMiliTech was incorporated as GMT Corp. Schweitzer said the name came to Studley after she had "a vision from God. . . . GMT stood for God's Mighty Team." Schweitzer was introduced to Studley by John Singlaub, a retired Army general who headed the World Anti-Communist League and served as a GMT consultant. The three met at a wreath-laying ceremony at the Tomb of the Unknown Soldier held by the veterans of the Bay of Pigs.[35]

GeoMiliTech wanted to become a central clearinghouse for all of the CIA's weapons purchases. The company was competing with a bevy of international arms dealers who sold weapons to the CIA. A principal competitor was Werner Glatt, a former Luftwaffe pilot who owned an enormous farm in Virginia named after the symbol of the Nazi air force: The Black Eagle.[36]

Singlaub brought a written proposal from GeoMiliTech to Casey in late November or early December 1985. It said the CIA should "create a conduit for maintaining a continuous flow of Soviet weapons and technology, to be utilized by the United States in its support of Freedom Fighters in Nicaragua, Afghanistan, Angola, Cambodia, Ethiopia, etc." The proposal went on to explain the beauty of this concept: it needed "neither the consent or awareness of the Department of State or Congress."

It was a self-sustaining, off-the-books source of weapons for CIA missions. It was a model for the network of private enterprise and covert weapons deals that unraveled in the Iran-contra affair.

GeoMiliTech's three-way deal was to work like this:

The government of China had large stockpiles of Soviet-style weapons. China wanted to upgrade its military forces and equipment.

The government of Israel wanted to sell modern weaponry to China. Israel's economy was cash-poor. It could not take long-term credit or barter arrangements.

Enter the CIA. The Agency would arrange for Israel to receive millions of dollars in credit toward the purchase of exotic military technology from the United States. Israel, in turn, would sell weaponry of equivalent value to China. China then would export an equal amount of Soviet-style weapons to a dummy corporation set up by the CIA and GeoMiliTech. The dummy corporation then would turn over the weapons to the CIA. Israel and China would be aware only of their own roles— never knowing they were helping to finance a secret CIA arsenal.

GeoMiliTech's idea was ingenious. But the concept of a CIA armory backed by secret funds and hidden from Congress was utterly unconstitutional. "It is totally outside the system of government that we live by and must live by," said Reagan's Secretary of State, George Shultz. "You cannot spend funds that the Congress doesn't either authorize you to obtain or appropriate. That is what the Constitution says, and we have to stick to it."[37]

The Constitution wasn't much on the minds of the men smuggling arms to the Afghans and the contras. Casey studied the proposition and talked it over with Oliver North in the first week of December 1985. He gave North a copy of the GeoMiliTech proposal. The Marine locked it in the safe in his National Security Council office. That same week North, for the first time, mentioned the idea of diverting money from the arms sales to Iran in a conversation with Israeli intelligence officials in New York. The GeoMiliTech paper dovetailed nicely with "a neat idea" that came to North—selling American weapons to Iran and skimming the proceeds to fund the President's secret wars.[38]

Efforts to arm the Afghans are woven throughout the web of America's secret weapons shipments to Iran. The U.S. and Iran had a common concern in Afghanistan. The Afghan *jihad* was a foundation for their covert compact.

Five Americans were being held hostage in Lebanon by terrorists trained and funded by Iran when President Reagan announced his firm resolve against dealing with the enemy on June 30, 1985: "The United States gives terrorists no rewards and no guarantees. We make no concessions. We make no deals." Iran, the president said eight days later, was part of "a confederation of terrorist states . . . a new international version of Murder Incorporated."

On January 17, 1986, President Reagan jotted seven words in his diary: "I agreed to sell TOWs to Iran." TOWs are tube-launched, optically tracked, wire-guided antitank missiles. They are generally regarded as excellent weapons.

Shipping the TOWs to the Iranians was a legal nightmare. Tom Twetten, then the deputy chief of the CIA's Near East division, called Major General Colin Powell in January to set up the transfer of the missiles from the Army to the CIA. Powell then was Defense Secretary Weinberger's chief assistant. Today he is the chairman of the Joint Chiefs of Staff.

Powell and Weinberger were forewarned that the plan was illegal. Glenn Rudd, deputy director of the Defense Security Assistance Agency, told them there was no lawful way to transfer the weapons without notifying Congress. Weinberger took the legal objections to the President. Reagan replied: "Well, the American people will never forgive me if I fail to get these hostages out over this legal question."

The legal question went back to Rudd. He concluded that the only way to handle the transfer was to do it outside the legal system. He told his superiors that the deal had to, in his words, "go black." By going black, the Army could sell the weapons to the CIA secretly. Then the CIA could ship them under a presidential finding, the legal document authorizing a covert action that the President must sign and submit to Congress.

By going black, the deal was kept secret—and the law was flouted. This finding was not going to be revealed to Congress, or so the CIA and the White House intended. As a lawyer for the Iran-contra committees put it, the President's men wanted the finding to "vanish into the black hole of history." Reagan never even saw the crucial document. His national security adviser, John Poindexter, briefed the president on the finding and then signed it himself: "RR per JMP." Thus the President agreed to sell the TOWs to Iran.[39]

On February 25, 1986, North and the CIA's Tom Twetten knocked on a door in the Sheraton Airport hotel in Frankfurt, Germany. Inside the room were Ahmed Kangarlu, the chief weapons procurer for Iranian prime minister Mir Hussein Moussavi, accompanied by two Iranian army colonels. A retired CIA official named George Cave served as translator. The Air Force general turned arms dealer, Richard Secord, and his Iranian-born business partner, Albert Hakim, joined in the negotiations. They told the Iranians they were military intelligence officers; they were mercenaries profiting from a secret foreign policy.

The United States delivered 1,000 TOWs to the Iranians that week. The deal produced $5.5 million in profits for Secord and Hakim, and for North and the contras. No hostages were released. But North reported to the White House and the CIA that an important understanding was reached at the meeting: "the Iranians agreed that if the United States government would provide TOW weapons to Iran, they would, in turn, provide same to the Afghan Mujahideen."[40] Twetten recalled that the Frankfurt deal was more specific: "ten percent of the weapons we delivered to Iran, Iran would pass on" to the Afghans.[41]

In March 1986, George Cave, the retired CIA officer, sent a long cable to CIA director Casey detailing the arms-for-hostages negotiations. Cave told Casey about an enticing idea that came up in the talks: "that we use the profits from these deals and others to fund support for the rebels in Afghanistan. We could do the same with Nicaragua."[42]

On April 4, North dictated a long memorandum for Poindexter to his secretary, Fawn Hall. It laid out the details of his plan to use the profits from the Iran deal for the contras. The memo also spelled out ways in which the United States sought Iran's aid on behalf of the Afghans. "We have told the Iranians," North said, "that we are interested in assistance they may be willing to provide to the Afghan resistance and that we wish to discuss this matter in Tehran. . . . The Iranians will undoubtedly want to discuss additional arms and commercial transactions as 'quids' for accommodating our points on Afghanistan [and] Nicaragua.''

North then proposed talking the Iranians into joining the CIA's pipeline to the Afghan resistance. He listed ''terms of reference'' for the meeting:

> —May be of real value for Iran and U.S. to find ways to cooperate against Moscow in Afghanistan.
> —U.S. can provide . . . lethal aid for Mujahideen.
> —We need to know who you work with, what you already provide, and devise strategy.[43]

On the evening of May 26, North and his old boss, former national security adviser Robert McFarlane, sat down in a suite atop the Independence Hotel in Teheran with a member of the Majlis, the Iranian parliament. The balding, bearded politician was Hossein Najafabadi. He was the head of the foreign relations committee in the Majlis and a close confidant of the powerful speaker of the parliament, Ali Akbar Hashemi Rafsanjani. Najafabadi was cultured, intelligent and politically adept. His English was excellent.

The first meeting of high-ranking representatives of the American and Iranian governments in nearly seven years had an extraordinary agenda: swapping American weapons for American hostages, joining forces against the Soviets, sharing secret intelligence on the Middle East. But the two sides first had to feel each other out, to seek a common ground. ''We were prepared to enter a dialogue to determine where there might be common interests,'' McFarlane reported to Poindexter in a cable from Teheran. ''Afghanistan appeared to be a leading case in point.''[44]

North told Najafabadi that the Americans had come to establish a working relationship with Iran. They had a common enemy in the Soviet Union. ''This is not a deal of weapons for release of the hostages,'' North said. ''It has to do with what we see regarding Soviet intentions in the region.'' Najafabadi listened with interest as the Americans painted a dark picture of the Soviets' plans against the nations of Islam. He told them that Iran was doing its part to support the Afghans' *jihad*.

''There are training camps for *mujaheddin* in Iran,'' Najafabadi told the Americans. ''Weapons and logistics support are provided. We are ready to send troops into Afghanistan. The Russians already complain about Iranian bullets killing Russians.'' He said the Afghans' struggle was at one with the Iranian revolution. ''You see many pictures of Khomeini in the Afghan trenches," Najafabadi told the Americans. "He is their leader."

North asked if Iran would help to provide the *mujaheddin* with some of the TOWs the Americans were shipping to Teheran. "We can cooperate with you in this area," Najafabadi replied.

"We have a famous saying," Najafabadi told North. "Enemy of your enemy is your friend."

Iran, the sworn enemy of America, agreed to become part of the CIA's arms pipeline by shipping American weapons to the Afghan rebels. They actually sent 100 of the TOW missiles to the Afghans, as they had promised—or so the White House believed.[45]

By the summer of 1986, nearly $50 million a month from CIA accounts was buying missiles, mules, machine guns and a military quagmire for the Soviets. The missiles were destroying Soviet tanks and aircraft. The mules carried weapons through Afghanistan's mountains. The machine guns were killing Soviet soldiers. And the quagmire was sapping the Soviet Union's will to fight. The new Soviet leader, Mikhail Gorbachev, described the war as "a bleeding wound." It was Afghanistan that was bleeding, but the import of Gorbachev's statement was obvious. The *jihad* was turning into Russia's Vietnam.

The congressmen who supported the *mujaheddin* most passionately now believed with all their hearts that the rebels could win a military victory over the Soviets. After two years of infighting, the CIA bowed to their strongest wish. The Agency began sending the first of 900 Stinger missile launchers to Afghanistan. The Stingers were sent despite well-founded fears that the devastating weapons would fall into the hands of the Iranians. The Stingers made their impact: they downed as many as 350 Soviet aircraft.

The steady increases in the CIA's spending continued. More and more weapons poured into the pipeline. More than $600 million was spent on the *mujaheddin* in 1987, $700 million in 1988. Gorbachev decided that he'd had enough. The Russians were not losing the war, not by any means. But for years the war had been a bloody stalemate, with the Soviet army securely holding Afghanistan's cities, the guerrillas freely roaming the countryside, and neither force able to dislodge the other. The war was pointless, and the Soviet government's lies to its people about why their boys were in Afghanistan were becoming embarrassingly obvious. Gorbachev had bigger domestic concerns. It was time to declare victory and pull out.

For nearly six years United Nations-sponsored peace talks on Afghanistan had gone on in Geneva, in total secrecy and without result. Now the Soviets were seeking an exit from Afghanistan more graceful than the American departure from Vietnam. They were haunted by that image of desperate men clinging to the struts of the last helicopter leaving Saigon. On February 8, 1988, Gorbachev announced that the Soviets would begin leaving Afghanistan on May 15, and pull out completely in nine months—if the accords were signed by March 15.

The United States scrambled to decide what its position on peace in Afghanistan would be. The diplomatic jockeying went on as the March 15 deadline passed. On April 10, as if to signal the volcanic tensions underneath the veneer of the diplomats' finesse, an explosion destroyed a huge arms cache near Islamabad where tens of millions of dollars of the CIA's weapons were stored. Nearly 100 people were killed and more than 1,000 injured as missiles and mortars from the secret armory shot wildly through the streets.

Four days later, the talks in Geneva suddenly brought forth accords. What had been a dialogue of the deaf now seemed transformed into a triumph of diplomacy. In principle, the accords outlawed "foreign intervention in Afghanistan." In practice, they were a farce.

The Soviets would withdraw their "uniformed forces." But the accords did not bar Moscow from providing the Afghan government with military aid. The Soviets fully intended to do so. The United States said that "if the U.S.S.R. undertakes . . . to provide military assistance to parties in Afghanistan, the United States retains the right . . . to provide such assistance." The United States fully intended to do so. This policy was elegantly entitled "symmetry." The accords meant the Soviets could go, but the war would go on.

On February 10, 1989, as the Soviets hurried to complete their withdrawal, two meetings aimed at shaping Afghanistan's future took place in two foreign capitals.

In Washington, the new President of the United States, George Bush, convened a meeting of the National Security Council to decide whether to continue the CIA's $700-million-a-year weapons shipments. As the day of the Soviet withdrawal approached, Bush decided that the CIA's guns and ammunition would keep flowing to Afghanistan.

In Islamabad, the rebel leaders met at the urging of their American backers. The Supreme Council of the Islamic Alliance of the Afghan Mujaheddin convened a *shura*, a council of elders, to attempt to form the next government of Afghanistan. Veterans of Peshawar politics viewed such gatherings with the utmost cynicism. "So far we have had eight alliances," Gulbuddin Hekmatyar's political spokesman, Nawab Salim, told me. "And they have all fallen apart."[46] The *shura* quickly collapsed into angry babble. The ninth and perhaps final alliance of the *mujaheddin* was an anarchists' convention.

For years, General Matuniddin of Pakistan's Institute for Strategic Studies had watched and worried as the rebels' anger simmered and boiled. "There will be a tremendous struggle for power," he said. "You can see it developing just now—the splits between the seven parties, their factions, and their commanders inside Afghanistan. The Afghans have always fought among themselves, and they have always been armed. But when you talk about Stingers, mortars, recoilless rifles that they have acquired—then the danger of civil war breaking out is greater.

"Many people believe that all the elements are here for another Lebanon," he said. "The *mujaheddin* have been incapable of agreeing on the distribution of weapons and money. How are they going to agree on the future of Afghanistan?"

A handful of Americans who knew Afghanistan and the costs of covert action had deep fears of what would happen to the rebels after the Soviet withdrawal. "You've got chaos," a CIA analyst at the Agency's headquarters said, shaking his head in dismay. "There is no structure, no party, no unity. And now you've got the *mujaheddin* stockpiling weapons. Now they can shoot one another instead of slitting one another's throats."[47]

Arnold Raphel, the U.S. ambassador in Pakistan in 1987 and 1988, foresaw bedlam and bloodshed. "When the Soviets leave, the killing won't stop," he said. "The commanders will take one another out. It'll be a blood bath, and the commanders with the most guns will make the decisions."[48]

On the afternoon of February 15, 1989, the champagne began flowing at CIA headquarters. A rare exultation filled the air. After fifteen years of failure and humiliation, the Agency had won a famous victory. The last Soviet troops had left Afghanistan. The Agency's biggest covert action since the height of the Vietnam war had achieved its goal. The CIA had won its *jihad*.

Ten thousand miles from Washington, on the outskirts of Peshawar, a drunken celebration broke out at the American Club. The club was the only legal bar in the rigidly Islamic town. The American Club barred teetotaling Muslims, but served all manner of expatriates, from diplomats down to the scruffiest freelancers. The club went wild that night. In their boozy exultation, the celebrants placed bets in a pool. They were trying to guess the date that the government of Afghanistan would fall.

So were the more sober analysts back at the CIA. They were sure the Soviet-backed regime would crumble like a sand castle in the surf now that the Soviet army was gone. They were certain the *mujaheddin* would be marching through the streets of Kabul in a matter of months, firing the CIA's weapons in the air in triumph.

They were wrong. The war did not end after the Soviets went home. The *mujaheddin* could not stand and fight as one. They were incapable of forging a common strategy for victory. As the war ground on, it went badly for the rebels. The month after the Soviet withdrawal, exhorted by the CIA and Pakistani military intelligence, they mounted their largest attack of the war, an assault on the city of Jalalabad. The campaign was a disaster. After five months and perhaps 5,000 dead, the rebels gained not an inch of ground. As their assaults faltered and their offensives collapsed, their rage turned inward.

Soon they were firing the CIA's weapons at each other. They killed each other by the hundreds, and their war became a caravan of mayhem and betrayal. The most powerful rebel leaders, who sought to establish an Islamic republic that had little to do with democracy, concentrated on ambushing and killing each other's troops. Hekmatyar's Islamic party, in particular, made war on rival rebel groups. "Hekmatyar is making a play for total power," said Robert G. Neumann, a former U.S. ambassador to Afghanistan. Freedom fighter fought freedom fighter in a bitter struggle over the nation's broken remains.[49]

And now the holy warriors were destroying their own people. From their mountain redoubts, the guerrillas fired tens of thousands of rockets and mortars into villages and cities, shattering mosques and bus stations and homes where innocents died cringing. In Kabul alone, more than 1,000 civilians were killed by rebel rocket attacks in 1989, according to Western relief agencies. Thousands more died in the countryside. The killing continues to this day.

The CIA kept pumping weapons into the battlefront, unwilling and unable to control the violent whirlwind it helped unleash. The weapons pipeline that was the sole source of the rebels' power could not be turned off. The CIA was fueling a civil war that would not stop. It could not abandon the guerrillas. Nor could it control them. The war promised nothing but more death and destruction. This was the cost of the CIA's greatest triumph of the 1980's.

As murderous as the Soviet war in Afghanistan was, the rationale for the CIA's covert action had ended on the day of the Soviet withdrawal. The reason the CIA armed the *mujaheddin* was to oust the Soviets. They were gone, yet the covert action continued. The day after the withdrawal, Gorbachev proposed that the superpowers suspend their weapons shipments and work as guarantors of a cease-fire. The White House reflexively rejected the offer.

A year later, a decade after the Soviets' invasion and the CIA's weapons shipments began, Afghanistan's immediate future was an unceasing civil war. "The war is a day-to-day, month-to-month, year-to-year affair," a State Department analyst, Craig Karp, had told me in Peshawar. "You have to take a twenty-, thirty-year perspective on it." In the winter of 1990, as heavy snows slowed the fighting in Afghanistan, the men at Foggy Bottom and across the river in Langley were taking the long view. They spoke of the need for "another season" of war. The CIA's *jihad* went on.

Yet the CIA knew, as did the politicians who shaped the CIA's war in Afghanistan, that the Agency could not stop the guerrillas from destroying one another. "I don't see that we have any leverage at all over them," said Senator Gordon Humphrey, the leader of the Afghan caucus in Washington. "I'm sure the *mujaheddin* have stockpiled a great deal of our weaponry," he said. "I have no doubt that there will be a struggle for power, especially by Hekmatyar. There'll be a long period of tumult and political infighting and bloodshed."

Congressman Charlie Wilson had more faith in the holy warriors. "The best we can hope for is an independent Afghanistan where people have tolerance for one another," he said. "It also could be a blood bath. It could be the most god-awful blood bath in history."

The CIA director who set up the arms pipeline to Afghanistan weighed the lives in the balance. "You were giving arms to people who were going to go out and get ground up in battle," Stansfield Turner reflected. "Now, it seems, they will use the same weapons to kill each other. It's one of those undesirable spinoffs."

7

From Lebanon
to Leavenworth

ADASHING and much-decorated lieutenant colonel found himself in
deep trouble in November 1986, the week the lies and revelations
about secret weapons shipments to Iran started swirling around Washington.

The officer's superiors had called him to account for millions of
dollars drawn from the Pentagon's black budget. He'd spent the money
on covert operations in Central America and around the world. He'd used
front companies, set up secret bank accounts, filled them with laundered
money. His paper shredder had been working overtime. His superiors
wanted answers. His explanations didn't add up.

The soldier in question was not running arms to Iran. He was Lieutenant Colonel Dale C. Duncan and he was part of a secret army within
the United States Army.

This army didn't advertise for recruits on television. It had no uniforms and no honor codes. It was part of the cadre of gung-ho colonels,
retired generals and CIA agents that came close to hijacking a fair amount
of power in this country in the 1980's.[1]

The secret soldiers started their work the week President Reagan
came to office. They ran the United States Army's most sensitive secret
operations. They aimed to implant the brains of the CIA in the body of
the Green Berets. What the CIA lacked the will to do and the Army

lacked the intelligence to do—that was their mission. Free hostages. Thwart terrorists. Take action and take revenge.

They had hundreds of millions of dollars at their disposal. They siphoned the money out of other Pentagon programs, buried it in black bank accounts, and bought helicopters and planes and boats with suitcases filled with cash. They set up operations in Central America, the Middle East and Europe that were hidden from Congress and the Army's civilian leadership. They operated under the authority of the highest-ranking generals in the Army. But ultimately they were accountable to no one.

This force was set up to fight the shadow wars that confronted the United States after Vietnam. The enemies were bearded Muslims in the Middle East who took Americans hostage and blew up American soldiers. They were shaky communist governments in the tropics that the U.S. saw as Soviet beachheads in the Western Hemisphere. They were guerrillas fighting military juntas loyal to the United States.

The U.S. Army was unprepared to fight these wars. Its tanks and bombs and armored personnel carriers were useless against kidnappers and saboteurs. Force was no match for terror. It was the wrong weapon for Third World political intrigues. And the American experience in Vietnam left the country with little appetite for open warfare in jungle nations.

The CIA wasn't much good at waging these battles either. It could hire private armies, but they often proved corrupt and ineffectual. It could subvert communist governments, but rarely succeeded in devising new regimes to replace them. It couldn't free American hostages or even find them. It could tell you the gross national product of Lebanon, but it couldn't draw up a detailed street map of Beirut, not one that showed the back alleys and basements in the bombed-out southern slums where the Shiite kidnappers kept their hostages in chains.

The secret army rose from the ashes of the 1980 attempt to rescue the fifty-two Americans held prisoner by revolutionaries in Teheran. The CIA had next to no human intelligence on Iran during that long ordeal. Human intelligence is the kind of information that machines cannot gather, the knowledge only spies can provide. The military knew what the U.S. embassy in Teheran looked like, but what went on inside the embassy compound where the Americans were held was a complete unknown.

The President had ordered the nation's best commandos to rescue the hostages. They were asked to mount a dangerous assault in a strange and hostile country without knowing exactly where to go or what to do once they landed. The Pentagon threw together the hostage-rescue mission under the command of Army Major General James Vaught. It also set

up an intelligence unit which infiltrated four American agents into Teheran. On April 24, 1980, 132 ground troops aboard C-130 transports
and eight Sea Stallion helicopters crossed into Iranian airspace, heading
for a rendezvous at a patch of wasteland called Desert One.

The mission was a disaster. Three of the helicopters broke down
within five hours, scuttling the rescue's chances for success. At Desert
One, the commandos prepared to retreat. One of the helicopters crashed
into a transport plane as it took off. Eight men died in the inferno. Iranian
television sent pictures of the charred bodies and twisted wreckage around
the world. The humiliation was overwhelming.

In the aftermath, a military commission concluded that excessive
secrecy had subverted the mission. It said "the great emphasis on Op
Sec"—operational security, which is military jargon for secrecy—"se-
verely limited the communications necessary to coordinate the operation." The plans were so tightly held that no one analyzed or criticized
them. The helicopter pilots couldn't talk to one another in flight for fear
the Iranians or Soviets would overhear. Too much secrecy and too little
internal debate contributed to the catastrophe.

Vaught began planning a second rescue attempt. The new mission
was code-named HONEY BADGER, after a vicious, carnivorous little
mammal known to rip apart its prey. Vaught took on only a few trusted
confidants as he laid his plans. His deputy was Air Force Major General
Richard Secord, who'd flown more than 250 secret missions during the
CIA's wars in Vietnam and Laos. Secord knew Teheran inside out. He'd
served four years there in the late 1970's, selling billions of dollars of
the Pentagon's weapons to the Shah.

Honey Badger started life as a small animal, but quickly grew into
a hulking beast. More than 2,000 soldiers were enlisted in the secret
operation. The plans grew so elaborate that they came to resemble an
invasion more than a surgical rescue mission. To keep the mission hidden
from foreign enemies, Congress and the press, the Pentagon channeled
more than $200 million out of unclassified programs into black accounts.
Vaught used some of the money to commandeer scores of special long-
range helicopters and equip them with exotic radars, electronic countermeasures and communications gear.

"Our force was combat-ready, and we were ready to roll," Secord
later said. "But we did not. We were not able . . . to pin down the
location of the hostages." Nobody in the CIA or the Pentagon knew
where the Americans were held captive. Nobody in the Army could rescue
them without that certain knowledge. The lack of intelligence kept Honey
Badger locked in its cage.[2]

The Army decided it had learned three lessons from these failures,
three ideas that burned deeply into its memory. It would never rely solely

on the CIA for intelligence. It would never again improvise the plans for such a crucial mission. It had to form clandestine units capable of co-ordinating paramilitary actions and intelligence-gathering. What the Army never learned was how to guard against the corrosive effects of excessive secrecy, or how to control covert forces set free from the everyday stric-tures of authority.

On January 20, 1981, the day Iran finally released the hostages, Ronald Reagan became President of the United States. He vowed to strengthen American forces so that the United States never again would be humiliated in this way. Out of this promise came a host of new military and intelligence initiatives. The CIA would be given new freedom and new vigor. The armed forces would receive billions upon billions of dollars in new funds for commando units. There would be new faces, new missions, new forces.

A week after his inauguration, Reagan formally welcomed the fifty-two hostages home. The White House reception was a smashing success, with flags and flourishes and fervent words. The President delivered a vivid warning that day: "Let terrorists beware that when the rules of international behavior are violated, our policy will be one of swift and effective retribution." With that ringing call to arms, the Army began to create the forces to carry out the President's vow of vengeance.

That very day, down in the basement of the Pentagon in Room BF741C, Lieutenant Colonel James Longhofer put the finishing touches on the top-secret plans to fulfill the promise. The forty-four-year-old soldier was a bemedaled Vietnam veteran with a sterling record. He had just been named the commander of the Army's newly born Special Op-erations Division. The subterranean office in the Pentagon was the di-vision's headquarters. Its leaders quickly became known within the Pentagon as "the crazies in the basement."

They were the junior officers of Vietnam come to power. They were the cream of the corps.

"Some of the best people usually go into special operations, the most talented in the widest variety of ways," said Timothy Enneking, a captain in Army intelligence who came to know the secret army well. "You're talking about people who have to be multilingual, and people who can also take a rucksack and hump it a hell of a long way. They're special people. They're doing the neatest missions, the highest-speed stuff, the stuff that gets the money and the attention. They're 'the best and the brightest.' "[3]

The father of the Special Operations Division was the Army's high-est-ranking general: the Chief of Staff, General Edward "Shy" Meyer. The division was a crowning achievement for General Meyer, who'd fought for years to create such a unit. His vice chief of staff, General

John Vessey Jr., a hard-nosed, plain-spoken commander who rose to become the chairman of the Joint Chiefs of Staff in 1982, also championed the secret soldiers.

Meyer wanted men who could perform almost any assignment on short notice. The post-Vietnam Pentagon was a bloated and sluggish bureaucracy. It took months of paperwork to accomplish the simplest task. Longhofer's orders were to cut through that paper swamp and take the hill. Shy Meyer said he demanded that the division develop a host of new capabilities "in the counter-terrorist and human intelligence areas, in conjunction with and in support of other agencies"—specifically, the Central Intelligence Agency. And he wanted it done now.[4]

The general wanted these missions kept completely secret. "We had a tremendous concern in the operational security area," General Meyer said, "and we would have used every means to keep the people involved from being known." The men and the machines assembled for Operation Honey Badger became the nucleus of General Meyer's new special operations division. "Shy Meyer took all the personnel with him. They reported directly to him," said Captain Enneking. The general placed the new division under the aegis of DCSOPS, the Army Deputy Chief of Staff for Operations and Plans. Lieutenant General James E. Moore was the DCSOPS commander in 1981 and 1982. "Most of the way we did our business originated from the Iran rescue mission," General Moore said. "The guidance from the Chief of Staff and Vice Chief of Staff was to get the job done while maintaining the strictest Op Sec."[5]

The division bypassed the chain of command, slashing through layers of bureaucratic control. Its missions were concealed from nearly everyone in the Pentagon. They were "stovepipe" operations, flowing directly from the basement to the top of the Army, past the architecture of authority. "Some were so sensitive that only two or three people within the Army staff would know about them," said Lieutenant General James Merryman, the Army's deputy chief of staff for research and development.[6]

"These black operations cut the lines of authority. The other generals just accepted that they were being bypassed by the 'crazies in the basement,' " Captain Enneking said. "The guys were left to whatever they could do as quickly as they could do it with very, very few restrictions, and the rules started getting in the way."

The secret units needed funds that were off the books, money that could not be traced. The division's financing systems were modeled on the CIA's. Proprietary companies, firms that looked like normal businesses, served as fronts for the supply of money and weapons. Covert bank accounts and cover stories were devised.

But first the money had to start flowing from the Treasury. General

Meyer said Larry Keenan, a deputy comptroller of the Army, was the initial "point of contact" for the division's covert funds. General Vessey wrote to Keenan asking him to help set up the division's finances. "There ought to be a bag of money identified that we can reach into," the general said.[7]

Throughout 1981, Keenan filled the money bag. He reached into the Army's coffers and took out millions of dollars of funds Congress had appropriated for other projects. When the division needed money, Longhofer and his finance officer, Lieutenant Colonel Keith Nightingale, could pick up the phone and call Keenan. The money would be available within the week. With that seed money, the Special Operations Division took root.

Keenan worked like an agent running an intelligence operation, performing a covert mission while going about his job in an everyday manner to evade enemy detection. Among those who never discovered the underground pipeline fueling special operations was Keenan's boss, Lieutenant General Ernest Peixotto, the Comptroller of the Army. "I was never consulted on any special funding arrangements," General Peixotto said. "I was totally unaware of such funding activities. The senior Army leaders apparently established some system without ever consulting me."[8]

Several such systems took shape. In October 1981, the Special Operations Division's leaders trooped up to Capitol Hill to brief the ranking members of the armed services and intelligence committees on their new regime. The Congress agreed to give the Special Operations Division $90 million.

Of those millions the Congress willingly and openly appropriated, $20 million disappeared into the black world. The $20 million created a secret unit called the Intelligence Support Activity, or ISA. The ISA's purpose was to gather intelligence for covert operations around the world. It was the Army's own secret espionage brigade, and it was hidden from the members of the Congress who financed it.

The Army danced around the subject of the ISA in the classified briefings it gave to the intelligence and armed services committees. The briefings were handled by the "action officers"—the majors and lieutenant colonels who ran the programs. Often they were one-on-one sessions with the committee chairmen, just like the CIA's scattershot briefings in the 1950's. "Only a few people within these congressional committees—possibly the chairman—would know all the details. That's how sensitive some of these projects and missions were," said Lieutenant General Merryman.[9]

But the chairman didn't know all the details either. The ISA briefings concealed more than they revealed. "I don't believe that they actually briefed Congress,'' said an ISA officer. "I thought that their maintaining that they had actually briefed Congress was a gross overstatement of fact. I did not have too much confidence in the information relayed. They were too footloose and had too many easy answers. . . . The entire time I was at ISA, I did not feel comfortable with the financial arrangements. I had many doubts about how the moneys were controlled. It was not a good situation. . . . There was some hanky-panky going on.''[10]

The competition for money, power and status between the Intelligence Support Activity and the Special Operations Division became increasingly intense as the secret forces grew. The ISA quickly expanded from a force of about fifty officers to nearly 300. It set up shop all over Central America—El Salvador, Guatemala, Honduras, Nicaragua, Panama—to support the war against the Sandinistas and their left-wing allies. It created private companies to serve as fronts for espionage, including a butcher shop and a meat warehouse in Panama. It set up safe houses, secret airfields and caches for money and weapons, breaking a trail for future operations against the enemy in Nicaragua.

As the ISA expanded, so did Longhofer's forces. He quickly came to realize that his division was becoming too large to stay hidden under the normal cloaks of classification. He decided to bury his entire operation in complete blackness. In January 1982 he proposed, and General Vessey authorized, a covert operation code-named FORESHADOW.

Operation Foreshadow eliminated all mention of the division from open Army records and accounts. General Vessey initialed an order on February 12 calling for the Special Operations Division's records to be destroyed as a matter of routine. The men and their missions disappeared from the public ledger.

The division couldn't subsist only on the funds supplied from time to time by Keenan. It needed an unfailing source of black money. It found a wildcat well in a fifty-nine-year-old civilian named Autmer Ackley Jr. Ackley was a bursar at INSCOM, the Army's Intelligence and Security Command, the unit that in theory commanded all the Army's espionage and counterespionage efforts. He had been in the military-intelligence business for more than thirty years, and he had grown utterly frustrated with the financial restrictions the Army bureaucracy had placed on intelligence operations. So when the special operations forces came to him looking for funds, he had the answer to their problems ready and waiting.[11]

Ackley was something of an alchemist. He had a way to turn an ordinary piece of paper into cash. The paper was a standard Army document—Form 1080, Voucher for Transfer Between Appropriations and/or Funds. One way the form is used to allow money to flow from the Treasury to the Army, or from one Army account to another, is for an officer to fill out the 1080. The bursar then signs the form and issues a Treasury check. The 1080 vouches that the money has been used to pay for the costs of authorized programs. It creates an audit trail—a paper path showing money flowing.

Ackley discovered that he could use the 1080s to channel Treasury checks to the Army's secret soldiers. He became the conduit for the money that kept the covert soldiers solvent. He could transfer unspent funds from a score of different programs into the covert forces' accounts. He could cut a check for their future needs, and at the same time vouch that the money already had been spent and accounted for on the Army's books. The soldiers turned the checks into cash. And then, by transferring the cash to clandestine checking accounts they controlled, they turned the greenbacks black. To serve the cause of secrecy, they wiped out the audit trail.

"Ackley suddenly realized that this system could work," said Captain Enneking. "He realized he didn't need to account for the money. Slowly things got looser and looser. . . . He could take a white sheet and turn it into green, take one white eight-and-a-half-by-eleven sheet of paper and literally turn it into tens of millions of dollars."

Cash without accountability was a godsend for the secret soldiers. There was a great demand for Ackley's unique accounting system. "The demand met the system, and the thing exploded," Enneking said. With its own treasury of covert cash, its own cover organizations and its own loose set of rules, the Special Operations Division started running on all cylinders.

Longhofer had created a secret aviation unit called Seaspray and hidden it inside a CIA-owned company, Aviation Tech Services. Longhofer had coordinated the purchasing and refurbishing of the exotic long-range helicopters for Honey Badger. Now those helicopters were Seaspray's. The unit's pride and joy were its Hughes 500MD choppers, so advanced that they could hug the ground at 150 miles an hour in total darkness, their whirring blades barely louder than an electric blender.

Seaspray's first assignment came in an urgent call from the CIA in August 1981. The Lebanese Christian leader, a warlord named Bashir Gemayel, was on a secret visit to Washington to meet with the Director of Central Intelligence, William Casey. He needed a lift back home. Could Longhofer secretly ferry him back to Beirut?

Three days later, two of Seaspray's helicopters swooped over the black Mediterranean at midnight. They made landfall at Junieh, nine miles north of Beirut. The choppers touched down on the beach, their rotors churning dust into the high beams of headlights piercing the night

air. Gemayel hopped out, shook hands with an officer from the CIA's
Beirut station, and jumped in the waiting car for the final leg of his
journey home.

A working relationship between the CIA and Seaspray was forged.
The connection proved fruitful. Seaspray's pilots spent much of 1982
flying near the Nicaraguan border, electronically intercepting Nicaraguan
army and government communications. The intercepts were fed to the
CIA, which fed the information to the contras to help them coordinate
attacks on Nicaragua. The Congress wasn't told about any of it.

As the division grew and its missions proliferated, Longhofer decided
that he needed a new unit assigned solely to preserve the division's
secrecy. In the summer of 1982, he created an outfit unique in Army
history. It was based in an innocuous-looking office building a few miles
from the Pentagon in Annandale, Virginia. From the outside, the office
was a consulting firm called Business Security International. From the
inside, it was a covert operation code-named YELLOW FRUIT.

Yellow Fruit was run by Lieutenant Colonel Dale Duncan, a thirty-
eight-year-old Georgia farmboy who excelled at almost everything he
had done in his Army career. Duncan's operation provided deep cover
for all the division's soldiers. The financing came through Autmer Ackley's magic money bag. The cover came from Duncan's fertile imagination, from secret checking accounts he created and dummy companies
he incorporated. Neither the Army's civilian leaders nor the Congress
knew anything about Yellow Fruit.

The Special Operations Division was becoming more than simply a
secret Army squadron. With its unaccountable financing and its corporate
fronts, it was beginning to look a lot like the CIA itself. The wily CIA
director William Casey received a briefing on the Special Operations
Division, and quickly saw a world of potential. The Army is not legally
bound to report its secret operations to Congress in advance, as the CIA
must. The Army's secret soldiers and the CIA already were doing a fair
amount of business together in Central America. Why not join forces?
If the CIA could have its own man running Army operations, and the
Army operations had their own covert funding, the possibilities were
limitless. The CIA could have its own secret paramilitary force. Casey
asked the Army to post a lieutenant colonel at the CIA to serve as liaison
with the Special Operations Division. He had a specific man in mind.[12]

And so it was that Lieutenant Colonel Longhofer came to work for
the CIA. He was appointed as the chief military assistant to the CIA's
covert-operations directorate on October 4, 1982. He worked with the
CIA's Office of Special Activities, setting up deliveries of weapons and
intelligence to the contras. And he secretly continued to control the Special
Operations Division.[13]

By the spring of 1983, it looked as if Longhofer, Duncan and their crews were untouchable. The stream of covert cash and the secret liaison with the CIA transformed the division. It had been set up as a counter-terrorist force, a hostage-rescue unit, a human-intelligence team. It hadn't countered any terrorists. It hadn't freed any hostages. Its energies were focusing on fighting the CIA's wars in Central America.

The division's men and planes and choppers and speedboats were at work in El Salvador, Costa Rica and Honduras, running operations for the CIA and the National Security Agency. The division's men were training contras in Honduras, California and Florida, building airstrips in Costa Rica, flying over Nicaragua in the dark. Secret Army units had set up shop in the Caribbean, Lebanon, Morocco, Nigeria, Saudi Arabia, Somalia, Syria and the Sudan, even in Iran. Unseen by Congress and the Army's civilian leadership, the secret soldiers had gone global.

The secrecy and power they possessed was a heady brew. It was also a recipe for moral rot. The secret army had no rules and no laws to guide it. No outsider was responsible for fixing its boundaries or steering its course. It existed in its own world. Inevitably, its world began coming apart.

The unraveling began slowly. First the Intelligence Support Activity's cover was blown—by a former Green Beret. James "Bo" Gritz, a retired lieutenant colonel, had long contended that some American soldiers missing in action during the Vietnam War were still alive and being held prisoner in Laos. He was working with the ISA on plans for a secret mission to find these Americans, if they existed.

Gritz's derring-do made its way into the news. Reporters for the *Boston Globe* and the *New York Times* mentioned a mysterious squad called the Intelligence Support Activity in their stories. Major General Harry Soyster, then the Army deputy chief of staff for intelligence systems, began receiving letters from congressional committees asking, in effect, General, what exactly *is* the Intelligence Support Activity? General Soyster had found out about the ISA by reading the newspapers. It was an unpleasant surprise, but it wasn't the last. General Soyster was never briefed on Yellow Fruit, either.[14]

Gritz wound up being called before a House Foreign Affairs sub-committee in March 1983 to tell his tale. He said the ISA "hoped to obtain the charter for the rescue of American POWs in Laos" and planned to "put an American across into Laos to verify, using various recording means, the presence of Americans thought to be at specified locations." It was a fascinating story, but troubling. Hardly anyone in the Congress knew anything about the Intelligence Support Activity. Sone members were disturbed to learn secondhand that the Pentagon had a secret detachment of spies and Rambo prototypes running around the world with satchels full of cash. Congress was not opposed to the idea in principle —far from it. But it wanted to be consulted about the nation's intelligence operations, and in advance. That was the spirit of the law.

A second problem with the ISA's secret venture was that the Joint Chiefs had their own POW rescue mission going in Laos. The ISA had stumbled all over it. When Defense Secretary Caspar Weinberger heard that the ISA was operating in Laos, he furiously ordered the unit disbanded. Nothing of the sort happened. The ISA survived Weinberger's death sentence and lives today.

The Army told the intelligence and armed services committees in April 1983 that it knew there were some problems with the ISA and that they'd been solved. Checks and balances had been imposed. The Congress was assured that things were under control.

Things most assuredly were not. A vicious battle for control of the Special Operations Division broke out that spring between a two-star general and a CIA colonel in civilian clothes. The general lost.

When Longhofer went over to the CIA in October 1982, Shy Meyer appointed Major General Homer Long commander of the Special Operations Division. Yet General Long found himself unable to assert his command. The general discovered some months later that he wasn't running the division at all. Longhofer was secretly controlling it from his post at the CIA.

Generals, as a rule, do not appreciate colonels usurping their power. "Longhofer was trying to run that show at the same time while over at CIA," General Long said. "And one of the unpleasant experiences I had with Longhofer was to call him into my office and tell him he was to have nothing to do with that outfit." Long told him that "he wasn't in charge of anything. Now, that infuriated him. I think if he had a knife he would have cut my throat."

Long was sure that his subordinate ignored his order. "I don't trust Longhofer as far as I can throw him," the general said. "My belief is that he went to the Chief"—Shy Meyer—"by notes and personal contacts, and also he kept his contacts going, pulling strings. He was a real operator."[15]

In June 1983, Shy Meyer retired from the Army after a long and distinguished career. He had been the Special Operations Division's godfather, creating the new team with a skillful assault on the bureaucracy. Now the team had lost its greatest ally. Longhofer lost his champion. And the Army lost the man who knew the most about what was going on inside the division.

By now, with General Meyer gone, General Vessey promoted to chairman of the Joint Chiefs, and General Long's command subverted, the secret soldiers were beyond the reach of authority. The new Army

Chief of Staff, General John Wickham, and his vice chief, General Maxwell Thurman, knew little about the secret operations. The Secretary of the Army, John O. Marsh Jr., came to realize that the division was creating and running black programs that were deliberately hidden from him. The most powerful men in the Army came to understand that the secret units were spending money on missions controlled by no one at the top of the chain of command.

An extraordinary order came down from on high to the Special Operations Division: the Secretary of the Army, his under secretary, the Army Chief of Staff and vice chief of staff hereby command you to tell us what you're doing.

"The announcement was made that the Vice, the Chief, the Secretary and the Under will be told, will be briefed on all black programs," General Long recalled. "Now don't give me any bullshit, don't, don't give me any [backtalk about] security clearances. . . . There's nothing goes on in the United States Army that those four will not be told about. We're saying it tough because that's actually the way it was told to us. Because they obviously had been stonewalled."[16]

The wall was beginning to crack, but it stood throughout that summer. The Army knew it had to get a grip on its black programs. Confronted with a serious problem, the Army did what any big bureaucracy would do: it formed a committee. The Special Access Program Oversight Committee tried to answer some questions for the Army's leaders. How many black programs existed? What were they? How could the Army control them?

Lieutenant General James Merryman chaired the committee. He ordered up a list of all black programs. It took months to assemble. "The list was quite large and surprised quite a few," he said. The Army leadership was alarmed to discover that its soldiers had created at least fifty or sixty black programs about which they knew absolutely nothing.[17]

Lieutenant General Willam Odom, who'd been so influential in revamping the nation's nuclear war-fighting plans in the late 1970's, was a member of the committee. Odom then was the Army's assistant chief of staff for intelligence, and would come in for his share of the blame for failing to control the division. But Odom said years later that he'd long been "suspicious of the special operations." He said no one took responsibility for overseeing the division. "There were no formal procedures," Odom said, because "special operations wanted no system" of control. The result was "the absence of any coherent fiscal control structure at all."[18]

The Special Access Program Oversight Committee was supposed to tell the Army's leaders how to police black programs. On that count it was a dismal failure. "The SAPOC effort was enormously confused,"

General Odom said. "The SAPOC never came to grips with the basic issues." It wasted its time inventing new security compartments and code words instead of instituting controls. It barely could define what a black program was, much less handle the slippery issue of responsibility. "The idea was to get a messy house in order for the future," he said. But that never happened. "The essential confusion still lingered."[19]

On August 15, 1983, the committee published its definition of a black program: a super-secret project "removed from normal procurement, fiscal and security channels." And there the problem lay. No other channels existed save the normal one. "Another method other than the 'normal' was to be followed," General Soyster said. "Another system was not in place."[20]

"The key here is 'normal,' " General Odom said. "The purpose was to deny hostile intelligence knowledge of the program's existence. The problem the SAPOC did not solve was how to maintain fiscal and policy accountability under this security criterion."[21]

The secrecy needed to defeat the KGB was defeating law and order inside the Army.

That same week, a new face turned up at Yellow Fruit. William T. Golden had twenty years in the military-intelligence business under his belt. He'd been serving in the American Embassy in Managua, Nicaragua, as the assistant Army attaché. A U.S. military attaché in a communist country has a clear-cut set of duties. Golden was a spy in the Sandinistas' lair.[22]

"I was assigned from there to a project called Yellow Fruit under the cover of Business Security International in Annandale, Virginia," Golden later testified. "I worked directly for Colonel Duncan. When I arrived in August of 1983, one of the first jobs that I was given was to establish accountability for covert funds that had been advanced to individuals and had been expended by the organization." Establishing accountability was a dangerous assignment—dangerous for Yellow Fruit.

As Golden began poring over Yellow Fruit's records, Duncan went on a European vacation with his wife, a vacation, Golden quickly discovered, financed with government funds. That was the least of it. Golden found two receipts totaling $89,000 that Duncan had turned in for reimbursement. "The receipts were bogus," he said. "They were fabricated receipts." Everywhere he looked he found clues to a crime. He quickly came to the conclusion "that there was some large-scale fraud on the part of Colonel Duncan and possibly other members of the organization."

Golden blew the whistle. He drew up a report on September 13 calling for an immediate probe of Yellow Fruit by the Army's Criminal Investigative Division. He sent the report to the division's deputy commander, Lieutenant Colonel Frederick Byard. Byard was knee-deep in the division's financial shenanigans. The report hit his desk like a live grenade.

Byard sent the report to Colonel Longhofer at the CIA. Longhofer got on a plane and flew to Berlin to meet the vacationing Duncan. A week later, Golden received a call at the office on one of Yellow Fruit's secure phone lines. It was Longhofer.

"Go home," the CIA's colonel said. "Don't ever come back to the office again. We'll call you, don't call us."

Golden went home and waited. He mulled over what he had seen at Business Security International. One item that stuck in his mind was a document Longhofer had brought over to Yellow Fruit from the CIA. The document was an elaborate plan, thirty or forty pages long, typed on plain paper. It was sitting in Business Security International's safe, next to an unlocked cash box holding tens of thousands of dollars.[23]

"This plan was a contingency plan that would be implemented in the event funding for the contras was cut off," Golden recalled. Nine months earlier, Congress had passed the first Boland amendment, prohibiting the CIA from spending money "for the purposes of overthrowing the Government of Nicaragua." In July 1983, three weeks before Golden left Nicaragua, the House passed a bill barring support for "military or paramilitary activities in Nicaragua." And now Congress was talking about beefing up the Boland amendment—and forbidding the Department of Defense, the CIA and every other U.S. intelligence agency from supporting the contras.

"Everybody was worried," Golden said. "What was talked about in the office was the Boland amendment. It was going to cut off funds for the contras and we would all be out of a job and how are we going to get around this thing."

The plan in the safe "talked about the various ways of supplying the contras indirectly" if and when Congress outlawed direct support, Golden said. One way was padding military-aid programs to Honduras or El Salvador with covert contra aid—"with the understanding under the table that those items that had been padded would be given to the contras." Another was "a supply system that would require aviation assets and an airfield that would have to be constructed." The airfield was to be built on the hacienda of "John Hull . . . an American living in Costa Rica who owned this huge ranch."*

"There was no question about it," Golden said. "The whole purpose of the plan was to circumvent the Boland amendment."

The plan called for the Department of Defense, the CIA and the

---

*At this writing, Hull is under indictment in Costa Rica on charges of cocaine trafficking and violating national security. The government in Costa Rica charges that Hull let pilots use his airfield to carry weapons to the contras and cocaine to the United States from 1983 to 1985.

Army to work through the Special Operations Division and Yellow Fruit. Their guns and money would flow to the contras through Lieutenant Colonel Duncan's elaborate network of cover organizations. Parts of the plan already were under way in September 1983, Golden said. The airfield was almost ready. Yellow Fruit's front companies were set up. Its secret bank accounts were open and waiting. But Lieutenant Colonel Duncan and Yellow Fruit were about to take a fall. Luckily for the contras, there was another lieutenant colonel to fill the role, a tireless soldier who would work eighteen- and twenty-hour days putting every part of this plan into action. And he worked for the President of the United States.

The call Golden had been waiting for came on his birthday, Friday, October 14. The secretary at Business Security International, Darlene Rush, telephoned him at home. "Colonel Duncan is back," she said. "He's in command. You are to show up Monday morning with your keys to the office."

Golden returned to Business Security International ready for a show-down. "Colonel Duncan stood up and said, 'I have been vindicated of all the charges against me and now I am back in command and certain people are going to be fired immediately.' . . . And I was first on his list."

Golden went home, picked up the phone and called the FBI. "They thought I was a nut and put me in their crank file," he said. "They had never heard of anything like this before." Nor had anyone else outside of a handful of people at the CIA, the Pentagon and the White House. Golden had to ask a friend who was an FBI agent in Albuquerque to vouch for him. He finally talked to the FBI. He talked to a military lawyer. And he talked to a federal prosecutor.

At that point, all hell broke loose. The Army's secret soldiers had run amok. Millions of dollars—at that point, nobody knew how much —had been siphoned into their black coffers. At Yellow Fruit, officers had spent money for their personal pleasures and tried to cover up their crimes. The Army quickly realized that it had a scandal brewing. Three separate investigations took shape. The Justice Department and the Pentagon's Criminal Investigative Division looked for evidence of crimes. A team of Army intelligence and finance officers tried to follow the dollars that had funded the division, and tried to figure out who was accountable for them.

The Army's initial attempt to investigate itself was almost comically incompetent. Investigators from the Army's Office of the Inspector General made a cursory check of Yellow Fruit's records in the fall of 1983 and advised the group's members that "a day of reckoning would come"—someday. After the inspectors left, Yellow Fruit's officers resumed feeding their records into their shredder. Auditors from the Army's

Finance and Accounting Center examined Yellow Fruit's books between January 1984 and June 1984. Their audits showed nothing amiss.[24]

More than a year passed before the Army's investigators came to grips with the case. Among them was Timothy Enneking, then a twenty-six-year-old first lieutenant. Enneking's previous assignment was taking things black—making Army weapons-development programs secret and making sure they stayed secret. He originally was detailed to the investigation to provide it with operational security. But the Army investigators were swamped, and they asked Enneking to help them take the network of black programs apart.

It took the investigators all of 1984 and the better part of 1985 to add up the money that had gone through Autmer Ackley's hands and out into the black world. The grand total of money missing and unaccounted for was $324 million.

"When the Army found out that there was, as near as they knew, a $324 million black hole, the first place they went was Yellow Fruit. Then they went to Seaspray—and then they said, 'Christ, let's shake down the world,' " Enneking said. "Nobody knew where this $324 million had gone. If what we knew had hit the news, you would have been able to say: 'Covert programs have lost, misused, stolen or abused more than $300 million in the first part of this decade. Criminal investigations are currently taking place. It's in the most highly secretive organizations in the Department of Defense. No one has any idea where it's going. Its limits at this point in time are unknown.' "

The Army thought it extremely important that this information would never hit the news. In October 1984 Enneking sat down with Brigadier General Charles Scanlon, the deputy commanding general of INSCOM. He asked him for his guidance. How much information should be classified in the investigation?

"Everything must be classified," General Scanlon said. "If this gets out it will probably affect the election."

Enneking was shocked. "It scared the living daylights out of me," he said. "That is a reason *not* to classify something. You cannot classify something for political reasons. It really bothered me, this guy telling me, 'We need to support the administration, we don't want to do anything to shake the chances of the President's reelection.'

"He clearly indicated that the election was coming up, and if this information was released, it would adversely affect the election," Enneking continued. "The message was very clear and very troubling.

"I was given an order I thought I could not follow. You get into the My Lai situation, and that sort of situation is scattered all over this. Most people here had to follow orders. If you do it, it's illegal. If you don't, you're dead.

"I was faced with that with Scanlon," he said. "But I just sort of very quietly went ahead and did what I thought was right and got away with it. I was lucky. He could have been really pissed. He could have killed me."

Enneking was only one among many Army investigators flying around the country and around the world, trying to figure out where the money was, trying to determine what had gone wrong. The answers, as it turned out, were difficult to find. No one assumed responsibility. No one pointed fingers.

For nearly four years, the Army tried to trace the missing money. It wasn't easy. Officers throughout the Special Operations Division had started shredding their cash blotters, vouchers, checkbooks and any other records they could find the week that Golden reported his allegations on September 13, 1983. They destroyed evidence for the next seventeen months.

The destruction of government records was forbidden by law and by official regulations. But General Vessey had initialed orders authorizing the destruction of the division's records. So, it appeared, had General Odom. Vessey was now chairman of the Joint Chiefs. Odom had just been named director of the National Security Agency, the nation's biggest espionage office. The investigation was going to wind up confronting some of the most powerful men in the military.

By the spring of 1985, a year and a half into the investigation, the investigators had pieced together a partial mosaic of what went on inside the Army's secret units. The picture was unnerving.

They found $64,292,335.50 on deposit in clandestine checking accounts. These were public funds in private accounts controlled by undercover Army officers.

They found that the secret soldiers blew an untold sum of money —untold, because the records were shredded—on $600-a-night hotel suites, $1,200-a-month liquor bills, first-class air travel, sharp suits and expensive luggage, entertaining their wives and sweethearts, dental bills, day-care fees and health-club memberships. None of this seemed to have much to do with the war against terrorism.

They found scraps and shreds of evidence suggesting that members of the Quick Reaction Team, a clandestine Army unit, had tastes more ornate than four-star hotels and Nautilus machines. "There were rumors that QRT members were flying hookers around, flying drugs around," according to one Army investigator.

There was theft of government funds. There was fraud. There was obstruction of justice. There was perjury. There was more, much more, but the investigators never found it all. The investigation "never got to the worst stuff, never traced as much of the outright thievery as there may have been, never traced as much of the abuse," Enneking said. "There was really a feeling of, yeah, we were able to dig up some of it, but there's a lot more out there. It was really awful. . . ."

Enneking worked under a colonel named Hector Perez-Lebron, who was officially in charge of the Army's administrative inquiry. The records of the investigation show clearly that Perez was overwhelmed by his task, that there was a vacuum to be filled, and that Enneking filled it. The investigation staggered forward slowly, reeling under the weight of its task. In June 1985, Perez and Enneking met with Autmer Ackley at Fort George G. Meade, Maryland, home of the National Security Agency. Ackley had been transferred out of his job as the Army's premier black money–man and now investigated the security clearances of Pentagon personnel.[25]

They listened as Ackley told his story. For thirty-six years, in and out of uniform, he'd served in military intelligence, growing more angry and frustrated with the Army's bureaucratic regulations with each passing year. The frustration boiled over when he was a second lieutenant sitting in an office in Saigon in 1965.

"I went through this in Vietnam," he said. "I set up the contingency funds for General Westmoreland," the senior U.S. commander in Vietnam from 1964 to 1968. Contingency funds are a stockpile of rainy-day money to be spent on whatever a commander wants.

Ackley's job was to free up money for secret intelligence operations, "to react to targets of opportunity," he said. Military intelligence units had to react quickly to those moving targets. "And there was just no way. It could not be done. You could not circumvent this bureaucratic nightmare that has been created to get things done when they have to be done. . . .

"Army regulations are not written for intelligence operations. They just don't work that way," Ackley said. "One of the first things I learned as a second lieutenant was that an Army regulation is only a guide. And I still maintain that they are only a guide."

So Ackley long ago had begun thinking about ways to end-run the bureaucracy's rules and regulations. And by 1981 he had come up with a way of channeling public money into black programs that was unprecedented in the annals of secret Army operations.

Ackley had reached into a dozen different unclassified Army accounts—money Congress had authorized for guns and tanks, missiles and ammunition, operations and maintenance—and helped divert the money to the secret soldiers. He had also gained authorized access to CIA accounts, further blurring the line between the Army and the Agency. In fact, Ackley said he had learned "the modus operandi" he used "from the intelligence community."

"We were plowing new ground here," he said. "This had never been done before. It was a new procedure completely."

Why was the Army relying on him for to provide these huge sums of untraceable funds for secret missions? Perez asked.

"It was the Department of the Army's reluctance to go to Congress," Ackley said.

"Are you saying that maybe these procedures were used because the Department of the Army did not want to go to Congress for more money?" Perez asked.

"I would bet my life on it," Ackley said.

President Franklin D. Roosevelt once said that the Constitution was "like the Bible; it ought to be read again and again." The Army appears to have needed a mandatory refresher course. The Army was reluctant to go to Congress for more money to finance its secret operations. So it sought and found secret financing. That served the cause of covertness and convenience, but it contradicted the Constitution. The Army is constitutionally barred from entering the Treasury. The Congress, not the Army, has the power to spend the public's money. This, among many other things, is what makes the United States different from the world's military governments.

"No Money shall be drawn from the Treasury, but in Consequence of Appropriations made by Law," the Constitution commands. Federal law based on this principle demands that appropriated funds "shall be applied solely to the objects for which they are respectively made, and no others." The Army cannot take money appropriated for C rations and spend it on covert operations. These are the rules that the black budget corrodes. [26]

"What Ackley did was to turn white to black," Enneking said later. "He converted money which the Congress intended to stay visible. Where there was money that was supposed to stay in the open world, the audit trail was cut off." An obscure Army bursar became the comptroller of a secret treasury. And that was how the division's missions were kept hidden from Congress and the Army's civilian leaders.

As their interrogation of Ackley stretched into the afternoon, the investigators' heads began to spin. Ackley wasn't a loose cannon. Someone—they weren't quite sure who—had authorized what Ackley had done. The entire purpose of the scheme was to disguise accountability for the funds. Who was accountable? Who was responsible?

"Here you give a guy two, three, four thousand or two, three or four million dollars that does not belong to them," Perez told Ackley. "It belongs to the taxpayers. They're public funds. . . . An officer in the United States Army, shouldn't he keep some sort of accountability for those funds?"

Look, Ackley told the investigators, my orders were to convert this money to cash and my accountability ended there. "I will be the first to admit that I was mission-oriented," he said. "I had one goal and that was to provide a service, to get a job done. And to me this was legal and sufficient."

He argued that the money belonged to the Army, not the taxpayers. Once the money passed through his hands, it was no longer green—it was black. It was invisible. "You maintain that the money still exists," Ackely said. "I maintain that it does not."

Perez saved his best shot for last. "Would it surprise you to know that the total money that flowed through your account was more than $300 million?"

Ackley was flabbergasted. "God *damn*, that's a lot of money," he said. "I—I—I hadn't realized it was that large."

"It surprises you to learn that there's more than $64 million left in cold cash?" Perez said. "The exact figure on cash in the bank or in a checking account was $64,292,335.50. So we're not talking about a very small amount of cash."

"No, we're talking about a lot of money."

"We're talking about a lot of money. That's why everybody's interested in what happened the last four years," Perez said. "Let me give you some examples of what I have found. I have found cold cash missing. . . . Some money actually disappeared. I have found records destroyed—"

"Sir," Enneking cut in. "Clothing, wives, girlfriends. . . ."

"Misuse of funds," Perez continued, ". . . and on and on and on. And all in the name of 'security.' "

Ackley said the top money men in the Army had to have been aware of what was going on. He singled out Oliver Kennedy, the assistant comptroller of the the Army for fiscal policy. "He knew exactly what we were doing," Ackley insisted. "He couldn't help but know."

Perez and Enneking went to see Kennedy in October 1985. He was appalled.

"Frightening!" Kennedy exclaimed. "No accountability? I do not believe that anyone in the government has the authority to approve such a procedure. . . . A sterile method of making payments would be okay, but no accountability? Hell, no! The CIA has special legislation concerning their activities, but to my knowledge the Army does not." He said the system the investigators had described could serve only one purpose—to circumvent the will of Congress.[27]

The Army Criminal Investigative Division's agents also were looking for answers to the question of accountability. They went to visit General Glenn Otis, the commander in chief of the United States Army in Europe.

General Otis had been the Army deputy chief of staff for operations and
plans, the DCSOPS commander, the man nominally responsible for the
Special Operations Division, when the division was first created in 1981.[28]

Otis was supposed to have kept tabs on the Special Operations
Division. He had not. "I don't have any reason to suspect that funny
money" funded the secret units, he said. How then, Special Agent Michael Keith asked him, did the division buy $17 million worth of aircraft
and millions more in high-tech equipment without anyone in Congress
knowing? "Where did this money come from?" Keith asked. "What
controls were established? And who was responsible for establishing those
controls?" General Otis said he did not know.

Yellow Fruit, the agent told the general, had set up "what they
called this Operational Contingency Fund." The unit had created the fund
out of thin air to act as a conduit for their laundered cash.

And now, said Keith's partner, Kenneth Haynes, "the money is
gone and there is nothing to support the expenditures and the Operational
Contingency Funds do not exist as a line item."

The general was dumbfounded. "I know of no funds that they had
entrusted to them," he said.

Keith kept pressing. "In other words, they shouldn't have had brief-
cases full of cash, for instance, or a safe full of cash?"

"There was never any cash that I know of," the general said. "I
never heard of greenback dollars being on hand."

The agents went to interview General Homer Long, who had just
retired. Keith asked about the millions of dollars the soldiers had spent
in secret on aircraft and weaponry. Was the Army leadership aware that
"an Army soldier in civilian clothes went out with a suitcase full of
money or a check in hand and said 'I want one of those [aircraft]'?"
Keith asked.

"I don't think that was their understanding at all," Long said.

Did the general know that the division had torn up Army regulations
so that they could deal in cash, shred their records and evade any oversight?

"I'm not surprised because that was consistent with the way they
were operating," Long said. "That gets you back to the question of
whether they were honest or not. But the way they were operating was
to avoid all those controls."[29]

Perez and Enneking read the transcripts of the interviews with Otis
and Long in wonderment. They kept searching for someone to hold
accountable. They sat down with Major General Albert Stubblebine, the
head of the Intelligence and Security Command from 1981 to 1984. The
general conceded that he was asleep at the switch. "I did not question

the procedures,'' Stubblebine said. ''I made the assumption that the system was honest.'' In retrospect, he said, that was a sad mistake.[30]

Who authorized this system? Perez asked. Who approved it? Stubblebine ducked the bullet. ''I don't think I want to answer that directly,'' he said. ''You should be able to make your own conclusions.''

Well, General, Perez asked, did *you* authorize it?

''The system was already in existence when I arrived'' at INSCOM, General Stubblebine said. ''I assumed it represented the wishes of the Army leadership.'' The investigators realized that he was talking about Generals Meyer and Vessey.

Nearly three years after they began their investigation, Perez and Enneking paid a visit to the two men who had been at the top of the chain of command. General Meyer said he should have paid closer attention to what the division was doing, but that security considerations took precedence over everything. As for the division's financing, ''I was sure that there was a system established to perform these functions.'' There wasn't.

General Vessey had recently stepped down as chairman of the Joint Chiefs and was enjoying life at his home in Garrison, Minnesota. He was not particularly happy meeting with his interrogators in Washington. He acknowledged authorizing the destruction of records, but said the authorization was in an annex of a long memorandum he'd signed. He said he had never heard of Yellow Fruit. He said he'd never heard of the unique financial methods of the division. And he said that whatever security methods were used were justified.

''There was no intention that anyone get rich doing this,'' he said. ''The intent was to protect the people . . . to preclude their identity as military personnel.''[31]

The search for accountability was leading to an inevitable conclusion. Everyone was responsible. And no one was.

The final report on the affair filled eight volumes and nearly 2,000 pages. I obtained a censored version of the report from the Army under the Freedom of Information Act. The report remains the only publicly available audit of a set of black programs in existence. It shows a consistent pattern of crimes, a complete lack of control, and a clear illustration of how secret power grows when no one knows enough to say no.[32]

The report got to the point quickly. ''An unauthorized system for handling [black money] was devised, condoned and accepted by the Army,'' it said. It was ''a novel, unique and unauthorized method.'' And ''after the system was in place, it proliferated. . . . The system was totally devoid of clearly delineated regulations, procedures, internal controls and effective oversight.''

In all, eight of the Army's most powerful generals "knew of, condoned or approved the unauthorized Special Mission Funds system." At the top of the list were three familiar names.

"General Vessey"—chairman of the Joint Chiefs of Staff from 1982 to 1985—"knew of, supported, condoned and approved procedures that clearly violated Army and Defense fiscal regulations."

"General Meyer"—Army Chief of Staff from 1979 to 1983—"enhanced the atmosphere of laxity. . . . [He must] share in the responsibility."

"Lieutenant General Odom"—director of the National Security Agency from 1983 to 1989—"either knew of the system, should have known about it, condoned it" or "was remiss in discharging his responsibilities."

Any question of disciplining the eight generals was quashed by two Army lawyers who reviewed the report. They concluded that a general is "cloaked with the authority of his office." A general "is entitled to the presumption that his subordinates acted in accordance with the law." They said a general may make, bend or break a military regulation as he pleases. And as for the criminal law forbidding the destruction of government records, "there exists no evidence" that Generals Vessey and Odom "were aware of this law when they ordered destruction of the records."

A general, the Army lawyers appear to have concluded, is above the law. Case closed.[33]

What's good for a general is not necessarily good for the rank and file. The Army meted out administrative discipline to more than 500 lower-ranking personnel in the Special Operations Division. The retribution ranged from slaps on the wrist to fines. In all, thirty-six officers were fined, penalized or punished.[34]

Criminal investigations and indictments of the special-operations soldiers continue to this day. Eighty members of the Delta Force, the secret commando squad, have been disciplined for financial abuses. At least three members of the Navy's Sea, Air and Land (SEAL) Team 6, another clandestine unit, have been court-martialed for theft and fraud. At this writing, Army Major Michael Smith, the Intelligence Support Activity's officer in charge of procuring guns and ammunition, is under federal indictment for stealing at least 200 weapons from the ISA's arsenal. The list goes on, and it's a long one.[35]

Yet soldiers who'd stolen thousands of dollars went scott-free or lightly scolded. "There was a lack of reaction to people who were actually found guilty of things," Enneking said. "One guy who admitted stealing $8,000—at the end of his tour they gave him a medal and made him first sergeant of a unit. Guys who stole a thousand, two thousand dollars, they'd get a letter of reprimand put in their files. It was a good-old-boy network. We protect our own. You just can't have that sort of attitude, but it's pervasive."

The Army lawyers who absolved the generals made one trenchant observation: "The Army leadership was obsessed with operational security." Secrecy was paramount. Everything else—the financial free-wheeling, the operational failures, the conduct of the men—was secondary.

The generals never stopped to ask whether their clandestine units were accomplishing anything. What successes did the special-operations units have to show for themselves? Ferrying Bashir Gemayel back to Lebanon? A nice piece of logistics, but Gemayel was assassinated in 1983 and any benefits accrued from that mission were with him in the grave. The division had played a supporting role in the capture of the terrorists who'd hijacked the cruise ship *Achille Lauro* in 1985, and that was surely praiseworthy. But that was about it. The national security was not notably enhanced by the special-operations forces.

And the extreme secrecy surrounding the division's funding wasn't necessary to protect the men or the missions. "The regular security channels can handle covert processes," Captain Enneking said. "Only about 10 or 20 percent of the money went through Ackley for real operational security reasons."

Ultimately, "secrecy became an end in itself," Enneking said. "You could see it happen. There's no oversight, there's no control. You don't have any fiscal control, logistic control, legal control—we're talking about money, property and the law—and those are the three areas where all the screw-ups take place. You have no oversight in this special branch of the force. Eventually it gets into trouble. Eventually somebody's going to find out about it. You have a fiasco. . . .

"It's just a very good thing that Ollie North never met Autmer Ackley," Enneking said. "They almost did. In six months they would have. It was ready to happen. The people Ackley supported were starting to get close to the players in the NSC. All it would have taken is one meeting—'Ackley, this is Ollie; Ollie, this is Ackley'—and this thing would have just freaked."

The Yellow Fruit affair foreshadowed the Iran-contra debacle in ways that are still coming to light: the overreaching ambitions, the addiction to secrecy, the deception, the crimes. While North was still carrying easels at the National Security Council in 1981 and 1982, the secret soldiers already had gone black, siphoned off funds, bought planes and helicopters and ammunition, and deceived Congress about their activities. They set the pattern.

Yellow Fruit was a topic of some interest in the closed-door depo-

sitions given to the Iran-contra committee, the testimony too secret, too
sensitive or too strange to be taken in public. The Secretary of the Army,
John O. Marsh Jr., had some thoughts on the subject of Yellow Fruit.
Marsh had an unusually deep perspective on political control of the military and the intelligence community. He'd been President Ford's national
security adviser during the post-Watergate struggles to reform the CIA.
He'd been a four-term congressman from Virginia during the war in
Vietnam. As the Army's top civilian, he'd been circumvented and deceived by the secret soldiers.

The committee's lawyers asked him what went wrong with Yellow
Fruit. Marsh said it was an ingrained belief, held by everyone involved
with covert plans and missions, from the top of the chain of command
to the bottom: "If it's secret, it's legal."[36]

"When you take the view that if it's secret it's legal, then all existing
regulations and laws and norms and customs very frequently fall by the
wayside," Marsh testified. "People go forward with this objective because it's secret and therefore it's legal."

That was precisely what North had told the committee: "We operated
from the premise that everything we did do was legal," he said. Colonel
North had the President behind him. Colonels Duncan and Longhofer
had an open-ended authorization from the Army's top generals. They
thought anything they did in secret was blessed by a power higher than
the law.[37]

The parallels between Yellow Fruit and North's secret funding of
the contras were "disturbing and troublesome," Marsh testified. Both
had sought to create a network of soldiers and spies free from all control.
They freed themselves by finding sources of black money, spending
unaccountable funds unrecorded in the government's open books.

That kind of subterfuge "subverts the system and the institution,"
the Secretary of the Army said. The American system of government
demanded oversight and review of secret operations. The Army as an
institution demanded control by legitimate authority. Most of all, Marsh
said, "there must be a system for financial controls. There must be. . . .
If you do not have a financial control system I guarantee you will get in
trouble."

The nation needed to conduct secret missions, Marsh said. "In the
world in which we live intelligence operations are vitally important. They
are vitally important. And they are more difficult to structure at times in
a free and open society, but they can be done. But if you short-circuit
that system because it's difficult to establish those operations you are
courting disaster. . . .

"These black operations," he said, "have caused us some enormous
problems and a great deal of national embarrassment."

The crazies in the basement of the Pentagon and the military men working for the President grew frustrated with the controls Congress had imposed on covert operations. So they set up their own self-financing subterranean intelligence units run by men whose power flowed from secrecy. The secrecy created an anything-goes ethic, a feeling that nothing was forbidden. Without rules and laws to control them, the secret soldiers self-destructed.

The marriage of spies and soldiers, the merger of the Army's power with the CIA's secrecy, created militias that could not meet the standards of common sense. "You have a lot of rogue elements coming together" in the special-operations forces, Captain Enneking said. "These are high-speed, can-do people with a get-the-hell-outta-my-way mentality. You take that and cut it off from the rest of the world and you get some very weird things happening. . . . You learn how to lie. . . . You erode the bright lines. . . . And once you break that down it's hard to go back.

"The problem, the tension with this kind of unit is—it's very secret, it's very neat, it's very high speed. There are a lot of very good people who did not do their jobs with regard to the special-operations stuff precisely because it was secret, it was neat, it was high speed. There were lawyers who didn't look at it closely enough. Finance guys didn't look at it closely enough. People signed 1080s for millions of dollars, blind. Idiots! If it hadn't been a high-speed, high-pressure, black, covert thing, would they have done it? They temporarily suspended their own rationality. They suspended their normal thinking processes. They were co-opted and corrupted."

And three were court-martialed and convicted.

The Army investigations produced clear evidence that Colonel Longhofer, his second-in-command, Lieutenant Colonel Byard, and Lieutenant Colonel Duncan had gone off on a serious tangent from authority. With a grim sense of obligation, the Army began gearing up for its first secret courts-martial in twenty years.

Colonel Longhofer came before the court on March 31, 1986. He was charged with dereliction of duty for secretly controlling the Special Operations Division after his transfer to the CIA. He was charged with disobeying General Long's direct and lawful order to relinquish his command of the division. And he was charged with conduct unbecoming an officer for covering up the crimes of Yellow Fruit.

The trial lasted thirteen days. The verdict was guilty on all counts. Longhofer was sentenced to two years in the stockade. His career as a commander of the secret army had taken him from the shores of Lebanon to a cell in Leavenworth.

In May, Lieutenant Colonel Byard was tried and convicted on

charges of larceny for pocketing some of Yellow Fruit's funds. He was sentenced to eighteen months of confinement and fined $5,000.

On November 10, Lieutenant Colonel Dale Duncan stood before the secret tribunal in a tiny, tightly guarded room at the Army's Intelligence and Security Command. Duncan was found guilty of forgery, for filing $157,816 in phony receipts and false claims for reimbursement from Yellow Fruit. He was found guilty of theft, for pocketing $6,684 of Yellow Fruit's black money. And he was found guilty of obstruction of justice, for trying to conceal his crimes under the cover of military secrecy.

Military justice was severe: ten years in prison. Forfeiture of ten years' pay. A $50,000 fine. And dismissal from the United States Army.[38]

Two weeks later, on the night of November 24, 1986, Duncan steeled himself for the journey to Fort Leavenworth. Longhofer lay in his cell, hoping that his appeal would be heard. And Oliver North was up all night shredding his files, one step ahead of the FBI.

8

Laws and Lies

"Midshipmen will not lie, cheat or steal. . . ."
—FIRST SEVEN WORDS OF THE U.S. NAVAL
ACADEMY'S HONOR CODE.

**"In the U.S. Naval Academy, nobody taught me how to
run a covert operation."**
—TESTIMONY OF OLIVER L. NORTH, U.S.
DISTRICT COURT, WASHINGTON, APRIL 11, 1989.

OLIVER North sat before the television cameras in his crisp Marine
uniform, trying to educate Americans in the ways of the secret
world. The seminar started ten minutes after his testimony to the congressional Iran-contra committees began that hot July morning in 1987.

North's voice was a hoarse quaver, full of passionate intensity. "I
think it is important that we somehow arrive at some kind of understanding
right here and now as to what a covert operation is," he said. "By their
very nature, covert operations or 'special activities' are a lie. There is
great deceit, deception practiced in the conduct of covert operations.
They are at essence a lie. We make every effort to deceive the enemy
as to our intent, our conduct, and to deny the association of the United
States to those activities. . . . And that is *not wrong*."[1]

North thought lies were a legitimate instrument of the President's
power, a power limited by little in the Constitution or the law. So his
lies multiplied. He lied to the CIA, lied to the Congress, lied to his
colleagues in the White House. From the time he took the stand before
Congress to the day of his criminal conviction, North maintained that
lying is the common language of the secret world. The gospel of deceit
he preached and practiced was simple. Lies were the essence of covert
operations. Covert operations were the heart and soul of the President's
foreign policy. So the foreign policy of the United States was driven by
lies. And that was not wrong.[2]

North's dogma was dangerous nonsense, and veterans of the secret war knew it well. "I disagree with Colonel North as strongly as I can disagree with anyone," said Clair George, the CIA's chief of covert action, testifying in a secret session of the Iran-contra committees one month after North's appearance. "This is a business of trust," he said, "a business of being able to trust and have complete confidence in the people that work with you. And to think that because we deal in lies, and overseas we may lie and we may do other such things, that gives you some permission, some right or some particular reason to operate that way with your fellow employees—I would not only disagree with, I would say it would be the destruction of a secret service in a democracy."[3]

North, a devout Christian and a frequent visitor to CIA headquarters, must have been familiar with the thirteen words from the Gospel of John that the CIA has inscribed on the wall of its marble lobby: "And ye shall know the truth, and the truth shall make you free." Those words were carved into the wall for a reason North never understood. In a world of secrets, the truth is the only code to live by. When the players in a covert operation start lying to one another, things fall apart.

North brought the lies and cover stories required of covert operators abroad back home to Washington. Three years of painstaking investigation failed to sort the wheat of what really happened from the chaff of his lies. When he shredded, burned and hastily rewrote the documents recording his exploits, he was cheating history, trying to steal the truth. Creating false documents and shredding real ones were everyday acts in the secret world, or so North protested. In the eyes of the law, they were crimes.

North had stared into the eyes of Clair George and Alan Fiers, chief of the CIA's Central American task force, and swore that he was not running covert operations in Central America. The CIA officials transmitted what North told them to the congressional intelligence committees, spreading his lies like a virus. The CIA men were betrayed. "Lying in my business is a kiss of death, a Judas kiss," a chastened Fiers said in his own secret Iran-contra testimony. "You can't lie. You have got to believe in each other. Believe me, in the world in which I live and work, you have got to have a moral compass, a moral anchor. . . . If you don't, you will go and crash."[4]

Without that moral anchor, the Marine colonel and a martinet admiral, the tight-lipped National Security Adviser John Poindexter, embarked on a course that ran the ship of state aground. What little we know about their lies and self-deceptions was accidently preserved for posterity in the memory of a computer. The mainframe saved the mendacious memoranda they wrote to one another over a special secure communications system created by Poindexter, a system only the two of them could use. The memory banks held a tangle of facts and fabrications that may never be unraveled. The system was code-named PRIVATE/BLANK CHECK.

What transpired over the circuits of Blank Check transcended the legal code of control over covert action. The carefully crafted laws required a common understanding between the CIA and the Congress. The lies North and Poindexter told to Congress destroyed that bond. "I want you to know that lying does not come easily to me," North told the Congress in his sincere tremolo. But didn't they see? He had to lie to protect the secrecy of his missions, the arms shipments, the Swiss bank accounts, the bungled tasks. There were lives in the balance, he said, so he "had to weigh in the balance the difference between lives and lies."[5]

Laws didn't enter into North's equation. His argument was a weak echo of Winston Churchill's defense of lies during wartime, the idea that secrets are so important to victory in war that they must be protected by a bodyguard of lies. But the United States wasn't at war; it was running guns to Iranian radicals and Nicaraguan rebels. And the lies weren't merely sentinels for the secret policies North supported. The body and soul of the policies were a lie: the policies were covert actions, and covert action to North was at essence a lie.

The lies grew from a common root: the will to finance secret operations in defiance of the law, to create a cache of guns and money to carry out the President's commands. The secret funding of the arms shipments to the Iranians and the contras cheated the Constitution's checks. It plundered Congress' power of the purse. "This power over the purse," wrote James Madison, the Constitution's principal author, is "the most complete and effectual weapon with which any Constitution can arm the immediate representatives of the people."[6] This is part of the architecture of American democracy. Thomas Jefferson said the power of the purse created "one effectual check to the dog of war by transferring the power of letting him loose . . . from those who are to spend to those who have to pay."[7] The men who broke that leash were breaking the Constitution's clearest rules. They knew exactly how dangerous a game they were playing. On June 25, 1984, Secretary of State George Shultz told Reagan that it would be "an impeachable offense" to wheedle millions of dollars from other countries for the contras when Congress refused to provide the money. Shultz said this opinion came from a good lawyer—James Baker, then White House chief of staff and now the Secretary of State.[8]

Reagan ignored the warning. He put his men to work cutting deals for the contras with dictators and communists, enemies and allies alike. Going down the list of nations the United States used to aid the "Nicaraguan Democratic Resistance''—China and Brunei, Guatemala and Panama, Saudi Arabia and Iran—it's hard to find a democracy in the lot. They were by and large nations ruled by kings and generals. It was natural that Reagan felt free to solicit millions for the contras from King Fahd of Saudi Arabia. His compact with the king was a covenant between two royalists. The secret financing of an outlawed war had nothing to do with the democratic tradition. The pool of private cash for covert operations was a throwback to the monarchy of seventeenth-century England. In those days the kings used and abused the privy purse, a cache of funds set aside for public defense in peacetime. The kings dipped into the purse and spent its contents on personal whims without Parliament's knowing. In the 1980's the President and his men took millions of dollars off the books to finance their own solutions to their foreign-policy obsessions. The covert funds became the privy purse for the President's secret policies.

The secret treasury was controlled by North, the retired major general Richard Secord and his Iranian-born business partner Albert Hakim. It financed the renegade operation that Secord dubbed ''the Enterprise.'' The Enterprise was patriotism for profit, a covert corporation of CIA agents turned arms merchants, dummy companies and Swiss bank accounts. The Enterprise took in $48 million selling weapons to the Iranians, the contras and the CIA. The sales spun off roughly $14 million in cash. Some was pocketed by Secord and Hakim. Some helped pay for North's botched attempts to ransom hostages in Lebanon, for the contras' futile campaigns and for a series of unauthorized and fruitless missions in cahoots with Israeli intelligence agents.

The Enterprise was supposed to be a fairly accurate scale model of the national-security complex built by the black budget, the vault from which it drew its seed money, its technology and expertise. ''General Secord set up a number of organizations to do what the CIA had done before,'' North testified at his criminal trial. ''He basically created a mirror image outside the government of what the CIA had done.''[9] That image was a warped parody of a secret service in a democracy. The Enterprise existed to make money off of covert operations, and to generate profits for more covert operations. Its comptrollers were a disreputable crew. Secord's standing with his own government was so low that he couldn't get a security clearance. Hakim was a sticky-fingered salesman with visions of billions of dollars of weapons deals dancing in his head. North appears to have been practically pathological—''delusional, power-hungry, and a danger to the president and the country,'' in the words of Jacqueline Tillman, a fellow National Security Council staffer and an ardent conservative.[10] This covert operation's chief informant was the Iranian swindler Manucher Ghorbanifar, known to the CIA as a drug dealer, a gunrunner and a charlatan who lied so baldly that the Agency issued a rare worldwide "burn notice" against him, warning all CIA personnel to slam the door in his face if he ever approached them.[11]

But the Enterprise was more than a collection of failed schemes and subterfuges concocted by miscreants. In the words of Senator Daniel Inouye of Hawaii, chairman of the Senate Iran-contra committee, it was "a secret government—a shadowy government with its own air force, its own navy, its own fund-raising mechanism, and the ability to pursue its own ideas of the national interest, free from all checks and balances and free from the law itself."[12] It was not an aberration. It was not some mutant creature sprung from the imagination of a confused lieutenant colonel. It was a natural result of a system in which huge sums of secret funds can flow to a closed society of military men and clandestine operators, soldiers who can seize the reins of policy and power. It was the quintessence of the black budget.

Perhaps the lies that were the Enterprise's stock-in-trade proliferated because the truth was too unpleasant to reveal. In the name of democracy and freedom, the President's men joined forces with tyrants, thugs and thieves.

Ronald Reagan had been President for less than two months when he invited General Roberto Viola to the White House. Viola was the commander of the Army in Argentina. He had just been chosen as the new leader of the Argentine military junta. The Carter administration had severed military and intelligence ties with the junta because the generals were killing and torturing their domestic opponents with unusual vigor. Viola eventually was sentenced to seventeen years in prison for murder, kidnapping and torture, for commanding death squads responsible for abducting and killing at least 9,000 people during the junta's dirty war against its citizens.

Reagan told Viola back in 1981 that the United States was going to stop criticizing his government and start selling it weapons. "We have had a good discussion on bilateral and multilateral issues of concern to our respective countries," Reagan said after getting to know the general. "I look forward to efforts by both governments to further improve our relations, and I have extended to General Viola my best wishes for his tenure as president."

High on the list of multilateral issues of concern between the Argentina junta and the United States was a tiny band of insurgents that William Casey's CIA thought could overthrow the left-wing government of Nicaragua—the contras. The rapprochement between Reagan and Viola opened up channels between the CIA and Argentine military intelligence. The wintry week in which the two leaders met was when Casey first proposed covert action against Nicaragua. By the summer of 1981,

Argentina was providing money and training for the contras. The Argentines infiltrated intelligence operatives into Honduras, where the contras made camp near the Nicaraguan border. In August, the newly selected chief of the CIA's covert operations in Latin America, an epicurean dandy named Duane Clarridge who spoke poor Spanish and had no experience in the region, flew down to the Honduran capital of Tegucigalpa in the company of Colonel Mario Davico, the vice chief of Argentine military intelligence. There they met with Honduras' president, its intelligence chief and the head of its national police. Clarridge introduced himself as Dewey Maroni. He said the United States, Argentina and Honduras needed to unite to support an armed struggle against the Nicaraguan government. He said he spoke in the name of the President of the United States. He was lying; he had no legal authority. Then and there the secret war took shape.[13]

Four months later, on December 1, 1981, Reagan signed a finding authorizing a covert action against the Sandinista government of Nicaragua. The administration falsely told Congress that its only goal was to stop Nicaragua from exporting its revolution to the rest of Central America. Reagan's speeches conjured up visions of a communist tide sweeping north through Mexico to Texas, a red dagger aimed at the heart of America. Neither Congress nor the public bought this dire warning. A year after the covert action began, the Congress passed the first of a series of laws barring the administration from spending funds to further its true goal—toppling the government of Nicaragua.

On April 27, 1983, Reagan addressed a joint session of Congress. The subject was Central America. Three weeks earlier, contra leaders had declared that they were "fighting to liberate Nicaragua" and vowed to "cut the head off the Sandinistas."[14]

Reagan told the Congress:

Let us be clear as to the American attitude toward the Government of Nicaragua. We do not seek its overthrow. . . . Our purpose, in conformity with American and international law, is to prevent the flow of arms to El Salvador, Honduras, Guatemala and Costa Rica.[15]

Those three sentences contained three lies. First, the United States *did* seek to overthrow the government of Nicaragua. And, to that end, it violated both international law and American law, as the World Court and the Congress later determined. Furthermore, rather than stopping the flow of arms to El Salvador, Honduras, Guatemala and Costa Rica, the United States moved heaven and earth to send as many weapons as it could, from as many nations as possible, to generals and guerrillas in those four countries.

In April 1983, the same month that Reagan made his speech professing the good intentions of his administration, CIA director Casey began his worldwide search for secret sources of arms for the contras.[16] Casey asked Defense Secretary Weinberger if the Pentagon had a man who could obtain arms for the contras in secret. Weinberger knew a man for the job. He selected Major General Secord, a man who knew his way around an arms deal, having served as the Pentagon's official arms salesman to the Shah of Iran and the Saudis. Despite his experience, Secord was not in good repute in the intelligence community. "The good General Secord's reputation inside the CIA was not of the highest," as the CIA's Clair George put it. "He was in our minds, in my mind as a manager of the American clandestine service, an individual with whom I would not do business."[17]

Secord had been unable to clear his name of the tarnish he had accumulated from his business and personal ties to Ed Wilson, a derelict CIA officer now serving a fifty-five-year prison sentence for selling tons of high-grade explosives to Libya and plotting to murder his prosecutor. Secord's association with Wilson would forever block him from promotion at the Pentagon. The third star could wait, though. Secord now had the chance of a lifetime. He could serve his country by shedding his uniform and going black. He could get out from under the infuriating ethical cloud. He could use his skills to make millions in the global arms bazaar. And perhaps, if all went well, he could realize his dream of replacing Clair George as the CIA's director of covert operations.

Secord officially left the Department of Defense in May 1983. Sometime that year he began arranging secret weapons shipments to the Afghan *mujaheddin*. He secured a $1,260-a-week consulting job at the Pentagon's office of special operations. The Pentagon hired him as a member of the Special Operations Policy Advisory Group, a group of retired generals who were asked to provide disinterested expert advice on covert operations. Secord was without question an expert on the subject. Whether he was entirely disinterested is another story.

In late May 1983, Secord met with Major General Menachem Meron, the director general of Israel's ministry of defense. Their discussions were brief and the outcome favorable. Over the next year, Israel secretly gave the Pentagon several hundred tons of weapons captured from the Palestine Liberation Organization, more than $10 million worth of guns. The Pentagon gave the weapons to the CIA. The CIA gave them to the contras. And the CIA lied to Congress about the weapons' destination, saying they were bound for the Afghan resistance and other causes more popular than the Nicaraguan rebels. Most of the weaponry was funneled to the contras after the guerrillas' legally appropriated funds ran dry in 1984.

By 1984 the tone was set. The administration was prepared to lie to preserve its power to do as it pleased. It was prepared to deal with unsavory governments such as Argentina's to achieve its goals. CIA director Casey was prepared to work at the very edge of the law, and beyond. Though the law now forbade arms shipments to the contras, the White House, the Pentagon and the CIA tried "to avoid complying with an established law by going black," said Senator William Cohen, Republican of Maine, during the Iran-contra hearings. When the administration could not win the consent of Congress, it would circumvent the legal system. Secret operations would supplant open policy.

"One of the risks" of covert action, the former CIA director Stansfield Turner has written, "is that it may get out of control." Covert agents given broad authority by their superiors "gain sufficient momentum of their own at some point to go on without us if necessary." When Congress outlawed weapons shipments to the contras, Reagan wistfully asked Poindexter to help him break that law. "Isn't there something I could do unilaterally?" the President pleaded. That plea provided the broadest possible authorization for the national security adviser. The next act in this shadow play was the private financing of covert action. Black money freed the President's men from the nagging leash of the law and constitutional restraints.[18]

The kind of conduct covert action condones was illustrated by the kind of company the President's men kept. In 1985, North telephoned a British mercenary by the name of David Walker. The two had been introduced by John Lehman, the Secretary of the Navy. Walker ran a skulduggery and sabotage outfit called Keenie Meenie Services—Keenie Meenie being an African idiom describing the undulations of a snake in the grass. North put the mercenary on Secord's burgeoning payroll. Together North and Walker coordinated commando missions in Nicaragua. Keenie Meenie's men managed to burn down a hospital in the process of blowing up a Sandinista arsenal, an act accomplished with the assistance of a Panamanian bomb-maker. The bomber was in the employ of General Manuel Noriega, the murderous military strongman who then ruled Panama.[19]

Noriega, who'd been a CIA agent when George Bush ran the Agency, saw an opportunity to do a little business with the boys at the National Security Council. He needed some assistance from his American friends. He was under investigation by the U.S. Justice Department for providing protection in Panama to the Medellín cartel, the world's biggest cocaine ring. He now faces trial in Florida for receiving millions of dollars from the cartel in exchange for giving sanctuary to their cocaine. American intelligence officials also had overwhelming evidence that Noriega recently had ordered his most prominent political opponent kidnapped, tortured, and beheaded.

Noriega dispatched an emissary to meet with North. Noriega's man proposed that if the U.S. would help clean up Noriega's sullied image and lift its ban on weapons sales to Panama, Noriega could do the U.S. some favors. He could assassinate the Sandinista leadership. He could sabotage Sandinista assets. North and Noriega met at least twice to discuss these propositions in 1985 and 1986. North carried Noriega's offers to his boss, Vice Admiral Poindexter. Poindexter said assassination was inappropriate. But if Noriega could carry out acts of sabotage on behalf of the American government, that was another matter entirely. Such was the secret foreign policy of the United States in those years.[20]

The members of the congressional Iran-contra committees, men not noted for radical thoughts, tried to put things simply and directly: "Excessive secrecy in the making of important policy decisions is profoundly antidemocratic."[21] It is profoundly foolish as well. Not only did North conspire with a dictator like Noriega to further the President's secret foreign policy; he ran a series of illegal and inept operations to ransom five American hostages in Lebanon. Reagan authorized North's ransom plans, although he later said he was "having some trouble remembering" that he did. The operation came as a shock to nearly everyone else in the American government.

While his superiors constructed their grand strategy of selling weapons to Iran to win the hostages' freedom, North concocted a separate scheme to buy the hostages from their kidnappers. He paid nearly half a million dollars in bribes to swindlers for information on the hostages—information that invariably proved worthless. North worked on the ransom plans with two Drug Enforcement Administration agents, like himself absolute amateurs at espionage. The DEA and the CIA kicked in seed money for the mission, illegally keeping the funding secret from Congress. For daily expenses, North skimmed $90,000 from a secret cash account set up for the contras. For serious capital, North turned to H. Ross Perot, the Texas billionaire who in the past had proved a reliable source of private funds for U.S. intelligence. Perot eventually put up $2.3 million in cash for North's bribery and ransom schemes. More than $400,000 was lost chasing false leads before the efforts collapsed. The Marine fell for "case after case of bums, crooks and petty thieves trying to sell hostages," said the CIA's Clair George.[22] An Iranian con man convinced North he was a Saudi Arabian prince with superior intelligence contacts and snookered him out of more than $15,000. An Armenian informant claiming to know a hostage's whereabouts got $100,000 from North and promptly disappeared in Syria. Lebanese informants with drug connections sought and received hundreds of thousands of dollars more.

North's prize informant went to Beirut in June 1985 and returned to Washington with a hot property—a copy of a Beirut newspaper that the informant said had been initialed by hostage William Buckley, the kidnapped CIA station chief in Beirut. Buckley's secretary was shown the handwriting on the paper and told CIA officials they'd been duped. It wasn't Buckley's. In fact, as the CIA later determined, Buckley already was dead, the victim of more than a year of torture and neglect. Exasperated, Clair George declared North's ransom operation "hocus-pocus" and "a scam." He assumed a decision had been reached that summer to shut the mission down. North thought otherwise. He continued to believe the Buckley signature was genuine and kept the Lebanese informant on the payroll. Far from scrapping the operation, North arranged for the informant to receive $200,000 more of Perot's money for more information, as well as $11,000 in contra funds for his expenses. The informant produced nothing else of value. The operation continued for another sixteen months.

The first of the secret arms sales took place in August and September 1985. North and the CIA helped Israel ship 496 American antitank missiles to the Iranians. The missiles were seized by Iran's Revolutionary Guards, the most radical faction in a radicalized nation. The $6.2 million transaction broke U.S. laws and tough presidential vows. But it raised profits and produced results. One American hostage, the Reverend Benjamin Weir, was set free on September 15. Elated, North spent the fall and winter tirelessly churning out new ideas, working eighteen-hour days and finally hitting on the ingenious method of selling arms to Iran at the highest possible price to generate cash for the contras.

Sometime in early 1986, North began ricocheting between fact and fantasy. He returned bleary-eyed from overseas flights to boast of his exploits, telling his cohorts he had Muslim hostages in cages all over Europe and the Middle East, ready to be bartered for American captives. "God bless poor Colonel North," Clair George said with measured sarcasm. "Everything was his, the world is mine, I'm going to see the President, I'm going to see the King, I'm going to fly down to Central America and have a private conference. How would you like some tickets to the Redskins game? *Christ. . . .*"

By the time North's missions finally exploded in his face, there were three more American hostages in Beirut than when he began. In early 1990, six remained captive, if they were indeed still alive. The ransom and the bribery and the arms sales were all "an exercise in enormous coup. It looked to Moscow for support. Armed rebellions against the Kabul government broke out in March 1979. The Soviets sent tanks and helicopter gunships to the Afghan capital. By mid-summer, 1,500 Soviet advisers were running what passed for the government in Afghanistan; 4,000 Soviet officers and technicians controlled an increasingly rebellious army. In August, an Afghan army regiment revolted and sent tanks rolling toward the regime's headquarters in a futile attack. Soviet helicopter pilots destroyed them. As the Afghan state began disintegrating, the Red Army began mobilizing for an invasion. Soviet military advisers and KGB agents filtered into Kabul in September. In mid-October, Soviet officers seized control of the strategic Shindand air base in western Afghanistan, less than 600 miles from the Persian Gulf. America's spy satellites observed Soviet troops massing near the Afghan border throughout November and December 1979.

Afghanistan, as big as Texas and as poor as Ethiopia, has had the enduring misfortune of lying landlocked amid high mountains, harsh deserts and huge empires. Surrounded by Russia, China, Iran, and what was the British raj in India, it had been sacked and pillaged and subdued over the millennia, yet never truly conquered. Its ancient cities had survived the onslaughts of Alexander the Great, Genghis Khan and Tamerlane. Now it faced the most brutal attack in its 6,000 years of civilization.

The first of 115,000 Soviet troops flew into Afghanistan on Christmas Eve on military transports and Aeroflot planes. Their assault was the first Soviet military seizure of a foreign land since World War II. Moscow's agents killed the inept Afghan leader, Hafizullah Amin, and installed a rigidly pro-Soviet ruler, Babrak Karmal. Film footage of Karmal's first public appearance after the invasion, on New Year's Day 1980, shows him waving jerkily to a crowd from a balcony, like a puppet on a string.

President Carter told Americans on December 28 that the invasion was "a grave threat" to world peace. On January 8, he said it was "the greatest threat to peace since the Second World War." A secret State Department report concluded that the United States could not stop the Soviet Union from driving into Iran and on to the Persian Gulf. If that happened, the report said, the United States should consider using tactical nuclear weapons against the Soviets. The stakes were about as high as they can be.[4]

Before the invasion, the CIA had confined itself to financing demonstrations among Afghan exiles, beaming radio propaganda into Afghanistan, and cultivating alliances with exiled Afghan guerrilla leaders by donating medicine and communications gear. Ever since the April 1978 coup in Afghanistan, the rebels had been training in camps inside Pakistan, and the CIA kept in touch with their political elders. One of them, Zia Nassery, warned a State Department official against the idea of a coalition of rebel groups. He said it would be like "putting five different animals in the same cage."

The CIA ordered its station chief in Kabul to keep his eye on the Soviets, rather than organizing and supporting resistance groups. The CIA and the State Department also had been keeping watch over the Arab nations' support for the Afghan resistance. The American ambassador in Libya reported that Muammar Qaddafi was sending the rebels $250,000. Secretary of State Cyrus Vance cabled his ambassadors in the region that Saudi Arabia also was funding the guerrillas. A CIA field report sent from the American embassy in Pakistan in October 1979 describes one of the resistance leaders, Syed Ahmed Gailani, meeting with "a Pakistani army major who would provide the Afghan dissenters with ammunition for the tribal insurgents."[5]

The Soviet invasion gave Afghanistan's "tribal insurgents" a new stature in the eyes of their countrymen. Now they were *mujaheddin*, a word with powerful religious meaning in Islam: part freedom fighter, part avenging angel—holy warriors of Allah. Their God commanded them to do battle. But Allah's soldiers were ill-equipped. To stand a chance against the Soviets, they needed missiles to repel the fearsome helicopter gunships and rocket-propelled grenades to pierce the armor of tanks.

President Carter decided within a week after the Soviet invasion to send arms to the Afghans. But the weapons could not come from American stockpiles. The guerrillas had to be able to claim their arms were captured from the enemy, not supplied by the CIA. Hiding one's hand in this way was standard procedure in a covert action. Carter later wrote in his memoirs that he ordered the CIA to begin "arranging for Soviet-made weapons (which would appear to have come from the Afghan military forces) to be delivered to freedom fighters in Afghanistan."[6]

The CIA was ready. After years of post-Watergate investigations, firings and doubts, here was an opportunity for the Agency to test itself in a war against the Soviet Union.

At first an ethical question confronted the CIA. Was it right to encourage outgunned and disorganized guerrillas to fight against the bombers and helicopter gunships of the Red Army? Was it willing to fight to the last Afghan? The *mujaheddin* were more than willing to die for their cause; to die in a holy war was the swiftest path to heaven. They would have fought the Russians with or without the CIA's help.

"We had some moral dilemmas in the beginning," said Admiral Stansfield Turner, Carter's CIA director. "The question in the beginning was, is it right for the United States to give weapons to people who wind up being killed in order to keep the Russians off balance? I thought that futility," said Francis McNeil, a former senior intelligence official at the State Department. "We didn't get any hostages out to speak of. A couple of hostages out and a couple of hostages taken." North's passion for secrecy proved futile as well. "Most of the Executive branch charged with dealing with sensitive actions, the Congress and the American people are all frozen out of it," McNeil said, "but you know that every [hostile intelligence service] knew exactly what was going on, and you know that every sleazy arms dealer in Western Europe knew that somebody was trying to make a killing on the Iranians with the U.S.'s blessing. . . . You know the reason they cut everybody off was they knew people would object to it. The noise would become too loud for this stupid initiative to bear."[23]

Naturally, no one in the Reagan administration told Congress about the DEA caper, the arms sales to Iran or the weapons shipments to the contras. The failures to notify Congress were flagrant violations of law. The law governing congressional notification of covert action—the 1980 Intelligence Oversight Act—explicitly covers every agency in the government. To say, as North and Poindexter did, that the National Security Council or the Drug Enforcement Administration could run covert operations with the CIA's help but without congressional approval, without appropriated funds, was to sever constitutional and legal control of covert action.

The law had to be short-circuited for the President's policies to continue. Of course Congress had outlawed weapons shipments to the contras, but the President, his CIA director, his national security adviser and his favorite foot soldier decided they didn't like the law. They needed secret financing to fund their foreign policy. The black money they generated allowed a clandestine arm of the government to run itself, check itself, finance itself and expand its power free from outside control. This was a direct assault on the constitutional system. In the end, the laws of the United States were trampled by a long parade of lies.

What justified the lies? For North and Casey and Poindexter, a state of war existed between the United States and its enemies—not only communists, but congressmen who opposed Reagan's policies and had the power to stop them. They felt this state of war made anything they did legal and constitutional. During the Iran-contra hearings, Senator George Mitchell, the Maine Democrat who is now the Senate majority leader, asked North to tell him about this martial code. "During your discussions" with Casey and Poindexter, the senator asked, "did the question ever arise among you as to whether what was being proposed was legal?"

North appeared confused by the question. He took on the startled expression of a jacklighted deer in a high beam. "Oh, no—I don't think it was—I mean—" he stammered. "First of all, we operated from the premise that everything we did do was legal."

This was a false premise. It was the rationale of a man at war. In war laws are suspended, lies are legitimate, and even murder is moral. From 1984 to 1986 the nation's most important foreign policies were conducted in secret by a handful of men in thrall to this imagined state of war. For Casey, World War II continued; for North and Poindexter, Vietnam raged on. The unreal war burned inside them, consuming the parchment of laws and charters. A battlefield ethic prevailed and the rule of law was suspended.

This fire in the minds of men in power was explained eloquently a while ago by William C. Sullivan of the FBI. Sullivan was the Bureau's deputy director in the 1960's and 1970's, the number-two man during and after the reign of J. Edgar Hoover. Sullivan held a seat on the U.S. Intelligence Board, a presidential executive committee on espionage. He was privy to most of the highest secrets in the land.

"During the ten years that I was on the U.S. Intelligence Board—a board that received the cream of intelligence for this country from all over the world and inside the United States—never once did I hear anybody, including myself, raise the question: 'Is this course of action which we have agreed upon lawful? Is it legal? Is it ethical or moral?' " Sullivan said in a talk with congressional investigators. "We never gave any thought to this. Legality was not questioned. Lawfulness was not a question; it was not an issue."

Sullivan attributed this blind spot to "a war psychology," a state of mind carried over from the Second World War after the war was over. "We could not seem to free ourselves from that psychology," he said. "Along came the Cold War. We pursued the same course in the Korean War, and the Cold War continued, then the Vietnam War. We never freed ourselves from the psychology that we were indoctrinated with, right after Pearl Harbor, you see. I think this accounts for the fact that nobody seemed to be concerned about raising the question: 'Is this lawful, is this legal, is this ethical?' It was just like a soldier in the battlefield. When he shot down an enemy, he did not ask himself: Is this legal, or lawful, is it ethical? It is what he was expected to do as a soldier. We did what we were expected to do. It became part of our thinking, part of our personality."[24]

Sullivan was explicating the covert creed: "If it's secret, it's legal." Or, as Richard Nixon once explained: "When the President does it, that means it is not illegal." So it was. The White House deemed the law an irritating impediment and ignored it. The CIA director and the Marine and the Navy admiral did what was expected of them, and carried out

the President's outlaw policy. That no one has been held responsible for
that lawlessness, and no one is likely to be, is a lasting testament to the
power of secrecy.

On the witness stand at his criminal trial in April 1989, North was
smaller, grayer, sadder than the Marine we all remember. He seemed
diminished. North recalled how the President of the United States praised
him as "an American hero." Now he heard the prosecutor, like himself
a heroic Marine, damn him for "a flat-out, one-hundred percent, old-
fashioned American lie." North's defense was a patchwork of discredited
and disreputable theories. First was the Nuremberg defense: I was only
following the President's orders. Then came plausible deniability: I had
to destroy the documents to preserve the President's secrets. And finally
the theory of executive privilege: the President can do whatever he
pleases, the courts and the Congress be damned.

When a President takes the oath of office from the Chief Justice of
the Supreme Court, he swears to take care that the laws are faithfully
executed. To fail in that duty is an impeachable offense. Reagan's televised lies in November 1986—arms were not swapped for hostages, the
United States had no connection to the weapons shipments to the contras
and to the Iranians—stemmed from his reading of false documents prepared by North and his superiors. North was convicted of felonies for
creating those false documents. He had said he was forced to choose
between lies and lives. Poignant as his choice may have seemed to him,
he chose lies, broke the laws of the United States, and caused a credulous
President to break his oath of office and commit an offense against the
Constitution.

There is no executive privilege to lie. Even North appeared to rec-
ognize this at his trial: "I was raised to know the difference between
right and wrong," he testified, choking up and choosing his words carefully. "I knew it was wrong not to tell the truth. I felt like a pawn in a
chess game being played by giants. . . . I was put in a situation where,
having been raised to know what the Ten Commandments are, that I
knew it would be wrong to do that, but I never dreamed it would be
unlawful." It was. But North was convicted only for the lies he told and
the documents he destroyed to save himself after the schemes were exposed, and of the humiliating act of taking $13,000 or so from the
Enterprise's profits to build himself a security fence around his suburban
home.[25] Poindexter, too, was convicted of covering up crimes, not com-
mitting them.

No one ever stood trial for the true crimes of the Iran-contra conspiracy. No one ever will. The White House, the Justice Department and
the CIA made sure of that.

At each turn in the legal process, the government tried to scuttle the central charges against North, Poindexter and their co-conspirators. At every step of the way, the courts tried and failed to rebuff their efforts. Before North's trial began, the judge, Gerhard Gesell, said he was faced with "an absurd situation": the White House, the Justice Department and the CIA had declared that reams of information, facts previously printed by the press and thus presumably known to the public, were actually deep secrets that could not be divulged in open court at North's trial. "The press is accurately reporting information in the public domain while the court is confronted with representations that the same facts must never be officially acknowledged," the judge said. The Attorney General of the United States, Richard Thornburgh, acting on behalf of Reagan, Bush and the nation's intelligence agencies, insisted that scores of details, names and locations—most of them plain facts already printed and published—were secrets so sensitive that their revelation would cripple the United States.

The secrets he strove to protect included the names of countries, such as Great Britain and South Africa, whose help the Reagan administration had sought in its war against the Sandinistas. These secrets included the fact that CIA officials operate out of American embassies in foreign capitals such as San Salvador, El Salvador, and Managua, Nicaragua. Any careful reader of the *Washington Post* or the *Wichita Eagle-Beacon* was well aware of all this.

Thornburgh confessed when questioned by reporters that he had not actually read the documents containing these secrets. But he had received assurances from high-ranking intelligence officers at the CIA and the White House that disclosing the facts the documents contained would endanger the nation. In fact, he conceded in a secret affidavit, the existence of these CIA stations and their locations were publicly known. Yet he argued that to acknowledge such facts openly would gravely damage the national security.[26]

And so the Justice Department drove a stake into the heart of the criminal cases against North, Poindexter and Secord. It effectively prevented the independent prosecutor appointed to try the cases from functioning independently. It denied the defendants documents they wanted to use in their defense. And it compelled judges to deep-six the crux of the cases. Judge Gesell was forced to dismiss the central charges against North: stealing profits from the Iran arms sales and spending them on the contras. Similar charges of conspiracy, theft and fraud against Poindexter and Secord were dismissed for the same reasons: the refusal of the government to reveal supposed secrets of state.

Then the Justice Department torpedoed the criminal case against Joe Fernandez, the former CIA station chief in Costa Rica. Fernandez was supposed to have helped plan shipments of weapons to the contras in defiance of the congressional ban. He was charged with lying to investigators from the CIA and a presidential commission about what he and North had done. The case against Fernandez was summarily dismissed at Thornburgh's insistence. The Attorney General barred the disclosure of the locations of CIA field offices in three American embassies in three Central American capitals. Again, this set of facts was hardly a state secret. It was not news to informed citizens of Costa Rica, El Salvador, Nicaragua and the United States.

"To call that a secret vital to national security or an unacceptable risk seems very hard to accept," said the independent prosecutor in the Iran-contra cases, Lawrence Walsh, a former federal judge, a lifelong Republican and a past president of the American Bar Association. What the government kept under seal were "fictional secrets." Walsh took the extraordinary step of warning President Bush directly that the refusal of the White House and the CIA to declassify these imaginary secrets posed "a very serious danger" to the rule of law. The secrecy would "insulate most if not all officers responsible for national security from prosecution," no matter what their crimes. The obsession with secrecy had become "ritualistic," a "fetish" within the government, Walsh told reporters as his cases fell apart. "I think we're getting to an extreme position here," he said. "What can occur is the development of an enclave of important national-security officers who are beyond prosecution because the intelligence agencies will not release the information necessary to their trial."[27]

What had occurred was a drift away from a government of laws. Crimes against the Constitution could not be prosecuted if they involved facts the government deemed secret. The greater the crime committed in the name of national security, the less likely was the accused to come to justice.

A trial is supposed to be a search for the truth. Secrecy had subverted that ideal. The government declared its secrets more important. The law was overpowered by the invocation of national security. There would never be sworn testimony in open court on the central facts of the Iran-contra conspiracy. No one would be held accountable. No one would ever know the whole truth. What would remain was a litany of lies. The lies shielded the workings of a secret government. What went on within it was impenetrable to the laws of the United States.

9

An Open Book

I N the old world, government was secret and its secrecy was sacrosanct. The king's mandate came from heaven. His command held the power and mystery of the church's holy rites. No one could question his authority, much less peer inside his purse. His word was law.

"None shall presume henceforth to meddle with anything concerning our government or deep matters of state," King James I of Great Britain warned the Speaker of the House of Commons. "Concerning government, it is a part of knowledge . . . deemed secret," the philosopher Francis Bacon, one of King James' subjects, wrote in 1605. "We see all governments as obscure and invisible."[1]

This was the government the American revolution rejected. The Framers gave a great deal of thought to the question of secrecy. They concluded it should be checked. They allowed for secrecy in diplomacy, in time of war and in executive sessions of Congress. But the men who wrote the Constitution wanted their government to be visible. They wanted it to be an open book.

The Framers thought the best way to do this was to let the people know how their government spent their money. They thought this knowledge was essential for the people to exercise their political power, to control their elected representatives and to live up to their responsibilities as citizens. So they required public laws and public budgets to keep the government open, honest and accountable for its actions.

The social compact the Framers sought to create was an engine that would run in perpetual motion. The people's money would power the machine of government, and the government would empower the people with information. Money was power; information was power; these powers would be exchanged in the constitutional machinery. The people would finance their government through taxes and receive in return an open accounting of how their money was spent.

"When the Public Money is lodged in its Treasury, the People who give their Money ought to know in what manner it is expended," James McHenry of Maryland said in the debates over the Constitution's language. Patrick Henry of Virginia insisted that a free people could not "allow the national wealth . . . to be disposed of under the veil of secrecy." His fellow Virginian, George Mason, "did not conceive that the receipts and expenditures of public money ought ever to be concealed." The people, he said, had "a right to know the expenditures of their money."[2]

This elegant idea, the right to know, was the source of democracy's power. Public information about the government gave power to the people. A secret government left them no better off than a serf under a king. "A popular Government without popular information, or the means of acquiring it, is but a prologue to a Farce or a Tragedy; or perhaps both," President James Madison said. "Knowledge will forever govern ignorance. And a people who mean to be their own Governors, must arm themselves with the power which knowledge gives."[3]

An open government sustained by public knowledge and funded by lawful appropriations could not conduct a secret war. The President could not spend a nickel to raise an army or ransack an enemy, not unless Congress gave it to him after open debate and an open decision. The power to make war depended on the power to finance an army; the Constitution separated those powers by locking the treasury and the arsenal in separate rooms. "The purse and the sword ought never to get into the same hands, whether legislative or executive," George Mason said at the Constitutional Convention.

The canon shaped in this crucible was Article 1, Section 9, Clause 7 of the Constitution:

No Money shall be drawn from the Treasury, but in Consequence of Appropriations made by Law; and a regular Statement and Account of the Receipts and Expenditures of all public Money shall be published from time to time.

The genius of this sentence was that it simultaneously pierced the veil of government secrecy, controlled the power to make war and expanded the power of public knowledge.

The Framers also thought a public budget would prevent political and financial corruption. They saw it as "a most useful and salutary check upon profusion and extravagance, as well as upon corrupt influence," wrote Joseph Story, a Justice of the Supreme Court from 1811 to 1844, in his commentaries on the Constitution. "It is wise to interpose . . . every restraint by which the public treasure, the common fund of all, should be applied with unshrinking honesty to such objects as legitimately belong to the common defence and the general welfare."[4]

As democracy took root in the new world, those who loved it warned against the power of secrets. In 1814, John Taylor, a defender of Jeffersonian democracy, wrote of the ignorance and impotence that clandestine government could create. "Executive secrecy is one of the monarchial customs . . . and certainly fatal to republican government," Taylor said. "How can national self-government exist without a knowledge of national affairs? Or how can legislatures be wise or independent, who legislate in the dark?"[5]

The Cold War eroded these ideals. It transformed the way the American government spent its money and used its power to achieve its goals. The nation's military and political leaders decided that the United States could not be ruled by the gentle assumptions of a bygone civilization. This new war made those old notions outdated. They belonged to a world where gunpowder, not plutonium, defined the power of the state.

The secrecy of the Manhattan Project was a mutant chromosome in the American body politic. The explosion of the secret weapon engendered a secret bureaucracy within the government. Soon the bureaucracy began creating secrets to keep. It issued security clearances and invoked security classifications and devised a secret lexicon of code words. It made policies and laws and appropriations in secret. It used secret weapons and secret wars to expand the nation's power. Secrecy itself became a weapon of the state.

Secret weapons cannot be built and secret wars cannot be fought without a secret treasury. The Central Intelligence Agency Act of 1949 legalized secret government spending and made shadow wars and clandestine programs possible. In time, the secrecy that shrouded the CIA's covert actions would envelop the nation's most expensive weaponry and its most elaborate foreign policies.

The Framers did not conceive a government that spent the nation's wealth and planned the nation's most important strategies behind the veil of secrecy. The architects of American power in the postwar world created a national-security state behind that veil. Given the power to spend money unchecked, it grew into a government accountable only to itself.

For a generation after World War II, no citizen challenged the constitutionality of secret spending. Few knew the system existed. Few knew the Constitution forbade it. Very few had the combination of knowledge and courage required to oppose the power of secrecy. And then, in 1967, William Richardson, a forty-nine-year-old insurance claims examiner in a small town in western Pennsylvania, decided to take a stand.

Richardson knew of and believed in the communist threat. He was well aware of the value of secret intelligence.

Richardson speaks in the banjo twang of his native land, the Tennessee Appalachians. He is an angular man, tall and thin, and now a bit bent with age. He is patriotic, but without sanctimony. He is a man who loves his country well. He had served as a communications and intelligence officer in World War II. When the Korean War came, he had served in civilian intelligence. His respect for the proper uses of secrecy is such that, forty years later, he will not discuss what he did during the war in Korea.

He is, in his own words, "a regular citizen," no different from most Americans, except in one respect. Between the wars he'd earned a law degree at the University of Tennessee, and in those years he'd come to know the Constitution by heart. He became, he said, "a constitutionalist more than anything else."

The practice of law didn't agree with Richardson, and so he took up work at an insurance company and settled down in Greensburg, Pennsylvania, a town in the Allegheny foothills thirty miles outside Pittsburgh.

In February 1967, he picked up his morning paper and read a story about the CIA. The story said the Agency was secretly funding organizations in the United States—student associations, trade groups, publishing companies and the like.

"It kind of floored me," he recalled years later. "I had no idea the CIA did anything in the United States. Of course we don't want communism in this country. Of course there's nothing wrong with an intelligence agency that does intelligence work, collecting foreign intelligence. Nothing wrong with doing that in secret outside the United States. Though that kind of went against the American grain, it was necessary. But I thought the American taxpayer, if he believed in the Constitution, didn't want his money spent to fight political wars in our own country.

"That started me looking into the Central Intelligence Agency Act, and *that* started me looking back into the Constitution," Richardson recounted. "The CIA Act said the CIA director didn't have to account for how he spent money. The Constitution said that a regular statement and account of the receipts and expenditures of all public money shall be published. Well. Here we wake up suddenly and there must have been a hundred of these organizations inside this country that the CIA was funding. . . ." Richardson mulled it over and decided that the secret-spending provisions of the CIA Act were unconstitutional. He decided to challenge the system on his own.

"We shouldn't undercut our Constitution even though we need intelligence," he said. "The people are sovereign and if they don't know what the government is doing they can't function in that capacity."

Richardson wrote a letter to the U.S. Government Printing Office on May 12, 1967. He requested a copy of the CIA's budget "published by the Government in compliance with Article I, section 9, clause 7 of the United States Constitution." The Agency used public money; the Government Printing Office published the federal budget provided by the Treasury; the constitutional command for publication was clear. Three months passed before he received a reply. The letter came from the Department of the Treasury's deputy commissioner for central reports and accounts, H.A. Turner. It was polite. It apologized for the tardiness of the response. And it in no way responded to Richardson's request. Turner enclosed copies of the federal budget, but the information Richardson sought could not be found in them.[6]

Richardson tried again. He sent Turner a letter quoting the CIA Act and asking whether the Agency's unaccounted spending did not "cast reflection on the authenticity" of the budget the Treasury published. The response was less polite this time: "We have no other information with respect to the Agency mentioned in your letter."

Richardson wrote back to Turner at the Treasury on September 25, 1967. His letter was a direct challenge:

Dear Sir:
 . . . The statement that you have no information available with respect to the Agency is not consistent with the [Treasury's] Constitutional mission. The Constitution . . . clearly requires the Treasury to make freely available to the Public an accurate statement and account of the receipts and expenditures of *all* their money. . . . The Treasury is only the instrument for presenting this document to the People and neither the Treasury, the Bureau of the Budget, the Congress, nor any other group in the Government has license to make the statement and account misleading. If the Treasury issues a document purporting to be a statement published in compliance with Article I, Section 9, Clause 7 of the Constitution, it must include all Government agencies spending money. I cannot conceive legislation as Constitutional that operates to withhold from public scrutiny the expenditures of public money by any Government agency. This letter respectfully requests that the Treasury terminate its present publications until

a ruling is given by the Attorney General's office as to what should be published in compliance with Article I, Section 9, Clause 7. . . .

A prompt reply advising how you intend to proceed will be appreciated. I would advise a careful consideration of the legal aspects involved. If the Government takes a position adverse to me, I would like to know the basic reasoning.

Sincerely yours,
William Richardson

One month later, Richardson received a reply from S.S. Sokol, the Treasury's commissioner of accounts. Sokol said, in so many words, that Richardson hadn't a prayer. He had no legal right to challenge the system of secrecy, no right to a legal opinion on its constitutionality, no right to the full accounting he sought, and no right to request that the Treasury alter its publishing practices to comply with his reading of the Constitution.

Richardson sat down at his typewriter and composed his response. When it was complete, he went down to the federal courthouse in Pittsburgh and filed it with the clerk of the court.

William B. Richardson v. United States of America was a sophisticated legal argument against government secrecy. Introducing himself to the court as "a member of the electorate, a loyal citizen of the United States [and] a taxpayer," Richardson based his complaint "upon authority of the United States Constitution." He argued that the CIA Act was "repugnant to the Constitution," for it "operates to falsify the regular Statement and Account of all public Money" called for by the Constitution. He said the omission of the CIA's spending made the federal budget "a fraudulent document. . . . a misrepresentation inconsistent with responsible government."

Richardson cited all the proper federal laws calling for open appropriations and forbidding the falsification of government documents. He petitioned the court to uphold the laws. He asked it to order the men at the Treasury to "perform their duties . . . as prescribed by the United States Constitution." He sought nothing from the United States government but a copy of the true account the Constitution required.

The *Pittsburgh Post-Gazette* published an article about Richardson's suit. It was the kind of story that can spur a reporter's interest, an ordinary citizen taking on the CIA. It was also the kind of story that can shock the sensibilities of a small town or a small mind. "A lot of people thought I was some kind of subversive," Richardson said. "Soon I was getting dark glances at work. . . . I was fired by the Old Republic Insurance Company in 1969. I surmised it was because of the case." He was out of work for a year after losing his job. He finally found employment as a legal investigator for the newly created public defender's office in his home county.

Richardson was opposed at every turn in court by the United States Attorney for the Western District of Pennsylvania, a young, politically ambitious prosecutor named Richard Thornburgh, now the Attorney General of the United States. Thornburgh and his assistants told the federal judge in Pittsburgh, Joseph P. Willson, that Richardson had no right to sue the government for the redress of his grievance.

Judge Willson agreed. The judge threw the case out of court. He said Richardson did not have standing to sue the government. Standing simply means the legal right to file a lawsuit under the rules of federal law. In this case, Richardson's right as a citizen to sue his government was at issue. The law said he had to have a personal stake in the outcome of the case; he also had to raise a specific constitutional challenge. On June 16, 1970, after nearly three years of technical wrangling and delays, Judge Willson said Richardson did not meet this standard.

A higher court said he did.

Richardson sought a hearing from the United States Court of Appeals in Philadelphia. The appellate judges sat in a Depression-era courthouse four blocks from the eighteenth-century red-brick buildings where the Constitution was signed, where the nation's first Supreme Court sat and the Liberty Bell rang out.

The federal appeals courts lie one rung below the Supreme Court of the United States; they can reverse a trial court's judgment on questions of legal precedence or constitutional interpretation. The appeals court normally hears cases in three-judge panels. It first heard arguments in *Richardson v. United States* on June 25, 1971. Richardson had written a thirty-three-page legal brief, a studious document save for one impassioned passage:

> The complaint now before this court is not without merit. Never in the history of this country has so much money been spent without the traditional safeguard of openness and in direct defiance of constitutional provisions.* Wars can be fought by mercenaries paid out of the Treasury of the United States for which there is no accounting. Corporate structures are secretly formed to act as instruments of destruction or suppliers of war materials whose capital assets come from tax receipts. . . . Billions are

---

*Richardson was right; the CIA had been pouring hundreds of millions of dollars into undeclared wars in Chile, Laos, Vietnam and elsewhere while his case was pending.

spent each year by unknown entities and this amount is spread throughout the Treasury's reporting system to confuse the public and belittle the Constitution.

. . . . None of the questions presented by the complaint have previously been precisely decided by the Federal courts in any full opinion.

Since Richardson was not a lawyer admitted to the Pennsylvania bar, and because his suit raised complex constitutional questions, the court decided to appoint a distinguished law professor, Ralph Spritzer, as *amicus curiae*, or "the friend of the court," to write a brief on Richardson's behalf. Professor Spritzer refined the argument:

The issue, put in its bare bones, is whether the public is entitled to know, because the Constitution confers the right, how much the CIA gets and spends. . . .

The Framers were seeking to assure the public's right to know. . . . A revolution had been fought largely because of popular resentment of a distant sovereign who taxed and spent without public accounting. . . .

It is hardly an accounting in any meaningful sense if the expenditures of the CIA are shown as welfare payments or aid to undeveloped countries—any more than it would be a satisfactory accounting if a taxpayer were to file a tax return showing items of income as capital gain and expenditures for personal pleasure as contributions for charity.

The government's argument was terse: Richardson had no standing to sue for disclosure of the CIA's budget. He was making a political argument in a court of law. Congress in its wisdom had chosen to keep this information secret—secret even from the vast majority of the Congress itself. Neither the law nor the Constitution gave Richardson the right to challenge the CIA's secret spending. The United States owed him nothing.

After hearing arguments, the court decided to review the matter *en banc*, meaning all nine appeals judges appointed to the court would consider the case—an unusual forum generally reserved for important and legally novel issues.

On July 20, 1972, the court ruled for Richardson. In a six-to-three decision, it said he had the right as a taxpayer to challenge appropriations that flew in the face of a constitutional prohibition.[7]

Circuit Judge Max Rosenn wrote the opinion of the court:

In contrast to the case frequently heard on appeal, in which the Government seeks an accounting from the taxpayer, here it is the taxpayer who seeks an accounting from the Government. . . .

[Richardson argues] that the constitutional duty to provide a regular account of the receipts and expenditures of public money is one owed to the taxpayer, for its obvious design is to provide members of the electorate with information lying at the core of public accountability in a democratic society. . . .

The Government argues that no specific duty exists because the Congress has, by the Central Intelligence Agency Act, relieved the Secretary of the Treasury of the obligation to publish a statement pertaining to the funds received and expended by the CIA.

The court rejected the government's legal position. It did not decide whether the CIA Act was constitutional. But it said that Richardson's challenge to its constitutionality was a live issue. The law creating the CIA *might* be unconstitutional, and the government could not base its defense on a dubious law.

Nor could the government say that the Secretary of the Treasury had no obligation to Richardson to account for the CIA's spending. The Framers wanted the statement of receipts and expenditures published and "widely circulated . . . for the benefit and education of the public." The relevant law said the reports were "for the information of the President, the Congress and *the public*." The court said Richardson "has set forth a clear duty owed to him by the Secretary of the Treasury."

The court next addressed the difficult question of standing. The issue had confounded the nation's federal judges for years, and the law was still murky. Richardson's standing rested on two questions. Did he, as a citizen and a taxpayer, have a personal stake in this case? Did his challenge go to the heart of a constitutional question?

Richardson had the legal right as a taxpayer to challenge unconstitutional expenditures, the court said. And here was the gist of the issue:

How can a taxpayer make that challenge unless he knows how the money is being spent? . . .

A responsible and intelligent taxpayer and citizen, of course, wants to know how his tax money is spent. Without this information he cannot intelligently follow the actions of the Congress or the Executive. Nor can he properly fulfill his obligations as a member of the electorate.

The Framers of the Constitution deemed fiscal information

essential if the electorate was to exercise any control over its representatives and meet their new responsibilities as citizens of the Republic; and they mandated publication . . . of the Government's receipts and expenditures. Whatever the ultimate scope and extent of that obligation, its elimination generates a sufficient, adverse interest in a taxpayer.

Richardson had passed the first part of the test. At stake was his right to information guaranteed to him by the Constitution. Now, was the case a constitutional matter for the courts to decide, or a political question best left to politicians?

"It would be difficult to fashion a requirement more clearly conveying the Framers' intention . . . to require public accountability," the court said. Richardson wasn't raising a general complaint about his government; he wasn't trying to destroy the CIA; he didn't want the details of the CIA's daily life. "He only seeks an accurate statement of account for the tax money extracted from him and spent."

If Richardson, "as a citizen, voter and taxpayer, is not entitled to [sue] to enforce the dictate of the United States Constitution that the Federal Government provide an accounting for the expenditure of all public money," said the court, "then it is difficult to see how this requirement, which the framers of the Constitution considered vital to the proper functioning of our democratic republic, may be enforced at all."

The court noted that Richardson's suit was unprecedented. "Nevertheless," it noted, "the Government would have us conclude that the question raised is plainly without merit." The government was wrong. Richardson was attacking a law "allegedly repugnant to a specific constitutional mandate." The Constitution clearly could be read in Richardson's favor, and "there is nothing in prior decisions of the Supreme Court which forecloses such interpretation." The appeals court had ruled that Richardson had the law and the Constitution on his side.

The court's ruling came at an auspicious time. The CIA was spying on American citizens, opening their mail and tapping their phones, conspiring to overthrow a freely and democratically elected government in Chile. The Agency was being used as an instrument of imperial power, accountable to no one save the President. Four weeks earlier, President Nixon had secretly ordered the CIA to block the investigation of the Watergate burglary, an obstruction of justice, an impeachable offense. Secrecy and deception were at their zenith in American government.

Now the United States government appealed to the nation's highest court to stop this citizen from opening the black budget's books.

Six years after he first walked into the federal court in Pittsburgh, William Richardson, now fifty-five, stood on a sidewalk in Washington looking up at the Corinthian columns and the classical Grecian figures that grace the American temple of justice. Behind him stood the dome of the Capitol. He took a deep breath, crossed the street, ascended the marble steps of the Supreme Court and stepped inside. He was awed and grateful. "I was just a regular little old person . . . but I'd found this discrepancy in the law that should be taken care of. I remember giving thanks for the government that we have and the government that we should not lose."

What Richardson had done reached all the way back to the beginnings of democratic government. The architecture of the Supreme Court recalls ancient Greece not merely for the aesthetics of design, but to evoke the essence of democracy. The court is open to the public and to the challenge of a citizen because the democratic tradition respects openness and rejects secrecy. Twenty-four centuries ago, the world's first democracy, the city of Athens, was locked in the first year of a long war with Sparta. The great Athenian general Pericles rose to address the citizens gathered at the city's annual memorial for the war dead. He reminded them what they were fighting for: "Our constitution and the way of life which has made us great. Our constitution is called a democracy because power is in the hands not of a minority but of the whole people. Our political life is free and open. . . . There is a great difference between us and our opponents, in our attitude toward military security. Our city is open to the world, and we have no periodic deportations in order to prevent people observing or finding out secrets which might be of military advantage to the enemy. This is because we rely not on secret weapons, but on our own real courage and loyalty."[8]

Courage, loyalty to the Constitution and a gut sense that secrecy was undemocratic had brought William Richardson to the Supreme Court. His case, now styled *United States v. Richardson*, for it was the government's appeal, came before the Supreme Court on October 10, 1973, as the floodtides of Watergate engulfed Washington. The United States was represented in court by its chief lawyer, the Solicitor General, an acerbic, sharp-tongued attorney named Robert Bork. Richardson remembers Bork well. "He was quite a remarkable-looking character. A pudgy guy, little red beard, and he came out in full tails and everything," wearing the formal morning coat the Solicitor General traditionally dons when coming before the court.

Ten days later, Bork carried out President Nixon's command to put into motion the Saturday Night Massacre, firing the Watergate Special Prosecutor, Archibald Cox, after the Attorney General and Assistant Attorney General of the United States refused to do so and resigned on principle instead. Fourteen years later, the United States Senate would deny him confirmation as a Supreme Court justice, finding his vision of the Constitution intolerably narrow.

Richardson now was represented by a lawyer from the American Civil Liberties Union, Osmond Fraenkel. As he watched and listened to Fraenkel make his argument before the court, hearing the fine-tuned repetitions of the ideas he had lived with for so long, he sensed a chill emanating from the Chief Justice, Warren Burger. The Chief didn't seem receptive to the civil-liberties lawyer. Fraenkel left the court downcast. "He had the impression afterward that things were not going to go our way," Richardson said. "I thought we were going to suffer if we lost."

During the six years it took for Richardson's case to come before the Supreme Court, the government of the United States time and again insisted that its national-security powers outweighed citizens' rights and freedoms. Time and again the justices of the high court had rejected that notion.

Can the wartime power of government overrule the powers of the law and the Constitution? No, said Justice Potter Stewart, in a 1967 case upholding the rights of a laborer with left-wing views to hold a job in a defense plant:

> "War power" cannot be invoked as a talismanic incantation to support any exercise [of government power]. . . . "National defense" cannot be deemed an end in itself, justifying any exercise of legislative power designed to promote such a goal. Implicit in the term "national defense" is the notion of defending those values and ideals which set this nation apart.[9]

Can national security close off the open government envisioned in the Constitution? Can it curtail the people's right to know what their government is doing in their name? Not in this country, said Justice Hugo Black, in the 1971 case allowing newspapers to publish the Pentagon Papers, the government's secret history of the Vietnam War:

> The word "security" is a broad, vague generality whose contours should not be invoked to abrogate the fundamental law [of the Constitution and the Bill of Rights]. The guarding of military and diplomatic secrets at the expense of informed representative government provides no real security for our Republic.[10]

Is there really a public right to know in the secret realm of nuclear weapons and classified stratagems? Absolutely, said Justice Stewart in the Pentagon Papers case:

In the absence of the governmental checks and balances present in other areas of our national life, the only effective restraint upon executive policy and power in the areas of national defense and international affairs may lie in an enlightened citizenry—in an informed and critical public opinion which alone can here protect the values of democratic government.[11]

These voices are in the mainstream of American political thought. One power, and one power alone, outweighed the government's invocation of national security: the fundamental rights of the citizenry to speak, write and think freely. All these freedoms flowed from the right to know. What was at stake in these cases, and in Richardson's, was the use of national security as a sword to cut off popular dissent and a shield to protect the government's power. The justices had chosen to protect values and ideals they deemed more important than military secrecy and national security.

Democracy is a dogfight, an unending battle between the rights of the people and the powers of the government. For every famous victory there are a hundred people whose spirits have been crushed because they fought for something they believed in and lost, and suffered the defeat of their ideals, and felt something inside of them die a small and quiet death.

William Richardson lost. On June 25, 1974, the Supreme Court ruled that no citizen had the right to know—or to challenge—the government's secret spending. The vote was five to four.

Chief Justice Burger spoke for the bare majority. The Chief Justice wrote that Richardson had no standing to sue the government; his rights were not at stake; the books would not be opened to him.

"It can be argued that if [Richardson] is not permitted to litigate this issue, no one can do so. In a very real sense," Burger wrote, that was true. The courts were closed to the citizens in this case. The release of the information Richardson sought was up to Congress, not the courts.

"The subject matter is committed to the surveillance of Congress and ultimately to the political process," the Chief Justice said. "Any other conclusion would mean that the Founding Fathers intended to set up something in the nature of an Athenian democracy or a New England town meeting to oversee the conduct of the National Government. . . ."

The court did not have to listen to every man in the street with a constitutional grievance. If Richardson didn't like the law, let him vote for different lawmakers. Let him and any other like-minded "dissatisfied citizens convince a sufficient number of their fellow electors that elected representatives are delinquent in performing duties committed to them." With that wave of the hand, the Chief Justice dismissed Richardson. He had no right to know—none that the court was bound to uphold. His right to know could be enforced only through the "slow, cumbersome and unresponsive" electoral process.[12]

"One has only to read constitutional history to realize that [Burger's] statement would shock" the Founding Fathers, Justice William O. Douglas wrote in a fiery dissent.

"Secrecy was the evil at which Article I, Section 9, Clause 7, was aimed," Douglas said. "The Framers inserted it in the Constitution to give the public knowledge of the way public funds are expended. . . . Secrecy of the government [now] acquires new sanctity."

Douglas continued:

> Congress of course has discretion, but to say that it has the power to read the clause out of the Constitution when it comes to one or two or three agencies is astounding. . .
>
> [This] decision . . . relegates to secrecy vast operations of government and keeps the public from knowing what secret plans concerning this Nation or other nations are afoot. . . .
>
> History shows that the curse of government is not always venality; secrecy is one of the most tempting cover-ups to save regimes from criticism. . . .
>
> The sovereign in this Nation is the people, not the bureaucracy. The statement of accounts of public expenditures goes to the heart of the problem of sovereignty. If taxpayers may not ask that rudimentary question, their sovereignty becomes an empty symbol and a secret bureaucracy is allowed to run our affairs.[13]

By a single vote, the Supreme Court cut off a citizen's access to information guaranteed by a clearly delineated constitutional right. It locked away the government's books. The power of secrecy proved greater than the power of the Constitution itself.

Douglas' dissent was also a strong current in the American mainstream. Now this stream was diverted, dammed by the construction of the black budget, and by the court's failure to inspect the constitutionality of its construction. Richardson's suit had raised enormous questions: Could the Constitution's command for a public budget be overridden by an act of Congress? Could the government ever be compelled to comply with that command? Was secret spending a breach of the Constitution's social compact with the citizenry? The Supreme Court left these issues unresolved. It said only that a citizen had no power to expose the black budget. The question of whether secret spending was constitutional was not addressed. Nor has it been addressed by the courts to this day. For now no citizen could ask that question, and the Congress would prove that it lacked the courage to answer it. The consequences of the failure to resolve these issues have been great.

In the months that followed the Supreme Court's rejection of William Richardson, the constitutional crises that secrecy had brought to the American government crested and broke like waves in a storm. Four weeks after the ruling, the President who had used secrecy as sword and shield against his own people fell from power. By the year's end, Americans began to learn that the CIA had become a secret police force in this country and, as President Lyndon Johnson once said, "a Murder Incorporated in the Caribbean" and in Africa. Saigon fell, ending a thirteen-year war that began as a small covert action and slowly spun out of control. The long struggle to reform the CIA and restrain the power of secrecy began.

By the time Ronald Reagan came to power in 1981, not seven years after the Court's ruling, the spirit of reform had faded. The CIA's budget doubled. Its agents began more than fifty major covert actions against foreign enemies both real and imagined. Covert action came to be the basis of American foreign policy. When the Congress cut off funding for the CIA's war in Central America, a private army run by a Marine in mufti found its funds in arms deals with a foreign enemy. The secrecy the Founding Fathers thought best reserved for the subtleties of diplomacy came to conceal foreign policies so foolish that they could not withstand the light of day.

The Pentagon began to bury its costliest weapons in the black budget, hidden from the proving ground of open debate. The production lines for secret armaments began running full-bore, creating Stealth bombers, MILSTAR satellites, advanced cruise missiles and a score more of nuclear war–fighting weapons. Now some ten billion black dollars a year are spent in secret on this weaponry, and a price is being paid that cannot be measured in money alone.

For these weapons are fundamentally useless. If they are used, they can destroy creation. Public information and open debate about these weapons must not be prohibited. By stamping the subject secret, the Pentagon leeches power from the citizenry.

As if we were still at war—and we are not at war in any sense that respects law and language—the government justifies secrecy and deception by higher reasons of state. In the war against Hitler and Hirohito, military secrets had a rationale. The citizenry had to be kept ignorant to keep the nation's secrets from the enemy. Today, in an era when the enemy appears evanescent, we are kept ignorant to keep us from questioning our own government.

Where the workings of government are wrapped in secrecy, they can be conducted outside laws and charters and constitutional restraints.

And that leads to plans and policies that frighten even hardened covert operators. In 1987, the CIA's director of covert action, Clair George, testified to a kind of mania that grips men empowered by secrecy. "If you were ever on any given day to know all the plans that were being made inside the American government on all the subjects, you would be so terrified you would leave," the spymaster said. "You can't stop people from planning. You've got to stop them from acting." It has proven difficult to stop them from acting. For what takes place behind this veil is, in Clair George's words, "a business that works outside the law . . . a business that is very difficult to define by legal terms because we are not working within the American legal system."[14]

A system that exists outside the law breeds lawlessness. It can produce, as Senator Inouye said, "a secret government. . . . free from all checks and balances and free from the law itself."[15]

The black budget is a challenge to the open government promised by the Constitution. Today close to a quarter of every dollar in the Pentagon's budget for new weapons is cloaked in blackness. This was not what Jefferson and Madison had in mind. Their vision is violated daily by the workings of the black budget. Every dollar spent in secret defies the Framers' intent that the balance sheet of government should be a public document. The Constitution's high standard of honesty and accountability is mocked by weapons and policies concealed by fraudulent disguises, labeled as something they are not, or simply erased from the public record. Our democracy denies its heritage by spending secret funds.

In the name of secrecy, political debate has been stifled. In the ensuing silence, the Pentagon has built exorbitant weapons of questionable value. The White House has carried out polices that have shamed the nation. And Congress has abdicated a power it held in trust for the people: the power of the purse. "The purse of the people," Jefferson wrote, "is the real seat of sensibility." Unwise, illegal and unconstitutional acts are the natural consequence of a black budget, since clandestine spending stands on an unsettled legal and constitutional foundation. The secret treasury was built on swampland.

Secrecy conceals the costs, and suffocates criticism, of the search for a magic bullet to make us invincible in war. The bomb was classified from its conception, and as its power grew, silently and unseen, casting lengthening shadows on the political landscape, it evolved into a national factory of warheads, computers, scientists and soldiers, a complex hidden in the highest realm of national-security secrets. In the realm of the bomb, military minds shaped political questions. Military technology shaped political thought. Military secrecy controlled political power. The secrecy prevented even Presidents from knowing and controlling the size and nature of the nation's nuclear forces. Secret powers naturally expand when unchecked; two bombs became nearly 25,000 in less than twenty years. Nearly 25,000 remain. We have found no way down yet from the Everest of warheads we built.

Perhaps, in the depths of the Cold War, the age demanded unlimited spending for secret weapons of every sort. "We are rightly spending billions" on nuclear weaponry, and "we must similarly deal with all aspects of the invisible war . . . in an era of unique and continuing danger," the CIA director Allen Dulles said in 1962.[16]

The era of danger is ending. The world in which the black budget was born and raised is vanishing. The emergency is over. The day when the fear of the enemy validated everything under the shield of national security is done. Communism is dying a natural death. It cannot subvert or destroy us.

For nearly fifty years the idea of national security has been expressed by nuclear weapons and covert actions. The world is changing in ways that make that definition self-defeating. We have spent ourselves into debt financing secret weapons: are we stronger? We have chosen these weapons over human needs: are we safer? We have fought scores of secret wars: are we more secure?

Security is freedom from danger and fear. We need fear the destruction of the ecology, the skewing of the economy and the scourge of poverty more than a nuclear attack by the Soviets. They have chosen to scale down their military because their people lack decent food and shelter and a third of their harvest rots in the field for want of trucks and fuel. Their national security no longer can be measured in weapons. Neither can ours.

Even Presidents have expressed their doubts about the wisdom of defining national security solely by military strength. President Eisenhower warned that "this world in arms is not spending money alone. It is spending the sweat of its laborers, the genius of its scientists, the hopes of its children." President Kennedy said the superpowers were "devoting massive sums of money to weapons that could better be devoted to combating ignorance, poverty and disease. . . . We all inhabit this same small planet. We all breathe the same air. We all cherish our children's future. And we are all mortal."

We as a nation can decide freely to spend our sweat and our genius and our treasure on weapons and wars. We cannot do so in secret and still claim our uniqueness as an open democracy. From the creation of the atomic bomb through the building of the Stealth bomber, from the covert funding of the CIA's secret wars through the clandestine conspiracies of the Iran-contra fiasco, the costs of secrecy have been high. We the people pay the highest price. As Justice Douglas said, what a secret treasury costs us is a rudimentary question. The simplest answer is an eleven-digit sum, some thirty-four billion dollars a year. But when we cannot ask that question of our government, we have lost the right to know, and without the right to know we are without power.

"It's natural for an army to have secrets," says William Richardson, now seventy-one years old and contemplating the end of his days. "But what is natural for an army is not necessarily what's best for a democracy." The secrecy best suited for a nation at war can be an enemy to a people seeking peace.

AFTERWORD
TO THE PAPERBACK EDITION

A s I write, the United States is at war again, fighting to restore the Emir of Kuwait to his throne. In the first great giddy flush of the battle, Americans have been dazzled by high-tech weaponry at work. But the greatest of the black weapons programs—the B-2 Stealth bomber, MILSTAR and the A-12 attack plane—are not in battle. They are serving only to drain the Treasury and sap strength from the forces in the Persian Gulf.

Since this book first went to press in the summer of 1990, a little more light has illuminated these weapons, and as the light grows, the costs of secrecy become clearer.

"The real problem with the B-2," Senate Armed Services Committee chairman Sam Nunn told me, "is that it was kept too secret too long." Nunn spoke on the day the Air Force declassified devastating reports describing years of chaos on the Northrop Corporation's B-2 production line. By then the company was under eleven criminal investigations. Justice Department officials had proposed barring Northrop from future Pentagon contracts. But with $28 billion down the drain, the Congress decided it was too late to stop the bomber cold. Throwing good money after bad, it approved $4.1 billion more for the B-2.

In the only public report ever to mention MILSTAR, the Senate Armed Services Committee said the system's cost had risen to more than $35 billion, and declared that "the Department of Defense has not justified the extraordinary expense of this over-designed system." Yet the Congress, without benefit of full debate, then approved another $950 million for MILSTAR.

The first audit of the Navy's biggest black program, the A-12 attack plane, revealed that dramatic problems, including a $2 billion overrun in the early stages of development, had been concealed under the cover of national security. The Pentagon's procurement czar and the Navy admiral in charge of the plane lost their jobs after auditors concluded that the Navy had used the covertness of the program to keep those problems concealed. Among those kept in the dark were the Congress and Defense Secretary Dick Cheney. In his chagrin, Cheney canceled the $58 billion program.

These three programs, paradigms of excessive secrecy, survived as long as they have because the Pentagon hid their birth and growth under the cover of the black budget, keeping their costs and their failures secret. I believe the lesson is clear. The Congress should forbid the Pentagon from concealing what we must pay for its armaments. The procurement of arms should not be conducted in secret, as if it were a covert operation. There should be far fewer blank spaces in the Pentagon's weapons budget. Once weapons programs reach a certain threshold—say, $50 million a year—they should be unveiled and debated like any other immensely costly undertaking.

A struggle more important than the fate of any one weapon went on behind closed doors. The Senate defense appropriations subcommittee reported in October 1990 that the White House, the Pentagon and the CIA had for years "ignored or challenged" the secret law passed by the defense and intelligence committees governing how the black budget must be spent. "The executive branch chose to regard" the law as a mere suggestion "which it could comply with or ignore as it saw fit," the report said. The result was that Congress had submitted unwillingly to "a sweeping abdication of authority"—its constitutional authority over the black budget.

President Bush's overt response was to veto the entire 1991 intelligence authorization act, the bill containing the bulk of the black funds hidden in the Pentagon's budget, saying he could not accept its restrictions on covert action. In a stroke, he nullified the laws governing how some $29 billion of black funds were to be spent—but continued to spend the money.

This cannot continue. No real or imagined threat to our national security justifies abrogating any part of the Constitution. The White House, as President Reagan once conceded, does not have the authority to spend a nickel—much less tens of billions of dollars—by executive fiat.

One way out of the present conundrum would be for Congress to allow itself more open debate on the spending of the nation's secret agencies. Congress should publish the aggregate budgets, discuss the priorities, debate the findings of these agencies. In an era when KGB and CIA officials can meet and seek common goals, this openness will not help our enemies, nor will it hurt us.

The CIA provides an invaluable service to the nation by analyzing political, economic and military events in a fiendishly complex world. Its independent-minded gathering, analysis and dissemination of intelligence should be strengthened and defended. But its role as the president's secret army should be curtailed. Covert action should begin only in extraordinary circumstances, only by congressional consensus, and only when checked regularly to make sure it is working in the way its controllers conceived it. Secret operations are not the best means of achieving democratic goals.

Nor should American ends be served by undemocratic means. The White House has fought to a garrison finish for the idea that it has the power to spend secret funds as it pleases, make secret foreign policy, undertake secret acts of war. While it wages this battle, it funds such operations with black money. It invoked the talisman of national security to thwart the criminal trials of CIA and White House officers in the Iran-Contra affair, and in the end subverted the law to preserve its secrets.

"Every thing secret degenerates," Lord Acton said, "even the administration of justice." The nation can have both secrecy and democracy if those in power will follow the rule of law. But the ruse of turning the Pentagon's balance sheet into a cover story should stop. The practice of black budgetry is a relic of the Cold War and should now come to an end. The creation of secret weapons and secret wars began four decades ago with an obscure passage in an opaque law giving the CIA and the Pentagon power to spend the public's money unaccountably. Slowly and silently, that power grew unchecked. The costs of secrecy have been billions of dollars wasted on useless weapons, a set of renegade foreign policies, and a people grown cynical of their democracy.

"I believe," James Madison said two hundred years ago, "there are more instances of the abridgment of freedom of the people by gradual and silent encroachments of those in power than by violent and sudden usurpations." If we want freedom unabridged, the public ledger of the government must be an open book.

—January 20, 1991

ACKNOWLEDGMENTS

THIS book began with the freedom granted me by Gene Roberts, executive editor of the *Philadelphia Inquirer*, to undertake an open-ended investigation of the Pentagon's secret spending. I am grateful to him for running his newspaper as if it were a Zen university instead of a frozen TV-dinner factory.

In Washington, I received guidance from Dina Rasor and Donna Martin, both formerly with the Project on Military Procurement; A. Ernest Fitzgerald and Thomas Amlie, the Pentagon's staunchest in-house critics; John Pike of the Federation of American Scientists; Gordon Adams and Stephen Alexis Cain of the Defense Budget Project; and Jeffrey Richelson, Jeff Nason and Steve Galster of the National Security Archive.

On my way to and from Afghanistan, the late Ambassador Arnold L. Raphel was generous with his time and his honesty during long interviews at the American embassy in Islamabad, Pakistan. His death in 1988, in an airplane crash that smelled of sabotage, was a rude shock to me and a great loss for the United States.

Many of the documents cited in chapters 2 and 3 were declassified at the request of the historian David Alan Rosenberg and the journalist and author Fred Kaplan. Their work has been a beacon to me. Bob Walsh, chief of the Freedom of Information Act office of the U.S. Army Intelligence and Security Command, at Fort George G. Meade, Maryland, was helpful in declassifying the documents on Yellow Fruit on which Chapter 7 is based.

William Richardson was kind enough to open up his thoughts and memories to me. Timothy Enneking patiently and forthrightly guided me through the maze of the Yellow Fruit affair.

Many thanks go to Faith Hampton Childs, my literary agent, and to Jamie Raab, my editor.

Finally, I am grateful to the friends who helped me write this book: Barbara Demick, Luisita Lopez, Catherine Manegold, Andy Maykuth, Jerry Mindes, Matt Purdy, Dale Russakoff, Margaret Scott, Lena Sun and Helen Winternitz. They are the art and the architecture of my life.

NOTES

Chapter 1 THE BLACK BUDGET

Unless otherwise noted, financial facts and figures in *Blank Check* are derived directly from the author's study of Department of Defense budget documents and the testimony of Department of Defense officials before Congress.

1 Figures are from *Department of Defense Budget For Fiscal Year 1991, RDT&E Programs (R-1)*, Department of Defense, January 29, 1990.

2 *Acquiring Strategic Weapons: Are Working Nukes Just Flukes?*, privately printed report by Rep. Les Aspin, June 1988.

3 The GAO's findings are outlined in "Special Access Programs," U.S. General Accounting Office, unclassified summary of classified report GAO/NSIAD-89-133 (Washington D.C.: Government Printing Office, May 1989) and "Special Access Programs: DOD Criteria and Procedures for Creating Them Need Improvement," U.S. General Accounting Office, unclassified summary of classified report GAO/NSIAD-88-152 (Washington D.C.: Government Printing Office, May 1988).

4 Richard Halloran, "Pentagon Official Accuses 8 Concerns on Secret Data," *New York Times*, December 22, 1988, p. A1; Mark Thompson, "Pentagon: 8 firms paid for secrets," *Philadelphia Inquirer*, December 22, 1988, p. A1.

5 Interviews with House Armed Services Committee staff, January 1990.

6 Interviews with former Army officers and House Armed Services Committee staff, June and September 1989.

7 Marty Overbeck-Bloem's assessment of the National Reconnaissance Office's research and development spending is not an isolated opinion. In his sober and sympathetic book

262728293031323840424445464748495052535455565758596061626364656667686970717273747576777879808182838485868788899091929697989910010110210310410510610710810911011111211311411511611711811912012112212312412512612712812913013113213313413513613713813914014114214314414514614714814915015115215315415515615715815916016116216316416516616716816917017117217317417517617717817918018118218318418518618718818919019119219319419519619719819920020120220320420520620720820921021121221321421521621721821922022122222322422522622722822923023123223323423523623723823924024124224324424524624724824925025125225325425525625725825926026126226326426526626726826927027127227327427527627727827928028128228328428528628728828929029129229329429529629729829930030130230330430530630730830931031131231331431531631731831932032132232332432532632732832933033133233333433533633733833934034134234334434534634734834935035135235335435535635735835936036136236336436536636736836937037137237337437537637737837938038138238338438538638738838939039139239339439539639739839940040140240340440540640740840941041141241341441541641741841942042142242342442542642742842943043143243343443543643743843944044144244344444544644744844945045145245345445545645745845946046146246346446546646746846947047147247347447547647747847948048148248348448548648748848949049149249349449549649749849950050150250350450550650750850951051151251351451551651751851952052152252352452552652752852953053153253353453553653753853954054154254354454554654754854955055155255355455555655755855956056156256356456556656756856957057157257357457557657757857958058158258358458558658758858959059159259359459559659759859960060160260360460560660760860961061161261361461561661761861962062162262362462562662762862963063163263363463563663763863964064164264364464564664764864965065165265365465565665765865966066166266366466566666766866967067167267367467567667767867968068168268368468568668768868969069169269369469569669769869970070170270370470570670770870971071171271371471571671771871972072172272372472572672772872973073173273373473573673773873974074174274374474574674774874975075175275375475575675775875976076176276376476576676776876977077177277377477577677777877978078178278378478578678778878979079179279379479579679779879980080180280380480580680780880981081181281381481581681781881982082182282382482582682782882983083183283383483583683783883984084184284384484584684784884985085185285385485585685785885986086186286386486586686786886987087187287387487587687787887988088188288388488588688788888989089189289389489589689789889990090190290390490590690790890991091191291391491591691791891992092192292392492592692792892993093193293393493593693793893994094194294394494594694794894995095195295395495595695795895996096196296396496596696796896997097197297397497597697797897998098198298398498598698798898999099199299399499599699799899910001001100210031004100510061007100810091010101110121013101410151016101710181019102010211022102310241025102610271028102910301031103210331034103510361037103810391040104110421043104410451046104710481049105010511052105310541055105610571058105910601061106210631064106510661067106810691070107110721073107410751076107710781079108010811082108310841085108610871088108910901091109210931094109510961097109810991100

7 Groves, *Now It Can Be Told*, p. 265; Fletcher Knebel and Charles W. Bailey, "The Fight Over the A-Bomb," *Look*, August 13, 1963. Full accounts of Stimson's first discussions about the bomb with Truman are in Isaacson and Thomas, *The Wise Men*, pp. 273–74; and Donovan, *Conflict and Crisis*, pp. 45–46.

8 Berlin's ruins made a mark on Truman. "I thought of Carthage, Baalbec, Jerusalem, Rome," he wrote in his diary. "I hope for some sort of peace. But I fear that machines are ahead of morals by some centuries and when morals catch up perhaps there'll be no reason for any of it." Harry S Truman, *Off the Record: The Private Papers of Harry S. Truman*, edited by Robert H. Ferrell (New York: Harper & Row, 1980), pp. 54–56.

9 Richard Rhodes, *The Making of the Atomic Bomb* (New York: Touchstone, 1987), pp. 681–86.

10 Eisenhower's recollections are from *Newsweek*, November 11, 1963.

11 Groves, *Now It Can Be Told*, p. 265; Knebel and Bailey, "The Fight Over the A-Bomb"; Groves' "push the button" statement is from an interview in Len Giovannitti and Fred Freed, *The Decision to Drop the Bomb* (New York: Coward-McCann, 1965), p. 251. After weighing the evidence on Truman's role in making the decision, I have stuck with General Groves' account.

12 Groves, *Now It Can Be Told*, p. 265.

13 Rhodes, *The Making of the Atomic Bomb*, p. 638.

14 Donovan, *Conflict and Crisis*, p. 96.

15 On the military's decision to drop the second bomb, see Donovan, *Conflict and Crisis*, pp. 97–98.

16 The Joint Chiefs' advice and the President's acquiescence are in Truman, *Memoirs*, Vol. I, pp. 575–80.

17 Norman A. Graebner, "The Sources of Postwar Insecurity," in Graebner, ed., *The National Security: Its Theory and Practice, 1945–1960* (New York: Oxford University Press, 1986), p. 13.

18 Donovan, *Conflict and Crisis*, pp. 359–61; Isaacson and Thomas, *The Wise Men*, pp. 439–40.

19 On NSC-30 and Truman's ignorance on atomic weapons and weapons policy, see Donovan, *Conflict and Crisis*, p. 424; David Alan Rosenberg, " 'A Smoking, Radiating Ruin at the End of Two Hours': Documents on American Plans for Nuclear War with the Soviet Union, 1954–1955," in *International Security*, Winter 1981–82 (Vol. 6, No. 3); Peter Pringle and William Arkin, *S.I.O.P: The Secret U.S. Plan for Nuclear War* (New York: Norton, 1983), pp. 49–52.

20 Bundy, *Danger and Survival*, p. 201; David Alan Rosenberg, "The Origins of Overkill: Nuclear Weapons and American Strategy, 1945–1960," in *International Security*, Spring 1983 (Vol. 7, No. 4).

21 LeMay has been caricatured in part because his stated views could be extreme. In his memoirs, he described lyrically the power of the warheads carried by just one of SAC's nuclear bombers: "It lugs the flame and misery of attacks on London . . . rubble of Coventry and the rubble of Plymouth . . . burn up fifty-three percent of Hamburg's buildings and kill fifty thousand people into the bargain. Mutilate and lay waste the Polish cities and the Dutch cities, the Warsaws and the Rotterdams. Shatter and fry Essen and Dortmund and Gelsenkirchen, and every other town in the Ruhr. Shatter the city of Berlin. Do what the Japanese did to us at Pearl, and what we did to the Japanese at Osaka and Yokohama and Nagoya. . . . and make the canals boil around bloated bodies of people. Do Tokyo over again." LeMay sometimes was criticized for fighting the last war. He could have fought that war in an hour. Curtis E. LeMay with MacKinlay Kantor, *Mission with LeMay* (Garden City, New York: Doubleday, 1965), pp. 383–84; 495–97. The best researched (and most devastating) portrait of LeMay in World War II is Michael S.

Sherry's superlative *The Rise of American Air Power* (New Haven: Yale University Press, 1987). The "no innocent civilians" quotation is from Sherry's interview with LeMay; the others are from LeMay's memoirs.

22 Stockpile numbers—the number of warheads in and the megatonnage of the nuclear arsenal—remain classified to this day. The best estimates are in Thomas B. Cochran, William M. Arkin, Robert S. Norris and Milton M. Hoenig, *Nuclear Weapons Databook*, Vol. II, *U.S. Nuclear Warhead Production* (Cambridge, Mass.: Ballinger, 1987), pp. 18 ff. The authors' estimates cited here are believed accurate to within 10 percent.

23 David Alan Rosenberg, "U.S. Nuclear War Planning, 1945–1960," in Desmond Ball and Jeffrey Richelson, eds., *Strategic Nuclear Targeting* (Ithaca: Cornell University Press, 1986) pp. 35–45; Rosenberg, " 'A Smoking, Radiating Ruin' "; Curtis LeMay, with Dale Smith, *America Is in Danger* (New York: Funk & Wagnalls, 1968), p. 82.

24 Admiral Ofstie's argument that the American people would reject the war plans as immoral had been anticipated by the National Security Council. NSC-30 had ordered that the American public should not be told anything about the emerging plans for World War III. They had to be kept ignorant: "Deliberation or decision on a subject of this significance," NSC-30 said, "might have the effect of placing before the American people a moral question of vital security significance at a time when the full security impact of the question had not become apparent. If this decision is to be made by the American people, it should be made in the circumstances of an actual emergency when the principal factors involved are in the forefront of public consideration." The bomb was too secret to be subjected to the war powers of the Congress and the democratic process of informed consent. Not until war broke out would the secrets be revealed.

The admirals' revolt of 1949 is detailed in Gregg Herken, *The Winning Weapon: The Atomic Bomb in the Cold War 1945–1950* (New York: Knopf, 1980), p. 290; *The History of the Joint Chiefs of Staff*, Top Secret (declassified), Vol. II, p. 341; and Fred Kaplan, *The Wizards of Armageddon* (New York: Touchstone, 1983), pp. 232–33.

25 "Truman seemed to know nothing about the Super [the hydrogen bomb]" in October 1949, reported Sidney Souers, the NSC's executive secretary. Cited in Richard G. Hewlett and Francis Duncan, *Atomic Shield 1947–1953*, Vol. II (University Park, Pa.: Pennsylvania State University Press, 1969), p. 374.

26 Truman, *Memoirs*; David E. Lilienthal, *The Journals of David E. Lilienthal*, Vol. II, *The Atomic Energy Years 1945–1950* (New York: Harper & Row, 1964), pp. 295–306.

27 The war fever of 1950 is detailed in Marc Trachtenberg, "A 'Wasting Asset': American Strategy and the Shifting Nuclear Balance, 1949–1954," in *International Security*, Winter 1988–89 (Vol. 13, No. 3); Isaacson and Thomas, *The Wise Men*, pp. 469, 497; Gregg Herken, *Counsels of War* (New York: Knopf, 1985), p. 95; I.F. Stone, *The Hidden History of the Korean War, 1950–1951* (Boston: Little, Brown, 1988), pp. 92–93.

28 Acheson, *Present at the Creation*, p. 374.

29 Truman, to his credit, found the calls for war appalling. By the end of 1950 he'd fired Navy Secretary Matthews and Air War College director Anderson for their public warmongering. Many of the general officers in the Air Force privately agreed with General Anderson's call for a preventive war against the Soviets and thought that his sacking was an outrage. "General Anderson's difficulty in the postwar years lay in his outspoken evaluation of the basic moral issue involved in our confrontation of the Communist conspiracy," wrote Air Force General Nathan F. Twining, chairman of the Joint Chiefs of Staff from 1957 to 1960, in his memoirs, *Neither Liberty Nor Safety* (New York: Holt, Rinehart and Winston, 1966), p. 19.

30 "NSC 68: A Report to the National Security Council by the Executive Secretary on United States Objectives and Programs for National Security, April 14, 1950." Declassified and first reprinted in *Naval War College Review* 27 (May–June 1975).

31 On Nitze, numbers and nuclear strategy: Strobe Talbott, *The Master of the Game: Paul Nitze and the Nuclear Peace* (New York: Knopf, 1988), passim; Isaacson and Thomas, *The Wise Men*, pp. 485–504; Lord Zuckerman, "The Silver Fox," in *The New York Review of Books*, January 19, 1989.
32 Steven L. Rearden, *The Evolution of American Strategic Doctrine: Paul H. Nitze and the Soviet Challenge* (Baltimore: Westview Press/Foreign Policy Institute, Johns Hopkins University, 1984); Paul H. Nitze with Ann M. Smith and Steven L. Rearden, *From Hiroshima to Glasnost: At the Center of Decision* (New York: Grove Weidenfeld, 1989), pp. 93–100; Acheson, *Present at the Creation*, pp. 374–77.
33 Budget data are from *Historical Tables: Budget of the United States Government*, Executive Office of the President, Office of Management and Budget (Washington, D.C.: Government Printing Office, 1988).
34 Trachtenberg, "A 'Wasting Asset' "; Stone, *Hidden History of the Korean War*, p. 205.
35 Paul Bracken, *The Command and Control of Nuclear Forces* (New Haven: Yale University Press, 1983), p. 78; Bundy, *Danger and Survival*, pp. 231–32.
36 SAC spent roughly $100 billion in the 1950's, about one-quarter of every dollar the Pentagon received. Twining, *Neither Liberty Nor Safety*, pp. 88–89; Rosenberg, "The Origins of Overkill."
37 Stephen E. Ambrose, *Eisenhower*, Vol. II, *The President* (New York, Simon and Schuster, 1984), pp. 94–95.
38 Eisenhower's memo to Dulles is reprinted in U.S. Department of State, *Foreign Relations of the United States, 1952–1954*, Vol. 2, p. 461.
39 Ambrose, *Eisenhower*, Vol. II, *The President*, p. 206. The quotation from the secret meeting with the Joint Chiefs comes from the confidential diary of Eisenhower's press secretary.
40 Twining, *Neither Liberty Nor Safety*, p. 112.
41 Carte Blanche is described in Jeffrey Record, *U.S. Nuclear Weapons in Europe* (Washington, D.C.: The Brookings Institution, 1974) pp. 10–11.
42 Robert Scheer, *With Enough Shovels: Reagan, Bush and Nuclear War* (New York: Vintage, 1983), p. 77.
43 The war plans of 1955, LeMay's briefing and his first-strike philosophy are detailed in Rosenberg, " 'A Smoking, Radiating Ruin.' "
44 LeMay told Jerome Wiesner and Robert Sprague, one of Eisenhower's top defense consultants, about his plans for a preemptive strike on September 16, 1957. They were visiting LeMay at the Colorado Springs headquarters of NORAD, the North American Defense Command. They were concerned about SAC's ability to respond to a nuclear alert.
    LeMay told them to rest easy. "I will know from my own intelligence whether or not the Russians are massing their planes," LeMay said. "And if I come to that conclusion, I'm going to knock the shit out of them before they get off the ground."
    Sprague remembered his shock as he recounted the conversation twenty-five years later in an interview for a television documentary. "General," he spluttered, "that isn't national policy." Only the President had the power to fire a nuclear weapon. "You know that."
    "No, it's not national policy," LeMay said. "But it's my policy."
    The conversation was first described, in slightly different form, in Kaplan, *The Wizards of Armageddon*. Sprague's recollections were recorded for a television documentary, *War and Peace in the Nuclear Age*. WGBH interview with Robert Sprague, Tape #CO3005.
45 So much material on this subject remains classified that it isn't possible to know exactly when Eisenhower delegated the authority to launch nuclear weapons, or who beyond the SAC commander received it. What is clear is that he did delegate it. The discovery that battlefield commanders could fire a nuclear weapon on their own initiative

shocked the new civilian leaders of the Kennedy administration. Ten days after Kennedy took office, he was notified that "a subordinate commander faced with a substantial Russian military action could start the thermonuclear holocaust on his own initiative if he could not reach you [by failure of communication at either end of the line]." The "substantial Russian military action" could be troop movements in Eastern Europe or even signs that the Soviets were gearing up for a European invasion. *Memorandum to the President: Policies Previously Approved in NSC Which Need Review*, NSC Meetings 1961, January 30, 1961, folder 2, box 313, National Security Files, John F. Kennedy Library, Boston.

46 The recently declassified memorandum from General White to General Power is available at the National Security Archive in Washington and is cited in Scott D. Sagan, *Moving Targets: Nuclear Strategy and National Security* (Princeton: Princeton University Press, 1989), p. 142. General Power never renounced the idea of a surprise attack on the Soviets. He wrote in his memoirs that it was "evident that we may have to take military actions which . . . fall under the public's broad concept of preventive war." The National Security Council had rejected "the concept of preventive war" in December 1954. Power never did. Thomas Power with Albert Arnhyn, *Design for Survival* (New York: Coward-McCann, 1964), pp. 79–84.

47 No better explanation of the predelegation of the authority to launch nuclear weapons exists than the one set down by Air Force General Nathan Twining, chairman of the Joint Chiefs of Staff from 1957 to 1960, in his 1966 memoir, *Neither Liberty nor Safety*:

> Any responsible Chief Executive must consider what would happen to the nation if he were to be immobilized or incapacitated, or if Washington, D.C., were to disappear as the result of a surprise attack. Could the Chief Executive accept a command and control system which would paralyze the nation's military forces if he were unable to act personally?
>   . . . . In terms of basic logic, it would appear that he has only three basic options:
>   1. The President can shut his eyes to the facts and hope that nothing will happen.
>   2. He can maintain personal (and detailed) control at all times, making no provision for national response in event of massive damage to the seat of government.
>   3. He can predelegate authority to be exercised under certain grave circumstances.
>   With respect to the first option in terms of logic, no Chief Executive could be so derelict in his duty. With respect to the second, the Chief Executive would be inviting an enemy attack if the enemy knew that the United States would be paralyzed by the delivery of only one nuclear weapon on the seat of government.
>   On the basis of just plain common sense, therefore, it would appear that the third option—predelegation of authority to take military action in the event of certain circumstances—can be the only valid solution.

The "third option" has been the policy since Twining's day. The "certain circumstances" under which a general can fire a nuclear weapon are, naturally, secrets. Twining, *Neither Liberty Nor Safety*, pp. 242–43.

48 *Nuclear Weapons Databook*, Vol. II, p. 17. SAC's most conservative plan in 1959–1960 called for an "alert force" to attack 654 primary targets with 1,459 bombs. This plan yielded 2.1 million kilotons of destruction—more than enough, as Churchill once put it, to make the rubble bounce. Thomas Powers, "Choosing a Strategy for World War III," *The Atlantic Monthly*, November 1982; Rosenberg, "The Origins of Overkill."

49 A Strategic Air Command history of the preparation of the first SIOP (Single Integrated Operational Plan) notes that, in each of the nuclear-war exercises conducted between 1958 and 1960, the Joint Chiefs discovered that U.S. strategic delivery forces would commit fratricide—that is, our own bombs would destroy each other—in a nuclear war.

50 Eisenhower's conversations with national security assistant Gordon Gray and AEC chairman John McCone are in the Dwight D. Eisenhower Library, Abilene, Kansas, and cited in Bundy, *Danger and Survival*, p. 324.

51 Telephone calls of April 7, 1960, Dwight D. Eisenhower Library, Abilene, Kansas. Cited in Greg Herken, *Counsels of War* (New York: Knopf, 1985), p. 117.

52 Eisenhower's shock upon looking into the SIOP and his comments to Captain Aurand are recorded in the papers of Admiral Arleigh A. Burke, at the Naval Historical Center, Washington, D.C., and cited in Rosenberg, "The Origins of Overkill."

53 General Power's outburst is recorded in Kaplan, *The Wizards of Armageddon*, pp. 286–90.

54 Presidential control of nuclear weaponry had eroded beyond all reason by 1960. A congressional delegation visiting West Germany was shocked to discover that fighter planes armed with nuclear weapons were sitting on runways at American military bases with German pilots in the cockpits. "The embodiment of control was an American military officer somewhere in the vicinity with a revolver." John Steinbruner, *The Cybernetic Theory of Decision: New Dimensions of Political Analysis* (Princeton: Princeton University Press, 1974), p. 182. Stockpile numbers cited here are from "The Bulletin of the Atomic Scientists," November 1989, p. 53, and are believed accurate to within 10 percent.

55 Herken, *Counsels of War*, p. 131; Kaplan, *The Wizards of Armageddon*, pp. 286–90.

56 Kaplan, *The Wizards of Armageddon*, p. 297.

57 *SIOP-62 Briefing, JCS 2056/281*, presented to the President on September 13, 1961; partially declassified August 15, 1986.

58 As McNamara, Rusk, Bundy and three others in Kennedy's inner circle wrote twenty years later: "American nuclear superiority was not in our view a critical factor" in the crisis. "No one of us ever reviewed the nuclear balance for comfort in those hard weeks." Rusk *et al.*, "The Lessons of the Cuban Missile Crisis," *Time*, September 27, 1982, p. 85. President Kennedy's comments are from the declassified tapes secretly recorded during the crisis and reprinted in "White House Tapes and Minutes of the Cuban Missile Crisis: The ExCom Meetings October 1962," *International Security*, Vol. 10 (Summer 1985), pp. 164–203. Soviet force levels in 1962 are from Raymond L. Garthoff, "The Meaning of the Missiles," *Washington Quarterly*, Vol. 5 (Autumn 1982), pp. 77–79. The revisionist histories of the crisis proceed apace. See Richard K. Betts, *Nuclear Blackmail and Nuclear Balance* (Washington, D.C.: Brookings Institution, 1987), pp. 109–23; Bundy, *Danger and Survival*, pp. 391–462.

59 The failure of technology in Vietnam has been expressed best by the military historian Martin Van Creveld: "Intuition was to be replaced by calculation, and since the latter was to be carried out with the aid of computers, it was necessary that all the phenomena of war be reduced to quantitative form. Consequently everything that could be quantified was, while everything that could not tended to be thrown into the garbage heap. Among the things that were discarded in this way were precisely those factors that make war what it is." Martin Van Creveld, *Technology and War: From 2000 B.C. to the Present* (New York: The Free Press, 1989), p. 246.

60 Kissinger later tried to explain away this cry from the heart. "My statement reflected fatigue and exasperation" following a long arms-control negotiating session in Moscow, he told senators weighing the SALT II treaty in 1979. I still take it as a true expression of doubt and fear rather than a slip of the tongue.

61 Murrey Marder, "Carter to Inherit Intense Dispute on Soviet Intentions," *Washington Post*, January 2, 1977.

62 For a thoroughly convincing critique of the CIA's estimate of Soviet defense expenditures, see Franklyn D. Holtzman, "Politics and Guesswork: CIA and DIA Estimates of Soviet Military Spending," *International Security*, Fall 1989, pp. 101–31.

63 In NSC-68, Nitze said 1954 was the year of maximum danger, the year the Soviets would have the strategic edge, and thus the temptation to launch a first strike on the United States. In 1975 and 1976, he said it would be 1980 or 1981. The year of maximum danger always was just over the horizon.

64 The "window of vulnerability" was an illusion, as the Reagan administration quietly conceded with the publication of the Scowcroft commission report in 1983. Why was this frightening but false image allowed to persist? Dr. Herbert "Pete" Scoville Jr., a former CIA deputy director for science and technology, offered an interpretation in 1982: "One of the greatest myths that is being perpetrated on the American public is the story that the Soviet Union is ahead of the United States in military nuclear technology. This is just plain nonsense," Scoville said. "The myth of U.S. inferiority is being spread to try to panic the public in the United States." Scoville's comments are recorded in a 1982 documentary film, "War without Winners."

65 Colin Gray and Keith Payne, "Victory Is Possible," *Foreign Policy*, Summer 1980, pp. 14–27; see also Gray, "Some Selective Options and Deterrence," Hudson Institute, 1981; "Nuclear Strategy: The Case for a Theory of Victory," *International Security*, Summer 1979.

Gray's estimate of acceptable U.S. casualties in a nuclear war—twenty million dead—was not plucked from the air. It is, of course, the number of Soviet dead in World War II.

This kind of war-fighting talk apparently scared the wits out of the Soviets. In 1981, shortly after the Reagan administration took office, Soviet intelligence became convinced that the United States was preparing to attack the Soviet Union. The KGB ordered its agents in Washington and London to report anything that might give the Kremlin strategic warning of a preemptive strike: anything from lights burning late in the White House, to unusual nighttime travels of an Air Force general, down to blood drives and civil-defense drills.

The alert from Moscow was like nothing in memory, Oleg Gordievsky, the KGB's station chief in London—and, for a dozen years, a double agent for British intelligence—told his debriefers after his defection in 1985. For three years, this war scare preoccupied Soviet intelligence and the succession of aged Soviet leaders who preceded Mikhail Gorbachev. As Gorbachev himself told a Communist Party Congress in 1986, "Never, perhaps, in the postwar decades has the situation in the world been as explosive and hence, more difficult and unfavorable, as in the first half of the 1980's."

66 The least informed of all was Reagan. This was the President who assured people that nuclear missiles could somehow be halted in midflight and returned safely to their nesting places. "Those instruments can be intercepted," he said in a May 1982 press conference. "They can be recalled if there has been a miscalculation." York quoted in Scheer, *With Enough Shovels*, p. 269.

67 Quoted in John Newhouse, "Arms and Orthodoxy," *The New Yorker*, June 7, 1982.

68 Keeny quoted in Herken, *Counsels of War*, p. 318.

69 *Hearings Before the Subcommittee on Strategic and Theatre Nuclear Forces of the Committee on Armed Services, United States Senate*, 97th Cong. 1st Ses. (Washington, D.C.: Government Printing Office), p. 89.

Chapter 3   TOWARD A BETTER ARMAGEDDON

Principal on-the-record interviews for this chapter were with John Steinbruner and Bruce Blair of the Brookings Institution, Paul Bracken of Yale University, Ashton Carter of Harvard's Kennedy School of Government and John Pike of the Federation of American Scientists.

1 Hendricks' remarks were made in a presentation to the annual Air Force Conference, in Wakefield, Massachusetts, on April 26, 1982. See Thomas Karas, *The New High Ground: Strategies and Weapons for Space-Age War* (New York: Simon & Schuster, 1983), pp. 91–92. Karas obtained a printed transcript of the general's remarks, which are unusually straightforward.

2 The requirement that MILSTAR function for six months without ground support has been one of several unprecedented goals for the system's designers. See *The C^3I Handbook*, 3rd ed. (Palo Alto: EW Communications, 1988), pp. 64–65.

3 Paul Bracken, "Delegation of Nuclear Command Authority," in Ashton B. Carter, John D. Steinbruner and Charles A. Zraket, eds., *Managing Nuclear Operations* (Washington, D.C.: The Brookings Institution, 1987), p. 353; Bracken, *The Command and Control of Nuclear Forces* (New Haven: Yale University Press, 1983), pp. 238–43.

4 For the selected target list of the SIOP in the mid-1970's, see Senate Armed Services Committee, *Department of Defense Authorization for Appropriations for Fiscal Year 1981*, Part 5, p. 2721. For recent SIOP revisions, see Desmond Ball and Robert C. Toth, "Revising the SIOP: Taking War-fighting to Dangerous Extremes," *International Security*, vol. 14, no. 4, Spring 1990, pp. 65–92.

5 The best short study defining the problem is John D. Steinbruner, "Nuclear Decapitation," Brookings General Series Reprint 383 (Washington, D.C.: The Brookings Institution, 1982). This piece originally appeared in *Foreign Policy*, Winter 1981–1982, no. 45, pp. 16–28.

6 Department of Defense Directive 5100.30, "World-wide Military Command and Control System," December 2, 1971 (emphasis added).

7 Henry Kissinger, *Years of Upheaval* (Boston: Little, Brown, 1982), pp. 545–613; Bundy, *Danger and Survival*, pp. 518–25.

8 The steps associated with ascending levels of nuclear alerts are described in detail in Bruce G. Blair, "Alerting in Crisis and Conventional War," in *Managing Nuclear Operations*, pp. 75–120.

9 *Defense Organization: The Need for Change*, Report of Senate Committee on Armed Services, 99th Cong. 1st Ses. (Washington, D.C.: Government Printing Office, 1985), pp. 95–97; Bruce G. Blair, "Alerting in Crisis and Conventional War," in *Managing Nuclear Operations*, pp. 113–16. Blair is one of a very few civilians familiar with current SIOP structures.

10 Bill Gulley, *Breaking Cover* (New York: Warner Books, 1980), p. 225.

11 House Committee on Armed Services, *Review of Department of Defense Worldwide Communications*, Phase 1, Report, 92nd Cong., 1st Ses. May 10, 1971; James M. Ennes Jr., *Assault on the Liberty* (New York: Random House, 1979); and James Bamford, *The Puzzle Palace* (New York: Penguin, 1983), pp. 278–93. The fatal consequences of failures to communicate are the subject of much military lore. The U.S. invasion of Grenada saw a near-complete breakdown of communications. The invading soldiers had radios that couldn't reach Navy operators offshore because the Army and the Navy and the Marines were all on different frequencies; the ground forces did not have the codes and call signs necessary to communicate with the Navy even when they did link up. One exasperated commander had to make a credit-card telephone call to Fort Bragg in order to request fire support from a Navy ship. The coordination of air strikes and naval gunneries was a disaster; an unknown number of American soldiers and at least twenty-one innocent Grenadians at a mental hospital leveled by an air strike died without reason, in large part because of communications snafus.

12 *Command and Control and System Management*, Office of the Under Secretary of Defense for Research and Engineering, Department of Defense, July 1978; House Government Operations Committee, *NORAD Computer Systems Are Dangerously Obsolete*, March 8, 1982; Albert E. Babbitt, "Command Centers," in *Managing Nuclear Operations*, pp. 323–36; Pringle and Arkin, *S.I.O.P.*, pp. 133–36.

13 Scheer, *With Enough Shovels*, p. 29.

14 Thomas Powers, "Choosing a Strategy for World War III," *Atlantic Monthly*, November 1982.

15 Zbigniew Brzezinski, *Power and Principle: Memoirs of the National Security Adviser, 1977–1981* (New York: Farrar, Straus and Giroux, 1983), p. 457.

16 Desmond Ball, "The Development of the SIOP, 1960–1983," in Ball and Richelson, eds., *Strategic Nuclear Targeting* (Ithaca: Cornell University Press, 1986), pp. 70–82; Jeffrey Richelson, "PD-59, NSDD-13 and the Reagan Strategic Modernization Plan," unpublished ms. courtesy of author, December 1982; Blair, *Strategic Command and Control*, pp. 26, 62–64; Colin Gray, *Strategic Studies and Public Policy: The American Experience* (Louisville: University of Kentucky Press, 1982), p. 158.

17 *Hearings Before the Subcommittee on Strategic and Theatre Nuclear Forces of the Committee on Armed Services, United States Senate*, 97th Cong., 1st Ses. (Washington, D.C.: Government Printing Office), p. 282.

18 The substance of PD-59 and NSDD-13 are discussed in Richelson, "PD-59, NSDD-13 and the Reagan Strategic Modernization Program"; Desmond Ball, "Counterforce Targeting: How New? How Viable?," *Arms Control Today*, Vol. 11, No. 2, 1981; Pringle and Arkin, *S.I.O.P*, pp. 233–34.; Michael Getler, "Administration's Nuclear War Policy Still Murky," *Washington Post*, November 10, 1982, p. A24.

19 Fred J. Ricci and Daniel Schutzer, *U.S. Military Communications: A C³I Force Multiplier* (New York: Computer Science Press, 1986), pp. 107–111.

20 Richard Banks Landolt, "The Officers in Tactical Command and Tactical Information Display Systems and the Transition to the Military Strategic and Tactical Relay System," Naval Postgraduate School, Monterey, California, March 1987.

21 *DARPA Fiscal Year 1987 Program for Research and Development*, pp. II–57.

22 Senate Armed Services Committee, *Fiscal Year 1974 Authorization for Military Procurement, Research and Development*, Part 4, pp. 2210–11.

23 DARPA, *Justification of Estimates for Fiscal 1987*.

24 Paul Bracken, "War Termination," in *Managing Nuclear Operations*, p. 206.

Chapter 4   A WING AND A PRAYER

1 Rep. John Kasich, Republican of Ohio, described the briefings he received on the Stealth as "a song and dance" on the McNeil-Lehrer news show, July 13, 1989.

2. Private interviews with former Northrop executives; "Stealth Projects," *Aviation Week and Space Technology*, October 12, 1981, p. 17.

3 Private interviews; John Pike and David Bourns, "The Case Against the Stealth Bomber," Federation of American Scientists, November 16, 1988; Mark Thompson, "Aspin: B-2 Cost May Hit $1 Billion," *Philadelphia Inquirer*, July 13, 1989.

4 Interview with Robert B. Costello, July 1989.

5 See generally Michael Sherry, *The Rise of American Air Power: The Creation of*

Armageddon (New Haven: Yale University Press, 1987), especially Chapter 9, "The Triumphs of Technological Fanaticism," pp. 256–300.

6 T.A. Heppenheimer, "Stealth," *Popular Science*, September 1986, p. 76.

7 Bill Sweetman, "Stealth," *Special Electronics*, February 1984, p. 7. The discussion of Stealth technology in this passage is drawn largely from the primary open source on the subject: Sweetman, *Stealth Aircraft* (Osceola, Wisconsin: Motorbooks, 1986).

8 Pike and Bourns, "The Case Against the Stealth Bomber."

9 Thomas S. Amlie, "Our Radar-Laden Weapons Attract Their Own Doom," *Los Angeles Times*, May 14, 1987; Malcolm W. Browne, "Music and Debate Mark Stealth Bomber's Debut," *New York Times*, November 23, 1988.

10 Stephen Green, *Living by the Sword: America and Israel in the Middle East* (Brattleboro, Vt.: Amana Books, 1988), p. 92.

11 Bill Sweetman, "Stealth," *Special Electronics*, February 1984, p. 7.

12 Nick Kotz, *Wild Blue Yonder: Money, Politics and the B-1 Bomber* (Princeton: Princeton University Press, 1988), pp. 200–218.

13 For a portrait of Jones in the 1970's, see Anthony Sampson, *The Arms Bazaar* (London: Coronet, 1977), pp. 140–42.

14 Anthony Ramirez, "The Secret Bomber Bugging Northrop," *Fortune*, March 14, 1988.

15 Frank Greve, "B-2 bomber a $68-billion Secret," *Philadelphia Inquirer*, March 8, 1989.

16 Ronnie Dugger, *On Reagan* (New York: McGraw-Hill, 1983), pp. 273–76.

17 A subsequent congressional investigation of the Stealth disclosure concluded that Carter's purpose was to "look good" in an election year.

18 David Stockman, *The Triumph of Politics: How the Reagan Revolution Failed* (New York: Harper & Row, 1986), p. 283; William Greider, "The Education of David Stockman," *Atlantic Monthly*, December 1981.

19 Interview with Frank C. Conahan, April 1989.

20 Kotz, *Wild Blue Yonder*, p. 212.

21 Private interviews; Benjamin F. Schemmer, "Financial Analysts Estimate Stealth Bomber Costs Within 4% of Each Other," *Armed Forces Journal International*, October 1987, p. 26; Malcolm W. Browne, "Music and Debate Mark Stealth Bomber's Debut," *New York Times*, November 23, 1988; Andy Pasztor and Mary Ellen Read, "Full-Scale Output of Stealth Bomber Is Likely to Be Delayed Well Into 1990s," *Wall Street Journal*, December 8, 1988, p. 24.

22 Ralph Nader and William Taylor, *The Big Boys: Power and Position in American Business* (New York, Pantheon, 1986), p. 382.

23 *Hearings Before the Subcommittee on Strategic and Theatre Nuclear Forces of the Committee on Armed Services, United States Senate*, 97th Cong., 1st Ses. (Washington, D.C.: Government Printing Office), pp. 137–57.

24 Ibid. pp. 261–68.

25 Ibid. p. 279.

26 Interview with Donald Hicks, July 1989.

27 Greve, "B-2 Bomber a $68 Billion Secret"; Common Cause report on corporate honoraria, July 1989.

28 Rep. Les Aspin, "Are Working Nukes Just Flukes?," House Armed Services Committee, June 1988; *Aerospace Daily*, October 31, 1988, p. 155, and November 28, 1988, pp. 290–91; Dagnija Sterste-Perkins, "B-2 Advanced Technology Bomber," CRS Issue Brief IB87216, Congressional Research Service, December 5, 1988.

29 Off-the-record interviews with aerospace industry analysts and former Northrop employees.

30 Testimony of Craig Alderman, deputy under secretary of defense for policy, to the House Committee on Energy and Commerce, August 11, 1986.

31 George Ramos, "Ex-Northrop Engineer Pleads Guilty to Fraud," *Los Angeles Times*, March 20, 1986; Ronald L. Soble, "Ex-Con Who Worked in Stealth Program Gets 5 Years For Fraud," *Los Angeles Times*, August 12, 1986.

32 Sentencing memorandum, *U.S. v. Ronald Emile Brousseau*, United States District Court, Central District of California, CR 85-387-JMI.

33 A. Ernest Fitzgerald, *The Pentagonists: An Insider's View of Waste, Mismanagment and Fraud in Defense Spending* (Boston: Houghton Mifflin, 1989), p. 224.

34 *Defense News*, September 23, 1985.

35 Interview with Rep. John D. Dingell, July 1986.

36 Letter in author's possession from Rep. John D. Dingell to Caspar W. Weinberger, January 16, 1986.

37 Letters in author's possession: Weinberger to Dingell, April 17, 1986; Rep. Les Aspin to Weinberger, April 9, 1986.

38 Associated Press, "Pentagon Releases Heretofore Secret Cost Information on New Bomber," *Philadelphia Inquirer*, April 16, 1986, p. 3A.

39 Private interview.

40 Ibid; Aspin, "Are Working Nukes Just Flukes?"

41 James E. Lalonde, "Untested Parts in Stealth? Boeing Work on B-2 Bomber May Have Involved Questionable Nuts, Bolts," *Seattle Times*, February 19, 1989, p. A1.

42 Eileen White Read, "Justice Department Drops Investigation of Northrop Bomber Costs, Sources Say," *Wall Street Journal*, October 24, 1988, p. B12.

43 Roy J. Harris Jr., "Northrop Chief to Quit Amid Controversy," *Wall Street Journal*, April 26, 1989.

44 Only Citibank, NA, New York had more than $70.2 billion on hand in 1988. Only General Motors and Exxon had earnings in excess of that sum.

45 U.S. Department of Agriculture's budget for FY 1990 as submitted to Congress showed a total of $19.8 billion for federal food assistance.

46 Andrew Rosenthal, "Criticism Mounts on Stealth Cost," *New York Times*, June 24, 1989, p. A6.

47 Aspin and Schroeder spoke at a Capitol Hill press conference broadcast by Cable News Network, July 17, 1989.

48 E.J. Dionne Jr., "Poll Finds Public Favors Sharp Cut in Arms Funds," *New York Times*, March 12, 1989, p. 24.

49 Federation of American Scientists, "The Case Against the Stealth Bomber," pp. 41–48; Donald Hicks, "Stealth—Its Implications for the Future," *Armed Forces International Journal*, September 1986, p. 71.

50 Richard Halloran, "Stealth Bomber Is Key to Arms Talks, Administration Warns," *New York Times*, July 21, 1989, p. A12; Dagnija Sterste-Perkins, "B-2 Advanced Technology Bomber."

51 135 *Congressional Record* 102, H4288 (July 26, 1989).

52 The description of the debate in the House on the three Stealth bills is taken from the *Congressional Record*. 135 *Congressional Record* 102, H4279–4316 (July 26, 1989).

53 Associated Press, "Cheney Cites Lessened Threat by Soviets, Says Spending on Defense Will Be Reduced," *Philadelphia Inquirer*, November 20, 1989, p. 3A.

54 Letter to author from Rep. Patricia Schroeder, July 14, 1989.

Chapter 5   KEEPING SECRETS

1 *The Senator Gravel Edition: The Pentagon Papers* (Boston, Beacon Press, 1971), Vol. I, p. xi.

2 OSS Collection, Historical Intelligence Collection, Central Intelligence Agency.

3 William Casey, *The Secret War Against Hitler* (Washington, D.C.: Regnery Gateway, 1988), pp. 5–7.

4 Anthony Cave Brown, *The Last Hero: Wild Bill Donovan* (New York: Vintage, 1984), pp. 301, 792.

5 Thomas F. Troy, *Donovan and the CIA: A History of the Establishment of the Central Intelligence Agency* (Frederick, Maryland: University Publications of America, 1981), pp. 282, 423; Rhodi Jeffreys-Jones, *The CIA and American Democracy* (New Haven: Yale University Press, 1989), p. 16.

6 Jeffreys-Jones, *The CIA and American Democracy*, p. 54; Daniel Yergin, *Shattered Peace: The Origins of the Cold War and the National Security State* (Boston, Houghton Mifflin, 1977), pp. 216–17.

7 Central Intelligence Agency, "Lawrence Houston," *Studies in Intelligence*, 1974.

8 Dean Acheson, *Present at the Creation* (New York: Norton, 1969, revised, 1987), p. 214.

9 Grover S. Williams, "Legislative History of the Central Intelligence Agency as Documented in Published Congressional Sources" (Washington, D.C.: Congressional Research Service, 1975).

10 *Final Report of the Select Committee to Study Governmental Operations with Respect to Intelligence Activities* [hereinafter, Church Committee, *Final Report*], United States Senate (Washington, D.C.: Government Printing Office, 1976), 94th Cong., 2d Ses., Book IV, "History of the Central Intelligence Agency," by Anne Karelekas, pp. 6–9.

11 *Hearings on the National Security Act of 1947 Before the House Committee on Expenditures in the Executive Department*, 80th Cong., 1st Ses., 120–21 (1947).

12 John Ranelagh, *The Agency: The Rise and Decline of the CIA* (New York: Simon and Schuster, 1986), pp. 117–38.

13 Sissela Bok, *Lying: Moral Choice in Public and Private Life* (New York: Vintage, 1978), pp. 174–77, 326–27; Bok, *Secrets: On the Ethics of Concealment and Revelation* (New York: Vintage, 1983), pp. 171–210.

14 Church Committee *Final Report*, Vol. I, p. 493.

15 *Hearings on H.R. 1741, H.R. 2546 & H.R. 2663 Before the House Committee on Armed Services*, 81st Cong., 1st Ses., ser. 26 at 487, as declassified (1949).

16 *Washington Star*, June 1, 1949.

17 95 *Congressional Record* 1945–48 (1949).

18 95 *Congressional Record* 1945 (1949).

19 95 *Congressional Record* 1946 (1949).

20 95 *Congressional Record* 1947 (1949).

21 95 *Congressional Record* 6942–55 (1949).

22 The CIA Act is at 50 U.S.C. Sec. 403f, 403j(b).

23 James McCargar ("Christopher Felix"), *A Short Course in the Secret War* (New York: Dell, 1963, 1988), pp. 65–67. This is a brilliant book that really has no equal as a discussion of tradecraft.

24 The best—the only—history of the National Security Agency is Bamford, *The Puzzle Palace*.

25 In 1985, when a lone Congressman, George E. Brown Jr., a California Democrat, once dared to speak the name of the National Reconnaissance Office on the floor of the House, to criticize the expense of its satellites and the secrecy surrounding the agency, he came within a hair's breadth of official censure.

26 Braden's comments come from a Granada Television program broadcast in June 1975, "World in Action: The Rise and Fall of the CIA." Braden, who once wrote a magazine article entitled, "I'm Glad the CIA Is 'Immoral,' " was being more nostalgic than critical.

27 Harry Howe Ransom, *The Intelligence Establishment* (Cambridge, Mass.: Harvard University Press, 1970), p. 166.

28 Mansfield's warnings about the CIA are in 97 *Congressional Record* 2811–14 (1954). For Saltonstall's reticence and his fellow senators' protective relationships with the CIA, see Karalekas, "History of the Central Intelligence Agency," pp. 53–54.

29 "CIA: Congress in Dark about Activities," *Congressional Quarterly*, Vol. 21, pp. 1840–42, August 21, 1971; Church Committee, *Final Report*, Vol. IV, pp. 62–63.

30 Church Committee, *Final Report*, Vol. I, pp. 9, 50.

31 Philip Roettinger, a Marine colonel who joined in Operation Success, looked back in sadness and said: "What we did has caused a succession of repressive military dictatorships in that country and has been responsible for the death of over 100,000 of their citizens." Roettinger's comments are taken from a transcript of "The Secret Government: The Constitution in Crisis," a November 1987 PBS television documentary produced by Bill Moyers. For a complete account of Operation Success, see Stephen Schlesinger and Stephen Kinzer, *Bitter Fruit: The Untold Story of the American Coup in Guatemala* (Garden City, N.Y.: Doubleday, 1985).

32 The Congo case is the closest one comes to a direct order from a President to commit murder. Robert H. Johnson, a National Security Council staffer, later recalled that Eisenhower "said something—I can no longer recall his exact words—that came across to me as an order for the assassination of Lumumba." Church Committee, *Alleged Assassination Plots Involving Foreign Leaders. Interim Report of the Select Committee to Study Governmental Operations with Respect to Intelligence Activities* (New York: Norton, 1976), pp. 15–16, 56.

33 For the story of Zaire and Mobutu, see Helen Winternitz, *East Along the Equator* (New York: Atlantic Monthly Press, 1987).

34 The "disposal problem" arises in Arthur M. Schlesinger Jr., *A Thousand Days: John F. Kennedy in the White House* (Boston: Houghton Mifflin, 1965), p. 242.

35 The Board of Consultants' report is cited in Arthur Schlesinger Jr., "A Democrat Looks at Foreign Policy," *Foreign Affairs*, Winter 1987–1988, p. 270.

36 Houston's argument that Congress, by approving a budget containing the CIA's appropriation, thus gave approval to the CIA's covert actions was worse than specious. It was simply wrong. The same argument—that Congress had declared war on Vietnam by approving funds for the war—was rejected by federal courts in the 1970's. Lawrence R. Houston, General Counsel, "Memorandum for the Director of Central Intelligence: Legal Basis for Cold War Activities," January 15, 1962, OCC 62-0083; declassified and cited by Jay Peterzell, "Legal and Constitutional Authority for Covert Operations," paper presented to the International Studies Association, Washington, D.C., 1985.

37 On Congressional, NSC and State Department knowledge and control of CIA covert actions in the 1950's and 1960's, see Church Committee, *Alleged Assassination Plots*; Loch Johnson, "Covert Action and American Foreign Policy: Decision Paths for the 'Quiet Option,' " paper presented to the American Political Science Association Annual Meeting, Washington, D.C., 1986; Gregory F. Treverton, *Covert Action: The Limits of Intervention in the Postwar World* (New York: Basic Books, 1987), p. 230; John Prados, *Presidents' Secret Wars: CIA and Pentagon Covert Actions Since World War Two* (New York: William Morrow), pp. 229–32.

38 Merle Miller, *Plain Speaking: An Oral Biography of Harry S Truman* (London: Gollancz, 1974) p. 391.

39 Fulbright and Ellender: 42 *Congressional Record* 929–31 (1971).

40 Helms' use of the phrase "honorable men" in this time of crisis for the CIA seems to me unintentionally ironic.

The line is from Shakespeare's *Julius Caesar*, Act III, Scene ii, line 82: "For Brutus is an honorable man;/ So are they all, all honorable men." It is taken from the famous speech by Marc Antony ("Friends, Romans, countrymen . . .").

Antony's speech is a masterpiece of hypocrisy and deception. Caesar has just been assassinated. Brutus has Caesar's blood on his hands, and he is not entirely pleased with himself. He always has been of two minds about the plot to kill Caesar. "If I have veiled my look,/ I turn the trouble of my countenance/ Merely upon myself. . . . Poor Brutus, with himself at war" (I, ii, 37–41, 46). Yet he chooses to carry out the conspiracy, as he tells the plebeians in the Forum, for the good of Rome. "Not that I loved Caesar less, but that I loved Rome more. . . . As Caesar loved me, I weep for him. . . . as he was ambitious, I slew him" (III, ii, 21–26).

Shakespeare unmasks Antony as a demagogue in the same scene, after his cunning speech incites the plebeians to riot and murder: "Now let it work," says Antony, "mischief, thou art afoot,/ Take thou what course thou wilt" (III, ii, 260–61). It is hard to believe Helms was being consciously ironic. By choosing that line from all of Shakespeare to defend the honor of the CIA, he celebrated an act of psychological warfare and a successful conspiracy to assassinate a potential tyrant.

41 Helms and Koch: Norman Dorsen and Stephen Gillers, eds., *None of Your Business: Government Secrecy in America* (New York: Penguin, 1974), p. 147.

42 Fulbright, Ellender and Cranston: 42 *Congressional Record* 927–31 (1971).

43 Jeffrey-Jones, *The CIA and American Democracy*, p. 185. Ellender's comments were reported in the *Washington Post*, December 9, 1973, p. A9.

44 The two most reliable secondary sources for the CIA's role in Watergate are J. Anthony Lukas, *Nightmare: The Underside of the Nixon Years* (New York: Viking, 1976, revised 1988); and Thomas Powers, *The Man Who Kept the Secrets: Richard Helms and the CIA* (New York: Knopf, 1979).

45 Given the résumés of the Watergate burglars, there was understandably some suspicion and confusion over the CIA's role in the break-in.

The FBI was called in and then called off. The FBI director, L. Patrick Gray, had been on the job only six weeks; J. Edgar Hoover had just died. Gray telephoned Helms on June 22. He said the FBI was "thinking that we may be poking into a CIA operation." Helms assured him that it wasn't.

Gray shared his thoughts later that day with the young and obsequious White House counsel, John Dean. Dean spent the evening conferring with his mentor, John Mitchell, the wily lawyer who'd stepped down as Attorney General of the United States to run Nixon's reelection campaign. Mitchell had a brainstorm.

At 8:15 the next morning, June 23, Dean met with the White House chief of staff, H.R. Haldeman. "I spoke to Mitchell," Dean said. "He and I agree the thing to do is for you to tell Walters . . . [to] talk to Gray—and maybe the CIA can turn off the FBI." Walters was the CIA's new deputy director, General Vernon A. Walters, an old confidant of Nixon's.

Haldeman took the proposition to Nixon two hours later. Haldeman told Nixon the thing to do was "to have Walters call Pat Gray and just say, 'Stay to hell out of this.' " The President agreed: "They should call the FBI in and [tell them] don't go any further into this case, period!" Helms' passive refusal to use the CIA to obstruct justice led Nixon to fire him two weeks after his reelection.

46 William Colby and Peter Forbath, *Honorable Men: My Life in the CIA* (New York: Simon and Schuster, 1978), pp. 337–38. See footnote 40.

47 Schlesinger memorandum to CIA personnel in author's possession.

48 Colby does have the touch of the father confessor about him. After a long talk with him one winter afternoon in his townhouse on a shady side street in an elegant sector of Washington's loveliest neighborhood, I came away thinking he missed his calling as a missionary priest.

49 Interview with William Colby, April 1989.

50 The false testimony of Helms is cited and discussed, with the highest level of intelligence and wit, in Powers, *The Man Who Kept the Secrets.*
51 Colby, *Honorable Men*, pp. 390–91.
52 Hughes' lament: 120 *Congressional Record* S9607 (June 4, 1974). Findley's charge: 120 *Congressional Record* H3450 (May 8, 1973).
53 Ford as FBI informant: Seymour M. Hersh, "The Pardon," *Atlantic Monthly*, August 1983.
54 Colby, *Honorable Men*, pp. 14–15, 399–400.
55 Ibid. pp. 443–44.
56 Cord Meyer, *Facing Reality: From World Federalism to the CIA* (New York: Harper & Row, 1980), p. 225.
57 *Report to the President by the Commission on CIA Activities Within the United States*, June 1975, p. 81.
58 The Church Committee's decision on publishing the intelligence budget is reported and discussed in Senate Select Committee on Intelligence, *Whether Disclosure of Funds for the Intelligence Activities of the United States Is in the Public Interest*, Report No. 95–274, 94th Cong., 2nd Ses., June 16, 1977 (Washington, D.C.: Government Printing Office, 1977).
59 Proxmire's figures are in 119 *Congressional Record* 6868 (1973). The unpublished House Government Operations Committee report is cited in Walter Laqueur, *A World of Secrets: The Uses and Limits of Intelligence* (New York: Basic Books, 1985), p. 387.
60 Figures on the black budget in the mid-1970's come from private interviews with former members of the Church Committee and Senate intelligence committee staffs.
61 Bush's role in heading off the revelation of the black budget is in the Senate intelligence committee's report.
62 Senate Select Committee on Intelligence, *Whether Disclosure of Funds for the Intelligence Activities of the United States Is in the Public Interest* (Washington, D.C., GPO, June 1977).
63 Interview, William G. Miller, September 1989.
64 Colby, *Honorable Men*, pp. 453–54.
65 It is maddening to have nothing more than a footnote for James J. Angleton. His work as chief of CIA counterintelligence deserves a multivolume study, an encyclopedia, an opera. The theories of Soviet conduct he developed were so ornate, so complex and ultimately so mysterious that they created a kind of parallel universe in which the laws of physics, time and reason ran backwards, sideways and upside down. Angleton's angle on reality ruled the CIA's interpretations of the Soviets for the better part of two decades. If Angleton, now dead, was right about The Threat, as he always called it, then everything we now think about the Soviets in the days of *glasnost* is probably wrong, and we are being lulled to sleep. If Angleton was wrong—or if, as I rather suspect, he was half mad—we have spent a good deal of time and energy chasing shadows in a cave. Angleton's testimony is in Church Committee hearings, Vol. 2, p. 72, September 23, 1975.
66 Justice Robert H. Jackson's famous 1952 opinion in *Youngstown Sheet & Tube Co. v. Sawyer* said, "There is a zone of twilight in which [the President] and Congress may have concurrent authority, or in which its distribution is uncertain. . . . When the President takes measures incompatible with the expressed or implied will of Congress, his power is at its lowest ebb, for then he can rely only upon his constitutional powers minus any constitutional powers of Congress over the matter."
67 William L. Riordan, *Plunkitt of Tammany Hall* (New York: Dutton, 1963), p. 17.
68 Mineta's complaint is from David M. Alpern, et al., "America's Secret Warriors," *Newsweek*, October 10, 1983.
69 Speech at the Metropolitan Club, New York, May 1, 1985.
70 Testimony of Robert McFarlane to the Iran-contra committees, May 11, 1987.

Chapter 6   A HOLY WAR

1 This chapter is based on interviews with forty-two present and former officials of the Central Intelligence Agency, the U.S. State Department, the Pentagon and the Drug Enforcement Administration. Afghan guerrillas and commanders were interviewed during a three-week journey inside Afghanistan. Documents reviewed include copies of CIA field reports, State Department cables and transcripts of congressional testimony. Special thanks to Steve Galster of the National Security Archive for pulling together an Afghan file.

2 The Soviets' lies, their refusal to allow foreign correspondents to cover the war and the extreme remoteness of Afghanistan made it impossible to know how many people died in the Afghan war. For one among many reports of murder and torture by the Soviet-backed regime see Felix Ermacora, "Report on the Situation of Human Rights in Afghanistan," United Nations document E/CN.4/1985/21, February 19, 1985.

3 The conversation between the Shah and Bush is recounted in a cable from Ambassador William Sullivan in Teheran to the State Department, Secret cable #04062, April 30, 1978. Copies of State Department and CIA cables cited in this chapter are in the author's possession and at the National Security Archive, Washington, D.C.

4 The State Department's warning and its nuclear gambit were leaked by a former *New York Times* reporter, Richard Burt, then serving as an under secretary of state, to the *New York Times* in February 1980.

5 Details of CIA and State Department activities regarding the Afghan resistance before the Soviet invasion are taken from copies of cables from CIA stations in Islamabad, New Delhi and Jidda to CIA headquarters, September–November 1979, and cables from U.S. embassies in Islamabad, Tripoli and New Delhi to the State Department, April–November 1979. For an excellent overview of this crucial period, see Henry S. Bradsher, *Afghanistan and the Soviet Union* (Durham, N.C.: Duke University Press, 1985).

6 Jimmy Carter, *Keeping Faith: Memoirs of a President* (New York: Bantam, 1982), pp. 473–75.

7 Interview with Stansfield Turner, January 1988.

8 Interviews with present and former CIA officials.

9 Private interview in Islamabad.

10 Interview with Syed Ahmed Jhan, Narang, Afghanistan, November 1987.

11 Hekmatyar's crimes and political beliefs are well-known. They were recounted in detail during interviews with State Department officials in Peshawar and Islamabad, Pakistan, and CIA analysts at Langley, Virginia, in 1987 and 1988. Biographical material on Hekmatyar may be found in Edward R. Girardet, *Afghanistan: The Soviet War* (New York: St. Martin's, 1985) and Olivier Roy, *Islam and Resistance in Afghanistan* (New York: Cambridge University Press, 1986). See also, among many such reports, Henry Kamm, "Afghan Guerrillas Hijack Convoy of U.N. Aid for Rival Rebel Area," *New York Times*, December 1, 1988, p. A1, and Robert Pear, "30 Afghan Rebels Slain by Rival Band," *New York Times*, July 18, 1989, p. A7.

12 Interview with Gulam Ahmed, Narang, Afghanistan, November 1987.

13 Private interview with State Department official, Peshawar, October 1987.

14 Interview with Ambassador Raphel, October 1987.

15 Private interview with State Department official, U.S. Embassy, Islamabad, November 1987.

16 Private interview, U.S. Embassy, Islamabad, December 1987.

17 Private interviews with State Department and Drug Enforcement Administration officials in Peshawar, Islamabad and Lahore, Pakistan, September–December 1987.

18 Interviews with Congressman George E. Brown Jr. and Senator Dennis DeConcini, January 1988.

19 Interview with General Kemal Matinuddin, Islamabad, December 1987.
20 Private interviews with CIA analysts, State Department officials, members of Congress, congressional staffers and a former NSA official, June 1987–January 1989.
21 Interview with William Colby, April 1989.
22 Interview with Stansfield Turner, January 1988.
23 Interview with Senator DeConcini, January 1988.
24 Koran, 44:25–27; 9:12–14, 41.
25 The belief, held by many in Washington, that the rebels could win the war and install a pro-American government in Kabul was generated by the diplomatic equivalent of a children's game of telephone. American diplomats in Kabul and Islamabad received very little accurate first-hand information on the progress of the war. The *mujaheddin* dramatically inflated accounts of victories and war-winning strategies. The American diplomats conveyed these reports to Washington, where the State Department filtered them through an ideological screen. Officials in the State Department and the CIA who expressed skepticism put their careers in peril. By the time reports from the battlefront reached the Congress, the image of the war more closely resembled *Lawrence of Arabia* than reality.
26 Private interview with a member of the House Permanent Select Committee on Intelligence, January 1988.
27 Interviews with Congressman Charles Wilson, June 1987, January 1988 (Washington, D.C.); December 1987 (Darra, Pakistan).
28 Wilson's estimate of Soviet deaths in the Afghan war was probably far too high. The Soviets admit to some 15,000 killed in action, and CIA analysts concurred with that figure.
29 Deposition of Thomas A. Twetten ("C-NE"), *Report of the Congressional Committees Investigating the Iran-Contra Affair* [hereinafter, *ICA*], Appendix B: Volume 5, pp. 945–46. Twetten was identified in public records only as C-NE, Chief of the Near East and South Asia operations division, the position he held at the CIA in 1986 and 1987.

Following McMahon's resignation, the CIA veteran become a vice president in charge of black programs at Lockheed Missile and Space.
30 Private interviews, Islamabad and Washington, D.C., October 1987 and January 1988.
31 Interview with Stansfield Turner, January 1988.
32 The Saudi intelligence relationship with the CIA is documented exhaustively in the public and classified records of the Iran-contra committees.
33 Interviews with State Department officials, July 1987, October 1989.
34 Deposition of Charles Allen, *ICA*, Appendix B: Vol. 1, pp. 236ff.
35 Deposition of Lt. Gen. Robert L. Schweitzer, *ICA*, Appendix B: Volume 24, pp. 319ff.
36 Ibid; see also deposition of Ray Cline, *ICA*, Appendix B, Vol. 5, p. 712. Cline, a former deputy director of intelligence at the CIA, also served briefly as a GeoMiliTech consultant.
37 The GeoMiliTech proposal was entered into the public record at several junctures by the Iran-contra committees. Shultz was shown the proposal and gave the quoted response in his public testimony to the Iran-contra committees on July 23, 1987.
38 North's December 1985 meeting with Israeli officials is described in the final report of the Iran-contra committees, *Report of the Congressional Committees Investigating the Iran-Contra Affair, with Supplemental, Minority and Additional Views, November 1987*, [hereinafter, *Final Report*], p. 197.

As with so much of the Iran-contra imbroglio, so many lies and cover stories were told that it's hard to know for sure who did what to whom and when and why. But the

GMT paper may well have planted a seed. "If the [GeoMiliTech] paper got circulation within the White House, then it could provide the intellectual basis or the theory for what was being done" in skimming the proceeds of the Iran arms sales, General Schweitzer said. Schweitzer did not think the GeoMiliTech proposal was a neat idea. He called it "a crazy idea." Secretary of State George Schultz held the GeoMiliTech proposal in his hand at the Iran-contra hearings and said it was an insult to the Constitution. "This is not in line with what was agreed to in Philadelphia," he said. "This is a piece of junk." Schultz testimony, *Final Report*, p. 413; Schweitzer deposition, *ICA*, Appendix B: Volume 24, pp. 319–888.

39 The Iran-contra committees' *Final Report* describes the legal wrangling over the TOWs shipments at pp. 194–209. Weinberger was convinced that somebody was going to jail over this deal—possibly the President. "Visiting hours are Thursday," he told Reagan, in an apparent attempt at levity. Shultz recalled the Reagan-Weinberger dialogue in his public Iran-contra testimony. House Iran-contra committee lawyer Bruce Fein characterized the vanishing finding during the June 3, 1987, deposition of CIA counsel George Clarke, Appendix B: Depositions, Vol. 5, p. 383.

40 The passage is at page 9 of the "Maximum Chronology" prepared by North and the NSC staff during November 1986. A declassified copy with the passage included is at the National Security Archive, Washington D.C. The reference to the diversion of the TOWs to the Afghans was deleted from the public report of the Iran-contra committees.

41 Twetten deposition, *ICA*, Appendix B, Vol. 5, p. 950.

42 Cave memo, undated, to Twetten and Casey. Subject: "Results of Ghorbanifar meeting." Copy on file at National Security Archive, Washington, D.C.

43 North memo to Poindexter, undated. Subject: "Release of American Hostages in Beirut." This is the famous "diversion memorandum." It was marked as Exhibit N28835 by the Iran-contra committees. North's spellings of "Tehran" and "Mujahideen" are verbatim.

44 The dialogues in the Teheran talks are detailed in McFarlane's cables to Poindexter and reproduced in full in *Report of the President's Special Review Board* at pp. B-103 –119, and the Iran-contra committees' *Final Report*, pp. 237–42.

45 John Walcott and David Rogers of the *Wall Street Journal* first reported, in a page one story on November 24, 1986, that Poindexter and other intelligence officials told senior members of Congress that the Iranians had passed on 100 TOWs to the *mujaheddin*. I have independently confirmed that the intelligence committees were told that by Poindexter. But I do not know if Poindexter was telling the truth.

46 Interview with Nawab Salim, Peshawar, September 1987.

47 Interview at CIA headquarters, January 1988.

48 Interviews with U.S. Ambassador Arnold Raphel, September, October and December 1987.

On August 17, 1988, a C-130 military plane carrying General Zia, Ambassador Raphel, the American military attaché and most of Zia's ranking generals exploded and crashed in Pakistan. All aboard were killed. An investigation concluded that the crash was apparently "a criminal act or sabotage." The investigation of the crash that killed Zia and Raphel was botched, and only circumstantial evidence remains for anyone who wants to know who or what blew up the plane.

Zia had many enemies. But he and the ambassador had only one common enemy: the Afghan government. Ambassador Raphel was deeply involved in the CIA's weapons shipments. He supported the guerrillas' cause as a matter of policy and personal belief. I have no way of knowing, but I believe that he and Zia were murdered in an act of vengeance for their role in the *jihad*.

49 Interview with Ambassador Robert G. Neumann, February 1988.

Chapter 7 FROM LEBANON TO LEAVENWORTH

1 Unless otherwise noted, the facts and quotations in this chapter are drawn from more than 3,900 pages of Army documents released to the author under the Freedom of Information Act. The central document is the Army's Intelligence and Security Command's eight-volume investigative record of the Yellow Fruit affair, entitled *Article 15-6 Investigation into Special Mission Funds* [hereinafter *INSCOM/FOIA*]. Steven Emerson's *Secret Warriors: Inside the Covert Military Operations of the Reagan Era* (New York: G.P. Putnam's Sons, 1988) was an invaluable reference. Timothy Enneking was interviewed on the record; other Army and Justice Department Investigators spoke off the record.

2 Testimony of Richard V. Secord, *Joint Hearings Before the House Select Committee to Investigate Covert Arms Transactions with Iran and the Senate Select Committee on Secret Military Assistance to Iran and the Nicaraguan Opposition* [hereinafter, *JHSC*], May 6, 1987, pp. 148–49.

3 Interview with Timothy Enneking, June 1989.

4 Statements of Vessey and Meyer: *INSCOM/FOIA*, Vol. I, pp. 52–53, 529–40.

5 *INSCOM/FOIA*, Vol. I, p. 30.

6 *INSCOM/FOIA*, Vol. IV, pp. 967–74, sworn statement of Lt. Gen. James Merryman, August 14, 1986.

7 Vessey and Meyer on Keenan: *INSCOM/FOIA*, Vol. I, pp. 45–52; Vol. IV, pp. 1120–29, Vessey's sworn statement of June 26, 1986.

8 *INSCOM/FOIA*, Vol. IV, pp. 991–97, sworn statement of Lt. Gen. Ernest Peixotto, July 30, 1986.

9 *INSCOM/FOIA*, Vol. IV, pp. 967–74, sworn statement of Lt. Gen. James Merryman, August 14, 1986.

10 *INSCOM/FOIA*, Vol. II, pp. 729–32. The ISA commander's name was blacked out in the documents. I have since learned his identity, but he still is serving as an intelligence officer and to reveal his name would be unwise and probably illegal.

11 *INSCOM/FOIA*, Vol. II, pp. 302–496, sworn statements of Autmer Ackley Jr., June 18–20, 1985.

12 The Casey briefing is described in *Secret Warriors*, p. 135.

13 Longhofer's assignment to CIA: "Report of Investigative Activity," Falls Church, Va.: U.S. Justice Department, April 13, 1984 (FBI interview of Longhofer).

14 *INSCOM/FOIA*, Vol. II, pp. 750–58, sworn statement of Maj. Gen. Harry E. Soyster, August 18, 1986.

15 *INSCOM/FOIA*, Vol. IV, pp. 936–65, secret taped interview of Maj. Gen. (Ret.) Homer S. Long, March 22, 1985.

16 Ibid.

17 *INSCOM/FOIA*, Vol. IV, pp. 967–74, sworn statement of Lt. Gen. James Merryman, August 14, 1986; secret taped interview of General Long, p. 940.

18 *INSCOM/FOIA*, Vol. II, p. 699, sworn statement of Lt. Gen. William E. Odom, September 24, 1985.

19 *INSCOM/FOIA*, Vol. II, pp. 706–10, sworn statement of Lt. Gen. William E. Odom, September 26, 1986.

20 *INSCOM/FOIA*, Vol. II, p. 754, sworn statement of General Soyster, August 18, 1986.

21 *INSCOM/FOIA*, Vol. I., pp. 134–35, sworn statement of General Odom.

22 Golden testimony: *Report of the Congressional Committees Investigating the Iran-Contra Affair* [hereinafter, *ICA*], Senate Report 100-216, House Report 100-433 (Washington: 1988), Vol. 12, pp. 375–473. All quotations from Golden are from his declassified testimony to the Iran-contra investigators.

23 Unlocked cash box in BSI's safe: *INSCOM/FOIA*, Vol. I, p. 85.
24 Initial Army investigation: *INSCOM/FOIA*, Vol. I, pp. 96–106, 137; destruction of records authorized by Vessey and Odom: ibid.
25 Interrogation of Autmer Ackley Jr., *INSCOM/FOIA*, Vol. II, pp. 302–491, June 18–19, 1985. All quotations from Ackley are from his declassified testimony.
26 The federal laws cited are 31 U.S.C., secs. 11, 628 and 696 (1970).
27 *INSCOM/FOIA*, Vol. II, pp. 570–75, sworn statement of Oliver Kennedy, August 6, 1985.
28 *INSCOM/FOIA*, Vol. IV, pp. 889–922, Top Secret taped interview of Gen. Glenn K. Otis, commander in chief, United States Army, Europe and Seventh Army by Special Agents Kenneth S. Haynes and Michael Keith, February 28, 1985.
29 *INSCOM/FOIA*, Vol. IV, pp. 936–65, interview with Gen. Long.
30 *INSCOM/FOIA*, Vol. III, pp. 677–88, sworn statement of Maj. Gen. (Ret.) Albert N. Stubblebine, September 12 and October 1, 1985.
31 *INSCOM/FOIA*, Vol. IV, pp. 1120–29, interview with Gen. Vessey.
32 Lt. Col. Robert C. Rhodes and Capt. Charles K. Sweeney II, "Memorandum for Commander, Military District of Washington. Subject: Action by the Appointing Authority on the Perez Investigation," May 29, 1987 (Released to the author under the Freedom of Information Act).
33 Letter to the author, Office of the Secretary of the Army, July 19, 1989.
34 Interview with Joe B. Brown, U.S. Attorney for the Middle District of Tennessee; private interviews with Justice Department and Pentagon officials.
35 Deposition of John O. Marsh, *ICA*, Appendix B, Vol. 17, pp. 783–866, July 23, 1987.
36 North testimony, *JHSC*, July 13, 1987.
37 Longhofer was released from prison, his appeal pending, on November 26, 1986. His sentence was commuted and he was freed. The Army Parole and Clemency Board granted Duncan parole after two years in prison on February 23, 1989. He, too, has appealed his conviction. Letter to the author, Office of the Secretary of the Army, July 19, 1989.

Chapter 8 LAWS AND LIES

1 North testimony, *JHSC*, July 7, 1987.
2 "North admitted that he and other officials lied repeatedly to Congress and to the American people. . . . North's testimony demonstrates that he also lied to members of the Executive branch, including the Attorney General, and officials of the State Department, CIA and NSC." *Report of the Congressional Committees Investigating the Iran-Contra Affair*, Senate Report 100–216, House Report 100–433 [hereinafter, *Final Report*] (Washington, D.C.: Government Printing Office, 1987), p. 13.
3 Clair George's testimony is in *ICA, Joint Hearings in Executive Session as Declassified*, August 5–6, 1987, pp. 189–273.
4 Alan Fiers' testimony is in *ICA, Joint Hearings in Executive Session as Declassified*, August 5, 1987, pp. 121, 171–72.
5 The Iran-contra committees said that the public disclosure of the secret missions "did not result in any loss of life of which the Committees are aware." *Final Report*, p. 421.
6 Federalist 58; *Final Report*, p. 412.
7 Cited in Bill Moyers, *The Secret Government* (Washington, D.C.: Seven Locks Press, 1988), p. 104.
8 The minutes of the June 25, 1984, meeting at which Shultz delivered his warning have

been reproduced by the Iran-contra committees and are backed up by the sworn testimony of Shultz and McFarlane.

9 Trial testimony of Oliver North, *U.S. v. North*, April 6, 1989.

10 Tillman's description of North is in Constantine C. Menges, *Inside the National Security Council: The True Story of the Making and Unmaking of Reagan's Foreign Policy* (New York: Simon & Schuster, 1988), p. 194.

11 Deposition of Thomas Twetten ("C/NE"), *ICA*, Appendix B: Volume 5, pp. 33 ff. Twetten said Ghorbanifar was known to the CIA as a "drug dealer" and an "arms merchant."

12 Closing statement of Senator Daniel Inouye, Iran-contra hearings, August 3, 1987.

13 For the substance of Clarridge's statements, see Roy Gutman, *Banana Diplomacy: The Making of American Policy in Nicaragua 1981–1987* (New York: Simon & Schuster, 1988), p. 57. Gutman interviewed two participants in the August 1981 meeting.

14 *Washington Post*, April 3, 1983, p. A13.

15 1983 Public Papers of the President of the United States, Ronald Reagan, Vol. 1, pp. 603–604 (April 27, 1983).

16 This recitation of facts is drawn from a court document released jointly by government prosecutors and defense lawyers at the trial of Oliver North, outlining facts "that the United States has admitted . . . to be true." Stipulation, *U.S. v. North*, April 7, 1989.

17 George testimony, *ICA, Joint Hearings as Declassified*, p. 243.

18 Turner, *Secrecy and Democracy*; Poindexter testimony, Iran-contra hearings, July 15, 1987.

19 Stipulation, *U.S. v. North*, pp. 6–7.

20 Stipulation, pp. 38–40.

21 *Final Report*, p. 423.

22 George deposition, *ICA, Joint Hearings as Declassified*, pp. 189–273.

23 Deposition of Francis McNeil, *ICA*, Appendix B, Vol. 17, pp. 515–78.

24 Deposition of William C. Sullivan, deputy director, FBI, to Church Committee investigators, June 1975. Cited in Loch K. Johnson, *America's Secret Power: The CIA in a Democratic Society* (New York: Oxford University Press, 1989), p. 151.

25 Quotations are from contemporaneous notes I took while attending North's trial.

That North was convicted of the nickel-and-dime crime of stealing some of the Enterprise's profits to build his electronic security fence was most ignominious. But that offense was the easiest to grasp for the working-class jury, a panel chosen for its innocence of affairs of state, security compartments and operational security. The jurors' eyes had widened and then narrowed when North revealed he had stashed "upwards of $15,000" worth of pocket change in a steel box bolted to his closet floor, that he filled the box by emptying the change from his pockets at night. They had heard of such boxes.

When North revealed the existence of his steel box, it rang a bell. This famous colloquy, from a 1931 municipal-corruption investigation in New York City, between the stalwart Judge Samuel Seabury and the Hon. Thomas M. Farley, sheriff of New York County, in which Sheriff Farley attempts to explain how he had amassed a considerable fortune on a salary of $8,500 a year, is the proper antecedent of North's testimony:

SEABURY: Where did you keep these moneys that you had saved?
FARLEY: In a safe-deposit box at home in the house.
SEABURY: Whereabouts at home in the house did you keep this money that you had saved?
FARLEY: In the safe.
SEABURY: In a safe?
FARLEY: Yes.
SEABURY: In a little box in a safe?

FARLEY: A big safe.
SEABURY: But a little box in a big safe?
FARLEY: In a big box in a big safe.
SEABURY: . . . . And, Sheriff, was this big box that was safely kept in the big safe a tin box or a wooden box?
FARLEY: A tin box.
SEABURY: Is it the type of tin boxes that are specially manufactured and designed to serve as a receptacle for cash?
FARLEY: It is.
SEABURY: . . . . Where did the extra cash come from, Sheriff?
FARLEY: Well, that came from the good box I had.
SEABURY: Kind of a magic box?
FARLEY: It was a wonderful box.

26 Aaron Epstein, "Prosecutor Rebuffed on Secrets Plea," *Philadelphia Inquirer*, December 12, 1989, p. 18-A.
27 David Johnston, "Iran-Contra Prosecutor Says Secrecy Issue Blocks Justice," *New York Times*, December 2, 1989, p. A12; Aaron Epstein and Matthew Purdy, "Walsh: Secrecy Hides Truth," *Philadelphia Inquirer*, December 14, 1989, p. 1A.

Chapter 9 AN OPEN BOOK

1 King James I to the Speaker of the House of Commons quoted in Bok, *Secrets: On the Ethics of Concealment and Revelation*, p. 172; Francis Bacon, *The Advancement of Learning and New Atlantis*, ed., Thomas Case (London: Oxford University Press, 1951), p. 235.
2 The Framers' debates on the language that became Article 1, Section 9, Clause 7 of the Constitution are recorded in M. Farrand, *The Records of the Federal Convention of 1787*, and J. Elliot, *Debates on the Federal Constitution*, and cited in *United States v. Richardson*, 418 U.S. 166 (Douglas, J., dissenting).
3 Letter to W.T. Barry, Aug. 4, 1822, *The Writings of James Madison* Vol. 9 (G. Hunt ed. 1910), p. 103.
4 Justice Joseph Story, *Commentaries on the Constitution of the United States*, 1348, at 222–23 (5th ed., 1891). Cited in "The CIA's Secret Funding and the Constitution," 84 *Yale Law Journal*, 613 (1975).
5: The quotation from John Taylor is cited in Arthur M. Schlesinger Jr.'s preface to Steven L. Katz, *Government Secrecy: Decisions Without Democracy* (Washington, D.C.: People For The American Way, 1987), p. ii.
6 Mr. Richardson's correspondence with Treasury officials and copies of court records in his case were provided by Mr. Richardson and are in the author's possession.
7 *Richardson v. United States*, 465 F. 2d 844, 853, United States Court of Appeals for the Third Circuit, 1972.
8 Thucydides, *History of the Peloponnesian War*, translated by Rex Warner (New York Penguin, 1974), pp. 144–45.
9 *United States v. Robel*, 389 U.S. 258–64 (1967).
10 *New York Times Co. v. United States*, 403 U.S. 713, 719 (1971).
11 Ibid. at 728.
12 *U.S. v. Richardson* (418 U.S. 166), 167–80, June 25, 1974.
13 *U.S. v. Richardson* (418 U.S. 166) 197–202, Douglas, dissenting.
14 Clair George's testimony in a closed session of the Iran-contra committees is in *Report of the Congressional Committees Investigating the Iran-Contra Affair* [hereinafter, ICA],

Appendix B, Vol. 12, pp. 1–164, as declassified (Washington, D.C: Government Printing Office, 1988).

15 Closing statement of Sen. Daniel Inouye, *ICA*, August 3, 1987.

16 The quotation from Dulles comes from the final paragraph of his book, *The Craft of Intelligence*, and is cited in L. Fletcher Prouty, *The Secret Team* (Englewood Cliffs, N.J.: Prentice-Hall, 1973), p. 66.

SELECTED
BIBLIOGRAPHY

Here is a selective list of works whose ideas I found particularly useful. It might be the beginnings of a syllabus for a course in the history of the Cold War.

Arkin, William M., and Richard W. Fieldhouse. *Nuclear Battlefields: Global Links in the Arms Race*. Cambridge, Mass.: Ballinger, 1985. (Arkin is an extraordinarily adept interpreter of arcane nuclear-weapons data for the general reader.)

Ball, Desmond, and Jeffrey Richelson, eds. *Strategic Nuclear Targeting*. Ithaca: Cornell University Press, 1986. (Essays collected here tend toward the technical, but with moral underpinnings.)

Bamford, James. *The Puzzle Palace*. New York: Penguin, 1983. (No one ever had written a full account of the National Security Agency before Bamford, and no one is likely to write a better one. A unique work, extraordinarily well-documented.)

Beck, Melvin. *Secret Contenders: The Myth of Cold War Counterintelligence*. New York: Sheridan Square, 1984. (The author, a twenty-seven-year veteran of the CIA, had an interesting career, but the best writing here is the introduction by Thomas Powers.)

Bellin, David, and Gary Chapman, eds. *Computers in Battle: Will They Work?* Boston: Harcourt Brace Jovanovich, 1987. (Accessible essays on a crucial question.)

Betts, Richard K. *Nuclear Balance and Nuclear Blackmail*. Washington, D.C.: The Brookings Institution, 1987. (Forty years of nuclear brinksmanship; a policy primer.)

Blair, Bruce G. *Strategic Command and Control: Redefining the Nuclear Threat*. Washington, D.C.: The Brookings Institution, 1985. (A definitive book by one of the clearest thinkers in the field.)

Bok, Sissela. *Secrets: On the Ethics of Concealment and Revelation*. New York: Vintage, 1983. (A philosopher wrestles with the morality of secrecy.)

Bracken, Paul. *The Command and Control of Nuclear Forces*. New Haven: Yale University Press, 1983. (An unsurpassed study of the insurmountable problems of controlling a nuclear war.)

262 SELECTED BIBLIOGRAPHY

Bradlee, Ben Jr. *Guts and Glory: The Rise and Fall of Oliver North*. New York: Donald I. Fine, 1988. (Occasionally slapdash but often illuminating biography.)

Bundy, McGeorge. *Danger and Survival: Choices About the Bomb in the First Fifty Years*. New York: Random House, 1988. (Six hundred pages of honest and finely honed analysis of why we did drop the bomb in 1945 and have not since. The finest in its field. Part of a growing body of works by Vietnam hawks turned nuclear doves.)

Burnham, David. *The Rise of the Computer State*. New York: Vintage, 1984. (The computer as a tool of national-security powers; levelheaded and thorough.)

Burrows, William E. *Deep Black: Space Espionage and National Security*. New York: Random House, 1986. (The first detailed book on the National Reconnaissance Office; excellent on the technology, uses and abuses of space-based intelligence systems.)

Carter, Ashton B., John D. Steinbruner and Charles A. Zraket, eds. *Managing Nuclear Operations*. Washington, D.C.: The Brookings Institution, 1987. (How to run a nuclear war, by a variety of experts.)

Emerson, Steven. *Secret Warriors: Inside the Covert Military Operations of the Reagan Era*. New York: G.P. Putnam's Sons, 1988. (The best book to date on the special operations of the Pentagon.)

Fallows, James. *National Defense*. New York: Random House, 1981. (How the Pentagon worked and did not work before the advent of the Reagan administration.)

Ford, Daniel. *The Button*. New York: Simon and Schuster, 1985. (A scientist tours the nuclear command and control complex and finds it doesn't work; an excellent starting point for beginners interested in the C³I issue.)

Gutman, Roy. *Banana Diplomacy: The Making of American Policy in Nicaragua 1981–1987*. New York: Simon and Schuster, 1988. (Faultlessly documented account of the White House's covert war against the Sandinistas.)

Herken, Gregg. *Counsels of War*. New York: Knopf, 1985. (A superior history of nuclear strategy since Hiroshima.)

Isaacson, Walter, and Evan Thomas. *The Wise Men: Six Friends and the World They Made*. New York: Touchstone, 1986. (The formation of postwar American foreign policy, told through the lives of the men who formed it; a social and political history of the Washington establishment, and a gripping one.)

Johnson, Loch K. *America's Secret Power: The CIA in a Democratic Society*. New York: Oxford University Press, 1989. (Probably the most thoughtful one-volume study on the Agency.)

Jordan, Amos A., and William J. Taylor. *American National Security: Policy and Process*. Baltimore: Johns Hopkins University Press, 1981. (A college textbook more interesting for its biases than its basics.)

Kahn, Herman. *On Thermonuclear War*. Princeton: Princeton University Press, 1961. (An insane masterwork on the logic of nuclear war by the intellectual model for Dr. Strangelove: "Objective studies indicate that even though the amount of human tragedy would be greatly increased in the postwar world, the increase would not preclude normal and happy lives for the majority of survivors and their descendants.")

Kaplan, Fred. *The Wizards of Armageddon*. New York: Touchstone, 1983. (How a handful of "defense intellectuals" shaped America's thinking about the bomb; a beautifully written book, filled with understanding.)

Klare, Michael T., and Peter Kornbluh, eds. *Low-Intensity Warfare: Counterinsurgency, Proinsurgency and Antiterrorism in the Eighties*. New York: Pantheon, 1988. (Collected essays, a few of them excellent.)

Kotz, Nick. *Wild Blue Yonder: Money, Politics, and the B-1 Bomber*. Princeton: Princeton University Press, 1988. (The life and death and rebirth of a second-rate weapon: the one book to read to gain an understanding of how the military-industrial complex works.)

Lukas, J. Anthony. *Nightmare: The Underside of the Nixon Years.* New York: Viking, 1976, 1988 (2nd ed.). (Especially good on the CIA's role in Watergate.)

Luttwak, Edward N. *The Pentagon and the Art of War.* New York: Simon and Schuster, 1985. (A well-known Pentagon consultant argues for better ways to convert money into military power.)

Marchetti, Victor, and John D. Marks. *The CIA and the Cult of Intelligence.* New York: Knopf, 1974 (1st ed.); New York: Dell, 1983 (revised ed.). (The most censored book in print in the United States today. Varied standard, italic and bold typefaces show passages previously deleted at the CIA's request and reinstated after legal struggles; they also show the absurdity of the deletions. Still powerful, still practical analysis by two veterans, respectively, of the CIA and the State Department.)

Martin, David C., and John Walcott. *Best Laid Plans: The Inside Story of America's War Against Terrorism.* New York: Harper & Row, 1988. (Tremendous reporting and sympathetic analysis of 1980's counterterrorism planning.)

McNamara, Robert S. *Blundering into Disaster.* New York: Pantheon, 1986. (The former defense secretary argues that the effort to improve our nuclear war-fighting ability is an "absurd struggle.")

Mojtabai, A.J. *Blessed Assurance: At Home with the Bomb in Amarillo, Texas.* Boston: Houghton Mifflin, 1986. (God, Armageddon and the factory workers at the nation's nuclear-weapons assembly plant.)

O'Connor, Patrica Ann, and Colleen McGuiness, eds. *The Iran-Contra Puzzle.* Washington D.C.: Congressional Quarterly, 1988. (Useful compendium of testimony, documents and background on an unsolved case.)

Orwell, George. "Politics and the English Language," *The Orwell Reader.* New York: Harcourt Brace Jovanovich, 1956. ("Political language . . . is designed to make lies sound truthful, and murder respectable, and to give an appearance of solidity to pure wind.")

Patterson, Thomas G. *Meeting the Communist Threat.* New York: Oxford University Press, 1988. (Intelligent analysis of presidential anticommunism from Truman to Reagan.)

Pringle, Peter, and William Arkin. *S.I.O.P.: The Secret U.S. Plan for Nuclear War.* New York: Norton, 1983. (Still the best account of the sketchy game plan for World War III.)

Ranelagh, John. *The Agency: The Rise and Decline of the CIA.* New York: Simon and Schuster, 1986. (Seven hundred pages of well-documented history, but lacking a full appreciation of the tensions between secrecy and democracy in America.)

Rhodes, Richard. *The Making of the Atomic Bomb.* New York: Touchstone, 1987. (A triumph. The poetry of physics and the power of plutonium wedded in prose; a landmark in thinking about the unthinkable. 1988 Pulitzer Prize for history; 1987 National Book Award.)

Richelson, Jeffrey T. *American Espionage and the Soviet Target.* New York: William Morrow, 1987. (Richelson, an assiduous researcher, knows his facts and lays them out intelligently in this and the three following works.)

———. *Foreign Intelligence Organizations.* Cambridge, Mass.:Ballinger, 1988. (A useful overview of Western, Israeli and Asian intelligence services.)

———. *The U.S. Intelligence Community.* Cambridge, Mass.: Ballinger, 1985. (The structure of U.S. intelligence made tangible; an excellent tour through terra incognita.)

———, and Desmond Ball. *The Ties that Bind.* Winchester, Mass.: Allen & Unwin, 1985. (The intelligence relationships between the U.S., the U.K., Canada, Australia and New Zealand.)

Scheer, Robert. *With Enough Shovels: Reagan, Bush and Nuclear War.* New York: Vintage, 1983. (Scheer's transcribed interviews with the fortieth (and forty-first) Presidents and their Pentagon strategists, on the subject of winning nuclear wars, were so scary that they helped create the nuclear-freeze movement.)

Sherry, Michael S. *The Rise of American Air Power: The Creation of Armageddon.* New Haven: Yale University Press, 1987. (Technological fanaticism, apocalyptic fantasy and the destruction of Japan: a brilliant history of American strategic bombing through 1945.)

Stares, Paul B. *Space and National Security.* Washington, D.C.: The Brookings Institution, 1987. (The new frontier for nuclear war; why anti-satellite and anti-anti-satellite weaponry for space war is destabilizing.)

Stockwell, John. *In Search of Enemies: A CIA Story.* New York: Norton, 1978. (Probably the best of the handful of books by ex-CIA agents. Stockwell, who was the chief of the CIA's Angola Task Force, tells the story of a fruitless covert policy that marked a turning point in CIA history: the first covert action publicly halted by Congress.)

Tsipis, Kosta. *Arsenal: Understanding Weapons in the Nuclear Age.* New York: Touchstone, 1983. (A distinguished physicist explains nuclear weaponry and its flaws.)

Union of Concerned Scientists. *Empty Promise: The Growing Case Against Star Wars.* Boston: Beacon, 1986. (Steady-voiced refutations of the visionary "peace shield.")

Wise, David. *The Politics of Lying: Government Deception, Secrecy and Power.* New York: Random House, 1973. (Lies, damned lies and White House press conferences: secrecy defined as a threat to democracy.)

————, and Thomas B. Ross. *The Invisible Government.* New York: Random House, 1964. (The first look inside the Panorama box: a pioneering analysis of American espionage and covert action. The CIA attempted to suppress it upon its publication; soon it was the best-selling book in the nation. A classic, now out of print.)

INDEX

Acheson, Dean, 28, 30, 31, 115
Achille Lauro cruise ship, 195
Ackley, Autmer, Jr., 178–79, 180, 187,
    189–91, 195
Advanced cruise missile (ACM), 8,
    9–10, 95
Afghanistan, 143–71
Ahmed, Gulam, 150
Air Force, U.S., 34, 39, 53, 63, 113,
    115
    budget, 13
    Stealth bomber, 8–9, 73–107
    strategic weapons programs, 8–10
    see also Strategic Air Command
Ajax (covert operation), 124
Aldridge, Edward C., Jr., 73, 79
Allen, Lew, Jr., 86
Allen, Richard, 44
Allende, Salvador, 133–34
Amin, Hafizullah, 145
Amlie, Tom, 13, 79
Anderson, Orville, 28–29
Angleton, James Jesus, 39–140, 252n.65
Antisatellite weapons, 68–69
Arab-Israeli conflict, 53–54, 80
Arbenz Guzmán, Jacobo, 124

Argentina, 203–4
Arms control negotiations, 41, 42
Arms pipeline, 143–71
Arms race, 24, 27, 28
    see also Soviet Union, weapons
    strength
Army, U.S., 11, 13, 113
    Special Operations Division, 173–98
Aspin, Les, 9–10, 17, 75, 94, 95, 101,
    104, 105–6
ATB (Advanced Technology bomber),
    See Stealth bomber
Atomic bomb, 5, 18, 36
    cost of, 20, 23
    decision to use, 21–23
    see also Manhattan Project
Atoms for Peace, 35
A-12 attack plane, cost of, 11–12
Aurand, Pete, 37
Aviation Tech Services, 179
AWACS, 160–61

Babbitt, Albert, 58
Bacon, Francis, 214
Baker, James, 201
Bamieh, Sam, 161

Barker, Bernard, 130, 131
Bay of Pigs invasion, 125–26
B-52 bomber, 76, 77, 78, 81
Belgian Congo. *See* Zaire
Bhutto, Zulfikar Ali, 147
Black budget, 5–18, 44, 141, 228–31
  for Afghan war, 158–60
  and CIA, 111–22, 129–30, 137–42
  growth of, 5, 16, 94–96
  origins of, 19–20
Blair, Bruce, 61, 70, 102
Boeing Co., 11, 88, 98–99
Boland Amendment, 185, 204
Bombers, manned and long-range, 76–77
  see also B-52 bomber; B-1 bomber;
  Stealth bomber
Bombs. *See* Atomic bomb; Hydrogen
  bomb
B-1 bomber, 81, 83, 84–87
  problems with, 96–97
Bonner, Robert, 93
Bork, Robert, 224–25
Boston Globe, 181
Bracken, Paul, 49, 64, 69
Braden, Tom, 121
Broe, William, 134
Brousseau, Ronald, 91–93
Brown, George, 59
Brown, George E., Jr., 152, 249n.25
Brzezinski, Zbigniew, 60, 148
B-2 bomber. *See* Stealth bomber
Buckley, William, 208
Budget. *See* Black budget; Pentagon,
  budget; Soviet Union, defense
  budget
Bundy, Harvey, 22
Bundy, McGeorge, 25
Burger, Warren, 225, 226, 227
Bush, George, 47, 53, 102, 144, 213
  as CIA director, 42, 137, 138
  on winning nuclear war, 59, 61, 70
Bush, Vannevar, 19, 20
Byard, Frederick, 184–85, 197–98
Byrnes, James, 23

CARTE BLANCHE (war games), 33
Carter, Ashton, 66
Carter, Jimmy
  and Afghan war, 145, 146
  and Argentina, 203
  B-1 cancellation, 81, 83

1980 campaign and Stealth, 83
  nuclear weapons policies, 59–61
  and Pakistan, 147
Case, Clifford, 130
Casey, William
  and arms pipeline, 158, 160, 162
  as CIA head, 141–42, 180, 206
  and Iran-contra, 161, 164, 203, 205, 206
  mentioned, 113, 163, 165, 179, 209, 210
Castro, Fidel, 125, 127
Cave, George, 165
Celler, Emmanuel, 119
Central America, ISA in, 178, 181
Central Intelligence Agency. *See* CIA
Central Intelligence Group, 114–15
Chain, John T., 103
Chaos (covert operation), 134
Cheney, Dick, 75, 106
Chile, 133–34
China, 160, 162, 163
Chou Enlai, 162
Church, Frank, 136
Church Committee, 136, 137–38, 139
Churchill, Winston, 21
CIA (Central Intelligence Agency), 5, 15, 24, 42, 111–42, 172, 175, 179, 186, 212
  Act establishing (1949), 118–20, 121, 216, 217, 218, 219, 222
  beginnings of, 113–16
  black budget of, 111–22, 129–30, 137–42
  covert activities of, 124–42, 143–71, 202, 205–8
  as danger to democracy, 127
  philosophy of, 123–24
  and Special Operations Division, 180–82, 185–86
  and weapons pipeline, 143–71
Clarridge, Duane, 204
Clay, Lucius, 24–25
Cline, Ray, 42
Cohen, William, 103, 206
Colby, William, 113, 138, 139, 153
  disclosure of CIA secrets, 132–33, 134, 135, 136
Cold War, 18, 29–45, 216, 230, 233
  and creation of CIA, 111–13
  Eisenhower and, 32–33

Command, control, communications and intelligence network, *See* C³I network
Committee on the Present Danger, 43–44
Conahan, Frank, 10–11, 84, 89
Concurrency, 89, 97
Congress, U.S.
  and Afghan war, 157–60
  and atom bomb, 20, 123
  black budget, 16–17, 95, 122, 129–30, 138
  Boland Amendment, 185, 204
  lack of control over CIA, 112, 115–22, 126–42, 229, 250n.36
  Intelligence Oversight Act, 209
  Iran-contra investigation, 199, 206, 209
  Military Reform caucus, 94
  nuclear war study, 70–71
  Stealth bomber, 75, 85–88, 103–17
  STRATSAT, 62
  see also Church Committee; House Armed Services Committee; Senate Armed Services Committee
Contras. *See* Iran-contra affair
Costa Rica, 181, 204
Constitution, U.S., 38, 52, 164, 211
  threats to, 16, 113, 120, 127, 139, 140, 190, 201, 229
  and CIA, 214–31
  framers of, 201, 214–16, 222
Costello, Robert B., 75–76, 98
Cranston, Alan, 129–30
Credibility gap, 127
CREEP (Committee to Re-Elect the President), 131
C³I network, 49, 50, 51, 56–72, 245n.11
Cuba, 125–26, 127, 130
Cuban missile crisis, 40–41

DARPA (Defense Advanced Research Projects Agency), 67–68, 80
Davico, Mario, 204
Davis, Bennie, 86–87
DeConcini, Dennis, 152, 153
DEFCON (Defense Conditions), levels, 53–55
Defense, Department of, 6, 96, 100–101, 115
  see also Pentagon

Defense budget. See Black budget; Pentagon, budget; Soviet Union, defense budget
Dellums, Ron, 104, 105
Denfield, Louis, 27
Devlin, Lawrence, 125
Dickinson, Bill, 95
Dingell, John D., 93–95
Donovan, William J., 113–14
Douglas, William O., 227, 230
Douglas Aircraft, 77
Dr. Strangelove (film), 51
Drug Enforcement Administration (DEA), 151, 207, 209
Drug traffic, 151, 152, 206, 207
DCSOPS (Deputy Chief of Staff for Operations and Plans), 176
Dubs, Adolph, 144
Dulles, Allen, 113, 115, 116, 122, 125, 230
Dulles, John Foster, 33, 36
Duncan, Dale C., 172, 180, 184, 185, 197, 198

Edwards, Glen, 77–78
EHF radio transmissions (extremely high frequency), 62, 67
Einstein, Albert, 72
Eisenhower, Dwight D.
  and atom bomb, 22
  covert actions during administration, 124–25, 126, 127
  and nuclear weapons build-up, 31–33, 36–38, 39
Electromagnetic pulse, 66–67, 68
Ellender, Allen, 122, 128, 130
Ellsberg, Daniel, 40, 131, 132
El Salvador, 178, 187, 204
Emergency Rocket Communications Systems, 52
Enneking, Timothy, 175, 176, 179
  investigation of black budget, 187–97
Enterprise, The (covert operation), 202–3, 211, 258n.25
Erasmus, 118

Fahd, King, 161, 202
Fat Man (atomic bomb), 23
FBI (Federal Bureau of Investigation), 91, 186, 251n.45
Fernandez, Joe, 212–13

Fiers, Alan, 200
Findley, Paul, 135
Finletter, Thomas, 28
Fitzgerald, Ernie, 94
Football, The (briefcase), 56
Ford, Gerald, 135, 136, 137
Foreshadow Operation, 178
Forrestal, James, 28, 116, 117
Fraenkel, Osmond, 225
Fulbright, William, 128, 129

Gallery, Daniel, 27
Garwin, Richard, 17
Gemayel, Bashir, 179–80, 195
General Accounting Office (GAO), 10,
    84, 89, 94
General Dynamics, 11, 93
General Electric, 11
Geng Biao, 162
GeoMiliTech Consultants Corp., 162–64,
    254n.38
George, Clair, 141, 200, 205, 207, 208,
    229
Gesell, Gerhard, 212
Ghorbanifar, Manucher, 202–3
Gilstein, Jacob, 67
Glatt, Werner, 163
Glenn, John, 101
GMT Corp, 162–64, 254n.38
Golden, William T., 184, 185
Goldwater, Barry, 85
Gorbachev, Mikhail, 167–68
Gottlieb, Sidney, 125
Grass Blade, 11, 12
Gravel, Mike, 112
Gray, Colin, 43, 44, 60
Gray, Gordon, 36
Gritz, James, 181
Groves, Leslie, R., 19, 20, 21, 23
Guatemala, 124, 178, 202, 204
Gul, Hamid, 149
Gulley, Bill, 56

Haig, Alexander, 54
Hakim, Albert, 165, 202
Hall, Fawn, 165
Haskell, Richard, 91–92
Have Blue project, 80
Haynes, Kenneth, 192
Heather, Fred, 93
Heilmeier, George, 67

Hekmatyar, Gulbuddin, 149–50, 168,
    170, 171
Hello, Buz, 85
Helms, Richard, 113, 129, 130, 133–34,
    138
Hendricks, Gerald, 46
Henry, Patrick, 215
Hersh, Seymour, 134
Hicks, Donald, 88, 89, 102
Hillenkoetter, Roscoe, 116–17, 118
Hiroshima, bombing of, 22–23, 36
Honduras, 178, 181, 204
Honey Badger Operation, 174
Hostages
    American in Iran, 173–74, 175
    American in Lebanon, 164, 165, 166,
        207–8
    see also Iran-contra affair
House Armed Services Committee, 16,
    74, 94, 95, 96, 101, 104, 119
Houston, Lawrence, 114, 117, 126
Hughes, Harold, 135
Hughes Aircraft Company, 148
Hughes-Ryan Act, 135
Hull, John, 185
Humphrey, Gordon, 148–49
Hunt, E. Howard, 125, 130, 131–32
Hydrogen bomb, 27–28

ICBMs, 38, 39–40, 55
Ikle, Fred, 44
Inouye, Daniel, 203
INSCOM, (Intelligence and Security
    Command), 178, 187
Intelligence Oversight Act, 209
Iran, 124, 144, 145, 147, 160, 181, 202
    American hostages in, 173–74
    TOW missiles sales to, 164–65
Iran-contra affair, 161, 164–67, 199–213
ISA (Intelligence Support Activity),
    177–78, 181
Israel, 57, 80, 163, 205
    see also Arab-Israeli conflict

Jackson, Henry, 88
Jefferson, Thomas, 201
Johnson, Louis, 28
Johnson, Lyndon B., 127
Joint Chiefs of Staff, 14, 24, 33, 34, 35,
    52, 59, 71, 81, 113
Jones, David, 63

Jones, Ruth, 84–85
Jones, Thomas V., 81–83, 84–85, 87, 100

Kalmbach, Herbert, 82
Kangarlu, Ahmed, 165
Karmal, Babrak, 145
Karp, Craig, 170
Kasich, John, 96, 104–5
Keenan, Larry, 177, 178
Keenie Meenie Services, 206
Keeny, Spurgeon, 44
Keith, Michael, 192
Kennan, George, 29
Kennedy, John F., 39, 40, 41, 125, 127, 230
Kennedy, Oliver, 191
Khalis, Yunis, 151
Khan, Asraf, 156
Khrushchev, Nikita, 141
Kissinger, Henry, 42, 54, 162
Kneecap, 53
Koch, Ed, 128–29
Korean War, 31, 32

Landolt, Richard, 66
Langer, William, 118
Laos, 126, 128, 130
    American POWs in, 181–82
Lebanon, 179–80
    American hostages in, 164, 165, 166, 207–8
Lehman, John, 44, 206
LeMay, Curtis E.
    mentioned, 58, 61, 76
    and nuclear weapons, 32, 33, 34–35, 239n.21
    and SAC, 26–27, 31, 241n.44
Liberty, USS, 57
Libya, 146, 149
Little Boy (atomic bomb), 22, 36
Lockheed Missile and Space Company, 11, 28, 63
Long, Homer, 182, 192
Longhofer, James, 175, 178, 179, 180, 182, 185, 197
Looking Glass (code name), 53
Lovelace, A. M., 93
Lovett, Robert, 28, 126
LTV Corporation, 87
Lumumba, Patrice, 125

Madison, James, 201, 215
Manhattan Project, 5, 19–22, 216
    see also Atomic bomb
Mansfield, Mike, 122
Marcantonio, Vito, 119
Mark, Hans, 62
Marsh, John O., Jr., 183, 196
Marshall, George C., 20, 115
Martin, Joseph, Jr., 20
Martinez, Eugenio, 130–31
Mason, George, 215
Matinuddin, Kemal, 152, 168–69
Matthews, Francis, 28
McCargar, James, 120
McCone, John, 36
McCord, James, 130
McCormack, John, 20
McFarlane, Robert, 142, 166
McGovern, George, 130
McHenry, James, 215
McMahon, John, 158–59
McNamara, Robert, 39
McNeil, Francis, 208–9
Medellín cartel, 206–7
Meron, Menachem, 205
Merryman, James, 176, 177, 183
Meyer, Cord, 137
Meyer, Edward, 175–77, 182, 193, 194
Military-industrial complex, 38
Military Strategic, Tactical and Relay System. See MILSTAR
Miller, William G., 139
MILSTAR, 7, 8, 233–34
    cost of, 9, 48
    criticisms of, 63
    uses for, 46–47, 49, 54, 58–72
Mineta, Norman, 141
Minuteman missiles, 52
MIRV (Multiple Independently Targeted Reentry Vehicle), 41
Missile gap, 38–39, 51
Mitchell, George, 209
Mobutu, Joseph, 125
Moore, James E., 176
Moral Majority, 84
Mossadegh, Mohammed, 124
Moussavi, Mir Hussein, 165
Mujaheddin, 144–71
Multiple Independently Targeted Reentry Vehicle. See MIRV
MX missile, 59, 82

Nagasaki, bombing of, 23–24
Nagel, Conrad, 85
Najafabadi, Hossein, 166–67
Nassery, Zia, 146
National Command Authority, 52
National Emergency Airborne Command Post (NEACP), 53
National Reconnaissance Office, 5, 13–14, 55, 121, 234, 237n.7, 238n.10, 249n.25
National Security Act, 115, 116, 126
National Security Agency, 5, 55, 120–21, 153, 234
National Security Council, 25, 43, 115, 116, 168
    directives, 25, 29, 61, 116, 117, 240n.24
Navy, U.S., 11, 13, 26–27, 113
Nedzi, Lucien, 133
Neumann, Robert G., 170
New York Times, 134, 181
Nicaragua, 161, 178, 180, 181, 185, 203, 204
    see also Iran-contra affair; Sandinistas
Nightingale, Keith, 177
1984 (Orwell), 71
Nitze, Paul, 29, 30, 40, 43, 44
Nixon, Richard, 54, 82, 127, 131, 133, 210, 251n.45
Noriega, Manuel, 206–7
North, Oliver
    covert operations, involvement in, 199–202, 206, 208, 209–10
    criminal trial, 211–12, 258n.25
    and Enterprise, 202, 211
    Iran-contra, 164, 165–67
    mentioned, 161, 195, 198, 207, 210
Northrop, Jack, 76–77
Northrop Corporation
    B-1 bomber, 81–83, 84
    corruption, 11, 82, 99–100
    MX, 82
    Stealth bomber, 73, 74, 88–99, 103
Nuclear war
    games, 33, 44
    and human element, 67–69
    length of, 60, 64, 66
    limited, 40, 41
    scenario for, 53–55
    U.S. chain of command, 52, 55–56, 60, 241n.5, 242n.47

U.S. command centers, 52–53
U.S. decisions during, 55–56
U.S. plans for winning, 24, 26–27, 33–38, 50–72
Nuclear weapons, 31, 32, 35–36, 39, 41
    buildup of, 40, 41
    command and control of, 49–50
    need for human element, 67–69
    see also Arms control negotiations; Atomic bomb
Nunn, Sam, 87

Occupational Safety and Health Administration, 100
Odom, William, 60, 183–84, 188, 194
Office of Policy Coordination, 115
Ofstie, Ralph A., 27
Omega 7, 125
Oppenheimer, Robert, 22
Orwell, George, 71
OSS (Office of Strategic Services), 113–14
Otis, Glenn, 191–92
Overbeck-Bloem, Marty, 14, 137n.7

Pahlavi, Reza (Shah of Iran), 124
Pakistan, 147–62
Panama, 178, 202, 206
Peixotto, Ernest, 177
Pentagon
    black programs, 6, 10–11, 13, 15–16, 95, 173
    budgets, 7, 8, 10, 13, 14, 15, 16, 31, 44, 83–84, 94–96, 138, 233, 234
    concurrency, 89, 97
    lack of accountability to Congress, 16–17
    nuclear war command centers, 52–53
    procurement scandals, 11, 91–94, 98–99
    r&d programs, 14–15, 80
    see also C^3I network; Defense, Department of: Joint Chiefs of Staff; Stealth bomber; specific branches of service
Perez-Lebron, Hector, 189–91, 192–93
Perot, H. Ross, 207, 208
Pipes, Richard, 44
Plato, 118
Poindexter, John, 165, 166, 200–201, 206, 207, 209, 210, 211, 212

Porter, John Edward, 105
Powell, Colin, 164
Power, Thomas, 35, 37, 38, 40, 48
POWs (in Laos), 181–82
Presidential election (1980), 60, 83
Proxmire, William, 138

Qaddafi, Muammar, 146, 149
Quayle, J. Danforth, 86–87

Rahman, Mahmoud, 154
Rand Corporation, 39, 40, 89
Raphel, Arnold L., 151, 169, 255n.48
Rayburn, Sam, 20
Reagan, Ronald, 44, 135–36, 159, 203, 228
  Central American policy, 204
  covert activities policy, 141–42, 162
  and Iran-contra, 164–65, 201–2, 205, 206, 207, 211
  1980 campaign, 60, 83
  and nuclear forces buildup, 48, 61, 84, 244n.6
  on terrorism, 164, 175
Reagan administration
  secrecy, 17
  cabinet, 44
  covert operations, 142–71, 175–213
  military budgets, 6, 10, 44, 84
Rehman, Aktar Abdul, 148, 149
Reinke, William, 90–91
Republic, The (Plato), 118
RF Engineering, 91
RH Manufacturing, 91
Richardson, William, 217–28, 231
Rivers, Mendel, 94
Rockefeller, Nelson, 135–36
Rockefeller Commission, 135–36, 137
Rockwell International Corporation, 11, 81, 85
Roosevelt, Franklin D., 19, 113, 190
Rosenn, Max, 221–22
Rudd, Glenn, 164–65
Rusk, Dean, 39, 127
Russell, Richard, 122
Ryan, Leo, 135

Sadat, Anwar, 147–48
SALT (Stategic Arms Limitations Talks), 42

Saltonstall, Leverett, 122
Sandinistas, 141, 204, 212
SAPOC. See Special Access Program Oversight Committee
Satellites, intelligence, 14, 38, 39, 50, 55, 121
Saudi Arabia, 144, 146, 160–61, 181, 202
Scanlon, Charles, 187
Schlesinger, James, 131, 132
Schroeder, Patricia, 101–2, 107
Schweitzer, Robert, 162–63, 254n.38
Seaspray (secret aviation unit), 179–80
Secord, Richard, 161, 165, 174, 202, 205, 206, 212
Senate Armed Services Committee, 85, 87–88, 103, 119, 122
Shah of Iran. see Pahlavi, Reza
Short, Dewey, 119
Shultz, George, 44, 164, 201, 254n.38
Singlaub, John, 163
Skaggs, David, 103
Skelton, Ike, 104, 105
SIOP (Single Integrated Operational Plan), 36–37, 39, 40, 50, 55, 58
Smith, Denny, 17–18
Smith, Michael, 194
Sokol, S. S., 219
Souers, Sidney, 114
South Korea, 100
Soviet Union
  Afghanistan invasion by, 143–68
  atomic weapons test, first, 27
  defense budget, 102
  first strike, 43, 52, 244n.63
  weapons strength, 29–30, 33, 34, 38–39, 41, 42–43, 51, 59, 244n.64
  and Yom Kippur War, 53–54
Soyster, Harry, 181, 184
Space, military use of, 69
Special Access Program Oversight Committee (SAPOC), 183–84
Special Operations Division (U.S. Army), 173–98
Spence, Floyd, 105
Spritzer, Ralph, 221
Stafford, Thomas, 81, 82
START (Strategic Arms Reduction Talks), 103
Stealth bomber (B-2), 7, 13, 73–107, 233, 234

Stealth bomber (B-2) (*cont.*)
    cost of, 8, 12, 74, 76, 83, 88, 89, 96,
        100–101
    first flight of, 101
    and fraud, 99–100
    purposes for, 89
    technology, 78–79
Steinbruner, John, 63
Stennis, John, 122
Stewart, Potter, 225–26
Stimson, Henry, 20, 21, 22
Stinger anti-aircraft missiles, 143, 151,
    156, 161, 167
Stockman, David, 84
Story, Joseph, 216
Strategic Air Command, 26–27, 31, 36,
    113, 241n.44
Strategic Arms Limitations Talks
    (SALT), 42
Strategic Arms Reduction Talks
    (START), 103
Strategic weapons programs, 8–10
STRATSAT (Strategic Satellite System),
    61–62
Stubblebine, Albert, 192–93
Studley, Barbara, 162, 163
Sturgis, Frank, 131
Success (covert operation), 124, 125
Sullivan, William C., 210
Supreme Court, U.S., 225–28
Sweetman, Bill, 78
Symington, Stuart, 129–30, 133–34
Synar, Mike, 96, 104, 105, 106

Taylor, John, 216
Terrorism, 164, 175
    see also Hostages
Thornburgh, Richard, 212, 213, 220
Thurman, Maxwell, 183
Tillman, Jacqueline, 202
Tokyo, firebombing of, 26
Tower, John, 88
TOW missiles, 164–65, 167
Truman, Harry
    and atomic bomb, 20, 21, 22, 23, 24
    and CIA, 114, 127
    defense spending, 30
    and H-bomb, 27–28
TRW, 11
Turner, H.A., 218

Turner, Stansfield, 138, 146–47, 153,
    160, 171, 206
Twetten, Thomas, 159, 164, 165
Twinning, Nathan F., 33, 34, 240n.29,
    242n.47
Tydings, Millard, 119

United Fruit Company, 124
United States v. *Richardson*, 224–27
U.S.S.R. *See* Soviet Union
U-2 spy plane, 127

Vance, Cyrus, 146
Vaught, James, 173, 174
Vessey, John, Jr., 175–76, 178, 182,
    188, 193, 194
Vietnam War, 41–42, 127, 132, 134,
    243n.59
Vinson, Carl, 94, 118–19
Viola, Roberto, 203
Voi-Shan (company), 98–99

Wade, James P., Jr., 44
Walker, David, 206
Wallop, Malcolm, 139
Walsh, Lawrence, 212
War games, 33, 44
Warner, John, 86
War psychology, 210
Watergate affair, 82, 125, 130–32, 133,
    251n.45
Wavelengths
    EHF, 62, 67
    VHF, 79
Weapons, nuclear. *See* Nuclear weapons
Weapons pipeline to Afghan rebels,
    143–71
Weinberger, Caspar
    and B-1 and Stealth bomber, 85–86,
        95–96
    and black budget, 12, 95
    and covert operations, 164, 182, 205
    and defense spending, 61, 62
Weir, Benjamin, 208
Welch, Larry D., 74–75, 97–98, 102, 103
Westmoreland, William, 189
Wickham, John, 183
Wiesner, Jerome, 34
*William B. Richardson v. United States
    of America*, 219–24

Wilson, Charles, 157–58, 159, 160, 171
Wilson, Joseph P., 220
Wilson, Woodrow, 112
Wirth, Timothy, 103
World War II, 19–24, 26, 76
World War III, U.S. strategies for winning, 9, 25–72
World War IV, 5, 46–47, 72
Worldwide Military Command and Control System, 56–58

YB-49, 77–78
Yellow Fruit (covert operation), 180, 184–87, 192, 193, 195–96
Yom Kippur War, 53–54, 80
York, Herbert, 44

Zaire, 124–25
Zia ul-Haq, Mohammad, 147, 148, 152, 255n.48